BEYOND DAMNED QUARTER

THE POLK/POLLOCK FAMILY OF THE CHESAPEAKE EASTERN SHORE IN THE COLONIAL ERA

John F. Polk, Jr.

Colonial Roots
Millsboro, Delaware
2015

Colonial
Roots

Helping You Grow Your Family Tree

ISBN 978-1-68034-053-2

CONTENTS

List of Figures

ACKNOWLEDGEMENTS

This origin of this book can be dated, if memory serves, back to a visit to the Maryland Historical Society in Baltimore, circa 1998, naively expecting to find quick answers to a few basic questions about family history. Needless to say, the quest was not that simple, but was the start of a long and special journey that still continues and will no doubt never end. As one soon learns in genealogy, every answer generates a new question.

Along the way I have had the good fortune to meet and work with very special colleagues who have contributed greatly to this work and without whom it would be a much lesser product.

I first crossed paths with my good friend, John C. Lyon, years ago on a Saturday at the Maryland Archives. John is now retired from a long career as a systems engineer and project manager at NASA developing remote sensing data systems and software. He has extraordinary expertise in cadastral systems, and in retirement has undertaken an immense self-directed project to develop a unified map and database for all land tracts surveyed in "Old" Somerset County (including present-day Worcester and Wicomico and a large part of Sussex County). An excellent example of the socio-historical value of his work can be seen at Somerset GenWeb (http://rootsweb.ancestry.com/~mdsomers/lyonmaps/). John generously shared his full land tract database with me during my research on the Polk family, and it has been an invaluable tool in tracing the family's progress and spread over three generations. The tract maps appearing throughout this work were developed directly from his database.

My longtime e-mail colleague, Billy F. (Bill) Polk, of Kansas City, Missouri, is the only person who I will readily admit knows more about the Polk family than myself. Bill is well known to anyone doing serious research on Polk ancestry as the go-to guy with all the answers on Polk family lineages. He and I have corresponded for so long that I have only a vague idea of when it began – somewhere around 2000. He has been a wonderful sounding board for my research and has contributed much to it. Beyond that, he has performed a Herculean effort in editing and critiquing the full text of this book to the last comma.

Michael G. (Mike) Hitch, currently the Chairman of the Edward H. Nabb Research Center for Delmarva History and Culture at Salisbury University, joined John Lyon and myself during many sessions at the Maryland Archives at the early stages of my research. More recently Mike has worked closely with John to incorporate Sussex County surveys into the Lower Delmarva land tract database. This has proved very helpful in producing the Sussex area land tract maps appearing in Chapter 3.

Others who have provided help, comments, and encouragement to me are Mrs. Doris Polk Killingsworth, who generously shared her research materials with me; Dr. Jean E. Russo, a well-known Maryland colonial historian; Richard H. Pollock, former President of Clan Pollock; John G. Kester, a fellow Polk historian; Robert (Bobby) Forrest of Northern Ireland, a professional genealogist; Angus Lyon, a Guide for the National Trust for Scotland at Pollok House, Glasgow, and James Polk Farber of Middletown, Maryland. And of course, I owe a great debt to my wonderful wife, Anita, and my children, Theresa, Jack, and Tom, who have tolerated my obsession for family history for these many years without complaint.

FOREWORD

Somerset County, Maryland, has one of the most complete and well-preserved collections of colonial records of all early American counties, and they reveal much about our Polk/Pollock family history. These records are readily available in the Maryland State Archives, or Hall of Records, at Annapolis. They include probate records (wills, inventories, administration accounts and testamentary proceedings), judicial proceedings, land records, and tax lists. The records of Dorchester County and the Proprietary government of Maryland also contain much Polk/Pollock land and probate information. Among other items, Magdalen Polke's original will is preserved at the Maryland Archives, and her personal mark can be seen affixed to it.

The records of Sussex County, Delaware, are also rich in Polk/Pollock family information since, as events transpired, the second and third generation Polk/Pollock lands along the Nanticoke in Dorchester and upper Somerset County were ceded to Delaware by the Penn-Calvert boundary settlement of 1760. Thus the probate records of these erstwhile Marylanders are mostly found in the Delaware Archives for the post-Mason-Dixon period. They lived in Maryland, but died in Delaware, so to speak.

Because of the extent of these records, their availability, and the power of modern information technology in compiling and accessing databases, a much more complete examination of our colonial Chesapeake Polk/Pollock family history is possible now than ever before. Not that it is a simple task. There is a lot more to be found than might be expected, and it still requires persistent digging through old manuscripts to find the hidden nuggets. The aim of the present work is twofold—a more accurate family genealogy and a deeper insight into the character and environment of our ancestors. To this end, not just the land and probate records have been researched, but also the Somerset County Court, or Judicial, records. These convey a vivid flesh and blood picture of our ancestors and the world they inhabited. Using these records, it has been possible to develop much of the family history directly from primary sources, starting with Robert and Magdalen Polke of Damned Quarter and continuing through a good part of the next four generations.

Not surprisingly, this has led to conflicts with what has become the standard account of the early Polk/Pollock genealogy as contained in the well-known works of Mary Winder Garrett, William Harrison (W. H.) Polk, and Mrs. Frank Angellotti. The author is well acquainted with those works and recognizes the contribution which they made to our family history. They are certainly the base line from which any departure requires explanation.

Polk Family and Kinsmen (PF&K), published in 1912, was written by William H. Polk over a period of almost forty years as an avocation to his career as a newspaper publisher in Lexington, Kentucky. It is a monumental work, and we are very fortunate to have it as a family genealogy resource. (A searchable copy is available on line at https://archive.org/details/polkfamilykinsme00polk courtesy of Internet Archive.) After his death his collected papers were donated to the Library of Congress but are now found in the Special Collections at the Margaret I. King Library of the University of Kentucky in Lexington. These have been examined by the author and are quite useful in understanding the basis for some of W. H. Polk's accounts since he rarely identifies his sources in the book. What becomes clear from these papers is that W. H. Polk had only limited access to primary sources, and he relied primarily on correspondence for his information. Indeed, he complains in his introduction about the lack of responses from some branches of the family despite frequent requests.

A few of the colonial era Polk wills came to W. H. Polk's attention as he was writing his book, mostly through the help of R.C. Ballard Thruston of Louisville, Kentucky, and Earle B. Polk of Somerset County, and changed his understanding of certain genealogical facts. Most notably, the previously assumed descent of the Polks of North Carolina from John Polk, eldest son of Robert and Magdalen, through his son William, was ruled out by the discovery of William's will, probated in Dorchester County in 1726. In any case, only a fraction of the relevant original colonial records was available to W. H. Polk and Mary Winder Garrett, and inevitably this limited their understanding of the early family history. Today we are blessed to have much more complete, organized, and readily accessible collections of the records available than they did, and it is incumbent upon us to use them fully, just as they would have done.

It is hoped that readers will agree that it is time to re-examine our early family history in light of the records now available. This is the author's objective, and hopefully, in some measure, it answers the rather poignant challenge offered by W. H. Polk in his introduction to *Polk Family and Kinsmen*:

> *Realizing the uncertainty of life; doubtful as to whether any other member of the family might feel inclined to finish the work before he, also, is called to join the "great majority;" remembering the inscription* "Tempus edax rerum," *on the face of the old clock brought by Robert and Magdalen from Ireland and still ticking off in Maryland the seconds that go to make up centuries; and aware that Time might also consume him within a short time, the writer has sought to finish his task as soon as possible, leaving to those who may come after him the correction of any mistakes discovered. He has laid the foundation and now commits to future generations of the family the work of extending the history on through the coming years.*

The present effort is intended as just that—extending the history that began with the initial correspondence of Colonel William Polk of Raleigh and General William Winder of Baltimore in 1824 and continued through the work of Josiah

F. Polk, Mary Winder Garrett, William H. Polk, and Emma Angellotti. Another step along the path they began.

A final word about future efforts—this author's original intent was to cover a much broader range of Polk and Pollock family history than is included in this work. As is apparent, the volume of material for the Maryland Eastern Shore and Delaware was more than enough for one book. A second volume is in preparation which will cover a variety of topics quite different from those included here. Hopefully it will not be as long in coming.

John Fleming Polk, Jr.
Havre de Grace, Maryland
November 2015

Introduction

Robert Polke's first appearance in colonial records is in the survey of Polkes Folly. This cites a warrant issued to him on 20 November 1687, but it is likely that the family arrived some time before that and took time to assess their options before making a major financial commitment. The exact date of their arrival in Maryland will most likely never be known, but if a year had to be picked, the best estimate would probably be the year before—sometime in 1686.

Whenever their arrival, the challenge faced by Robert Polke and his family was truly daunting. The contrast between the climate and geography of Donegal, Ireland, whence they came, and their new home in Somerset County is extreme and gives special poignancy to the name, Polkes Folly, that Robert selected for his first land holding in the new world. Dames Quarter, then known as Damned Quarter or Damn Quarter, is now an official wildlife management area of the State of Maryland and nothing more than a primeval marshland. At the end of the 17th century it was probably woodland interspersed with marshes, barely above sea level, much like present-day St. Stephen immediately to the east. The land has certainly subsided and changed in the last three centuries, but even then there were large areas of swamp and marsh, specifically mentioned as such in the land records, and otherwise dense thickets of virgin forest. Today, in summertime, the dominant feature of the area is the hostile mosquito and deerfly population which in warm weather makes even the briefest unprotected exposure intolerable. Things could not have been much different back then—legend tells us that the very names of Damned Quarter and nearby Devil (Deal) Island are attributed to the insect population. One has to wonder just how Robert and Magdalen, a military man and lady of status, with their eight or nine teenage and younger children, possessing only the most basic resources, could have looked upon this wilderness with anything but despair.

Robert did not arrive on the scene a wealthy man. Presumably he sold whatever he owned in Ireland to finance the family's ocean passage and initial stake in the new world. He acquired only 250 acres of land during his years in Somerset— Polkes Folly (100 acres) and Polkes Lott (50 acres), for which he was issued land warrants on 20 November 1687, and the tract Forlorne Hope (100 acres) purchased from Augustine Stanford in 1697. The inventory of Robert's estate made in 1703 shows just how rudimentary their belongings were. It is valued at a modest total of £50/16/11, most of that attributed to livestock (28 hogs, 1 mare, and 13 cattle comprising £35 of the total). The remainder is a short list containing such items as a feather bed and covering, yard and a half of serge, frying pan, 3 iron wedges, 3 reaphooks, a parcel of linen yarn, and a tanned hide. Their dwelling place must have been a basic settler's cabin that was eventually abandoned by the next generation. The frequently repeated assertion that they lived in a manor house known as White Hall is certainly incorrect. The tract White Hall is in present-day Wicomico County. It was patented in 1795 by Judge William Polk as a resurvey

1

of the tract Fortune first acquired in 1744 by his father, David Polk, the son of Robert's second son William. None of this occurred during Robert or Magdalen's time.

By whatever means, the family managed to survive the initial pioneer years and in due course but not in Robert's lifetime, the family prospered. Their presence was gradually felt in Somerset and later in adjacent areas of Dorchester and Worcester counties, Maryland, and Sussex County, Delaware. As opportunities arose, the second and third generations moved to more desirable lands along the Manokin and Nanticoke, and by 1740 there were no Polks or Pollocks living in Damned Quarter. Their judgment was more than validated by the subsequent deterioration of the area into a primal wetland. Today, muskrats burrow in the marshland grasses of these ancestral lands, the waterfowl swim serenely in its waters, and in summer the mosquitoes and deerflies reign supreme. Somewhere within its bosom, lost to time and memory, the bones of Robert and Magdalen are resting in quiet peace, while their pilgrim spirits move ever onward with their departed seed—beyond Damned Quarter.

1. The New World

Before turning to the lives of Robert and Magdalen Polke and their children it will help to give a brief sketch of the new world into which they arrived. This will be done from three perspectives with increasingly specific focus—Maryland, Somerset County, and Damned Quarter.

A brief note is needed at the outset regarding colonial dates and how they are exhibited in this work. England did not adopt the Gregorian calendar until 1752. Before that, in the British Empire 24 March was the final day of the calendar year, and 25 March was New Year's Day. This introduces some confusion about the recorded dates for events occurring between 1 January and 24 March in years prior to 1752. The survey date for Polkes Folly, for example, was recorded in the Maryland land office as 7 March 1687, but should be understood as 7 March 1688 in our now standard (Gregorian) system. Such dates have sometimes been written, in secondary sources, in a compound form with both years indicated, e.g. as 7 March 1687/8. In this book, however, only the adjusted (Gregorian) date will be shown in these cases, followed by "(NS)" to indicate it is in the new system. The foregoing date will thus appear as "7 March 1688(NS)" in this notation. This will not be done in direct transcriptions of actual text from colonial records, such as in Appendix IV, which are printed in italic font.

Tract maps are included with the text to give a clear idea of where Polk and associated family properties were located in Maryland and Delaware. As mentioned in the Acknowledgement, these maps were produced from the extensive database developed by Mr. John C. Lyon from the original colonial survey records. A good overview of the database, and maps produced from it, is available on line at http://rootsweb.ancestry.com/~mdsomers/lyonmaps/. The software application that is used to produce the plots is Deedmapper©. This program works by inputting the metes and bounds data for individual land tracts, which are assembled and placed on a background map of the area. If the metes and bounds data are available for a group of contiguous tracts, they can be positioned and gathered as appropriate to form a unified tract map of an area. Mr. Lyon's database includes more than 13,000 land tracts from Lower Delmarva, including present-day Somerset, Worcester, and Wicomico Counties in Maryland and about half of Sussex County, Delaware. Subsets of the data can be extracted and plotted by filtering out ones of specific interest, such as those with which the Polk family were associated. The tract maps displayed in this work were developed in this way.

1.1 Maryland

Noe person or persons whatsoever within this Province professing to believe in Jesus Christ, shall henceforth bee in any waies troubled,

3

molested or discountenanced for or in respect of his or her religion....

A Law of Maryland Concerning Religion, 1649

The act of religious toleration passed by the Maryland Assembly in 1649 was the first such law enacted in the colonies and one of the truly enlightened, if little recognized, moments of our colonial heritage. It proved to be a strong attraction for groups facing religious oppression elsewhere and looking for refuge during an era of ceaseless and brutal sectarian conflict. The law was the basis for Maryland's reputation as a desirable place of settlement by non-conforming groups such as Quakers, Baptists and Presbyterians—a strong contrast in the 17th century with the more intolerant attitudes seen in the Puritan settlements of New England and with the establishment Church in Virginia.

It was exactly this circumstance that led to the initial settlement of Somerset County, Maryland, on the Eastern Shore of the Chesapeake. In March 1660, following the restoration of Charles II in England, the Virginia Assembly enacted laws against Quakers and began forthwith to enforce them with vigor, causing resentment and distress among the Quaker settlers of Accomac, then part of Northampton County, in the Virginia portion of the Eastern Shore. Casting about for relief and knowing of Maryland's tolerant religious policy, the Quaker settlers sent a petition to the Maryland Proprietor asking for help. Lord Baltimore, shrewdly seeing an opportunity to better secure the borders of his thinly populated Province, extended them an invitation in November 1661 to settle on his lands south of the Choptank River. The disaffected Quakers were not long in accepting this offer, and a sizable group of them moved a few miles north to become his loyal subjects and the staunch defenders of his territory against any claims by the royal colony they had just departed. Numerous land patents were granted by the Proprietor at this time, and Somerset was formally erected as a Maryland county on 22 August 1666.

Although they were the first major identifiable group, the Quakers were not the earliest or only European inhabitants of the county. There were other adventurers and pioneers from England, Virginia, and other parts of Maryland. With easy access along the extensive river and tributary system emptying into the vast Chesapeake estuary, the early settlers had little difficulty finding desirable land. Something of a land rush developed and large parts of the territory, especially along the rivers, was taken up in fairly short order. But ownership was only a record entered in a book; the land was still a raw wilderness needing to be tamed. In our time it is still possible to drive through uncleared areas of Somerset and catch glimpses of the dense thickets of woodland and mire of swamps that were ubiquitous in the 17th century. It is indeed humbling to consider the price that must have been paid by the first settlers of these tracts to convert them into productive agricultural lands in an era that relied exclusively on human and animal labor.

A major event that impacted Somerset's early history and which deserves mention in this short sketch is the Maryland Revolution, something that happened not long after Robert and Magdalen Polke's arrival. This was an essentially bloodless *coup d'etat* in which the Maryland Council was overthrown by a Protestant faction known as the "Associators" who had long harbored resentment to the domination of the Provincial Council by the Catholic inner circle associates of Lord Baltimore. It occurred in July 1689, and was led principally by John Coode and Kenelm Cheseldyne of St. Mary's County.[1] It was the product of festering religious tensions in the provincial government.

Maryland has frequently been characterized as a Catholic colony because the Calvert family, the Proprietors of Maryland, was Catholic, but as already noted, the colony was tolerant of all Christian religions. The majority of the population in most counties, especially Somerset, was not Catholic. Only a few were predominantly Catholic—St. Mary's and Calvert Counties, and barely settled Cecil, among them. As far as the practice of religion in Maryland was concerned, local populations were free to do as they chose. This was a pragmatic accommodation by the Calverts, who could not push their own faith on the colony because of their precarious situation back in England where the establishment (Anglican) church had controlled the Court since the time of Queen Elizabeth. The Calverts were in fact under constant challenge to explain their ineffectiveness in administering the official establishment religion in their colony. The Law Concerning Religion enacted by the Maryland Assembly in 1649 was largely a product of this tension between the Catholic faith of the Proprietors and the reality of the Protestant character, both establishment and non-conformist, of the population.

Some of the Protestant members of the Maryland upper class were resentful of Lord Baltimore's appointments of his Catholic associates to the key positions of power. As long as Lord Baltimore was on the scene in Maryland, and the Stuart family was in power in England, there was little that the Protestants could do about this, but they were not happy with it. In 1689, however, things were different. The reigning British monarch, James II, a Catholic Stuart, had been deposed by parliament and replaced by his daughter Mary and her husband William of Orange, a Calvinist. This was a pivotal moment in English history, now called the Glorious Revolution. It was the effective end of the divine right of kings and the emergence of Parliament as ultimate source of power in the land. The coronation took place on 11 April. James fled to France and raised an Army of continental Catholic forces to regain his throne. Their strategy was to invade Ireland hoping to defeat the Williamite forces there with help from the Catholic Irish before turning to England, but this proved unsuccessful and James never returned to power. The major events in the struggle were the unsuccessful siege of Derry in 1689 and James's defeat at the battle of the Boyne in July 1690. Both events became lasting fixtures in the iconography of Ulster Scots.

---

[1] See Carr for a detailed account.

While this was happening, Charles Calvert, the current Lord Baltimore, was in England fighting his own battles against the Penns and other enemies in the Court. It was an opportune moment for Cheseldyne and Coode to take power back in Maryland. They did so simply by taking over the government facilities and records in St. Mary's and evicting Lord Baltimore's son-in-law from his residence. This was done by force of arms, but there was no actual struggle or resistance and no casualties.

Although their initial step was a clear success, the Associators faced a critical problem—establishing their legitimacy as leaders of the Province in the eyes of the new royal powers in England. They had taken a large gamble by seizing power and could well be regarded as traitors to legitimate authority, for which the ancient penalty, still on the books, was to be hanged, drawn and quartered. The key to their position was to justify their actions as having been done on behalf of the new King and Queen, to ensure that they were recognized as the legitimate monarchs of the Kingdom in the face of "Papist" opposition. It was therefore an urgent matter for the Associators to demonstrate that they were accepted by the general populace and local authorities in the counties as the proper and acknowledged leaders of Maryland under the new Protestant regime in England.

To do this, the first step was to call an Assembly at St. Mary's and have the county representatives acknowledge them as legitimate authorities. This was done in August-September, but to ensure a favorable outcome no "Papists" were allowed to represent their respective counties. Catholics were also relieved from official positions in the counties. This was not an issue for Somerset where there essentially were no Catholics. The County was represented at the Council by one of its Commissioners, Francis Jenckins, and three others whose names are not known.

A second step was to have the Counties demonstrate their acceptance of the new Protestant monarchs in England, and by inference the new Protestant powers in St. Mary's, through the documents we now refer to as the Addresses of Loyalty. All counties were asked to do this, but not all did, notably those with predominantly Catholic populations and authorities. The documents that resulted were sent back to St. Mary's, combined and dispatched to London where they could be presented to the Royal Court, and hopefully win the case for those who had seized power in Maryland.[2]

The language in all of the documents is very similar and was probably prescribed by the Associators. The key assertion which they make is to defend "the Protestant Religion and your Majesty's title and interest against the French and other Papists that oppose and trouble us in soe good and just a cause..." in return for which they

---

[2] These are archived at the British Public Records Office at Kew, reference number CO5-718; the Somerset address is folio 64.

fervently desired that the King would secure "our Religion lives and liberty under Protestant Governors and Government."

The period that followed was one of intense tension back in the Province as they awaited word on how this was received by the King. No doubt Charles Calvert was at the same time marshalling all the forces at his disposal to put down this usurpation of his Proprietorship and have the Associators declared outlaws. It was not until the arrival of a new Governor in 1692, Lionel Copley, appointed by the King, that it became fully clear that Lord Baltimore was permanently removed as Proprietor and Maryland had become, for the time being, a Royal colony. (The next Lord Baltimore was reinstated in 1715, but by this time the Calverts had renounced their Catholic faith.)

1.2 Somerset County

On 6 November 1661 Governor Phillip Calvert issued the following proclamation which opened up the Maryland eastern shore for settlement: [3]

> *Taking into Consideracon the peticon of divers persons well affected to this Province now or late Inhabitants of Northampton County otherwise called Accomac in Virg'a who are desirous to transplant themselves and familyes into this Province ... I have nominated constituted and impowred ... to grant warr'ts for land upon the Eastern shoar of this Province in any part below the Choptank River.*

Settlers relocating from Virginia soon accepted the invitation and two new counties were formed from this area within a few years, Somerset (1666) and Dorchester (1668).[4] See Figure 1 for the map of this region originally published in *Polk Family and Kinsmen.*

Calvert's proclamation was issued as a response to the petition of the dissident Quakers and other non-conformists of neighboring Accomac, but they were not the only people to move across the border into these lands. Other settlers and eager land speculators followed almost immediately in the wake of those first inhabitants, staking out properties along the almost limitless shoreline. Most of the secondary group also came from Virginia. They were not necessarily dissidents, but simply people who saw an opportunity for land acquisition, and moved to take advantage of it. At that time the two Provinces were in effect different countries, both competing for settlers, so immigrants "transported" from Virginia were legally no different in Maryland from those arriving from across the Atlantic, and were afforded the same head rights. Entrepreneurs who could assemble a group of willing transportees could reap the collective head rights of the lot.

---

[3] AOM, Vol. 3, *Maryland Council 1636-1667*, p. 435-6.
[4] For a full account of the history of Somerset, see Torrence.

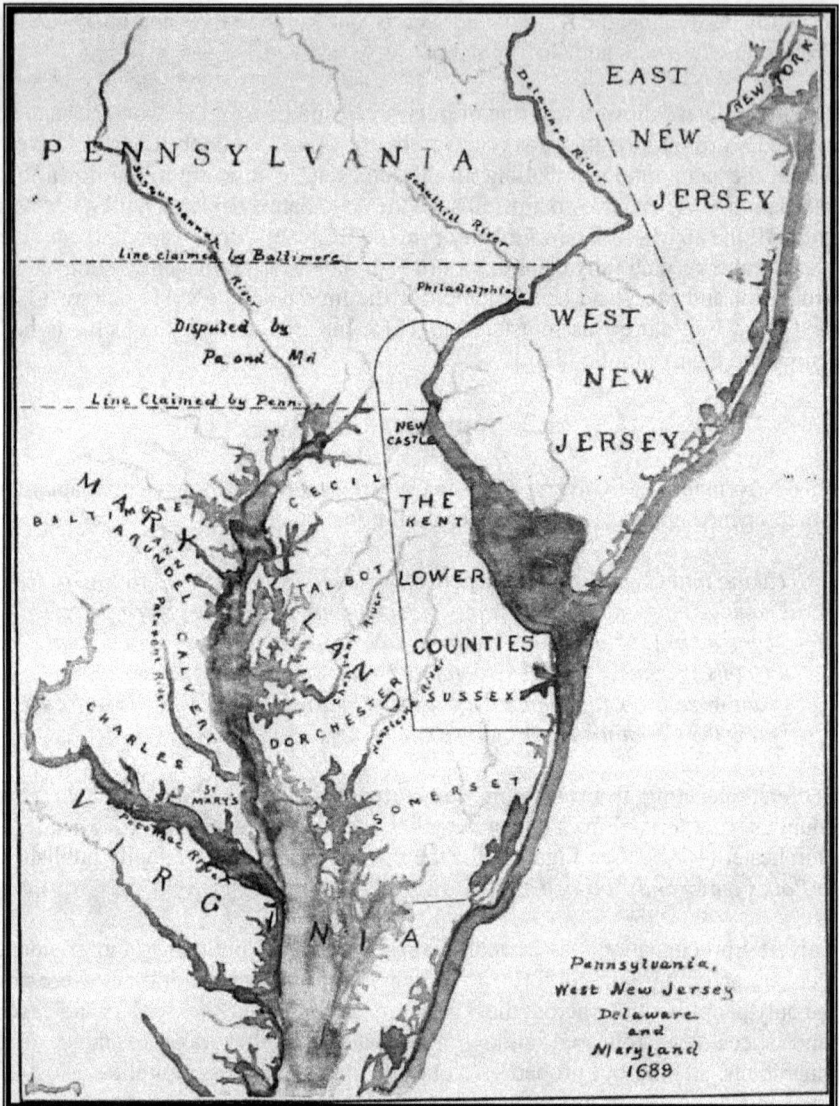

Figure 1. Chesapeake Eastern Shore in 17th century.
(From *Polk Family and Kinsmen*)

Somerset County was ideally suited by geography for settlement by these colonial pioneers. In the 17th century colonial world, commerce was conducted almost entirely by water and Somerset offered an enormous pristine complex of rivers and tributaries entering into the Chesapeake estuary. Somerset, as then constituted, was penetrated deeply from the bay side into its interior by five major river systems—Pocomoke, Annemessex, Manokin, Wicomico, and Nanticoke. Between these were the peninsular landforms or "necks" and their hinterlands going back into the head waters (see Figure 2). On the seaboard side was the great inland waterway behind the barrier islands of Chincoteague and Assateague below the Indian River inlet and Cape Henlopen to the north. The primary product and *de facto* currency of the early colonial world was tobacco, and all land tracts were patented with access to water for getting crops to market as an essential feature. All of the tract descriptions appearing in the land records at this time were specified in terms of the adjacent body of water, or as "back in the woods" therefrom. Unfortunately for later landholders, little care was given in the early land rush to the overall consistency of these descriptions away from the shorelines, and many legal conflicts resulted in the ensuing years. Fortunately for later researchers, many land commissions and resurveys also resulted, which are sometimes of considerable use in historical and genealogical studies. Some of the land disputes are being sorted out to this day as the improved precision of modern surveying technology just makes the inconsistencies of the early surveys even more apparent. Even the boundary between Delaware and Maryland, originally agreed between the Calverts and Penns in 1760, was still being refined by an interstate commission as recently as 1982. [5]

As may be expected, the first settlers of Somerset took up the most desirable lands along the waterways, and a collection of settlements quickly developed along the major rivers. The earliest nucleus was formed around the most southerly of Somerset's wholly contained rivers, the Annemessex. It was here that the initial colony of dissidents exiting from Virginia took up residence, just far enough inside Lord Baltimore's province to feel safely beyond the reach of the Royalist powers of their former colony. The first lands patented by the principal leaders of the non-conformist community were found here, including those of Arnold Elzey, Ambrose Dixon, George Johnson, Henry Boston, Thomas Price, and the most notable member of this community, its outspoken leader, Stephen Horsey.

A second cluster of settlers formed almost simultaneously around the head of the Manokin River, the next river northward from the Annemessex. This settlement had a distinctly different, less radical character, not being populated as much by dissidents, as by individuals attracted simply by the economic opportunity of cheap and viable lands. The community centered at Manokin, somewhat below the site of present-day Princess Anne, which had already been the location of an Indian trading post from the earliest days of English presence on the Eastern Shore peninsula.[6] Religiously, this group was probably more aligned to the establishment church, although it had little actual presence there at this time. A few years later this area would become the center for a strong Presbyterian community of Ulster Scots arriving from the North of Ireland.

Stephen Horsey, the first true citizen of Annemessex and Somerset, brought with him a well-earned reputation as agitator and general thorn in the side of the

---

[5] See Meade.
[6] See Rountree, p. 103.

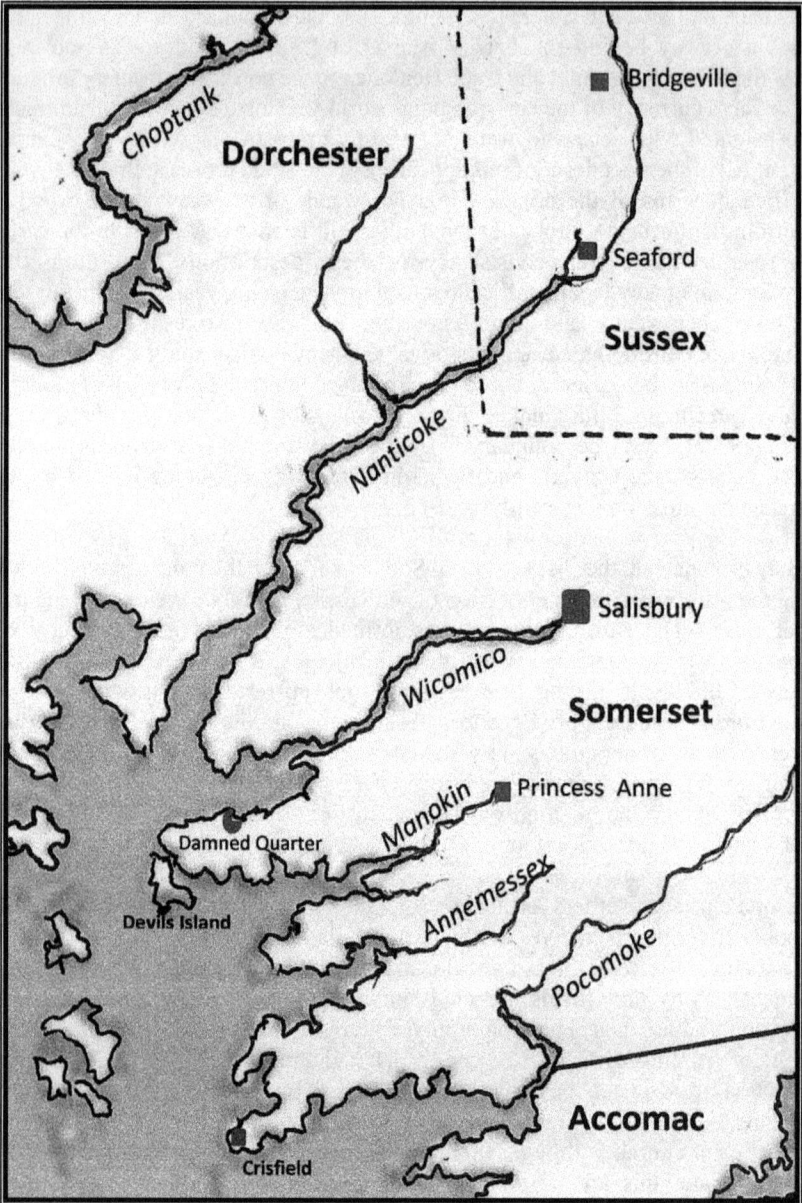

Figure 2. Chesapeake shoreline of Somerset County.

Royalist government in Virginia, having raised such issues as taxation without representation and disavowal of tithes to the establishment church. In 1653 he was selected to represent Northampton County in the House of Burgesses,[7] but was not allowed to sit in the proceedings because of objections raised against him by the Royalist faction. Back in Accomac, he managed to alienate the County Commissioners by calling them "asses and villanes" in their own court. After the punitive laws against non-conformists were passed by the Virginia Burgesses in 1660, Horsey was most likely the first person to pick up and transplant himself across the border. The records show him securing head rights for a group of thirteen, mostly members of his family, in early 1661, apparently anticipating the opening of soon-to-be Somerset.[8] In short order, he became not only the *de facto* leader of the new community in its earliest years, but the official one as well. Lord Baltimore was quick to appreciate the very qualities that made Horsey such a nuisance to the Virginia authorities and appointed him a commissioner of the peace for the area in February 1662/3. He held that position until the formal erection of Somerset as a county in 1666, when his preeminence was recognized as being the chief among the commissioners, appointed to administer the oaths of office to the others.

~~~~~~~~~

Very soon after their relocation into Somerset, the Accomac dissidents were faced with a serious, almost mortal, challenge from the same forces that they thought they had just escaped. This challenge was brought on them by the dominant personality of the Accomac/Northampton establishment, Edmund Scarburgh, who bitterly resented their departure and was determined not to let such audacious behavior go unchallenged. There was already no love lost between him and Stephen Horsey, whom Scarburgh had denounced years earlier as "a factious and tumultuous person; a man repugnant to all Government."[9] Scarburgh needed no special motivation, but to give himself a pretext for action, he undertook a campaign to discredit the legitimacy of the Maryland-Virginia border beyond which the erstwhile Accomac dissidents had just passed. The point of beginning for this border on the bay side had been fixed by the original Charter of Maryland at Watkins Point, located on the north side of Pocomoke Sound, from which it was supposed to run due east towards the Atlantic. With nothing more than the force of his personality to base it on, Scarburgh began to assert that Watkins Point was located almost thirty miles farther North, across the Bay from the Patuxent River, rather than at the Pocomoke. On the basis of this claim he asserted that the recently relocated dissidents were still the subjects of Virginia, and to his authority

---

[7] At that time Accomac was still part of Northampton County and did not become a separate jurisdiction until 1663.

[8] Patent for Colebourn, MD Patents 04, p. 580. In subsequent patent issued 1663 for tract Colebourn MD Patents 05, p. 440) Horsey cites himself, wife Sarah Horsey, children Stephen Horsey, Jun., John Horsey, Samuel Horsey, Mary Horsey, Abigail Horsey; Michael Williams, Thomas Williams, Sarah Williams, John Roche, Benjamin Sumner, Thomas Whitfield.

[9] See Court records, Accomac County, Vol. 1, p. 43; also transcribed in *Virginia Magazine of History and Biography*, Volume XIX, p. 173.

as the chief representative of the King in Accomac.

Scarburgh was a formidable person and was vested with considerable powers with which to enforce his will. He was both the Surveyor General and Treasurer of Virginia, appointed to these positions by the King himself since Virginia, unlike Maryland, was a Royal Proprietorship. Moreover, his brother, Sir Charles Scarburgh, was the personal physician to King Charles II back in England. Because of these appointments, Scarburgh was not directly answerable to the Governor of Virginia and, at such a remote distance from the Royal Court, essentially free to arrogate to himself whatever powers he found convenient for his purposes. He was also the chief Commissioner or Justice of the Peace in Accomac, and its representative in the Virginia House of Burgesses, where he had considerable influence.

Working from this power base, Scarburgh did not hesitate to force an astonishing law through the Burgesses in September 1663 which gave him the legal cover he needed to establish a claim over a large portion of Somerset. The law was entitled *An Act Concerning the Bounds of this Colony on the Eastern Shore.* It accomplished three things: 1) commanded all inhabitants of the Eastern Shore from Watkins Point southward *"to render obedience to his majesties government of Virginia and make payment of his majesties rent and all publique to his majesties colony of Virginia;"* 2) asserted that Watkins Point was north of the Wicomico River at a point *"on the south side of the straight line opposite to the Potuxent river... within which bounds his majesties subjects that are now seated are hearby commanded to yield due obedience at their peril;"* 3) put Scarburgh in charge of enforcing the law. Thus the law unilaterally extended the Virginia Eastern Shore thirty miles farther north into Lord Baltimore's province by a bold, but manifestly incorrect, assertion that these territories lay below what John Smith had designated as Watkins Point during his initial exploration of the Bay in 1608. It did make provision that if *"Lord Baltimore his lieutenants or deputies shall not be fully convinced of his or their actuall or pretended intrusions* (into the lands now claimed by Virginia)" then they could meet with Scarburgh and one of two other specified Virginians to resolve the matter. However, in the meantime *"all inhabitants on the Eastern Shore as aforesaid are required in his Majesties name to conforme due obedience to this act of assembly."*

Scarburgh did not wait for Lord Baltimore to voice any objections to this act, if indeed Baltimore was even informed of it, but immediately prepared an armed force to pay a visit to the newly enlisted subjects and extract suitable attestations of their obedience to the King and the Royal colony. On Sunday, 11 October, with a force of forty horsemen from the Accomac militia, he entered into Annemessex where the most refractory citizens were likely to be found. Steven Horsey was first on the list. Defiant as ever, Horsey refused to acknowledge Scarburgh's authority and was arrested forthwith and his house marked with the "broad arrow" indicating that it was escheated to the King. Scarburgh then proceeded to the house of Ambrose Dixon, where he and two other Quaker former residents of

Accomac, George Johnson and Thomas Price, were found. Like Horsey, both refused to acknowledge Scarburgh's right to exercise jurisdiction, and were similarly arrested.

Having made his point in the Annemessex area, Scarburgh moved on to Manokin where the citizenry was less particular about which province commanded its allegiance. This area was not generally inhabited by Quaker refugees from Accomac, but by new settlers of various backgrounds attracted by the cheap and viable lands of the newly opened frontier. Their major concerns were property rights and whether the governing authorities would provide effective protection from the Indians when called upon. When confronted by Scarburgh they accepted his claims to authority over them with little protest according to Scarburgh's own account of the events in his report to the Virginia authorities.

Scarburgh proceeded to hold a summary "Court of Survey" at Manokin to demonstrate in practice the reality of his claimed authority. He required all inhabitants to register their claimed land holdings, granting them in return his assurances of the protection of the Governor of Virginia, "as his Majesties subjects." He apparently had little difficulty in this regard although several of the officials temporized by asking for time to formally resign their commissions in Maryland. In truth, the citizens of Somerset were in a very ticklish position, since acknowledging the authority of Scarburgh put them in direct conflict with Lord Baltimore, for which they could be held accountable in his Province, should his authority be restored. However, the immediate presence of Scarburgh and his horsemen spoke with considerable more force than missives from the dilatory Maryland Council across the bay, so at least for the moment Scarburgh was recognized as the Lord of Manokin. Having made his point, Scarburgh adjourned his Court of Survey and returned to Accomac where further Court sessions were to be held in the usual jurisdictional seat of his newly augmented county. Horsey and the others who resisted Scarbrough were allowed to return to their homes.

Charles Calvert, then Governor of Maryland, shortly learned of the rapacious developments in Somerset and to his credit realized at once that it made more sense to go over Scarburgh's head than to take him on directly where he had a tactical advantage. Calvert headed directly down the Bay for a conference with the Virginia Governor, William Berkley, on the matter. Berkeley of course understood the legality of the situation and knew that the whole matter turned on the location of the beginning point of the Maryland-Virginia boundary at Watkins Point. He agreed to a joint commission to visit the sites in question and settle the matter permanently. The true location of Watkins Point was well-known, and the falsity of Scarburgh's claims readily apparent, so once his bluff was called, the conflict quickly abated and the beleaguered citizens allowed to resume their status as Marylanders. The full transpeninsular boundary between Maryland and Virginia from the Chesapeake to the Atlantic was marked off in 1668 and has remained essentially the same to this day.

~~~~~~~~~~

Somerset was formally established as a county of Maryland in 1666. As originally constituted it comprised all lands north of Virginia from Chesapeake Bay and the Nanticoke River in the West to the shores of the Atlantic in the East. This included all of present-day Somerset, Worcester, and Wicomico counties, as well as Sussex County, Delaware. William Penn did not arrive to start his colony to the north until 1682, so no competing claim had yet been lodged for the lands that now form Delaware, at least south of New Castle. Lord Baltimore's charter for Maryland covered the entire Eastern Shore peninsula to the Delaware Bay.

With the Scarburgh episode dispelled, and no subsequent crises other than relatively minor confrontations with the Indian population, Somerset grew steadily in population, economy, and governance in the ensuing years. A remarkably detailed picture of this period can be found in the surviving land, probate and court records of Somerset. The growth of the population, for instance, can be gauged from the number of tithables in the annual levy, as noted sporadically in the Somerset Court records:

October 1668	211
August 1671	386
April 1689	1266
September 1689	1312
March 1692/3	1428
Nov 1696	1388

This sprang from an original base of about 50 as noted in the Maryland Council in April 1662.[10] Tithables included all able-bodied males, and both male and female slaves, over sixteen; the actual population is usually estimated at about four times the number of tithables. A good indication of the extent of land speculation occurring in the early years of Somerset is clear from a comparison of these figures with the accumulated number of land tracts surveyed as of the same dates: 290, 349, 1486, 1542, 1548, 1646, respectively,[11] showing that throughout this period there were generally more surveyed land tracts than tithables to work on them. The median tract size was about 200 acres.

The government of Somerset was in the hands of the County Commissioners, or Justices of the Peace, who exercised both the judicial (civil and criminal) and executive functions at county level. These individuals were appointed by the Proprietor in a written charter, served at his pleasure, and were always selected from the large landowning class. Typically, there were six to eight commissioners, several of whom were designated as "quorum" members, meaning that their presence was required in order for a council meeting to proceed. We are very fortunate that the bulk of the original court records have survived and are available

---

[10] AOM, Volume 3, *Maryland Council 1636-1667*, p.452.
[11] Note that very few surveys occurred in the period 1689-1694 due to the disruptions caused by the Maryland Revolution. Surveys did not resume in earnest until November 1694.

at the Maryland Archives. Many of these have been either transcribed or abstracted and are accessible online at the Archives website. A large selection of representative passages from these records, including most of the items that refer to Polks/Pollocks, is contained in Appendix IV. They provide a fascinating portrait of the people and community of early Somerset and are a delight to read.

What seems most striking about the records is how clear and well-formed the governing process was from the very outset. From a historical perspective, 17th century Somerset might be regarded as a frontier community, but there was little uncertainty among its people about the line of authority and rules of behavior. And, as always, there was no escaping from taxes. These were collected both as land rent due to the Proprietor and as the annual county levy for services and expenses approved by the county commissioners. The composite picture that emerges from the collected records of Somerset is a community of industrious, efficient, purposeful people dedicated to the enterprise for which they had come— the advancement of their own prosperity under the Proprietary polity.

A great number of the early residents found their way into the Court records in one way or another—as petitioners, plaintiffs, defendants, jurors, witnesses, constables, overseers of roads, ferrymen, indentured servants, or just persons on the docket who settled out of court. From these we catch fleeting glimpses, and a few colorful appearances, of many persons of interest to our story. Robert Polke, for example, first appears as a juror in August 1690, and altogether is found in at least thirty-four entries before 1700.

As an illustration of the content of these records, here is the transcript of the opening of Somerset Court, November 1683 session:

> *At A County Co'rt helld the 13th Day of November in the eight year of the Dominion of the Rt hon'rble Charles over Maryland &c Anno Dom 1683 before his Lopp's: Justices thereunto appointed. Comm'rs Present Coll William Colebourne Capt Henry Smith Mr William Brereton Mr Thomas Newbold Major Ambrose London*
>
> *This day the Sherife of this County brought before the Co'rt the grand Jury of Enquest for the body of this County whose names are as followeth that were Sworn vizt Capt Wm Colebourne foreman William Winslowe Stephen Costen John Browne Donam Olandman John Parker Daniell Hast Richard Jefferson Jeremiah Hook Robert Willson Robert Catlin Jun Nehemiah Covington Thomas Shanck John Moore ferreman Robert Johnson Mathew Dorman Stephen Horsey John Harris George Downes Henry Hudson Sam'l Jackson Thomas Cottingham*
>
> *The Grand Jury having rec'd theire Charge Goe forth. And on the 14th day of the said month of Nov Anno Dom 1683: they appear & being Called by theire names & asked whether they were agreed they Said Yea And the*

Clerke bid them deliver theire presentments to the Co'rt: w'ch upon
delivery of them the Clerke Said you are Content the Courte Shall amend
formes alltering matter of noe Substance in these bills you have found w'ch
they allowed Presentm'ts as followeth, ~ ~
Edward Price of this County for the entertaining of John Kempe &
Florence Mecuom Serv't to Capt:John Winder from Munday the 12th of
March 1681/2 til Sunday following, ~ ~ ~ ~
Jane Gessell Servant to John Cropper for bearing a bastard Chilld about
June last ~ ~ ~ ~
Chocoho an Indian belonging to the King of Copomco for hogstealing
discovered about the last of march 1683
Matcha An Indian Comonly Called Dick belonging to the king of Tondetank
for hogstealing
Peter Whaples & Henry Phillips for falsly reporting that Tho: Shancks wife
was delivered of A negro or mullato chilld
Mathew Baker Servant to John Bossman for bearing a bastard Chilld about
the first of August 1683
Margarett Hall Serv't to Thomas Hobbs for bearing a bastard Chilld about
the first of May 1683
Elizabeth Williams Serv't to Jacob Waring for bearing Two bastard
Chilldren about the first of April 1683
Christopher Nutter & Wm Furnace being Summoned to be of the Grand
Jury & not appearing
Anne Vine for Comeing with William Vine pretending he was her husband
but afterwards disowned each other and did relate that he was none of her
husband for his name was William Massy though they lived together as man
& wife now the Said Anne Living at Wm Elmes Leading an Sole Life
Thomas Jones Charles Courteny at the Same house Robert Devie at the
Same house Emanuell Coll Colebournes Negro Joseph Night his Serv't Wm
Lewis Living at the Same house John Roch Sen. John Roch Jun. Wm
Gromer Living at John Roch Wm. Jenckins Thomas Wood Francis Martin
John Hill Nathaniell Evans & Wm Hart for not appearing to work on
Clearing the highwaies being Summoned by John Kirke one of his Lopp's
overseers In Annamessex hundred ~ ~

     Signed by Capt Wm Colebourne foremann

Ordered that these following persons be Constables And that they be
Sworne before Some magistrate
Robert Collier Constable for Nanticoke hundred
Phillip Askewe for Wiccocomoco hundred
George Mitchell for Manny [Monie] hundred
Miles Grey for Manoakin hundred Constables
Danack Dennis for Anamessex hundred
Teague Riggen for Pokomoke hundred

Mathew Scarbrough for Mattapeny hundred
John Smock for Boquetenorten hundred

Following these were the individual cases, both civil and criminal, that were heard and disposed of by the commissioners over the next several days until court completed its business and was adjourned until the next session.

~~~~~~~~~~

In 1680 Colonel William Stevens, one of the founders and original Commissioners of Somerset, sent a letter to the Presbytery of the Laggan (Donegal) in Ulster, asking that a "godly minister" be sent to look after the needs of the people of Somerset. The actual text of the letter has not survived, but it is referred to in the minutes of the Presbytery. The motives of Stevens can be seen as both enlightened and self-interested. He was probably speaking for entire Council, but Colonel Stevens certainly stood to benefit personally from an influx of new settlers that might follow the minister's lead. He had acquired very extensive land rights in the form of warrants and patented land, more than any other individual in the county at that time, and needed settlers to increase the value of these holdings and realize a profit. At the same time, one has to admire the open-minded liberality of Colonel Stevens, a member of the established church and leader of the local government, in turning to a non-conformist group with which he had no obvious ties, to provide spiritual leadership for the people of his domain. The followers of the Covenant were not known as strong supporters of establishment power, in fact, their reputation was quite the opposite. The records of the Presbytery do not indicate that he actually asked for settlers as well as ministers, but simply that "Col. Stevens of Maryland beside Virginia his desire of a godly minister is represented to us. The meeting will consider it seriously and do what they can in it," dated 29 December 1680.

Whatever its motivation, Colonel Stevens' letter arrived at a moment of great travail and no doubt had a profound impact on the entire Presbyterian community of Donegal. Following the restoration of Charles II in 1660 a number of repressive measures were taken against Presbyterians in Ulster which made their situation at least as difficult as that of the Catholics, a fact sometimes lost in view of the later Presbyterian ascendancy in Northern Ireland. They had struggled through the Ulster Plantation, the Catholic uprising of 1641, the Cromwellian devastation of Ireland, the restoration of Charles II, and faced the prospect of a Catholic restoration under James II. In 1670 there had been an aborted plot called Blood's Rebellion in which a number of Presbyterians were implicated. Most noteworthy in our context was Reverend William Traile, minister from Ballendrait near Lifford, the home of the Tasker family—possibly the man who united Robert Polke and Magdalen (Tasker) Porter in marriage and almost certainly the minister for their growing family. Reverend Traile was accused on purely circumstantial evidence of complicity in the plot and sent to Dublin for lengthy interrogations on his religious beliefs. He was released unconvicted but with strengthened faith, and returned to Lifford only to be held under arrest there during 1682. The affair was highly resented by the Presbyterians and gave them every reason to see their future prospects in Ulster as very bleak. The embattled fortress psyche which these people had developed since first settling in Ulster was ratcheted upward one more notch.

It is easy, therefore, to imagine that the letter found a very attentive audience in Donegal. The response was predictably vigorous and its repercussions have echoed through the course of American history. The Presbytery sent not just one, but four, able and dedicated ministers with a clear mission to establish the Presbyterian faith in the New World. First and foremost among these was the young Reverend Francis Makemie, now recognized by the Presbyterian Church in America as their founder and patriarch. He was newly ordained in 1682 and specifically selected for the task of going to America and planting the seeds of his faith, which he did to great effect. Makemie arrived in Somerset around the spring of 1683, and stayed for a time at the home of Colonel Stevens, Rehobeth on the Pocomoke, where the earliest Presbyterian church edifice in America was built. Either coming with him or following very shortly afterwards was William Traile, and within the next two years the Reverends Thomas Wilson and Samuel Davis also arrived. While the other three ministered to the people in Somerset, Francis Makemie journeyed around the Chesapeake region establishing numerous frontier churches and ultimately organizing the first Presbytery of the American Church at Philadelphia in 1706. When the great wave of Scotch-Irish migration from Ulster commenced a decade or so later, the Presbyterian structure was already in place to lead and enliven them. The subsequent Presbyterian impact on the American frontier as it pushed down the Great Wagon Road through Pennsylvania into valley of Virginia and the Carolinas, and afterwards west beyond the Appalachians, can truly trace its roots back to its precursor arrival in Somerset.

Along with these ministers, it is certain that some of the Presbyterian families of Donegal also elected to cast their lot in the new world, hopefully leaving behind the turmoil of the old. Among these would be the families of Knox, McKnitt, Wallace, Alexander, Owens, White, Galbraith, Caldwell, Gray - and Polk. Certainly Robert and Magdalen Polke came within a few years of Makemie and Traile. This influx of Ulster Scots did not escape official notice in the Chesapeake area. An interesting passage appears in a letter of Edward Randolph, a Virginia Official, writing to the Commissioners of Customs for James City County in Virginia, on 17 June 1692:

> *I hear he has continued Maj^r King to bee the Navall Officer in Somerset Co^{ty}, a place pestred with Scotch & Irish. About 200 families have within the two years arrived from Ireland & settled in your County besides some hundred of family's there before. They have set up a linnen Manufacture, Encouraged thereto by Co^{ll} Brown, a Scotchman, one of the Councill & by Maj^r King & other principall persons upon the place, who support the Interlopers, & buy up all their Loading upon their first arrival, & govern*

the whole trade on the Eastern shore, so that whereas 7 or 8 good ships from Eng^ld did yearly trade & load the Tob^co of that Co^ty I find that in these three years last past there has not been above 5 trading ships legally in all those Rivers, & nigh 30 Sayle of Scotch Irish & New Eng^ld men.[12]

The motivation to emigrate from Ireland greatly abated after the lifting of the siege of Derry in 1689 and the victory of William of Orange at the Battle of the Boyne in 1690. The removal of the Catholic Stuarts and the ascension of a confirmed Calvinist to the English throne quite reversed the prospects of the Presbyterians in Ireland. This was a watershed moment in their history and the emigrations to Maryland probably slowed to a trickle at about the time Edward Randolph wrote his letter quoted above. All the same, the Scotch-Irish community that had established itself by this time had a growing impact on the Chesapeake region. Some of the Ulster-Scot families of Somerset moved northward to the Newcastle, Delaware, area and adjacent Cecil County, Maryland, where Makemie was establishing additional churches. It is difficult to say whether their relocation was purely for their own economic advantage or was partly done in consort with Makemie's missionary efforts. A petition from some Presbyterians in Newcastle to the General Assembly of the Church of Scotland in February 1705/6 provides some insight. It begins

We undersubscribers and the greatest number of us born and educated in Ireland under the ministry of Mr. William Traill presbiterian minister formerly at liford are by a Divine providence setled with our families at Newcastle and about it in the province of pensilvania." [13]

The petition goes on to ask if they might be supplied with a minister lest they *"be cast desolate and to our great griefe we and our posterity left as a prey to superstition and heresies."* Almost all of the twenty signers of the petition (viz. Ninian Dunlop, John Stahl (Steele), various Wallaces, David and Andrew Miller, John Garner, Morgan Patton, John and Abraham Emmett) will be found in earlier records in Somerset. The mention of William Traile, who left Somerset and returned to Scotland in 1690, is strong testimony to the lasting impact he had on his flock and how his example led many of them to follow him from Lifford to Somerset two-and-a-half decades earlier.

1.3 Damned Quarter

The earliest settlements in Somerset at Annemessex and Manokin have already been discussed. A third cluster of settlements, or at least surveyed land tracts, began at almost the same time along the Wicomico, the next major river north of the Manokin, and its tributary, Wicomico Creek. At that time the upper part of the

---

[12] Bolton, p. 25.
[13] Scottish Record Office CH 1/2/28 fol. 4; see also Public Record Office of Northern Ireland, T3762; provided to author by R. K. McMaster.

Wicomico River was referred to at first as Cuttmatico Creek and later as Rokiawakin, and the lower Wicomico together with Wicomico Creek was known as Wiccocomico. The tracts surveyed in Wiccocomico at this time had a strong association with Northumberland County, Virginia, located almost directly across the Bay, and were acquired in large part as objects of land speculation by investors from that area. Ownership of some of these tracts changed frequently and it took some time before they were actually settled. Among the early property owners of this area the following were citizens of Northumberland: Thomas Brereton, William Brereton, Samuel Smith, William Thomas, Benjamin Cottman, Isaac Allerton, William Keene, James Dashiels, David Spence, Peter Presley, Francis Roberts, John White, Thomas Roe, John Winsor, and William Shores.[14] Of these, somewhat more than half eventually moved to Somerset while the others remained permanently in Virginia.

Damned Quarter was the name given to a small inlet issuing from the south side of Wicomico Sound, originally known as Williamsons Creek. It first appears in the records as the name chosen for a tract patented by William Stevens in 1666 and assigned to Major Thomas Ball, a 150-acre strip of land lying along the coast between Damned Quarter Creek on the east and Balls Creek on the west, described as follows:

> all that parcell of land surveyed for the aforesaid William Stevens
> called Damn Quarter lying on the Eastermost side of Chesapeak
> Bay being on the Southermost side or point of Wiccocomico
> beginning for breadth at the Westermost side of a Creek called
> Williamson's Creek[15] at a marked white oak standing at the Mouth
> thereof and from thence up the said Creek forty perches, bounded
> on the South with a line drawn West South West from the end of the
> former line for length six hundred and thirty perches to a Creek
> called Bales (Ball's) Creek, bounded on the West by the said Creek
> called Bales Creek, bounded on the North by the sound or Bay of
> Wiccocomico aforesaid containing and now laid out for one
> hundred and fifty acres more or less[16]

Whether Colonel Stevens had a special reason for selecting the name is not known. Its location in the lee of Deal Island, then known as Devil Island, may have been suggestive. The local legend quoted by W. H. Polk[17] is that the glow and density of the firefly population in the surrounding marshland during the steamy summer nights were intense enough to give it the appearance and feel of the underworld. In the land records of Somerset, the name appears variously as Damned Quarter, Dam Quarter, Damn Quarter, and Dame Quarter, but the

---

[14] These can all be documented either from the Order Books of Northumberland County, or the land records of Somerset.
[15] Earlier name for Damned Quarter Creek.
[16] MDLP 12:458.
[17] PF&K, p. 51.

20

meaning was implicit in any case and understood by all. The present names of Dames Quarter and Deal Island were a later 19th century development, more consonant with the gentility of that era.

Like many localities of the Eastern Shore, the area has its own distinctive character and history. There are stories that it was a haunt for pirates in the 18th century, but this is mostly an exaggeration. It was a hardscrabble community which survived primarily on agriculture as well as some shipbuilding activity. During the time of the Revolutionary War, Tangier Sound, which includes Devil Island and Damned Quarter, was a haven for the loyalist Picaroons[18] and several armed naval engagements occurred in its waters. Most notable was the battle of Kedges Strait in December 1782, a deplorable engagement from the American side which saw the last American blood shed in the Revolution, though it was not against a legitimate British force. The Picaroons were a lawless band of renegades beholden to no one other than their disreputable leader, Joseph Whaland. The war gave them license to engage in any mischief likely to yield a profit or provide entertainment, and they were never really defeated. In a later period, that remarkable individual known as the Parson of the Isles, Rev. Joshua Thomas, redeemed the reputation of this area.[19] He lived and is buried on Deal Island, but traveled throughout the region in his Chesapeake canoe known as *The Methodist,* carved from a single massive tree, preaching and conducting camp meetings that left a lasting and benevolent impression on the character of its people.

But these episodes were far in the future when the first settlers arrived in the 1670s. In their day the area was very sparsely settled, and acquisition of its lands had been done more for speculation than serious settlement. Prior to Polkes Lott and Polkes Folly, only eighteen tracts totaling 2800 acres had been patented in the Damned Quarter peninsula,[20] not counting Devil Island where an additional handful of settlers could be found. The tract Damned Quarter itself passed in quick succession from Colonel Stevens to Thomas Ball, to Major Thomas Brereton of Northumberland, and finally to John White of the same county in 1675. It was White who was the first among the succession of owners to actually take up residence on it with his wife and four daughters who are listed as transportees in 1680.[21]

It is difficult in this initial period to be sure when the area actually became the residence of *bona fide* settlers. It seems likely that the first group of permanent inhabitants of the Damned Quarter peninsula arrived in 1672 from Northumberland County, Virginia, about 25 miles across the bay. The Provincial

---

[18] A good account can be found in Footner, Chapter 4.
[19] Op. cit., Chapter 6.
[20] In chronological order of their surveys: Damned Quarter, Friends Content, Golden Quarter, Lumn's Improvement, Lumn's Encrease, Elliotts Choice, Davids Destiny, The Downs, Roberts Lott, Jones Adventure, Locust Hummock, The Hope, Oxford, Jesimon, Roberts Recovery, Forlorne Hope, Tilbury and Glascowe.
[21] MDLP WC2, p. 321.

Land Office records show that on 6 June 1672 Francis Roberts proved head rights to 550 acres of land for transporting "*himself, Rosamond his wife, Alice his daughter, Christopher Little, John Pelton (Pelkee?), Collet Seaverne, Rachel Grandee, Katherine King, Sarah Irish, Jone Little (wife of Christopher), and Abigail, an English woman servant*" from Virginia.[22]

This little band of transportees was a curious lot. Of their leader, Francis Roberts, there is much to be learned from the records of Northumberland. It is clear that he did not come to Somerset simply as an opportunist land speculator, although he certainly was that. He was fleeing a myriad of legal problems, one step ahead of the posse so to speak, and relocating to Somerset was for him an easy means of escape. The compelling need for such a course becomes clear from the litany of entries relating to Francis Roberts which may be found in the Northumberland Order Books (court records) over the period 1662-1673, including fourteen debt collections, all settled against him, and three cases involving bastardy.[23] The final mention of him is recorded on 21 May 1673: "*Whereas it appears to this Court that Fran. Roberts standeth indebted unto Mr. James Gaylard the summe of five hundred pounds of tobaccoe & caske, & is departed this Colony, an attachmt. is awarded the sd. Mr. Gaylard against the estate of the sd. Roberts for the sd. Summe with costs retorneable to the next Court.*"

Thus Roberts had simply fled the Province with his family and ragtag boatload of followers, most of whom were likely also absconding from obligations or indentures in Virginia. Collette Sevearne (Severin), for example, was adjudged age 12 as servant to Ralph Waddington only two years earlier in the Northumberland Court.[24] John Pelkee was indentured to Thomas Peryne and adjudged to be of age 15 in October 1668.[25] It seems unlikely that these two were actually released by their Northumberland masters so that Roberts could claim them as transportees in Maryland. Rachel Grandee was already a servant of Francis Roberts, aged 16 in July 1670. She became the mother of his illegitimate son John, who appears in Somerset records alternately under the surnames Roberts and Grandee/Grundy. There is no mention in the Northumberland Order Books for the other accompaniers, Sarah Irish, Katherine King, and "Abigail, an English woman servant," but we can surmise that they came from similar circumstances. No doubt they all had their own special tales to tell of the hardships that induced them to leave Virginia and follow a proven lecher like Roberts to a new life in a different Province.

---

[22] MDLP WT:708; also Liber 17:33. In 17:33 the name is spelled "Robertson" but on the following page, where the same individuals are cited, it is spelled "Roberts."

[23] More detail on these cases will be found in Chapter 4.

[24] Northumberland Order Book 1666-78, p. 96. Sevearne ended up in Monie as a servant to David Spence. See will of David Spence, MDW 18:297.

[25] Northumberland Order Book 1666-78, p. 20. In the Sparacios' transcription of this text the name is spelled "Pelker," but the author has examined the original document and found that "Pelkee" is at least as likely, if not more so, the correct spelling.

Just where these errant pioneers took up residence on their arrival and how they subsisted there is not known, but converting the marshy wilderness of Damned Quarter into a viable landholding must have been a daunting struggle. The two male members of the group, Christopher Little and John Pelkee, no doubt went about the business of clearing areas for cultivation and tending livestock. In time, they appear to have prevailed and raised families of their own. Both registered cattle earmarks on the same day in 1680. In 1682 Pelkee had a fifty-acre tract surveyed which he called Locust Hummock, and in 1683 Christopher Little purchased a 100-acre parcel from Francis Roberts to which he gave the name Bitts Folly. Pelkee died in 1703, leaving a rather peculiar will that did not provide for his wife or children. We only know of his children's existence from a later entry in the rent rolls for Somerset that cites the "relict and orphans of John Pelkee." Christopher Little also raised a family in Damned Quarter and apparently died sometime prior to May 1699, when Robert Polke wrote his will mentioning *"an orphan boy called Christopher Little"* as an indentured servant.

For his part, Francis Roberts probably did not put much effort into land cultivation, for he was buying and selling land at a rapid pace at this time. More than twenty separate land transactions involving Roberts can be found in the county and provincial land records during the period 1668-1684. At some point he took up residence permanently in a dwelling known as the "Fort House" alongside the western side of Williamsons, or Damned Quarter, Creek.[26] His first wife, Rosamond, passed on, probably soon after their arrival, and Rachel Grandee became the mother of his son, John Roberts, alias Grandee.

In addition to the boatload of Northumberland transportees, a handful of other new settlers arrived in the period from 1670 to 1680 to become permanent residents of the area. In the near vicinity of Damned Quarter were John White, Charles Williams, Samuel Jones, George Betts and John Richins; John Pelkee and Christopher Little, who arrived with Francis Roberts, as already mentioned, also settled in this area. On Devils Island were Thomas Roe, John Winsor, Henry Layton, and John Laws, and at Monie to the east were John Panter (Panther), John Rencher (Renshaw), Benjamin Sawser, George Phoebus, Thomas Bloyce, Roger Woolford, and Thomas Walter. Together, these few settlers and their families constituted the populace of the Damned Quarter peninsula when Robert Polke and family arrived in 1687. The location of their surveyed land tracts, along with those of Robert Polke, are shown in Figure 3. It was a sparsely settled primitive area, just barely on the edge of becoming cultivated, but such as it was, this was the world into which Robert and Magdalen entered at the end of their long transatlantic voyage. One has to wonder just how they came to select this remote and inauspicious woodland as their point of beginning in the New World. We may never have a complete answer to this question but a possible explanation is suggested in the next chapter.

---

[26] SOJR, 1730-33:.8.

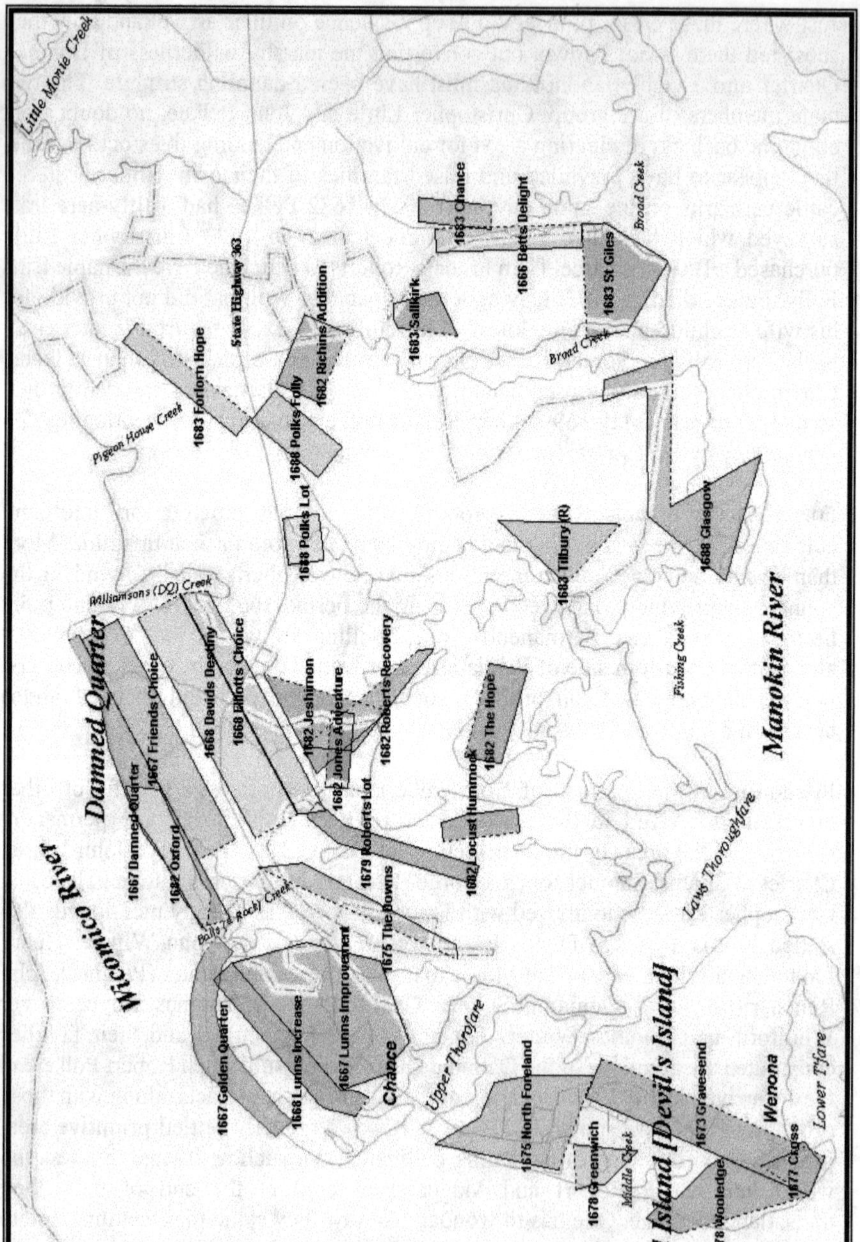

Figure 3. Surveyed land tracts in Damned Quarter, 1688.

24

2. Robert and Magdalen Polke

To the best of our knowledge, the story of Robert and Magdalen begins with the passion or ambition of a junior officer for the wife and estate of his departed commander. This is the tradition that has come down to us, not through their descendants in America, but as the legacy left behind in Ireland. There are two sources for this—a letter from a 19th century descendant of Magdalen's sister Barbara, and a supplemental account which was found more recently in the Pollock estate in Scotland.

John Keyes, a sixth generation descendant of Barbara Tasker and Captain John Keyes, in his letter to W. H. Polk, the author of *Polk Family and Kinsmen*, dated 17 October 1877 says with reference to the daughters of Roger Tasker:

> *Magdalen, the younger, was married to Colonel Porter. He died*
> *some time before the 'Derry Spree'. Then she ran off with one Polk,*
> *and she having no family to Col. Porter, his family obtained most of*
> *the property in the estate Moneen.*

The other account, which seems to come from the same source but expressed somewhat more forcefully, appears in handwritten notes (c.1880) discovered at Castle Pollock in Renfrewshire, Scotland, many years after they were written. These notes apparently originated from enquiries made by "E. F. T." in America, identified as a descendant of Robert and Magdalen's son Joseph, who refers to work being done at the time by W. H. Polk. A copy of these notes was given to Mr. Richard, then President of Clan Pollock, on a visit there in 1997. It reiterates the above account as follows:

> *From the descendant in Ireland of Magdalen's sister (Barbara the*
> *only other child of Col. Tasker and who married Capt. John Keyes)*
> *is learned that the marriage of Robert Pollok to Magdalen was*
> *bitterly opposed. There was great trouble over it but on the death of*
> *his commanding (officer) Col. Porter, with whom he was on*
> *intimate terms, he married the widow against all opposition and*
> *just after the siege of Londonderry, being obliged to quit the*
> *country, he placed in ship what effects he could hastily get together*
> *and set sail for America. After a long voyage they ascended*
> *Chesapeake Bay and landed in the Eastern Shore of Maryland at*
> *what is known as Dames Quarter.*

The timeline in this passage is certainly inaccurate, as the marriage must have occurred in 1665-66, and their arrival in America occurred some twenty years later, a year or two before the siege of Derry (1689). Another somewhat indelicate fact not mentioned in these accounts, but which may have been the source of some of the turmoil, concerns the timing of Robert and Magdalen's marriage. John Porter was still alive when the Donegal Hearth Rolls were compiled in 1665, and Robert and Magdalen's first child Anne was born in 1665-66, as we now know from the Somerset records. This would seem to indicate a rather precipitous turn of events, and not kindly regarded, especially if Magdalen's marriage of at least eleven years[1] to Colonel Porter was childless.

As noted in Chapter 1, the arrival of Robert and Magdalen in Maryland occurred about 1686 or 1687 and was probably inspired by the lead of Francis Makemie, William Traile, and the other Presbyterian ministers who responded to the invitation of Colonel Stevens. A good-sized contingent of Ulster Scots arrived in Somerset about this time, and their presence can be seen in the land and court records of Somerset. According to the 1874 letter of Colonel W. T. G. Polk quoted in *Polk Family and Kinsmen,* family tradition holds that Robert and Magdalen first arrived at Pigeon House Creek in the Damned Quarter peninsula. This is the next inlet from Wicomico Sound eastward of Damned Quarter Creek. The tract Polkes Folly is indeed located at the head of Pigeon House, as noted in its survey description, and the other Polk lands acquired in Damned Quarter all cluster about this area, so this tradition seems well-founded. Of course, it was not just a matter of arriving at Pigeon House, staking a claim, and beginning the clearing of land. Robert and Magdalen were probably welcomed by earlier arrivals, possibly formerly known to them in Ireland, who would have provided them with initial shelter and sustenance until they were properly settled.

Certainly the acquisition of land would have been their first priority although the formal transaction may not have occurred for a year or more after their arrival. The choice of land was a momentous decision as they probably had means enough to get started but not to compensate for any serious missteps. There was no doubt a period of time during which they stayed with one or more other families, working with them, and getting a grasp on what they had undertaken. Once a decision was made, there was a formal process of warrant, survey and patent to be followed for obtaining land from the Maryland Proprietors who, in principle, retained ownership of the land. Patents were issued under certain conditions, most essentially the annual rent "in free and common soccage," which was specified at two shillings per fifty acres at that time to be paid to the Proprietors at St. Mary's in two installments every year, at Michaelmas and the Feast of the Assumption.

We can only speculate on what led Robert Polke to select Damned Quarter as the place on which to settle his family and build the future, but it surely must have been based in part on advice from persons he trusted. One such person may have been Captain, later Colonel, David Brown, a leading figure in Somerset at that

---

[1] The Civil Survey of Donegal mentions John Porter as the son-in-law of Roger Tasker. The survey for all of Ireland was taken during the period 1654-56; that of Donegal is usually dated 1654, but may have been later, so the marriage may have only lasted nine years.

time and an acknowledged leader of the Scotch-Irish. There is a revealing coincidence in Brown's certificate of survey for a tract he called Glasgow, also located in Damned Quarter, with Robert Polke's certificates for Polkes Folly and Polkes Lott. These are all dated 7 March 1688(NS), and appear together on the same page of Land Office Patents Liber 22.[2] These tracts certainly appear to have been surveyed as a group, indicating a close association between Robert Polke and David Brown.

Captain Brown was one of the Somerset Commissioners at this time. His identification with the Scotch-Irish is made quite clear in the following indictment filed in Somerset Court June, 1690:[3]

> *Matthew Scarbrough of this County at the house of James Minor in the hundred of Bogetenorton Anno. '89. his Ma'ties peace then and their did not keep, but their M't'ies. Comrs did abuse and contemne, Calling Capt David Browne Rogue & Dogg, and **in an oppirous manner stile him the Scotch Irishmens God**, and upon the matter aforesd did beat and wound William Pattent of this County, taylor, saying affirming and his wicked intent wth a loud voyce declaring that it was no more sin to kill the sd Pattent than it was to kill a dogg not regarding that due respect by the law of God he ought and should give to Magistracy but in despite of their power & authority in it by law invested by particularizing the sd Capt David Browne in the name of the whole did tacitly imply his contempt to the sd power. Their Maties Attorney craves judgmt may be entered agt the sd Scarbrough according to Law in that case made and provided.*

Obviously, not all in Somerset were happy with the advent of the Scotch-Irish in the 1680s. Apart from the rancorous language, this passage is interesting in that it clearly places David Brown at the front of the Scotch-Irish in Somerset. Brown had arrived in Somerset from Glasgow, Scotland, about 1669-70 and quickly became one of its leading citizens. He was certainly a Presbyterian, for in his will, written in 1696, he bequeathed 10,000 lbs. of tobacco to Rev. Thomas Wilson, the Presbyterian minister of Manokin, and a similar endowment to the College of Glasgow where Rev. Francis Makemie had studied before his ordination. Based on these strong Presbyterian connections, it seems rather likely that David Brown was the real instigator of the letter sent to the Presbytery of Laggan by Colonel Stevens in 1680. Brown was in fact the foreman of the Somerset Grand Jury that made the following recommendation in 1672: [4]

> *It is the opinion of us Grand Jurors that Sermon shoulld be taught in foure several places in the County (vizt) one the first Sunday at the house of Mr. William Stevens at Pocomoke one the second Sunday at the house of Daniell Curtis in Annemessicks one the third Sunday at the house of*

---

[2] On the Manokin River side of the peninsula, about two miles due south of Polkes Folly.
[3] SOJR 1689-90: 103.
[4] SOJR 1671-75:79.

Christopher Nutter in Manoakin and one the fourth Sunday at the house of Thomas Roe in Wiccocomoco. And it is our desire the Mr Matix should there preach.

David Brown Foreman.

Robert Matix (Maddox) served as a minister in Somerset for several years, but there is no record of his presence there any later than 1675.[5] A few other ministers made appearances in this period, but none that remained permanently. By 1680 the case for a regular minister was probably addressed by the Somerset commissioners and produced Colonel Stevens' letter to Ireland. Unfortunately, the Court records for that period are lost, so no account of this is found in Somerset. All we have is the mention of it in the Laggan Presbytery minutes already quoted. Since David Brown was already on record on the need for regular religious services and was well-acquainted with the Presbyterians of Scotland and Ulster, it is highly likely that he would have been one of those pressing for a "Godly Minister" and very happy, in particular, to solicit a Presbyterian from Ulster.

David Brown continued to rise in prominence and became a member of the governing Council of the Province in the aftermath of the Maryland Revolution in 1689, and from that point his rank is indicated as "Colonel" in the Somerset records. His Presbyterian credentials were no doubt a factor in his selection since they aligned well with the Calvinist faith of William and Mary, the new monarchs of England. The other delegate from Somerset to the Provincial Council at that time was Major Robert King, also a Presbyterian. Brown and King were neighbors on the Manokin, at the head of the Damned Quarter peninsula, an area almost completely inhabited by Presbyterians.[6] It may well have been part of a general intent to populate the area with his co-religionists that led Brown to recommend Damned Quarter as a place of settlement to Robert Polke in 1687. However, it came about, Robert's choice of the name Polkes Folly for his new abode speaks rather wryly to us over the centuries about his misgivings for this endeavor, but, for better or worse, here began the history of the Polk family in America.

~~~~~~~

In what follows, information gleaned from various primary sources about Robert and Magdalen and their descendants is presented with commentary. Most of this comes from the author's personal research into the original colonial records of Somerset and Dorchester counties and the Province of Maryland.[7] This was done

---

[5] Torrence, p. 125.

[6] Robert King may in fact have come, like Robert Polke, from the Barony of Raphoe in Donegal – he used the name Leck for a tract of land he purchased in 1691. Leck is a Parish in Raphoe.

[7] The author is particularly indebted to Mr. John C. Lyon and Dr. Jean E. Russo for their assistance in this effort and generous sharing of indexes and extracts from the Somerset Judicials developed in their own private research.

as thoroughly as possible, but no claim is made that all the pertinent citations from those records have been retrieved. Anyone who has worked with these documents knows that would not be possible in a finite amount of time. It is indeed fortunate that so much information about these people has managed to survive from that distant and primitive community. Few other counties of the American colonial era are as rich as Somerset in this regard. The author has searched all the court, probate, land, and tax records of Somerset County for Polk family appearances. Combined with information from earlier family histories, this data has been used to develop a genealogy table or family tree for the Polk/Pollock family, beginning with Robert and Magdalen. The first four generations of the tree are presented in Appendix I.

2.1 Robert Polke (c.1638-1703)

Parents: not known
Date of birth: c.1638-1640, no definite record
Birth place: probably Ireland, no definite record
Will: MD Wills, 11:356; written 6 May 1699, amended 8 August 1702, proved
  5 June 1703
Inventory: 16 August 1703, appraised at £50/16/11
Spouse: Magdalen Tasker (c.1636-1727), daughter of Roger Tasker and widow
  of Colonel John Porter; marriage 1665-66, Donegal, Ireland
Children: Anne, John, Margaret, William, Ephraim, James, Robert, David,
  Martha, Joseph
Property: Polkes Folly (100A, patented 1687), Polkes Lott (50A, patented
  1687), Forlorne Hope (100A, purchased 1697), all in Damned Quarter

ROBERT'S first appearance on record may possibly be as the "Robert Poak" listed in Raphoe, within the Barony of Raphoe, in the 1665 Hearth Rolls for Donegal; a John Poak is also listed there. There is no further information to identify this person as the Robert Polke who married the widow of John Porter, but there are no other individuals of similar name listed for Donegal so it is not unreasonable to suppose that this was our Robert. His reputed commander, John Porter, is listed in the Rolls at "Monyn" in Lifford and presumably still alive at the time. Just one year later, in 1666, Robert was not only married to Magdalen, but their first child Anne was born.

Beyond this mention, there is only scattered evidence of Polk or Pollock presence in 17th century Ulster that has so far come to light. The rather fanciful claims in some family histories of vast land grants made by the King of Scotland to "Sir Robert of Ireland"[8] just do not have any basis in fact. There are no Pollocks appearing in the lists of undertakers and servitors that took up land in the plantation of Ulster following the ascension of James I (VI of Scotland) in

---

[8] PF&K, p. 5; also Garrett, AHM, Vol. 1, p. 378-9.

England and the escheatment of native Irish lands in Ulster. The John and Robert Poak of the 1665 Hearth Rolls did have land or would not have been listed, but it was of modest extent. No Poak, Pollock, or related name is found in the 1654-56 Civil Survey of Donegal, but that was limited to a smaller group of major land holders to which they did not belong.

The first appearance of a Pollok in the Ulster plantation is probably James Pooke, a merchant at Strabane, County Tyrone, who along with others "all of the Scotch nation or descent," was granted a certificate of denization by James I in 1617. These grants provided "that they be free from the yoke of Scotch or Irish servitude, and enjoy the rights and privileges of English subjects."[9]

Strabane was one of the plantation settlements that grew quickly as an urban center after its incorporation in 1613. This was primarily due to the leadership and energy of James Hamilton, Earl of Abercorn and undertaker for Strabane, who came from Paisley in Renfrewshire, Scotland. R. J. Hunter, a well-known historian of the plantation, comments on this as follows: "Strabane was thus fulfilling the trading needs of the Scottish colony of which it was the urban focus. The few surviving records of this trade show it to have been with Renfrew in Scotland, near to the home district of the Earl of Abercorn."[10] Renfrewshire is, of course, also the home of Polloks in Scotland, so it is quite reasonable to suppose that it was the origin of James Pooke, the merchant of Strabane. Polloks and Hamiltons in fact resided in the adjacent lands of Overpollok, Mearns, and Fingalton in the Eastwood District of Renfrewshire.[11]

Strabane was located directly across the Foyle River from Lifford and Ballendrait, so it is also reasonable to ask whether James Pooke was the father or grandfather of Robert Polke who married Magdalen, the daughter of Roger Tasker of Ballendrait. This is speculative, but does provide a plausible line to connect Robert Polke back to the Polloks of Renfrewshire based on an actual, documented person of Pollok or similar name in Ulster at the right place and time.

~~~~~~~~

Claims have also been made that Robert was in Cromwell's Army[12], but this seems unlikely. As a Scots Presbyterian, it is more likely that he, or his father, was one of the Lord Protector's opponents and slated by him for transport out of

---

[9] The date of the grant is 14 August, 14th year of James I's reign (1617). The original documents were lost in the Dublin Courthouse fire of 1922, but a list of persons issued such certificates appears in *Calendar of the Patent Rolls of the Reign of James I*, p. 306-7
[10] Hunter, p. 29.
[11] Welsh, pp. 50, 75-76.
[12] PF&K, p. 6; Garrett, AHM, Vol. 1, p. 380.

Ulster to other parts of Ireland (which was not actually carried out).[13] In any case, beyond his association with John Porter, Robert's military career is little more than speculation and will remain so until research into British military records provides something more definite.

Regarding John Porter himself, one contemporary record has been found which supports his military credentials. A John Porter appears in a list of officers to whom lots were allocated (possibly posthumously) in 1666 for service prior to 1649.[14] The list describes him as "Quartermaster" and provides compensation in the amount of £45/11/10. Inclusion in this list clearly implies that Porter served in the Royalist Army and was not a supporter of Cromwell since 1649 was the year that Charles I was tried and executed and Cromwell invaded Ireland. Compensation was made to Royalist officers after the Restoration and enthronement of Charles II in 1660. It is possible, of course, that this was not the same individual, but the presence of a John Porter in the Barony of Raphoe (which included Lifford and Ballendrait) in 1641 is established in the Irish Books of Survey and Distribution, wherein he is listed as a Protestant holder of sixty-six plantation acres.[15]

<p style="text-align:center">~~~~~~~~~~</p>

The date of Robert's departure for America is not known with certainty. He no doubt followed the lead of Rev. William Traile, who left Ballendrait, County Donegal, for Somerset in 1683. Robert's first appearance in colonial records is in the surveys for Polkes Folly and Polkes Lott dated 7 March 1688(NS), which mention a warrant issued to him on 20 November 1687. There is also a record of his daughter Margaret's marriage to Thomas Pollitt at Manokin (Princess Anne) in December 1687, so an arrival date of 1686-87 seems reasonable.

The John "Pelke" who appears in the cattle earmarks list of Somerset in 1680 was not Robert's son John as W. H. Polk suggests,[16] so there is no basis to assume that Robert had arrived in Somerset by 1680. Robert's son John could not have been more than thirteen in 1680, and Robert himself, rather than John, would have registered the earmark if the family was actually there at that time. Further research in the Somerset land records shows that John Pelke was the individual who patented the tract Locust Hummock as "John Pelkee" in 1682 and died in 1703. His will and inventory are transcribed in the records of the Maryland Prerogative Court at the Maryland Archives (with further variations in the spelling of the name).[17] As noted in the previous chapter, he probably came from

---

[13] Cromwell waged his brutal genocidal campaign against the Irish in 1649-50, followed by his battles against the Scots in 1650-52, after which he returned to affairs in England; he died in 1658.

[14] McKenny, Appendix C, 1649 Officers' Lots, p. 212.

[15] Ibid, p. 188.

[16] PF&K, p. 15.

[17] MDW 11:345.

Northumberland County, Virginia, with Francis Roberts, but there is also some indirect evidence of a close relationship to the family of Robert Polke.

~~~~~~~~~~

Robert mentioned eight children in his will written in May 1699. The other two, Anne and Margareth, are known from other documents. The birth years of Robert and Magdalen's children are either known or estimated as follows:

Anne	1666	(deposition, 29 Jul 1709, aged 43; Somerset Land Records, IKL: 125)
John	1668	(estimate, oldest son)[18]
Margaret	1670	(deposition, 7 Aug 1730, aged 60; Somerset Court, 1730-33: 9)
William	1673	(deposition, 11 Aug 1739, aged 66; Somerset Court, 1738-40: 184)
Ephraim	1675	(estimate)
James	1677	(estimate)[19]
Robert	1679	(estimate, see note in section on Robert, Jun.)
David	1681	(estimate)
Martha	1685	(estimate)
Joseph	1689	(deposition, 7 Aug 1730, aged 41, Somerset Court, 1730-33: 9)

With the exception of David and the two daughters Anne and Margaret, this age sequence follows the order as presented by W. H. Polk[20] and as appears in the Polk Family Tree of 1840. This order is also consistent with the fact that John, William, and Ephraim were the first three to acquire their own land holdings, in that order, and they appear to have been independent or nearly so by the time Robert made his will. His sons David, Robert, and Joseph are the only ones provided significant bequests in his will, in that order, and in nearly equal value in terms of price of land in tobacco. The inference is that they were younger and less established and Robert was providing for them with the relatively modest assets at his disposal. James would seem to be in between these groups. He did not acquire any land holdings until 1705, several years after his presumably younger brother Robert Jun., possibly because he was fully taken up with his principal occupation as a shipwright. He eventually acquired extensive land holdings, both in Somerset and Dorchester.

---

[18] The following entry appears in Derry Cathedral, p. 169: *Cristtenings in July 1668 ... John, the Sonn of Robert Poke, baptized 16th.*

[19] Ibid, p. 189: *James, the son of Robert Poke of Belimagrotyr, bapt. 10th* (January 1678(NS)). Ballymagrorty is a townland in Templemore Parish, Londonderry. It is not certain that Robert Poke mentioned in this and previous footnote is the Robert Polke that settled in Maryland, but these two citations certainly lend credibility to the estimated birth years for John and James.

[20] PF&K, p. 28.

David was not known as one of the children of Robert and Magdalen until a copy of Robert's will was found in the Maryland Prerogative Court records in Annapolis, just a few years before the publication of *Polk Family and Kinsmen* (1912). The will, written in 1699, mentions David as one of the principal legatees and appoints him and Magdalen as joint executors. However, David appears to have died by August 1702, when Robert amended the will making Ephraim and James executors. No other citation of David has been found by the author in Somerset probate, land, or judicial records, or any other Maryland colonial records. Moreover, the lands which David should have inherited according to the terms of Robert's will (Polkes Folly and half of Forlorne Hope) ended up in the possession of John, the eldest son. This is consistent with David predeceasing his father and having no heirs, since these lands would revert to the oldest son John in this case, absent any other conditions in Robert's will.

Regarding Margaret, there is no unambiguous primary source record that Robert and Magdalen actually had a daughter of that name (Robert's will mentions Martha, not Margaret), but it was clearly a family tradition when the history was being developed in 1840s and the indirect evidence is quite strong. This is discussed in greater detail in the section on Margaret in the next chapter.

~~~~~~~

As to the spelling of Robert's name, it is found numerous times in the records of Maryland and Somerset and is written almost invariably as "Robert Polke" or "Robt. Polke," with only minor variations. There is never any use of either the title Captain or the middle name "Bruce;" the latter would in fact be highly atypical in that era. The aggrandized name "Captain Robert Bruce Pollock" was not used by the family either in colonial days or in the early development of the family history, as in the notes of Josiah F. Polk or the Polk family tree of 1848. Nor was it used in some early correspondence (1874-75) between W. H. Polk and Mrs. William Hawkins Polk, wife of James K. Polk's younger brother, concerning family genealogy.[21] The middle name "Bruce" seems to have originated, along with the Pollock family lineage from Scotland, with Mary Winder Garrett who published the articles on the Polk family in the *American Historical Magazine* in 1896-1899.[22] Subsequent writers all accepted this account in their work,[23] and it has been widely used ever since. This is unfortunate, and based on primary sources, both the title, Captain, and the middle name, Bruce, are unfounded and inappropriate.

There are almost fifty citations of Robert Polke in existing Maryland colonial documents, the majority of which are listed below. The exact spelling of the name as it appeared in the document is shown in brackets. A more complete transcript

---

[21] Lucy Polk Papers, NC Archives Special Collection, Box 75.13.
[22] Garrett, AHM, Vol. 1, pp. 157 & 380.
[23] In addition to *Polk Family and Kinsmen*, see *Behind the Lines* by Mary Polk Branch and "Memories," by Esther Winder Polk Lowe.

or abstract of these citations can be found in Appendix IV.

7 Mar 1688(NS)	Patent for Polkes Lott and Polkes Folly [Robert Polke]
13 Nov 1689	Somerset Address of Loyalty to Wm.and Mary [Robert Polk]
25 Feb 1691(NS)	Testator, assignment to Anne Polk by Francis Roberts [Robert Polke]
12 Aug 1690	Member of Jury, Taylor vs. Hopkins [Robert Polke]
14 Aug 1690	Member of Jury, Trial of George Seaward [Robert Polk]
14 Aug 1690	Member of Jury, Trial of Daniel Selby [Robert Polke]
14 Aug 1690	Member of Jury, Crawford vs. Towers [Robert Polke]
15 Aug 1690	Member of Jury, Towers vs. Crawford [Robert Polke]
15 Aug 1690	Member of Jury, Smith vs. Holland [Robert Polke]
17 Oct 1690	Cattle earmark recorded [Robert Polyke]
10 Jun 1691	Security for William Mason [Robert Poke]
10 Jun 1691	Member of Jury, trial of Walter Taylor [Robert Poke]
9 Mar 1692(NS)	Member of Jury, trial of Margaret Kennedy [Robert Polke]
11 Mar 1692(NS)	Member of Jury, Gunby vs. Jones [Robert Polke]
11 Mar 1692(NS)	Member of Jury, trial of Thomas Porter [Robert Polke]
11 Mar 1692(NS)	Member of Jury, trial of Daniel Selby [Robert Polke]
Aug Court 1692	Defendant vs. Andrew Whittington, on docket [Robert Poke]
Sep Court 1692	Suit vs. Andrew Whittington, settled out Court [Robert Poke]
14 Nov 1693	Impaneled on Grand Jury [Rob't Polk]
15 Nove 1693	Grand Jury Informer vs. Jane Carr [Robert Poke]
Jan Court 1694(NS)	Subpoena to testify vs. Jane Carr [Rob't Poke]
Jan Court 1693(NS)	Defendant vs. Snee, listed on docket [Rob't Pollock, aka Robert Poke]
Jan Court 1694(NS)	Plaintiff vs.Patrick Quatermus, on docket [Robert Polke]
Jan Court 1694(NS)	Plaintiff vs. Edward Hagan, listed on docket [Robert Polke]
10 Jan 1694(NS)	Security on recognizance, bond for Jane Carr [Robert Poke]
11 Jan 1694(NS)	Suit vs. Patrick Quatermus, settled out of Court [Robert Polke]
11 Jan 1694(NS)	Suit vs. Edward Hagan, settled out of Court [Robert Polke]
Mar Court 1694(NS)	Subpoenas issued (3 times), case of Bryan Snee [Rob't Polke]
15 Mar 1694(NS)	Defendant vs. Bryan Snee [Robert Pollock, aka Robert Polke]
14 Jan 1696(NS)	Impaneled on Grand Jury [Robert Polke]
Jan Court 1696(NS)	Defendant vs. Robert Pirrie, on docket [Robert Polke]
Jan Court 1696(NS)	Subpoena to testify, listed on docket [Robert Polke]
Aug Court 1695	Subpoena issued, listed on docket [Robert Polke]
Novr Court 1695	Subpoena issued, listed on docket [Robert Polke, Sen.]
Jan Court 1696(NS)	Subpoena to testify, listed on docket [Rob't Polke, Sen'r]
10 Mar 1696(NS)	Impaneled on Grand Jury [Robert Polke, Sen.]
13 Jun 1696	Payment for attendance at Court (2 entries) [Robert Polke]
10 Mar 1697(NS)	Petition to alter road [Rob't Polke, Sen.]
9 Aug 1697	Deed for Forlorne Hope [Robert Polke]

6 May 1699	Will written [Robert Polke]
5 Jun 1703	Will proved [Robt. Polke]
10 Aug 1703	Inventory of goods and chattels [Robert Polke]

Several other "traditions" about Robert and Magdalen do not appear to have any verifiable basis, specifically his military record, her connection to the family of the Duke of Wellington, and Magdalen's father, Roger Tasker, having been a Chancellor of Ireland. While these cannot be absolutely ruled out, no corroborating records have been found to support them. They were not part of the oral tradition of the Somerset Polks, as reflected in the notes of Josiah F. Polk— and it was from the Somerset Polks that the Polks of North Carolina and Tennessee first learned of Robert and Magdalen. The knowledge of the family history at that time, and its limitations, can be understood from the correspondence in 1848-9 of James K. Polk, Josiah F. Polk, William H. Winder, and Leonidas Polk, who together developed the Polk Family Tree published in 1849. Their correspondence is transcribed in Appendix III.

The assertion that Roger Tasker was a Chancellor of Ireland comes from the Keys family of Donegal who descend from Magdalen's sister Barbara, the wife of Captain John Keys. It entered Polk family tradition when John Keys, a later descendant, made the statement in his letter to W. H. Polk in 1877,[24] and first appeared in published form in Dr. William Mecklenburg Polk's biography of his father, Bishop Leonidas Polk. Mary Winder Garrett repeated the claim in her articles on the Polk family which appeared in the *American Historical Magazine* (AHM) in 1897-1900.[25] These articles contain much genealogical information, but unfortunately also contain numerous errors and need to be read very critically. In fact Ms. Garrett's first two articles had to be revised because of new information that came to light after they were published and were republished a second time.[26] While it is not unlikely that Robert Polke had military experience and that he had been in a regiment of Magdalen's first husband, John Porter, any real knowledge about this remains a task for future research. With respect to Roger Tasker being a Chancellor of Ireland,[27] diligent searching by the author and others has revealed no Chancellor or other high level Irish official of that name. More to the point, Roger Tasker's status is known from the Donegal Civil Survey of 1654, where he is identified simply as a land holder with two sons-in-law, certainly not a lofty position.[28] Finally, concerning any relationship to Wellington, it could only be remote, at best, for the Iron Duke was born in 1769, more than 130 years after Magdalen.

---

[24] PF&K, p. 9.

[25] Garrett, AHM, volumes I-IV.

[26] In fact, W. H. Polk and R. C. Ballard Thruston made highly disparaging remarks about her work in their private correspondence. See W. H. Polk papers.

[27] The first instance of this assertion known to the author is in a letter from W. H. Polk to Mrs. William Hawkins Polk dated 20 January 1874. See Lucy Polk Papers in NC Archives Special Collection, Box 75.13.

[28] See below in Section 2.2.

The connection of Robert Polke with the Pollock or Pollok family of Refrewshire, Scotland, also greatly needs to be re-examined and further researched. Other than the James Pooke of Strabane mentioned earlier in this section, the author knows of no primary sources that establish this connection. Poak/Pollock/Pogue was not an uncommon name in Scotland and Ulster in the 17th century as a perusal of the Scottish Old Parish Registers or volumes of the Scottish Records Society will show, and persons of this name do not all necessarily trace back through a single line of descent from Fulbert, the progenitor. The commonly accepted lineage from Fulbert to Robert Polke of Donegal and Somerset also appears to have originated with Ms. Garrett, although she makes attribution to Mrs. William Hawkins Polk. This lineage appears to have been derived in part from the account of the Pollock family published in *A General Description of the Shire of Renfrew* by George Crawfurd and George Robertson (1818). A badly garbled version of it was published in the *American Historical Monthly* articles[29] and afterwards repeated almost verbatim in *Polk Family and Kinsmen*, surprisingly without attribution to Ms. Garrett.

This leaves unanswered the question of whether Robert Polke of Donegal descended from the lineage of Pollok-of-that-Ilk traced in Crawfurd/Robertson. Was there such a connection? In Burke's *Presidential Families of the United States of America*, it is suggested that Robert was the great-grandson of Sir John Pollok of Renfrewshire (13th Laird of Pollock-of-that-Ilk) and Janet Mure, through a son, Robert, with the caveat that the three generations of this lineage are "in fact unproven, but appear highly probable," although no source for this information is given. It should in fact be noted, to the contrary, that Sir John, the 13th Laird, left a will in which mention is made of one son, John, who succeeded him, and of two daughters, Janet and Edgedia, but not of a son Robert.[30]

Another possibility was suggested by Edward A. Langslow Cock in notes collected during his writing of *Pollock Pedigree, 1080-1950* and later in notes published by J. F. Engert.[31] Cock developed a lineage chart to explain "the probable origin of the Pollocks of Newry (Ireland)," which shows our Robert Pollok of Donegal and his son Robert Jr. as their progenitor. In this chart Robert is shown as the son of John Pollok, second son of John Pollok-of-that-Ilk (14th Laird, d. 1596) and Dorthea Stewart, but the explanation offered for this is a heuristic argument based on the incidence of family names.[32] The part of the lineage showing Robert Polk Jun. as progenitor of the Pollocks of Newry, Ireland, is certainly incorrect since Robert Polk Jun. lived and died in Dorchester County, Maryland. His son Robert (III) was born no earlier than 1711 and could hardly

[29] Garrett, AHM, Vol. 1, No. 2, pp. 154-156; Vol. 2, No. 4, pp. 376-79.
[30] Edinburgh Commissary Court, Johne Pollok 1578, Reference CC8/8/6; see also Engert, *Pollock: Letters, Queries and Notes*, p. 16.
[31] Engert, *Irish Pollocks: Letters, Queries and Notes*, p. 46.
[32] Op. cit., p. 18.

have been the father of John Pollock of Newry, born in 1718.

The scholarship in E. A. L. Cock's work is generally thorough as it relates to the Pollocks of Britain, but the information that he had concerning Robert Polk of Donegal/Somerset and his descendants in America was very limited. His notes offer no new information on Robert's lineage but do provide evidence that there was a John Pollock, Lieutenant of Foot (infantry), in Ireland in 1662. It is not unreasonable to suppose that this individual was Robert's brother, and that both may have indeed been sons of John Pollock as shown in Cock's lineage chart, but, once again, this is only speculation.

Another account, partly consistent and partly at odds with the others, is offered in the 1893 biography of Bishop Leonidas Polk by his son, William M. Polk:[33]

> *The branch of the Pollock family from which Leonidas Polk traced his descent was represented in the reign of James, Sixth of Scotland and First of England [James' reign was 1603-1625], by John Pollock, a gentleman of some estate in Lanarkshire, not far from what was then the small but important cathedral city of Glasgow. Those were troublous times in Church and State, and John Pollock, who was an uncompromising Presbyterian, left his native land to join the new colony of Protestants which had been established in the north of Ireland. It was a hazardous adventure; for although the last of the numerous petty kings of Ireland had professedly submitted to the English arms at the beginning of King James's reign, the Irish people cherished a vindictive hatred of their conquerors, and while the king's writ ran throughout the length and breadth of the island, the Scotch and English colonists were often compelled to maintain peace by drawing and using their good swords. Little more is now known of John Pollock than that he lived to a good age, and that he had a son of true-blue Presbyterian principles and of a strenuous temper like his own.*
>
> *Robert Pollock, a son of John Pollock, served as a subaltern officer in the regiment of Colonel Tasker in the Parliamentary army against Charles I, and took an active part in the campaigns of Cromwell. He married Magdalen Tasker, who was the widow of his friend and companion in arms, Colonel Porter, and one of the two daughters of Colonel Tasker, then Chancellor of Ireland, of Bloomfield Castle, on the river Dale...*

As is generally the case with genealogical works of that era, no sources are given. Considering these various accounts, one can only say, in short, that the authorities are at odds and the known primary source information is simply insufficient to determine the lineage, or even the parents, of Robert Polke with certainty. It

---

[33] W. M. Polk, pp. 2-3.

remains an open matter at this time.

~~~~~~~~

Another, totally different, lineage for Robert Polke was suggested in a recently published book, *Our Polk Family*, by Anna Lee Polk Comfort, now deceased. The suggested lineage is not presented as Mrs. Comfort's own work but as supplemental material given to her by another Polk family researcher, Mrs. Doris Polk Killingsworth of South Carolina, and simply included as "Additional Information" in Chapter V of the book. Mrs. Comfort does not endorse the material or the suggested lineage but states that she "has some doubts about the records," and leaves the reader to decide "whether you feel we are descended from Scotch-Irish or French-Irish." The material presented is attributed to a professional genealogist, Mr. Charles H. Starr of Salt Lake City, hired by Mrs. Killingsworth in 1984-85. Mr. Starr is no longer in business, but the author has corresponded with Mrs. Killingsworth who has generously provided him with much of the genealogical material that Mr. Starr developed for her.

The genealogy of Robert Polke suggested by Mr. Starr differs from the usual understanding of Robert's origin in several major respects. Specifically, it claims that:

1) Robert "Poague" was of French Huguenot descent;
2) Robert married his first wife, Jeanne Joyvelin, in a Quaker ceremony in Strabane, County Tyrone, in 1657;
3) Robert married his second wife, Margaret Mackie, in 1684, and she accompanied him as his wife when the family emigrated to Maryland c.1687; "Magdalen" was an alternative form of her name;
4) Magdalen's only child by Robert was his youngest son, Joseph.

The author has carefully reviewed these materials and has found many issues, both with respect to the sources cited and the veracity of some of the data. The bottom line, in his opinion, is that the evidence does not support the claimed lineage.

The principal sources cited by Mr. Starr are Quaker records. However, in all but two cases, the author has not been able to locate and verify these records. The most important is *Extracts of Quaker Records, Kingdom of Ireland*, which is cited as the basic reference for Robert Poague's suggested French lineage and his supposed first marriage, as presented on pages 235 and 236 of Mrs. Comfort's book. This work is attributed to William Wade Hinshaw, the well-known authority on Quaker records in America, but it is not listed in *WorldCat*, Family Search, the Library of Congress, or at the Swarthmore College Library, the acknowledged leading center for Quaker records in America. The Irish Quaker Historical Library in Dublin and the Ulster Historical Foundation in Belfast also have no record of it. One can only conclude that it does not exist.

In addition, the following references are cited as microfilms available through LDS Family Search:[34]

- GS Film 1,212,684—Protestant Church Records, Parish of Stabane
- GS Film 50330 – Quaker Monthly Meeting, West Nantmeal Twp, Chester PA

Neither of these could be found in the online Family Search catalog either by the microfilm number or by keyword search. Both are essential for validating the claimed Huguenot lineage of Robert Polke, or "Poague."

Finally, it is stated (p. 242) that Margaret "McKey", supposed second wife of Robert Polk, was from Moneen, Parish of Lifford, Donegal, Ireland. This is the basis for connecting Margaret Mackie with Moneen and Lifford. However, the actual record in the Register of Derry Cathedral, Templemore Parish, reads as follows:[35]

Marriages in May 1684: Robert Poog of this Parish and Margaret Mackie of the Parish of Faan, married by Licensce by Mr. Adam Reed, rector of Faan, the 14th.)

Faan is in the Barony of Inishowen in north Donegal. There is really no basis for connecting the Robert and Margaret Poog of this marriage with the Robert and Magdalen Polke who emigrated to Somerset circa 1686.

There are also some problematic factual issues in Mr. Starr's data relating to Robert's wife Magdalen. These will be addressed in the section on Magdalen below, after other information about her has been presented.

~~~~~~~~

An inventory of Robert's goods and chattels dated 16 August 1703 was made following his death, as usual in colonial Maryland, and was officially recorded in the Inventories and Accounts of the Maryland Prerogative Court.[36] It reads as follows:

An inventory of the estate of Robert Polke late of Somerset County deceased taken and appraised by us the subscribers -

	£	s	d
To 1 feather bed and covering a small chest at	02	02	06
To 1 yard and half of serge and handmill at	01	13	0
To 5 Books and 17 pound pewter and 1 Iron pot at	01	01	6

---

[34] https://familysearch.org/search
[35] Derry Cathedral, p. 277.
[36] MDIA 24:96.

To 1 frying pan and 3 Iron Wedges at 00 10 0
To 1 Grubing hoe and 1 small Gun at 00 09 2
To 2 Tin pans and 1 pot hanger at 00 04 6
To 3 Reaphooks and a parcel of linnen yarn at 00 17 9
To 38 pounds of bacon and a Grinstone at 00 13 6
To 1 Servant girl and 1 old Bed tick on at 06 05 0
To 28 head of Hogs and one Mare at 11 05 0
To 13 head of cattle at 24 00 00
To 1 Hide of tanned leather and 1 Iron pot at 00 15 00
To a parcel of old lumber at . . . . <u>01 00 00</u>
£50 16 11

Given under our hands and seals this 10th day of August Anno Dom 1703
George Hutchins
Richard Wallis

~~~~~~~~~~

The location of Polkes Folly and Robert Polke's other properties in Damned Quarter can be fixed with near certainty, probably within the order of a hundred feet or so, but a visit to the site will quickly show that such precision is not very meaningful in any case since the area is now just an open marshland. A view of the landscape as it now appears at the approximate location of Polkes Folley is shown in Figure 4. The original markers or "bounders" have long since disappeared, and the area has been subsumed into the Deal Island Wildlife Management Area, obliterating almost all remaining traces of the original properties. The actual locations can be closely reconstituted by extracting data from the original survey certificates and assembling the full database into a tract map for the area in the manner of a jigsaw puzzle, but this is not an exact process. The difficulty is that there were inherent errors, inconsistencies, and lack of precision in the original patents that were never fully resolved. These were generally issued with a basic metes and bounds description, usually citing a certain marked tree along a creek or swamp side as the point of beginning, frequently without any reference to other adjacent properties. In other parts of Somerset, Worcester and Wicomico these problems have in large part been settled by resurveys done in the latter half of the 18th or in the 19th century, but in Damned Quarter the need for such corrections was greatly diminished by the continual deterioration and abdication of the land.

The area on the north side of the old colonial road continued to be inhabited through most of the 19th century. A small community known as the village of Bethel grew up there, populated mostly by the Bozman family, as shown in the Dames Quarter map in the Atlas of the Eastern Shore of Maryland published in 1877. Besides the dozen or so homes there were also a church and grocery store on the site. The village thrived until the turn of the 20th century when the

Figure 4. Landscape at Polkes Folly as it now appears.

encroachment of the marsh on the town rendered the area uninhabitable. Some of the existing houses were actually lifted from their foundations and transferred to other nearby communities. Today, there are still vestiges of the wooded area where the village stood, and a small cemetery where graves of the Bozman family can be found.[37]

At the end of the 19th century ownership of a fair amount of land on the Damned Quarter peninsula reverted to the State of Maryland which constructed a new main road, State Route 363, through it to Chance and Winona on Deal Island in the 1930s. Maryland also reissued the same lands to private ownership again in the first half of the 20th century without any reference to the previous land patents. This seems to have been done mainly for the purpose of setting up hunting and fishing reserves. For example, 2488 acres were patented to the Manokin River Club in 1943. The area between Dames Quarter and Pigeon House on the north side of SR 363, once the domain of Robert and Magdalen and their children, was granted in 1923 to Brice Bozman as a 460-acre tract called Bozmans Marsh without any citation of its earlier history.

The original corner markers of Polkes Folly no longer existed even in the 19th century. However, four deeds in the 1850s from Thomas Shores to his sons Severn, William, Nehemiah and Thomas, help pin down the exact location of Polkes Folly along the original colonial road through the area. The deeds all conveyed lands described as parcels of Polkes Folly.[38] The posts that were placed at the corners of these parcels are gone, but using the orientation of the road and

---

[37] A short article, "Bethel, Maryland?," by T. Aaron Horner, appears in the Nabb Research Center quarterly, *Shoreline*, Volume 8, No. 1, Winter 2001.
[38] SOLR LW 1:328; LW 3:150, LW 4:408 and LW 4:543.

the parcels as described in the deeds effectively fixes the location of the original full tract as shown in Figure 5. The four parcels are identified as PF1, PF2, PF3 and PF4. The northwest boundaries of PF1 and PF2 are described in the deeds as being on the county (old colonial) road and the southeast boundaries of PF2 and PF3 are described as being on the second line of Polks Folly. These are not completely consistent, as may be seen in the figure, but the information is good enough to give us confidence in the basic placement of the tract.

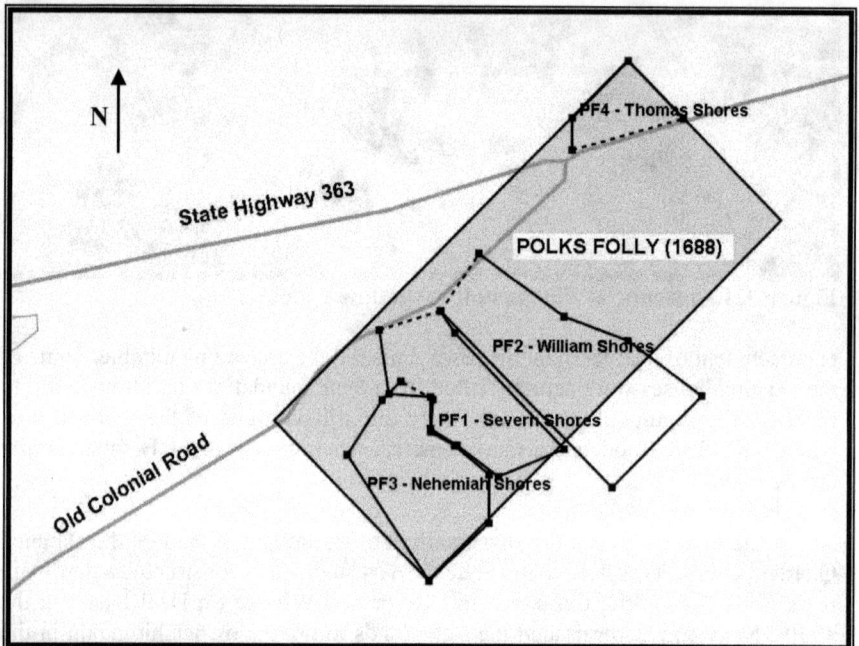

Figure 5. Location of Polkes Folly in Dames Quarter peninsula.

The trace of the old colonial road that wended its way through Damned Quarter from Monie to Deal Island is still maintained as an access road in the Wildlife Management Area and gives a good reference line for gauging the location of the colonial properties. The WSW direction that it follows for a section of the road immediately south of the Pigeon House inlet conforms to the basic lengthwise azimuth of the Polkes Folly, Clonmell, and Forlone Hope tracts. In Figure 6 the approximate location of Robert's three tracts, Polkes Folly, Polkes Lott, and Forlorne Hope are shown on a *Google Earth* image of the area.

~~~~~~~~

Finding the exact site of Robert and Magdalen's original dwelling house would seem an impossible task. Some remains of the original dwelling were still in place in mid-19th century. The following note is recorded in the papers of W. H. Polk at the Library of the University of Kentucky:

This section of Maryland has been steadily sinking for years. There are now perhaps 25 houses forming a little village at that place, probably all on "Polk's Folly" of the tract. There is only about 5 acres of it that is for sale that is high ground. The rest is low and marshy. This part that is for sale is the highest point down there and it is the spot where stood the original home of Robert Bruce Polk that was burned some 50 or 60 years ago. There is at present no house on it. (Letter from Earle B. Polk of Princess Anne, Md. to W. H. Polk, of Lexington, Ky. Dec. 11, 1908.)

This refers to land purchased by Colonel W. T. G. Polk from the Shores estate in 1868; the Shores property originally comprised Polkes Folly, Ballyhack, Clonmell, Polkes Meadow (James Meadow), Forlorne Hope, and Forlorne Hopes Addition, all of which Joseph Pollock sold to John and William Shores in 1748. The village that Earle B. Polk refers to was Little Bethel, on the north side of the road. The area is now an open stretch of marshland, interspersed with scattered clumps of bushes and shrubs and gives little hope to finding the actual site location. Nothing of significance has survived as far as is visible.

In his will Robert left "my now dwelling house and plantation" to Magdalen.[39] Since he bequeathed all of Forlorne Hope and Polkes Folly to sons Robert and David, it might be inferred that his "now dwelling place and plantation" was his other property, Polkes Lott, but this is probably not the case. This 50-acre tract was the first of the two tracts which were certified in Robert's name on 7 March 1688(NS), in the Maryland Patent Liber 22: 371. It is described as follows:

near the head of Damned Quarter bounded as followeth—beginning at a marked pine standing on the east side of the said Dame Quarter from there running South eighty perches thence running East one hundred perches thence North eighty perches thence running West one hundred perches to the first bounder containing and now laid out for fifty acres more or less to be holden of the Mannor of Somerset.

A perch or pole is 16.5 feet. In present times the head of Dames Quarter inlet is quite discernible and is located at the northwestern end of the Deal Island Wildlife Management Area. A small community is still found on the west side of this inlet, but to the south and east the area is nothing but marshland. It probably was little different back in the 18th century, since the tract Polkes Lott seems to have been abandoned by the family. In the Proprietary Debt Books for Somerset[40] the entries for Polkes Lott are annotated over various years as "land unknown," "no charge to," and "land not accounted for." It was not mentioned among the tracts conveyed in the sale of the Polk lands in Damned Quarter to John and William Shores in 1748, and there is no further mention of it in the Somerset land records.

---

[39] The phrase "my now dwelling place" was standard usage in wills written at that time and does not imply relocation from an earlier residence.
[40] MSA Series S12

Figure 6. Approximate location of Robert Polke's properties in Damned Quarter. (*Google Earth* image.)

The last will and testament of Robert Polke:

In the name of God Amen ~ this sixth day of May in the year of our Lord God 1699 I Robert Polke of Somerset County in the Province of Maryland being of Good health and of perfect memory at this present thanks be to God allmighty for the same yet knowing the uncertainty of this present Life and being desireous to settle my affaires doe make this my last will and testament in manner and forme following ~~

First and principally I commend my soul to God who gave it me assuredly believing that I shall receive full and free pardon of all my sins and be saved by the pretious death and merritts of my beloved Saviour and Redeemer Jesus Christ and my body to the Earth from whence it was taken to be buried in a decent and Christian manner at the discretion of my executor hereafter named and as touching such worldly estate as God in his mercy hath bestowed upon me it is my will that it be disposed of as is hereafter expressed ~

2dly ~ I leave to my son Robert Polke a parcell of land called Forlorne Hope formerly belonging to Augustin Standforth but now conveyed to me the sd land called Low Ridge beginning at a marked pine standing in a slash next to my said sons house and from thence running North East the number of poles specified in the pattent, soe leaving to my son Robert what land belongs to the said pattent on the North East side of the said slash to him the said Robert Polke and his heires for ever ~

3dly I leave to my said son David Polke the remainder of the abovesd tract of land called Forlorne Hope as also one hundred acres of land called Polks Folly bound per pattent will appear both said tracts of land to him the said David and his heires for ever

4ly I leave to my beloved wife Magdalen Polke my now dwelling house and plantacon during her naturally life and also a third of what goods and moveables I am possessed with or shall herafter to the day of my death the said goods and moveables to be at her disposing at her decease ~ Another third of my goods and moveables I leave to my daughter Martha be it little or much to her and her heirs for ever and as for the other third it is my will it be equally divided between my sons David and Joseph and if it should please God to remove me before I purchase a seate of land for my son Joseph it is my will that my son David give unto my son Joseph four thousand pounds of tobacco in the lieu of the above said tracts of land left to my said David and as for what cattle I have given to my son Joseph they being in his owne proper mark it is my will he enjoy and possess the same he and his heires for ever

~ for this boy Christopher Little must live with Magdalen Polke during her lifetime then

-5ly I leave to my son James an orphan boy called Christopher Little to

45

him the said James and his heires during the time of his Indenture. I leave unto my son Ephraim the choice of what stears I have or may have att the day of my death I leave unto my sons John and William Polke to each of them twelve pence ~

I constitute and appoint my sonn David Polke and my wife Magdalen Polke to be executors of this my will ~

I constitute and appoint my sons Ephraim and James Polke to be executors of this my last will and testament disannulling and making voide any former will or wills by me made either by word or writt ~ In witness whereof I have hereunto sett my hand and seale the day and year above written and being altered the eighth day of Aug't 1702

Richard Knight
Mary O English   *Robert **X** Polke*
Richard Whitty   *his mark*

And I desire that Martha Pock may have liberty to lett her cattle run on my plantacon until she gets plantacon ~ and as for Sarah Power she must have a heifer at her freedom day ~
Signed sealed and delivered
In the presence of us ~
Robt Polk
Rich Whitey
Rich'd Knight
Mary O English

Memorandum that the 5ᵗʰ day of June the within Will was proved to be the act and deed of the within named Robert Polke by the oaths of Richard Whittley, Richard Knight and Mary English before Peter Dent, Dep'ty Com'ry

~~~~~~~~~

Robert's will is rather complex considering the somewhat limited assets at his disposal, but it seems carefully constructed to provide for his children in the most equitable manner possible considering their individual needs at the time of its writing. Its main provisions are concerned with the distribution of Robert's lands to his three youngest sons, Robert, David, and Joseph. His two oldest sons, William and John, were both well established by this time in a jointly run coopers' business at Manokin (Princess Anne), so Robert bequeathed them twelve pence each, basically a legal formality to preclude any further claim they might make against his estate. The middle two sons, Ephraim and James, who were still living in Damned Quarter, were given somewhat more significant bequests–Robert's cattle to Ephraim, and the apprentice services of Christopher Little to James. His daughters Anne and Margaret were not even mentioned in the will; both were comfortably married and Robert apparently saw no need to provide for them. There was not even a need for the token twelve pence in their case. His unmarried daughter Martha, on the other hand, was specially provided for by the bequest of a third of his personal goods, the same as given to Magdalen, as well as the promise of access for her cattle to his lands.

The tracts Polkes Folly and Forlorne Hope (100 acres each) were split between David and Robert Jun. David received a larger share, but with the proviso that he should give his brother Joseph, Robert's youngest, 4000 pounds of tobacco if Robert [Sen.] were to die before making other arrangements for him. This would certainly have enabled Joseph to acquire property of his own, as Robert had purchased Forlorne Hope for a slightly higher amount, 5000 pounds, only two years earlier.

Magdalen is given right to the "dwelling place and plantacon" [Polkes Folly] for the balance of her life, after which it would belong exclusively to David or his heirs. As it turned out, David appears to have died intestate between the time Robert's will was drawn up in May 1699 and August 1702, when the codicil was added changing executors. Polkes Folly and the parcel of Forlorne Hope devised to David therefore reverted to John Polk as the oldest son and heir-at-law. When John also died intestate, these tracts were inherited in turn by his son and heir, William Polk, who devised them to his daughter Jane in his will written in 1726.

As already noted, Polkes Lott is not mentioned in Robert's will and seems to have already been abandoned by that time.

2.2 Magdalen Tasker Polke (c.1636-1727)

Father: Roger Tasker of Lifford, Donegal
Born: c.1636, Lifford, Donegal, Ireland
Spouses:
(1) John Porter (d.1665), Quartermaster, Royal Army
(2) Robert Polke, married 1665-66
Will: Somerset Wills (original), Box 3, folder 90; written 7 April 1726; proved
   20 March 1728(NS)
Children:
(1) by John Porter: not known; possibly a son, William Porter, who died in
Somerset County in June 1696
(2) by Robert Polke: Ann, John, Margaret, William, Ephraim, James, Robert,
   David, Martha, Joseph
Property: Moneen (Monyn), in Ballendrait, Donegal, inherited from her father

****

Magdalen's mark as it appears on her will
(Only the irregular lines between the given and surname were her mark.)

****

MAGDALEN TASKER was one of two daughters of Roger Tasker, an important local official in the Lifford area of Donegal. Tasker was responsible for maintaining crown authority at a key strategic location overlooking the River Dale, a feeder into the River Foyle, deep in the territory that had been escheated by James I from the O'Donnells. Claim is made by M. W. Garrett,[41] repeated by W. H. Polk in *Polk Family and Kinsmen*, that Roger Tasker was a Chancellor of Ireland, but no record of his holding such a position has been found. Roger Tasker does not appear in the 1665 Hearth Rolls so probably had passed on by then. Magdalen married John Porter, a Quartmater in the Royal Army, and her sister Barbara married Capt. John Keyes. Following is from Burke's *Genealogical and Heraldic History of the Peerage Baronetage and Knightage*, 1963, under "Keyes," p. 1350:

---

[41] Garrett, AHM, Vol. II, No. 4, p. 381.

Thomas Keyes served in the war in Ireland from 1578, first as
Assist. to the "Trenchmaster," Sir Richard Hansard. Hansard was
sent back to England to raise a Company, which he took to Ireland
in 1601, and was joined by Thomas Keyes and his son, John.
Hansard was eventually appointed Gov. of the Liffer, and
consolidated his hold on the fords across the Foyle River by
building a fort at Lifford. Thomas Keyes, who was then Hansard's
Capt., was granted a plot of land ("one sesiagh") in the vicinity on
which to build a house. His son John, and Roger Tasker, who were
Hansard's Lieuts. were given similar plots to build fortified houses
to guard another ford at Ballindrait. Hansard's officers did not
participate in the distribution of escheated lands on the
"Plantation" of Ulster; but Thomas Keyes and Roger Tasker took
up and developed land included in Clonleigh, originally granted to
the Bishop of Derry. Thomas Keyes's property was Clonfade
(afterwards Glenfade) and Roger Tasker's was Cavanacor. Thomas
Keyes settled in Derry, where he became Sheriff in 1623, and made
over Clonfade to his son, John Keyes, who settled there, and had a
son, John Keyes, m. Barbara, dau. and heiress of Roger Tasker, to
whom her father assigned Cavanacor, which estate henceforth
became their principal residence.

Magdalen was married to John Porter by 1654 as is shown by the following entry from the Civil Survey of 1654 for the Townland of Monyn in Donegal:

John Porter claims one sheshock of the sd. Qr. (Quarter) with a
house and garden plot in Ballendrait being given him by his father
in law Roger Tasker as a porcon with his wife, it being purchased
by him from Thomas Flood who held the same in freehold from the
sd Sr. Richard (Hansard).

If assumption is made that she was eighteen at this time, Magdalen would have been born no later than 1636. This is exactly consistent with the assertion of a family tradition that she was almost ninety-two when she died (in March 1728), as stated by Garrett [42] although the source of that information is not identified. It is also known that John Porter was still alive in 1665, as he appears at "Monyn" in Ballendrait in the Hearth Rolls (tax list) taken that year, so the marriage of Robert and Magdalen could have occurred no earlier than 1665. It was apparently opposed by the Porter family and caused quite an upset at the time, as already noted.

---

[42] Garrett, AHM, Vol. II, No. 4, p. 381

It is mentioned in the account by John Keys that there was no issue from the marriage of Magdalen and John Porter, but this may be questionable. They were married for at least eleven years, and she was certainly fertile, so children were a likely possibility. There are records of a William Porter in Somerset who had a close association with the two oldest Polk sons, John and William. He acquired land in the same area of the Manokin Hundred, near Princess Anne, at the same time as they did, and they were both witnesses to his will written in 1695. Moreover, Porter's marriage to Elizabeth Benton in 1687 was performed by Rev. William Traile who, as mentioned earlier, preceded Robert and Magdalen from Ballendrait to Somerset. These close links seem more than coincidental and are very consistent with Porter being a half-brother to John and William Polk and their siblings.

The birth year of Magdalen's last child, Joseph, was 1688-89, as known from his deposition in Somerset Court Records in which he stated his age as forty-one in August 1730.[43] This would mean that Magdalen was at least fifty, more likely fifty-two, when he was born—rather extraordinary in that day when so many women died at childbirth, and a testament to her enduring fortitude.

~~~~~~~~

The suggestion in *Our Polk Family* attributed to the genealogist, Mr. Charles H. Starr, that Robert Polke was of French Huguenot descent was discussed in Section 2.1. Some assertions were also made in the book about the Tasker family which should be commented on here. One is that Tasker was not a surname found in Ireland and that Robert's wife, Magdalen, was actually a member of the Keys family.[44] Furthermore it is claimed that the marriage of Robert and Magdalen was recorded as a marriage between Robert Poage and Margaret Mackie in 1684, and also that Joseph was Magdalen's only child by Robert.[45]

It is hard to understand how these claims can be made. The most basic point is that the cited marriage was for a Margaret (not Magdalen) from the Parish of Faan (Fahan) which is in Inishowen, in North Donegal, not Lifford where Magdalen lived. Secondly, per the entry in the 1654 Civil Survey quoted above, Roger Tasker was a landowner at Ballendrait at that time, with land held by his son-in-law John Porter. Porter is listed at "Monin" in the Donegal Hearth rolls of 1665 and Magdalen Polke bequeathed her land, Moneen, to her son Joseph in her will in 1728 (see below). As will be seen in the next chapter, Robert Polke's oldest son, John (born c.1668), gave the name Ballendrett to his property in Somerset and his second son, William (born c.1773), used the names Moneen and Donegal (Denegall) for two of his patented properties. This would not make sense if John and William were not Magdalen's children with roots in those places. Nor would the use of the name Magdalen by two of Robert's sons, Ephraim and James, for

---

[43] SOJR, 1730-33:9.
[44] Comfort, p. 243.
[45] Ibid, p. 235, 242.

their daughters if Magdalen was not their mother. None of Robert's children used the name Jeanne, the given name of Robert's alleged first wife, for any of their daughters.

There are several other factual issues with the information provided in the Huguenot lineage discussion. For one, it is stated (p. 239) that Margaret, the daughter of Robert Poague and Jeanne Joyvelin, was christened in 1661 at Londonderry (Protestant Church Record). The Register of Derry Cathedral actually reads "*Baptismes in February 1661 ... Margarett, the daugh: of John Poke, bap. ye 5th. George Poke. Jennett Poke and Isabell Donnell, gossips.*" The mother's name is not given.[46] Moreover, in an August 1730 deposition in Somerset Court, Robert's daughter, Margaret, stated her age as sixty, so her actual birth year was 1689-70.[47] Secondly, it is stated (p. 239) that Margaret married "William Pullet, Americanized from Guillermo Follett, or William Polled." Margaret's marriage, as actually recorded in Somerset Records, was to Thomas Pollitt.[48] Finally, it is stated that Joseph Polke was born about 1696-97 in Somerset County and joined the Quakers in West Nantmeal Township, Chester County, Pennsylvania, before 1735. However, as just noted, Joseph was actually born about 1689. He remained in Somerset County, appearing in its tax lists, through 1740 when he relocated to Dorchester County where he died in 1753.[49]

For these and other reasons not presented here, the author believes that the Huguenot lineage of Robert Polk and first marriage to Jeanne Joyvelin as suggested by Mr. Starr are not correct.

~~~~~~~~

Magdalen's original will is on file at the Maryland Archives, and bears her personal mark and seal. It is a rather rough document, in crude handwriting, certainly not written by a practicing clerk or scribe. Her mark is a poorly scrawled "X", little more than a chicken scratch. She was at least ninety and apparently very feeble at the time it was written, but did not go quickly. It is dated 7 April 1726 but was not proved until 20 March 1728(NS).

As noted by others, the spelling of her name is "Pollok" within the text and "Polke" at the signature, which was written by the scribe, not herself. Such inconsistencies were quite common in documents of that era and should not be interpreted as some deliberate choice by the individual. Spelling had more to do with the rather random preferences of the particular clerk or scribe. In this case, the script is rather crude and does not appear to have been the work of a skilled

---

[46] Ibid, p. 277.
[47] SOJR 1730-33:9
[48] SOLR IK1:213. Pollitt family researchers believe Thomas Pollitt came from Bolton, Lancashire, England. See Bryan Lane, *Some of the Descendants of Thomas Pollitt,* 2005 (http://home.earthlink.net/~bwlane2/bks/BK-Pollitt-pvt.pdf). See also Section 2.3 below.
[49] See Section 3.10 below.

hand. It may have been done by Magdalen Pollitt ("Magdlen Polet"), one of the witnesses, whose signature is very consistent with the script of the words "Magdlen Polke" to which Magdalen affixed her mark. Her Christian name, for example, is spelled as "Magdlen" which does not occur in other documents where the name is used. Following is a transcript:[50]

> *In the name of God amen. I Magdlen Pollok*
> *being weak and sick of body yeet of perfect*
> *mind and memory prais be to all mighty god do make*
> *and ordaine this my Last will and testament in*
> *manor and form as followeth. First I give my*
> *soul unto the hands of almighty god hoping through*
> *the marits of my Savor Jesus Christ to reseve a full*
> *pard of all my sins and my body I commit to the*
> *earth from where it was taken to be buried in*
> *Christian buriall at the discretion of my executor*
> *hear after nomenated. Item I give and bequeath*
> *a tract of Land called Moning lying in the king-*
> *dom of Ierland and in the barony of Rofo*
> *and County of Doneygall and in the parish of*
> *Leford unto my son Joseph Pollok and to the*
> *hears of his body forever with all the rest of my*
> *moveabel easteat and him to be hole executor*
> *of this my last will and testament hearby*
> *revocken all other wills and testaments by me*
> *maid either by word or writting in testemony*
> *wherof I set my hand and Seaill this 7 day*
> *of april 1726 Sined Seailled and delivered*
> *in sight and presents of us*
>
> *David Polk*
> *William Pollet*   *Magdlen X Polke*
> *Magdlen Polet*   *her marke*

[Note: David Polk is the son of Magdalen's son James who also resided in Damned Quarter. William Pollet was the son of Thomas Pollitt and Margaret Polk; he was listed at that time as a taxable in the nearby household of Charles Williams, Margaret's third husband. Magdlen Polet is most likely the daughter of James Polk,[51] and wife of William Pollet.]

It was rather uncommon for women to leave wills in these times and it seems to have been written for the sole purpose of passing on her rights to the estate

---

[50] Somerset Wills (original), MSA C1817, Box 3, folder 90; also MDW 19:125.
[51] James' will mentions a daughter Magdalen.

52

"Moning" (Moneen, Monyn) in Ireland to her youngest son, Joseph. No other items are mentioned, nor do any consequent probate documents (inventory or accounts) of her estate appear on record.

Magdalen's will might reflect her unhappiness with the devolution of the ownership for Polkes Folly and associated parcel of Forlorne Hope contrary to the intent of Robert Polke in his will. Due to the unexpected predecease of his son David, these lands had reverted to the possession of the oldest son John, and afterwards passed on to John's son, William, who still retained ownership at the time Magdalen drew up her will. Magdalen had the lifetime right to remain at Polkes Folly, but Joseph, who looked after her and had always lived there himself, could be dispossessed after her death. The provision in Robert's will to pay Joseph 4000 pounds of tobacco in lieu of land may have fallen casualty to the unforeseen circumstance of David's death and never honored. Joseph held no land in his own name at this time, and Robert's carefully considered legacy providing for all his children according to their needs seems to have been thwarted in Joseph's case. By devising Moneen directly to Joseph, Magdalen ensured that her one possession of value would be secured for him and not go the way of Robert's property. We have no idea if Magdalen had been in correspondence with anyone back in Ballendrait about the property or had any assurance that Joseph would actually be able to take possession of her bequest. There is no evidence that he ever traveled to Ireland and claimed his inheritance.

William Polk (son of John) wrote his will about a half year after Magdalen wrote hers, and left Polkes Folly and Low (Long) Ridge to his daughter Jane. He died just three months afterwards and the land presumably went to Jane as provided; she appears to have subsequently conveyed it to Joseph, although there is no record of the transaction, since he included it in his 1748 liquidation of Polk properties in Damned Quarter. Thus it may be said that Robert Polke's original intent to provide for his youngest son Joseph was ultimately realized, but by a far more circuitous route than intended.

It is also worth noting in this regard that Robert Polk Jun., living in Dorchester, had written a will in February 1726(NS), only six weeks before Magdalen, in which he left his own Damned Quarter properties, Ballyhack and part of Forlorne Hope, to Joseph. We might wonder why he chose not to give these to his own children—possibly this was a payback for the 200-acre warrant Joseph assigned to Robert in 1723, cited in Robert's survey for the tract Hazard.

3. The Children of Robert and Magdalen

Robert and Magdalen did not arrive in America wealthy or become so in their time in Damned Quarter, but they provided well for their children. As they came of age the sons were set up with land and trades, and the daughters were married into comfortable situations. By the time the second generation passed the torch to the third, the family was well established, and the foundations for wealth and prominence were laid. It was with the third and fourth generations that the harvest was realized.

Almost from the beginning it appears that the family determined that their long-term future was not in Damned Quarter and they should seek lands elsewhere. As the opportunity arose, the second generation or their offspring all moved farther inland along two principal rivers, the Manokin and the Nanticoke. The oldest sons, John and William, moved as soon as they came of age to the Manokin headwaters near present-day Princess Anne. The younger sons, Ephraim, James, and Robert, initially spread out into the remaining unclaimed lands of the Damned Quarter peninsula as shown in Figure 7, but during the decade of the 1720s, they or their children undertook a mass migration to the upper reaches of the Nanticoke River. This area was then contained entirely in Maryland, partly in Dorchester County, on the west side of the Nanticoke, and Somerset County on the east, but it all became part of Delaware following the Calvert-Penn settlement of 1760 which shifted the Maryland-Delaware boundary line substantially westward.

Robert and Magdalen's daughter Margaret followed her older brothers to Manokin when her first husband Thomas Pollitt purchased Pollitts Choice, a parcel of a larger tract called Shipways Choice, there in 1699. She returned to Damned Quarter with her later marriage to Charles Williams, but her children by Thomas Pollitt did not. Some remained in Manokin while others joined the move to the Nanticoke.

Of all Robert and Magdalen's children, only daughter Anne remained permanently in the Damned Quarter area, but for good reason. By virtue of her prenuptial arrangement with Francis Roberts, some thirty years her senior, she became mistress of more lands than any of her brothers, all in Damned Quarter. Her offspring were the only known descendants of Robert and Magdalen remaining in that area into the 19th century.

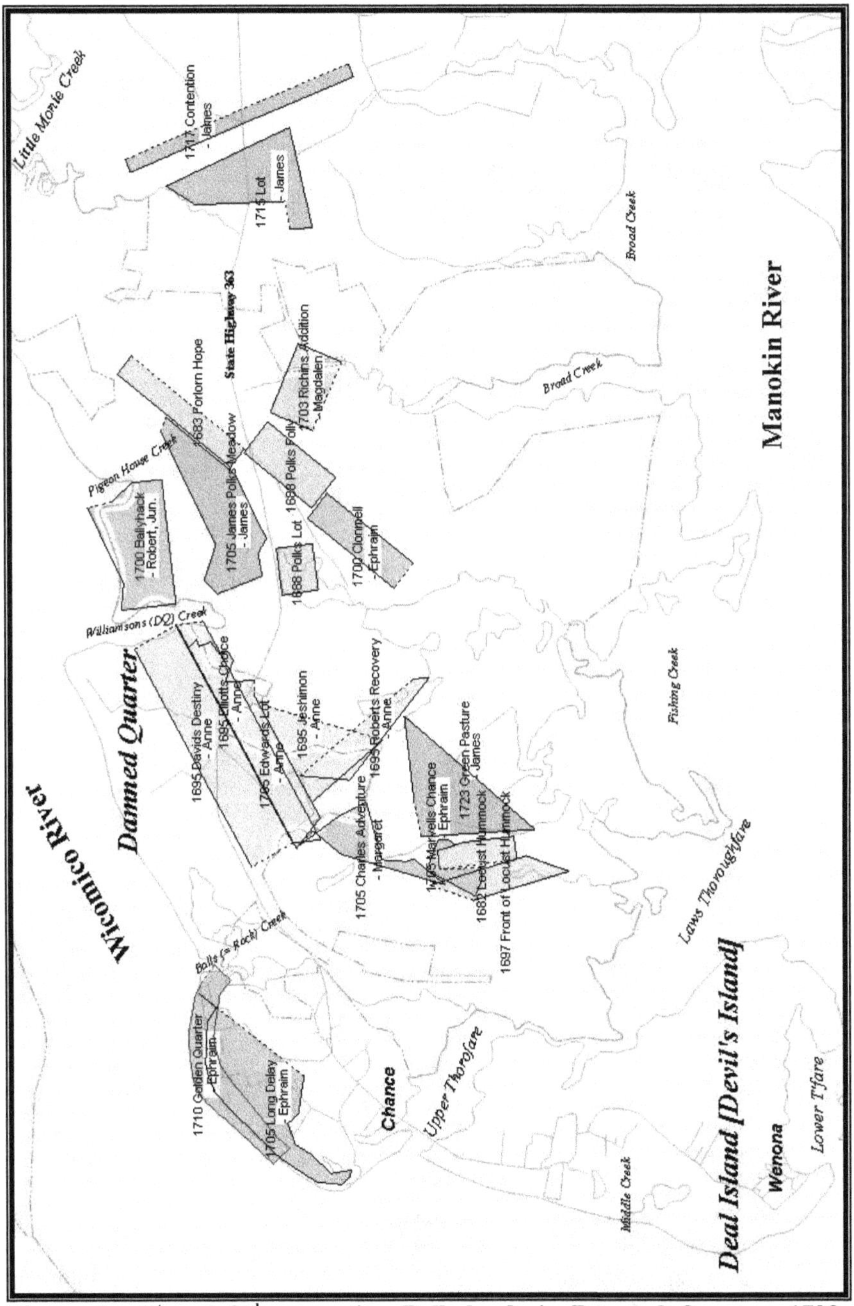

Figure 7. 1st and 2nd generation Polk lands in Damned Quarter, 1723, acquired by patent, purchase or marriage.

The family interest in the upper Nanticoke began at least as early as 1709, when the tract Hazard (300 acres) was surveyed for James and Ephraim in Dorchester, and continued steadily until the family had completed its exodus from Damned Quarter by 1740. The area was probably under consideration from the outset because other Scotch-Irish families such as Caldwell, Givans, Ross, Brown, and Knox had already settled along the Nanticoke and no doubt kept in contact with their fellow Ulstermen. There was probably also an association with the Nutter family, which had been in Somerset from its beginning and had a longstanding trading relationship with the Nanticoke Indians. The head of this family, Christopher Nutter (c.1638-1702), had established trading posts and patented land at Manokin, Nanticoke, and along the Wicomico. His tracts Attawattocoquin, (1200 acres, 1684) near what is now Bridgeville, Delaware, and Kilmaynham (150 acres, 1665) near Princess Anne, were among the earliest settlements in their respective areas. The latter tract was located quite close to the lands later purchased by John and William Polk in Manokin. The Nutters shifted from Manokin to an area now known as Nutters Neck on the lower Nanticoke, perhaps ten miles by water north of Damned Quarter. They surely crossed paths with the Polks and may have influenced them to consider the upper Nanticoke as an area to settle. Many of the lands purchased by the Polks in that area (Salem, Dublin, Little Goshen, Ramas, Moanen, Denegall) were in near proximity to Nutter family plantations. In time there were several intermarriages between the families and parcels of both Attawattacoquin and Kilmaynham ended up in Polk family ownership.

Although James and Ephraim took the first step towards the Nanticoke with the survey of Hazard in 1709 this tract was never patented and is not found in later records. The first patented tract was Polks Chance (200 acres), surveyed by Ephraim Polk in Dorchester in 1715, situated somewhere on the west side of Fishing Bay. The location of this land is not clear, nor does it appear in later records such as the Proprietary Debt Books, and Ephraim certainly never moved to it.

Robert Polk Jun. was the first to actually settle in Dorchester. In 1719 he purchased Venture (300 acres) on Clearbrook Creek from Samuel Jackson, and it was here that he lived his last years and died in 1726. Somewhat inexplicably, not long after Robert's death his children became the first of the family to move away from the Chesapeake area altogether, possibly relocating to Virginia and the Carolinas. This will be further discussed below (Section 3.7). As a more immediate consequence, Robert's move may have triggered the family's migration to the Nanticoke area in earnest. It came shortly after Ephraim's death and at a time when the third generation was just coming into its own. It seemed to have been a moment for taking a hard look at the family future and making major strategic decisions about the way ahead. We will never know exactly how this came about, but it seems clear from the course of events that James, Robert, and Joseph, with William as the family leader, resolved at this point on a wholesale exodus out of Damned Quarter and on to the Nanticoke.

The move began with William obtaining a warrant from the Land Office for 200 acres in August 1720. He assigned these to his stepsons Samuel and Robert Owens who used them in the survey of a tract they named Fellowship (200 acres) on the east side of the Northeast Fork of the Nanticoke in Johns Neck. Then William took out a warrant for 500 acres in September 1721, assigning 100 acres to his nephew Charles Polk, son of Ephraim, and another 100 acres to Samuel and Robert Owens. A flurry of other land transactions followed. To summarize:

12 Nov 1718	John Pollet	Purchase of Welshmans Kindness (400 ac, Dorch)
27 Jun 1719	Robert Polk, Jun.	Purchase of Venture (300 ac, Dorch) from Samuel Jackson
29 Aug 1720	William Polk	Warrant for 200 acres; assigned to Sam'l & Robt Owens
10 Aug 1721	James Polk	Purchase of Salem (800 ac, Som) from Thomas Layfield
16 Sep 1720	Sam'l & Robt Owens	Survey, Fellowship (200 ac, Som)
29 Sep 1721	William Polk	Warrant for 500 acres; assigned 100 ac to Charles Polk, 100 ac to Samuel & Robert Owens
20 Oct 1721	Charles Polk	Survey, Charles Purchase (100 ac, Som)
20 Oct 1721	Sam'l & Robt Owens	Survey, Goshen (100 ac, Som)
20 Oct 1721	William Polk	Survey, Moanen (100 ac, Som)
20 Oct 1721	William Polk	Survey, Dennigal (100 ac, Som)
20 Oct 1721	William Polk	Survey, Ramas (100 ac, Som)
17 Sep 1722	William Owens	Survey, Owens Venture (100 ac, Som)
18 Oct 1722	Thomas Smith	Survey, Rich Ridge (50 ac, Dorch)
11 Dec 1722	William (of John) Polk	Purchase of Colliers Adventure (250 ac, Dorch)
11 Dec 1722	James Polk (Pollok)	Purchase of Dublin (100 ac, Dorch)
10 Jan 1723 (NS)	James Polk	Warrant for 200 acres
10 Jan 1723 (NS)	Joseph Polk	Warrant for 200 acres
29 Mar 1723	Robert Polk, Jun	Purchase of Hazard (200 ac, Dorch)
12 Aug 1723	William Polk	Warrant for 164 acres
24 Oct 1724	William Polk	Warrant for 200 acres
5 Nov 1724	William Polk	Survey of Rich Land (200 ac, Som)
4 Mar 1725(NS)	William Owens	Survey of Owens Purchase (50 ac, Dor)
23 Jul 1726	James Polk	Warrant for 100 acres
9 Mar 1726(NS)	William Owens	Purchase of Morgans Venture (120 ac, Dor)
6 Aug 1726	Thomas Smith	Survey of Golden Grove (100 ac, Dor)
6 Aug 1726	Thomas & Wm Smith	Survey of Poplar Ridge (87 ac, Dor)
23 Nov 1726	William Owens	Purchase of Swan Pond (50 ac, Dor)
13 Jan 1727(NS)	William Owens	Survey, Owens Security (140 ac, Som)
19 Jul 1727	Thomas Smith	Warrant for 700 acres

6 Dec 1727	Robert (of John) Polk	Bequeathed Poplar Level (100 ac, Dor) by Thomas Smith
11 Jan 1728(NS)	Robert (of John) Polk	Assigned Margarets Fancy (50 ac, Dor) by Stephen Smith (bro. of Thomas)
1 Apr 1728	William Owens	Patent of Good Will (100 ac, Dorch)
12 Jul 1728	Charles Polk	Charles Advantage (50 ac, Som), assigned by John Caldwell
12 Jul 1728	Charles Polk	Polks Privilege (50 ac, Som), assigned by John Caldwell
11 Jan 1729(NS)	Thomas & Wm Smith	Survey of Good Will (100 ac, Dor)
10 Jun 1729	Sam'l & Robt Owens	Owens Chance (100 ac, Som); assigned by John Caldwell
9 Apr 1730	Sam'l & Robt Owens	Survey of Goshens Addition (100 ac, Som)
25 Sep 1730	Charles Polk	Special warrant for 400 acres
3 Nov 1730	John Knox	Survey of Knoxes Hazard (12 ac, Dor)
10 Nov 1731	David Polk (Pollock)	Survey of Addition
26 Mar 1734	Charles Polk	Warrant for 400 acres
20 Aug 1734	John Polk	Survey of Addition (26 ac, Som)
28 Aug 1734	Manuel Manlove (Ephraim's son-in-law)	Survey of Jonathans Lott (100 ac, Som)

These lands were mostly at the head of the Nanticoke, northeast of present-day Bridgeville, Delaware. See Figure 8. At the time this area was considered part of Maryland, and the surveys were filed in Somerset County. Several of the tracts were further west of the Nanticoke in the area known as the Northwest Fork in what was then part of Dorchester County. Almost all of this was ceded to Delaware (the "lower three counties" of Pennsylvania) in the Calvert-Penn settlement of 1760 and the subsequent survey of the Maryland-Delaware boundary by Mason and Dixon in 1763-65. The residents of this area thereby became citizens of Delaware and following a few years of confusion their land, tax, and probate records were thenceforth recorded in Delaware, not Maryland. The residents of the area at that time can truly be said to have lived in Maryland and died in Delaware, without moving.

A clear picture of William Polk's role as the family patriarch and protector emerges from the foregoing list if the family relationships are noted. William, Samuel, and Robert Owens were William's stepsons by his marriage to their widowed mother, Anne Owens; William and older brother John Owens had already settled in the Manokin on land conveyed to them by William Polk in 1713 in a reciprocal exchange for the tract they had inherited from their father (Golden Quarter and Smiths Hope for Widows Choice). Samuel Owens married Magdalen, oldest child of Ephraim Polk, during this period. Her brother Charles was Ephraim's second child and oldest son. William (of John) Polk was the ward of William (the elder) by John's deathbed request. Thomas Smith is included in

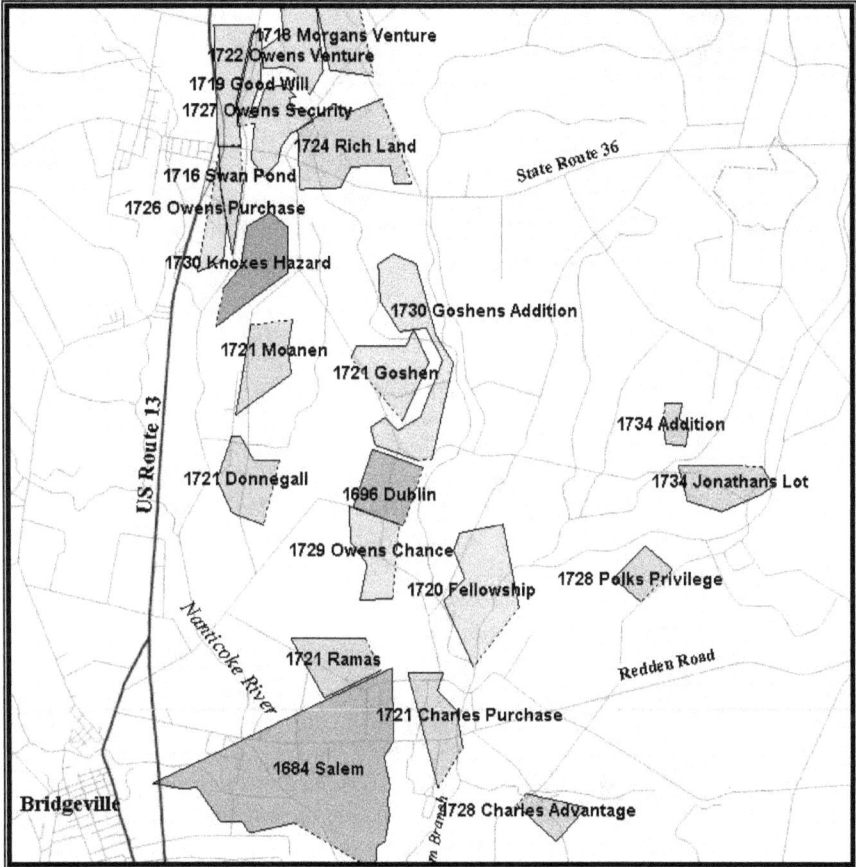

Figure 8. Polk family lands at head of Nanticoke, 1734.

the foregoing list because it appears likely he was the father of Johanna, John Polk's second wife and widow. This will be explained in Section 3.5. Although William was not the guardian of John's children by Johanna, he no doubt had concern for their welfare.

In the middle of this eventful period the family experienced a major transition that marked the passing of the torch from the second generation to the third. William, son of John and the eldest of Robert and Magdalen Polke's grandchildren, died in February 1726/7 at an early age, barely in his thirties. James and Robert Jun. followed soon afterwards in May 1727. And finally Magdalen, the matriarch, and no doubt a dominating presence in Damned Quarter, died in March 1728(NS) at an ancient age, certainly in her nineties. Of the original seven sons of Robert and Magdalen only William, at Manokin, and Joseph, the youngest, living at the original homestead, still survived. This chain of events appears to have spurred the children of both Ephraim and James to make the major decisions that shaped their own lives. Thus the period 1727-1728 can be seen as the pivotal time in the family's relocation from Damned Quarter to the upper Nanticoke and the moment of the third generation's ascendancy in the family.

Ephraim had died not quite ten years earlier and his offspring, living at the head of Deal Island with stepfather John Laws, were coming of age. The three sons, Charles, Joseph, and Ephraim (II), perhaps with William's guidance, must not have seen Deal Island as a viable place on which to build their futures. Their move from there is recorded in a deposition of Ephraim (II) transcribed in the Archives of Maryland: [1]

> *Sussex County on Delaware.*
> *The deposition of Ephraim Polke of the County afsd yeoman aged about Forty One years or thereabouts taken at Lewis in the said County* (Sussex, Delaware) *this Nineteenth day of May in the year of Our Lord One Thousand Seven Hundred and Fifty Nine. This deponent being Solemnly Sworn on the Holy Evangelists did depose & say that he was born in the County of Somerset in the Province of Maryland at the Lower end thereof, but that when he was about Eight years of age his Brother Charles Polke (who had care of him) became a Settler at the upper end of said County of Somerset, now called Worcester County; and the Deponent further saith that the Place his aforesaid Brother settled on at his Removal as aforesaid (being now about Thirty two years past) was Reputed to be on the borders between Somerset County as it is was then called and the County of Sussex aforesaid but then more generally called by the people of the Province of Maryland, Whorekill County, The Deponent further saith that he lived with his Brother Charles at his Settlement on the aforesaid Reputed Borders until he was upwards of Twenty Years of age; he then married and went to Settle on an Improvement made by a Certain George Bishop...*

Ephraim's second son, Joseph, also moved to Nanticoke and some of the daughters as well, though their lives are much harder to trace. It is known that Magdalen, Ephraim's oldest child, became the wife of Samuel Owens about this time.

The sons of James Polk also left Damned Quarter in this period as the tax lists of Monie Hundred readily show. James' second and third sons, Henry and John, disappear from the lists after 1728, and oldest son David after 1730. In 1731 only "widow Polk" is still listed in Damned Quarter with two slaves, and by 1732 she too is gone. All subsequent records of James' oldest son David are found in Dorchester County where he acquired land southeast of Bridge Branch, now Bridgeville, Delaware. Younger brothers Henry, John, and James inherited the nearby tract Salem, only a couple miles east of David's lands but in Somerset County. The presence of John and James in the Nanticoke Hundred is seen in the

---

[1] AOM, Vol. 31, p.367.

Somerset tax lists after 1731, but Henry moved to Queen Anne's County, perhaps twenty miles further northwest, where he settled on the Tuckahoe Creek and carried on his father's trade as a shipwright.

The transition from Damned Quarter to the Nanticoke was completed by 1740 when Joseph, by then the only surviving child of Robert and Magdalen and patriarch of the family, purchased Little Goshen to the west of Bridgeville. The next generation continued to grow and prosper in this new environment. Their land holdings along the Nanticoke in Delaware became quite extensive, comprising 77 separate land tracts and more than 12,000 acres as shown in Figure 9. The Polk lands in Damned Quarter, Polkes Folly, Clonmell, Ballyhack, Forlorne Hope, and Forlorne Hopes Addition were sold by "Joseph Pollock" to neighbors John and William Shores in 1748.[2] Ironically, at the Shores' estate settlement in 1868, part of this land including Polkes Folly was purchased by Colonel W. T. G. Polk of Princess Anne, a descendant of William Polk, who was unaware of its earlier history at the time.[3]

The Polk/Pollock sojourn in Damned Quarter thereby came to an end, and the family saga moved on to new chapters on yet another frontier. Like its antecedents in France, England, Scotland, and Ireland, this episode was a story of struggle, success, and the resilient spirit captured in the family motto—*audacter et strenue*. Looking back over the lives of Robert and Magdalen and their children one sees in them a prototypical passage from the turmoil of the old world to the promise of the new. Somewhere in that crucible of religious conflict, seventeenth century Ireland, a seminal moment came when they made the decision to risk all for an unknown future in an unknown land. And the same bold instinct which guided that first generation to a new frontier in America was surely passed on to the next, as we now see in the lives of Robert and Magdalen's children and grandchildren.

---

[2] SOLR MF:109.
[3] PF&K, p.52

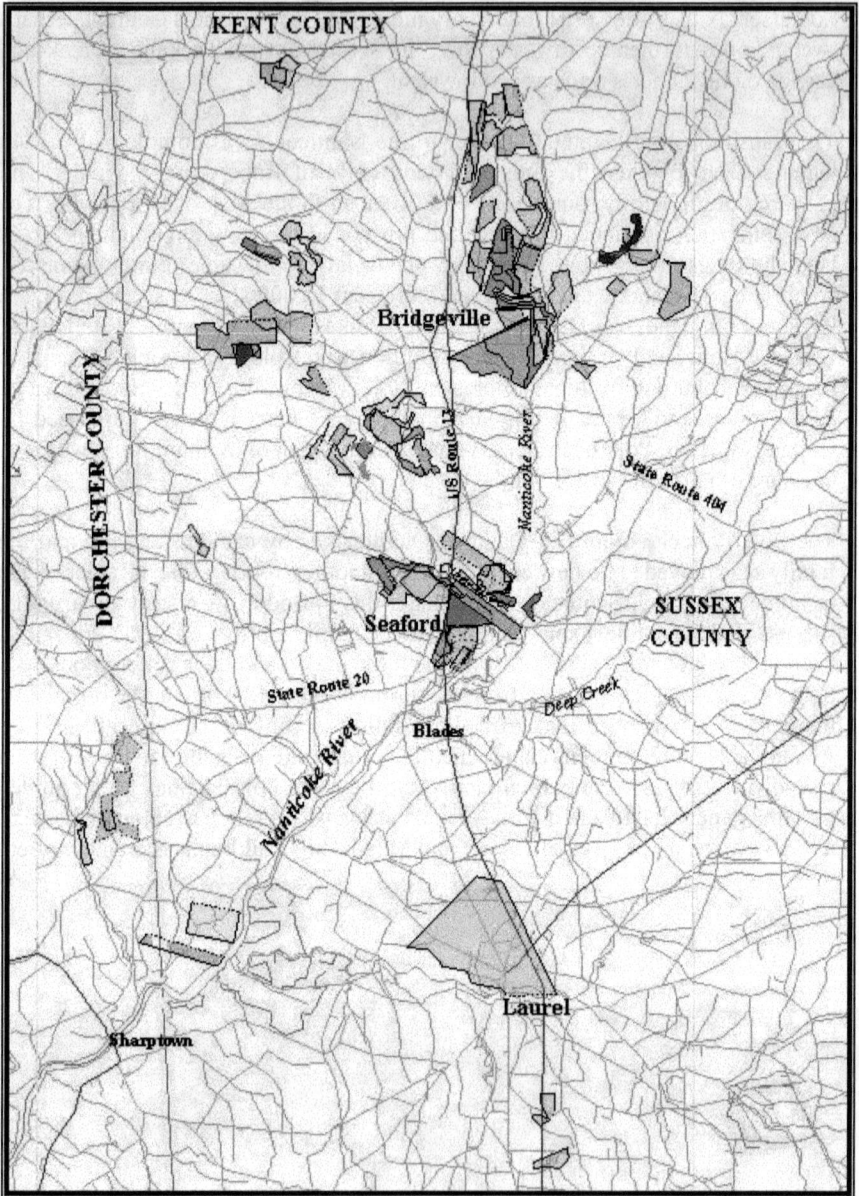

Figure 9. Polk family lands in Sussex County, 1770.

3.1 Anne Polk (c.1666-1738+)

Born: Ireland, most likely at Monyn, Ballendrait, Donegal
Probate: no records located
Spouses:
(1) Francis Roberts (c.1636-1703), m. 1690-91
(2) John Renshaw (d.1720/21), m.1711
Children (by Francis Roberts):
(1) Edward Roberts (c.1692-1774), m. Anne Polk, dau. of John Polk
(2) Priscilla Roberts (1694-1768), m. William Polk, son of John Polk
Property: Davids Destiny (350A), Elliotts Choice (20A), The Downs (100A),
Roberts Recovery (100A), Jeshimon (150A), New Found Land (125A),
Edwards Lott (220A)

~~~~~~~~~~

ANNE was the eldest of Robert and Magdalen's children, and her life may have been the most turbulent. From the outset some crisis or scandal was the dark companion to the principal events of her life. At her birth there was the question of the hasty marriage of her parents and conflict with the Porter family. At her marriage there was a coerced property arrangement with her husband to be, many years her senior and in court for fathering a bastard child. Following his death there was an open family conflict over the squandering of his estate. And in the end, only she and her son Edward remained permanently in Damned Quarter, while her siblings and their offspring dispersed in separate directions.

~~~~~~~~~~

In a deposition made in July 1709 Anne (Polk) Roberts stated her age as forty three.[4] This is a revealing piece of information since Magdalen was still married to Colonel John Porter in 1665. It tells us that Anne was born in 1665-66, was certainly the oldest of Robert and Magdalen's children, and that her parents must have married very shortly after Porter's death. It also means Anne was at least twenty-four at the time of her first marriage, which was relatively old in the context of the times. By comparison, her younger sister Margaret was at most seventeen when she married Thomas Pollitt in 1687.

But age was not the most peculiar circumstance in the marriage of Anne to her first husband, Francis Roberts, in 1690-91. An even more curious factor is revealed by the following entry in Somerset Land Records:[5]

> *Be it known to all men whome this present may concern that I Francis Roberts of Dam Quarter in the County of Somerset and Province of*

---

[4] SOLR IKL:125.
[5] SOLR L:266.

Maryland Planter I the said Francis doe for severall good reasons &
valuable considerations doe bind and firmly make over unto Anne
Polke of the County and Province afsd. all my goods lands and
chattels moveables and inmoveables and to be possest with the same
during her natural life, and if the aforesaid Anne Polke doth enjoy any
child or children by me the aforesaid Francis for they to enjoy and
possess the same estate above mentioned but if the aforesaid Anne
Polke should enjoy no child nor children by me the aforesaid Francis
then she only to enjoy the said estate during her natural life and I the
above said Francis doe give this as my free deed gift and grant and for
the true performance hereof I the aforesaid Francis Roberts bind
myself my heirs Extors admins firmly in the penalty of two hundred
pounds sterling money to be paid to the aforesaid Anne Polke and to
be paid upon at demand and in the true performance I sett my hand &
seal this twenty fifth day of February Anno Domini 1690/91.

Teste: John Planter, Robert Polke   Francis < FR> Roberts
Entered on Record this 30th day of April Anno Domini 1695
*   P J West Clr Cur*

This is an extraordinary document, possibly unique in colonial Maryland records.
It was very unusual for a man to convey property to a woman in that era for any
reason other than as a parent's bequest in a will. Prenuptial agreements conceding
property to the future wife were unheard of. Women's rights to landed property
were practically nonexistent at that time; ownership of property basically passed
from a woman to her husband with marriage, although he could not sell it without
her co-signature. In this case, Francis Roberts was a well-established planter thirty
years senior to his betrothed[6] and considerably wealthier than her father, Robert
Polke, in terms of real property holdings. As already noted in the opening chapter,
Roberts was the first real settler, and certainly the leading land owner, of the
Damned Quarter peninsula. One has to wonder just what led him to sign such a
document, and the only plausible explanation is that it was simply a matter of lust,
or else Roberts was in his dotage.

On the other hand, there is no mystery about why Robert Polke would have
wanted to exact such an agreement from Roberts. For one thing, Roberts already
had a bastard son by his consort, Rachel Grandee, who had accompanied him to
Somerset from Northumberland County, Virginia. Roberts was apparently quite
fond of this son and in fact afterwards attempted to circumvent the prenuptial
arrangement by a legal stratagem. And there was, of course, Roberts' well-
established record as a philanderer in his earlier days in Northumberland.[7] Any
claim that Roberts may have reformed himself was not supportable in light of very

---

[6] Northumberland County VA Court Records, 13 April 1657; Roberts made a deposition
in which his age is stated as "21 yeares or thereabouts."
[7] See section on Francis Roberts in Chapter 4.

recent behavior, as witnessed in the Court records at the time:[8]

> *10 June 1691. Case against Mary Mackenny for bastardy. The*
> *Grand Jury do present and find that Mary Mackenny of this County*
> *spinster and of Money* (Monie) *Hundred within the Jurisdiction of*
> *this Court hath most wickedly sinfully and shamefully commited*
> *fornication and born a child to the great dishonour of Almighty God*
> *scandall & evil example to all the good people of this Province and*
> *in contempt of the good laws and Institutions of the same.*

Mackenny confessed, and made oath that Francis Roberts was the father of her child. Due to her fits of sickness, punishment was remitted to twenty days' work for George Betts, overseer of Monie Hundred. Henry Haylor was then recognized and pledged security of £5 sterling as security for Mackenny's good behavior. Court ordered that Francis Roberts be summoned to appear next day.

> *11 June 1691. Case against Francis Roberts. Their Ma'ties Attorney*
> *came and says that the said Roberts hath most wickedly sinfully and*
> *shamefully committed fornication and upon the body on Mary*
> *Mackenny hath begot a Bastard Child against the laws of the*
> *Province.*

Roberts admitted the charge and agreed to make bond of £20 with his two securities, James Langrett and John Richins, who pledged £10 each. The condition of the bond was that Roberts

> *be of good behviour and aberrance to all their ma'ties liege people*
> *of this Province and shall keep this county harmless and*
> *indemnified from charges or trouble by reason of a Bastard Child*
> *born of the body of Mary Mackennie as also to pay all Court*
> *charges.*

Fornication, bastardy, and cohabitation were hardly unusual occurrences in those times. The court records are replete with such cases. In cases of illegitimate offspring, the usual punishment was for the offending woman to receive a certain number of lashes, typically twenty to thirty, "on the bare back, well laid on," which punishment was administered in public directly after it was pronounced. This was normally reduced or omitted if she revealed the male participant, who would be summoned into court, as in this case, fined, and made to post security against the child being a burden on the community. And life went on. So, in the social context of the times, this transgression, embarrassing though it was, hardly seems enough to have forced Francis Roberts, already in his sixties and an established man of property, into such a concession as was wrung from him in the prenuptial agreement. Exactly how this occurred must be left to conjecture, but it

---

[8] SOJR 1690-93:95.

is testimony to the force of Robert Polke's character that he was able to parlay this incident into the permanent transfer of Roberts' landed wealth to his daughter and her issue. The details of the conversation between the two gentlemen that preceded the sealing of this compact can only be left to our imagination.

~~~~~~~~~~

Anne Polk had two children by Francis Roberts, and none by second husband, John Renshaw, as far as is known. Her first child, Edward Roberts, was born about 1692 and Priscilla, the second, about 1694. They are said by tradition, as cited in *Polk Family and Kinsmen,* to have married their cousins Anne and William, the children of Anne's brother John Polk and his first wife Jane Knox. In the case of Edward, no records have been found which confirm the name of his wife, but for Priscilla the tradition is borne out by several records that cite William Polk's wife by name. The 1723 deed for the sale of William's two tracts, Friends Denial and Kirkminster, for example, mention a wife named Priscilla, and although his will does not state her name, both his inventory and probate account do.[9]

Priscilla presumably moved to William Polk's lands known as Kirkminster and Friends Denyall on the northeast side of what is now Salisbury when they were married. They sold these in 1723 after acquiring a tract called Colliers Adventure in Dorchester (1721), on the west side of the Nanticoke where William died just three years later, barely thirty years old. His will mentions three children, Ann, Jean, and John, who would have been minors at the time. The two daughters are untraced, but from land records we know that John moved to "the territories of Pennsylvania" after selling his inherited land in 1750.[10] He was apparently not married at that time since no wife is mentioned in the sale.

[Note—some confusion has been caused by William Polk's inventory[11] which refers to Priscilla (Presila) as the wife of Robert Clarkson in May 1727, no more than four months after William's death. Two years later the probate account[12] (June 1729) identifies her simply as Priscilla Polk. An error in the inventory seems likely, and is probably a mix-up with Phyllis, the daughter of Gabriel Cooper and widow of Matthew Cannon (died in June-July 1726), who actually became the wife of Robert Clarkson. It should be understood that the probate records of the Maryland Prerogative Court were compiled as transcriptions from the original documents sent from the counties, usually submitted in bundles containing multiple cases, and probate documents for Matthew Cannon and William Polk were being generated in the same time period. The author suspects there was a transcription error on William Polk's inventory, for Priscilla is clearly not the wife of Robert Clarkson. Robert Clarkson and wife Phyllis Clarkson are listed as the

---

[9] SOLR GH:102.
[10] DOLR Old #14: 480. Note – the "territories of Pennsylvania" probably means the lower three counties of Pennsylvania which we now know as Delaware.
[11] MDI 12:25.
[12] MDA 9:381.

executors for the probate account of Matthew Cannon on 3 August 1727, and Phyllis Clarkson is mentioned both as the daughter of Gabriel Cooper in his will (1737)[13] and as wife and executrix for Robert Clarkson's will (1746).[14]]

Sometime between June 1729 and August 1730, Priscilla married secondly a Mr. Quatermus, probably Patrick or Isaac, also of Dorchester County.[15] On 7 August 1730 she made the following deposition recorded in the land commission on Elliotts Choice:[16]

> *Priscilla Quatermus aged thirty six years being sworn on the Holy Evangelists of Almighty God deposeth and saith that Samuel Jones came to her mother Anne Roberts and said I am come to the bounder of Elliotts Choice and that the said Jones went to a pine stump where the deponent now sits near the side of a marsh about two hundred and fifty yards from the dwelling house of Edward Roberts and about South from the said house with the deponent and severall others and there set up a post at the root of the said stump and that Samuel Jones told them that the stump afsd was the first bounder of Elliotts Choice and the deponent further saith that John White Sen had laid his hand on the stump aforesaid and said it was the first bounder of Elliotts Choice and Richard Wallis Sen said father White it is, in the presence of the deponent she being then at the afsd stump and further saith not. Priscilla Quatermus.*

Priscilla Quatermus died by 8 January 1768 when an administrative bond was issued for her estate in Worcester County.[17]

Edward Roberts inherited the lands of Francis Roberts after his mother's death and remained in Damned Quarter throughout his life, dying in 1774. Records show he had at least five children: William, Francis, Priscilla, Edward, and Mary.[18] Of these only William remained permanently in Damned Quarter. He inherited and lived on the original homestead of his father at Elliotts Choice, but acquired additional lands in the area. When he died in 1794 his will mentions the following tracts in his possession: Elliotts Choice, Davids Destiny, Roberts Recovery, Ventures Privilege, Green Pasture, Father and Sons Desire, Dames Quarter, Polks (James) Meadows, Williams Begining, Friends Choice, Friends Contentment.

The other children of Edward Roberts all moved to the upper Nanticoke area. Francis and Priscilla married Elizabeth and David Pollock, respectively, the children of David Pollock, son of Robert and Magdalen's son James; Mary Roberts married Isaac Williams of Dorchester.

---

[13] MDW 21:818.
[14] MDW 24:410.
[15] Batchelder, p. 224.
[16] SOJR 1730-33:8.
[17] MDTP 43:7.
[18] See will of Mary Williams, probated in Worcester, 1754. MDW 29:286.

As it turned out, the prenuptial settlement with Anne Polk was not accepted by Francis Roberts at face value. In 1697 Roberts conveyed 100 acres to his illegitimate son "John Grundee otherwise called John Roberts" through the artifice of a 99 year lease—a very unusual, perhaps unique, transaction.[19] The tract name was not mentioned, but a later court record identifies it as Elliotts Choice.[20] This scheme was a legal loophole designed to circumvent the constraints placed on him by the premarital agreement and indicates a strong resentfulness by Roberts to his situation. The metes and bounds description of the land in the lease seems to have almost deliberately been contrived to create disputes since it was clearly incongruent with the defined boundaries of Elliotts Choice, far exceeded the nominal 100 acres, and was mathematically inconsistent in any case. This poisoned pill inevitably spawned a legacy of conflict in the family. Elliotts Choice was the subject of a land commission on at least three different occasions in the ensuing years. One of these occurred at the petition of Edward Roberts in 1730 and produced the following statement in a deposition by Joseph Polk:[21]

> The deponent saith that John Roberts interrupted James Polk on his oath (referring to an incident 25 years earlier) *and then Richard Wallis Sen standing by said that John Roberts was a liar for the afsd pine stump was the first bounder of Elliotts Choice. Likewise John White said John Roberts was a rogue for the pine stump aforesaid was the first bounder of Elliotts Choice and further saith not. Joseph Polk.*

In this light, one could expect relations between the two sons of Francis Roberts, John Grandee and Edward Roberts, to be problematic, but matters grew even more contentious when Anne Polk Roberts took John Renshaw Jun. as her second husband in 1710.[22] Renshaw was certainly related to, most likely the brother of, John Roberts' wife, Elizabeth Renshaw. This development immediately raised concerns among the other Polks in Damned Quarter that the lands and legacies due to Anne's son Edward Roberts would end up under the control of John Roberts and John Renshaw. The inventory of Francis Roberts' estate filed in June 1703 appraised his goods and chattels at £79, a suspiciously modest amount of for a man of his means, and an account of the estate was never filed by Anne, the administratrix. The family formed the opinion that the interests of Roberts' son Edward were not being properly looked after, and following Anne's marriage to John Renshaw they went to court. In November 1710 a petition was filed in Somerset Court[23] by Richard Tull and Thomas Hugg, acting in the place of

---

[19] SOLR Liber L:439.
[20] SOJR 1727-30:136.
[21] SOJR 1730-33: 8.
[22] Variously spelled Rensher, Rencher, Rinshaw, Wrencher, etc.
[23] SOJR 1707-1711:413.

Thomas Pollitt and John Polk, the original bondsmen for the estate, both deceased by then, to force John Renshaw and wife Anne to give a proper account. The petition was granted by the Court but apparently ignored, for a rather unhappy document was afterwards filed with the Maryland Commissary General for Probate by Joseph Polk on behalf of Edward Roberts against his own mother and stepfather:[24]

> *The Libell and Complaint of Edward Roberts the son of Francis Roberts late of Somerset County, dec'd (Which said Edward is a minor and under the age of twenty one years) by Joseph Polk his next friend humbly showeth unto your Hon.*
>
> *That your Libellants father Francis Roberts being possessed of a considerable personall estate consisting of sundry quantities of goods of several sorts household goods, cattle, horses, mony, mony debts, tobacco, tobacco debts, and diverse other sorts of necessaries on or about the year Seventeen hundred and two dyed Intestate, That in some short time after his decease, the said Francis, his Widow Anne Roberts now the wife of one John Rinshaw of Somerset County took out Letters of Administration on the said dec'ds Estate and returned an invnt'y of some part thereof about June Seventeen hundred and three wherein the goods and particulars therein expressed are not only much undervalued but also a great part of the said Intestates Estate wholly omitted and no Notice taken thereof Either in the said first inventory or by any Additionall Inventory thereof or other wise to make the said admn answerable for the same. That about the year Seventeen hundred and Eleven the said Anne married one John Rinshaw of Somerset County who in some short time after the Marriage Exhibited his account of Disbursements against the said Intestate estate unto the Office of this Court and had an allowance therein for sundry disbursements charged to the said Estate that the said John in the said amount did not only charge the said estate debtors for sundry disbursements wherewith said estate ought not to be burthened but also claimed and had allowance for sundry payments of tobacco, pork and such Like at unreasonable rates and even beyond what the same species of goods were appraised at in the Inv'ty of said estate Particularly the said Rinshaw is allowed therein for six thousand eight hundred & nineteen pounds of Tobco Twenty Eight pounds Eight shillings and three pence being at the rate of about one penny per pound whereas in the inv'ty there is two thousand four hundred forty and three pounds of tobacco appraised but at Six Shillings and six pence per Cwt.[25], that the sd. Rinshaw has not given the estate credit therein for the total amount thereof nor has he or the said Anne while sole ever returned any list of the dew debts as by Law they are obliged nor given the Estate Creditt for them, That altho the Said Anne well knowing the falsity of the said account*

---

[24] MDTP Box 21, File 9.
[25] Cwt is hundredweight or 112 lbs.

*has refused to take her Oath to the same Yet the said John has sworn
thereto and without your Libellants knowledge has procured an allowance
of the same with designs to Defraud your Libellant of the greater part of
that which most justly belongs to him of his Dec'd fathers Estate. All which
acting and doings as well of the said Anne as of the said John are against
all right Equity and Conscience & to the end that the said John and Anne
may answer upon their Oaths all and singular their premises and fully
Discover the said Intestates Estate, May it therefore please your Hon'r to
grant unto your Libellant her Majesty's Writ of Citation commanding them
to appear at a Certain time and place therein to be limited before your
Hon'r to answer your Libellants Libell in this behalfe And that the said
John and Anne may Stand to such Decree as your Hon'r shall think fitt to
make for your Libellants relief in the Premises*

And your Libell's shall pray etc ~~

per Bordley, for Libellant

This case dragged on for several years and is noted in numerous entries in the
Prerogative Court Testamentary Proceedings which also cite a contempt charge
against John Renshaw and wife. Eventually a settlement was reached, as seen
from the cryptic note "Agreed" entered in the Prerogative Court record dated 15
Feb 1714/5.[26] Seven months later, on 9 September 1715, the 220 acre tract,
Edwards Lott, in Damned Quarter, was conveyed as a gift to Edward by John
Renshaw and wife Anne. The "for love and affection" clause usually included in
deeds of gift to family members was omitted in this case.

An almost comic incident also occurred during this period which no doubt
exacerbated the already fractious situation. It arose over the petty theft of a piece
of beef in 1711, when Anne's brother James Polk was serving as Constable for
Monie. John Renshaw was accused of this theft and, as Constable, James was
responsible for bringing him before the Justices for a hearing. Following is a
transcript from the Somerset Court record:[27]

*The examination of James Polk taken before me George Gale etc. This
examinant being sworn on the Holy Evangelist to declare the truth saith
that by virtue of the warrant above mentioned he did search the milk house
of John Rensher and then found the piece of beef which is above mentioned
which the wife of the above said John Austin did suppose to be the stolen
beef was given him by the wife of John Marvell and this examinant further
saith that he did then go to the wife of John Marvell and asked her if she*

---

[26] MDTP 22:380.
[27] SOJR 1711-13:104

*had given John Roberts that piece of beef and she answered that she would
not satisfy him wheather she had or not.*

*The examination of John Marvell taken before me George Gale etc. This
examinant being sworn on the Holy Evangelist do declare that the piece of
beef above mentioned could not be any part his beef he having none in his
house but cow beef and the piece that was found and produced by the
Constable was part of the cod piece of a steer.*

*The examination of Wm. Harris taken before me George Gale etc. This
examinant being sworn to say the truth saith that he was with Thomas
Rensher and a Mulatto wench belonging to John Austin at Dam Quarter
Creek on Wednesday and Thursday last they having a canoe which had on
board her a carcass of steer beef belonging to John Austin and that during
their stay at the said creek part of the said beef was cut and stolen away
which was perceived by Thomas Rensher but who stole it knoweth not.*

*The examination of John Austin taken before me George Gale etc. The 19ᵗʰ
of November 1711 This examinant being sworn on the Holy Evangelist to
say the truth saith that he doth realy believe the beef produced by the
Constable to be found at John Renshers milk house to be part of that which
was stolen from him, and John Rensher and John Roberts had this day
deposed him and puts up this complaint and offered to give him a steer and
some other considerations if he would proceed no further against them.*

*The examination of John Rensher taken before me George Gale etc. This
examinant saith that he is not guilty of stealing any beef or other things
from John Austin or any other person and that he was not at his house when
the beef was found there.*

*The examination of John Roberts taken before me George Gale etc. This
examinant saith that he is not guilty of stealing said beef but that he found
the said piece of beef (produced by the Constable) hanging on a cedar after
the canoe above mentioned was gone from Dam Quarter and he carrying it
into John Renshers Milk House and put it there with intent to send it to John
Austin believing it to be some of the beef the said Austin had lost. He owns
that when the Constable found it he did say that he had it of Betty Marvell
but that was not true and the reason why he said so was that he was taken
at a nonplus and did not know what to say.*

The charges against Renshaw and Roberts appear to have been dropped, since no
further record of this case is found in the Judicial records. However, there was a
later case brought against James Polk by the Court and John Renshaw,[28] probably
related to this proceeding, but that too was eventually dropped. Although nothing
came of these proceedings in the end, they give a clear indication of the rankled

---

[28] SOJR 1711-13:234.

undercurrent running between the Polk and Roberts/Renshaw factions in Damned Quarter. This seems to have been sufficiently intense to cause the Roberts family to adopt the use of their mother's maiden name, Grandee or Grundee, in lieu of their usual paternal surname. This occurs intermittently in both the Court records and Somerset tax lists.[29]

~~~~~~~

John Renshaw died in 1721, and Anne is listed as the administratrix on his estate. After that date few records are found of her. Surprisingly, there are no probate records at all, even though she was a substantial property owner. She is cited as "Widow Ann Roberts" (not Renshaw) in the 1733 and 1738 Debt Books for Somerset as the taxpayer for her Damned Quarter properties, Davids Destiny, Elliotts Choice, etc. In the intermediate years 1734 and 1735 her son Edward Roberts is listed for the same properties. The next extant Debt Book for Somerset is 1745. Edward Roberts is the indicated landholder for that year and in subsequent Debt Books through 1774. On this basis we may infer that Anne Polk Roberts Renshaw died sometime after 1738, although the debt books are admittedly not the most reliable source in such matters.

~~~~~~~

Following are the entries for Roberts and Renshaw in the extant tax lists for Monie Hundred through 1740:[30]

1722 and earlier No tax lists survive
    1723   Edward Roberts,
                    John Roberts, William Roberts, Negro Bess
                    (no entry for Anne Rensher or Roberts)
    1724   Edward Roberts
                    John Roberts, Bess
    1725   Edward Roberts, Richard Whitty
                    John Roberts, William Roberts
    1726   No list extant
    1727   Edward Roberts
                    Widow Roberts Plantation—John Roberts (only one taxable)[31]
    1728   John Roberts, Widow Roberts (only one taxable)
                    Edward Roberts, Richard Wallis, Jeffrey, Edward Martin
    1729   No extant tax list for Monie Hundred
    1730   Edward Roberts, Negros Jeffrey, Sarah

---

[29] John Roberts was the son of Francis Roberts by his mistress Rachel Grandee/Grundee (d. 1672); see Batchelder, p. 220.

[30] Note: each line in this annual listing represents a separate household.

[31] This refers to the widow of John Roberts who died in 1727. His probate is filed under the name "Grundie." The John Roberts appearing in this and subsequent entries is the son of the first John Roberts.

	John Grundey, Rensher Grundey[32]
	no entry for Anne/Widow Roberts
1731	Edward Roberts, Negros Jeffrey, Sarah
	Widdow Roberts, Jn° Roberts, Rencher Roberts
1732	No extant tax list for Somerset
1733	Edward Roberts, Negro Jeffrey
	John Roberts, Ranshaw Roberts
1734	Edward Roberts, Negro Jeffrey
	John Roberts, Thomas Roberts[33]
	Daniel Jones, Renshaw Roberts
1735	Edward Roberts, Negro Jeffrey
	John Roberts, Thomas Roberts
1736	Edward Robarts, Negros Jeffrey, Binah,
	John Roberts, Thomas Roberts
1737	Edward Roberts, Negros Jeffrey, Binah,
	Jn°. Roberts, Tho. Roberts
	Rencher Roberts
1738	Edward Roberts, Negros Jeffrey, Binah.
	John Robbards, Thoms Robberts
	Rancher Roberts, Negro York (in Nanticoke Hundred)
1739	Edward Roberts, Negros Jeffrey, Cuffie, Binah,
	Jn°. Roberts, Thomas Roberts,
	Rencher Roberts (Wicomico Hundred)
1740	Edward Roberts, Negros Jeffry, Cuffee, Binah,
	John Roberts, Thomas Roberts
	Rencher Roberts (Wicomico Hundred)

---

[32] John and Rencher Grundie/Roberts was the son of John Grundy/Roberts and Elizabeth Rencher.

[33] Rencher Roberts left the household of John Roberts at this time, moving first to household of Daniel Jones in Monie and afterwards to his own household in Wicomico.

3.2 John Polk (c.1668-1708)

Born: Ireland, most likely at Monyn, Ballendrait, Donegal
Occupation: cooper
Probate: died intestate; admin bond issued to wife Johanna, 20 Aug 1708,
Somerset County; inventory: valued at £66/9/1, 2 September 1708
Spouses:
(1) Jane (Jean) Knox, died 1700 at childbirth
(2) Johanna (Smith?); Johanna married secondly Thomas Hugg, by 1710; died
after 1731
Children by Jane Knox:
(1) William (1695-1726), m. Priscilla Roberts, dau. of Anne Polk & Francis
Roberts
(2) Anne (1698- ?), m. Edward Roberts, son of Anne Polk & Francis Roberts
(3) John (1700), died one week after birth
Children by Johanna:
(4) Robert of Dorchester (c.1707-1771), m. Alice Covington
(5) John of Little Creek (c.1708-1788), m. Sarah Vaughan
Property: Ballendrett (150A, 1692, sold 1707), Friends Denyall (300A, 1707),
Kirkminster (200A, 1707)

****

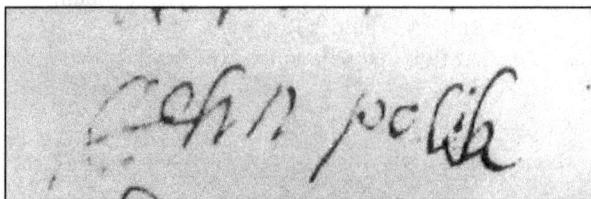

Signature of John Polk on will of William Porter, 6 December 1695

****

JOHN was the oldest of Robert and Magdalen's seven sons, and the first of
their children to settle outside Damned Quarter.

On 15 March 1693(NS), John Polke purchased a 150-acre parcel of Smiths
Recovery from Captain Henry Smith and gave it the name "Ballendrett" for his
childhood home in Donegal. For this he paid a premium price of 10,000 lbs. of
tobacco. (His father paid 5000 lbs. for Forlorne Hope, 100 acres, in 1697). This
tract was located between Smiths Branch and Kings Branch which feed into the
Manokin River, slightly more than a mile south of Princess Anne.

This purchase was part of a collective move involving a group of allied families that remained together over several generations. On the same day, John Knox and William Owens also acquired 150-acre parcels of the tract Illchester from Capt. Henry Smith, which they renamed Brothers Agreement and Ballyshannon respectively. Knox was probably the brother of John's wife (or wife to be; the marriage date is not certain), Jane Knox, and Owens' wife's [Jane] sister, Anne Knox, would later marry William Polk after Owens' death in 1698.

Manokin was a significant departure from Damned Quarter, about fifteenn miles eastward and not an easy journey in the conditions of the time, but the move was a well-considered choice that placed this group in the heart of the burgeoning Presbyterian community in Somerset. Families long identified with the Manokin Presbyterian Church in later years were already in the area. David Brown, Robert King, and Charles Ballard, three of Somerset's prominent citizens and sitting members of the court, were near neighbors. See Figure 10.

Rev. Thomas Wilson had also settled along the east side of Smith's Branch on a tract called Turner's Purchase in January 1685 very soon after his arrival from Donegal. John Polk's new dwelling place was located on the west side, just across from Wilson. Rev. Wilson was one of the ministers who followed shortly after Francis Makemie in answer to Colonel Stevens' letter of 1680, and it was Wilson who remained permanently in Somerset to minister to the faithful while Makemie traveled the Chesapeake region organizing mission churches.[34] The Presbyterian congregation in the Manokin area gathered for worship a short distance up the river from its juncture with Smith's Branch. Today the Manokin Presbyterian Church of Princess Anne stands at this same location, perhaps the oldest site in continuous usage by the Presbyterian faith in the new world.[35] No doubt this is where Margaret Polk and Thomas Pollitt were married by Rev. Wilson in December 1687 as well as Robert and Magdalen's other children as the occasion arose. Sadly, no records survive from this period of the church's history due to a fire which occurred in 1849.[36] Otherwise we would surely know considerably more of the Polks and other Presbyterian families of early Somerset than we do.

John's brother William followed him to Manokin not long afterwards and the two went into business together as coopers. William patented Golden Quarter in 1697, and their brother-in-law Thomas Pollitt purchased Pollitts Choice in 1699, both close to Manokin. Other families which took up land in this area and had close ties with the Polks for many years were Guillett, Heath, Alexander, Strawbridge, Chambers, and Gray.

---

[34] See also Torrence's account of Rev. Wilson, *Old Somerset*, pp. 226-33.
[35] See discussion in Torrence, pp. 234-248.
[36] Garrett, AHM, Vol. IV, No.1, p. 65.

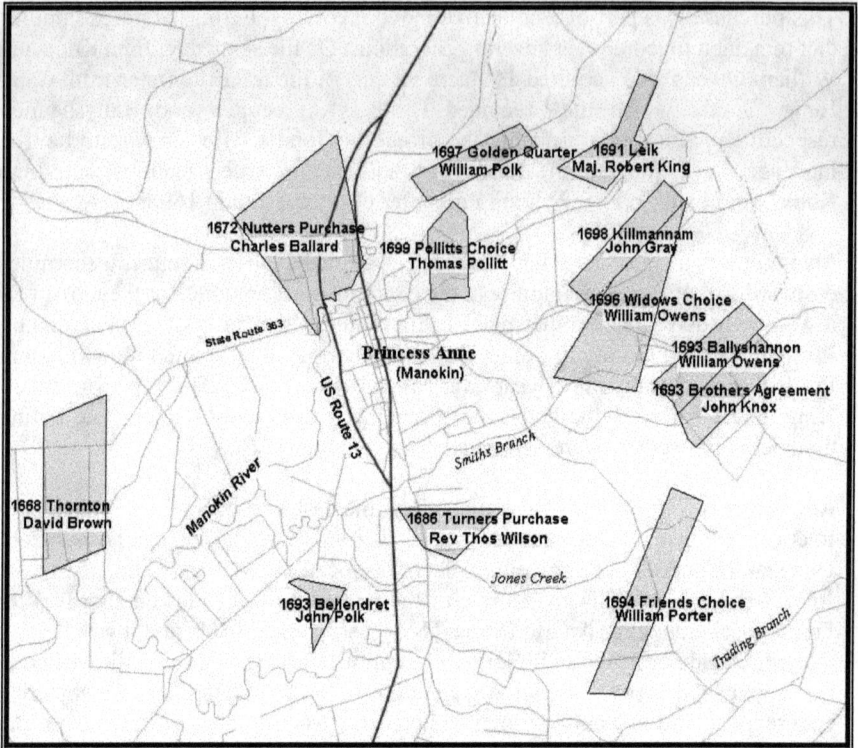

Figure 10. Land tracts of Presbyterian families near Princess Anne, at the head of the Manokin River.

~~~~~~~~

John was a cooper, as mentioned in numerous documents including his will. In the colonial world the cooper's principal task was fabricating hogsheads and other casks, the essential containers used for the transport of tobacco and comestibles. The craftsmen who constructed barrels for holding liquids in the holds of ships were known as wet coopers or tight coopers. This was a fairly lucrative trade and both John and younger brother William prospered in due course. They both learned their craft by 1690 from a George Parks who lived in the Annemessex area of Somerset to the South of Damned Quarter. Interestingly, John and William simply paid in tobacco for the needed instructions and worked for him as laborers rather than becoming apprentices to Parks. This arrangement later led to an unsettled account for which they eventually brought suit against Parks. In June 1696 John submitted the following account to the Court:[37]

---

[37] SOJR 1696-98:28.

George Parks Dft	Contra
To the 4th part 8000 pounds tbco	*By 600 lb allowed for instructing*
by the setting up in caske in ano 1690	*me in the Coopers trade——— 600*
by George Parke, Wm Polke & myself	*By the 4th of 1600 lb tbco for*
of Sundry prod——— 2000 lb tbco	*Staves to make up the Cask— 400*
	By two bar'll Indian Corn - 200
	1200
	Balance due 800

Errors Excepted, Per me
John Polke

The court ruled in John's favor, but collection of the debt was another matter, even as it is in our own times. The suit resurfaced three more times in court,[38] and the record does not show if John ever obtained satisfaction. Since Parks left the county at some point, further legal action was required to attach the assets Parks left behind. In any case, both John and William prospered in the long run from the skills they acquired from Parks and, in fact, formed a joint partnership when William moved to the Manokin area. This continued until John's death in 1708.[39]

~~~~~~

Several actions relating to John Polk's apprenticeship agreements appear in the Somerset land and court records. In August 1705 he entered into a contract with John Mulky for a six-year term as a cooper's apprentice. In December 1706 an arrangement with John Ryne, alias Mulrine, was ordered by the court to remove and protect Mulrine from an abusive stepfather. Following John's death in 1708, Mulrine petitioned the court for release from this agreement "and be restored to his mother." However, John's widow, Johanna Polk, objected and the court ruled that he stay with her, provided "the said widow Polk give security to learn the said Mulrine the trade of a cooper."

In light of this, it might seem surprising that John's own son William was not brought up as a cooper but as a blacksmith, as we know from later records.[40] This choice was probably made by the elder William Polk, who became the younger William's guardian after John's death. William no doubt saw this as a more lucrative trade.

~~~~~~

John married Jane, or Jean, Knox, probably very near to the time of his move to Manokin in 1692. We know that Jane was the sister of William Knox (Nox) from the latter's will probated in 1698 in which he appoints "my two brothers James Nox and John Polke to be overseers and aiding and assisting to my afsd. wife as need shall require." (Referring to a brother-in-law simply as a brother was

---

[38] SOJR 1696-98:302 and 1698-1701:25, 477.
[39] SOJR 1707-11:265.
[40] William describes himself as a blacksmith in his will.

common at that time.) Jane became the mother of John's children William and Anne whose births in 1695 and 1698 are recorded in the Somerset Parish records.[41] She gave birth to a third child, John, in October 1699, but tragically both mother and child died within a week.[42]

~~~~~~~~~

John married secondly a woman whose given name was Johanna. There is some confusion about her in the earlier accounts of the family history, and it is suggested that she was a sister to John's first wife, Jane Knox,[43] but this is almost certainly not the case. It seems more likely that she was the daughter of Thomas Smith, who bequeathed 100 acres to her son Robert Polk in his will probated 1727 in Dorchester.[44]

John had at least two sons by Johanna: Robert born c.1706-7, and John born c.1708-9. This has not been noted in the earlier Polk family histories, but it is clear from the tax lists of Somerset where these two sons are included as taxables in the household of Thomas Hugg, Johanna's second husband.[45] Robert Polk is listed in 1723 (the first year for which records are extant), and it may be inferred that he was born no later than 1707, since males became taxables at age 16.[46] He is also in the 1724 list, but disappears thereafter, most likely having moved to Dorchester at that time to take up residence with either his half-brother John, or Thomas Smith, from whom he inherited a tract called Poplar Level in 1727.[47] In February 1725/6 Robert signed as a witness to the will of his uncle, Robert Polk Jun., who lived near Smith in the Clear Brook Branch area of Dorchester. Unfortunately, no tax lists for Dorchester survive so it is not as easy to trace the movements of individuals in that county, but Robert appears regularly as rent payer for Poplar Level and other properties in the Proprietary Debt Books for Dorchester which commence in 1734. In due course he became a very substantial land owner and

---

[41] Somerset Parish was one of the four parishes into which Somerset County was divided in 1688. Parishes were administrative units to which, in principle, a minister of the established church would be assigned. But few established church ministers were available and inclusion in the parish records does not imply any association with the established church. Somerset Parish included the Manokin and Monie Hundreds.

[42] Somerset Parish Records; microfilm copy available at the Nabb Research Center for Delmarva History and Culture, Salisbury University, Salisbury, MD; also quoted in PF&K, p. 34, and referred to as records of "the Old Monie Church."

[43] PF&K, p. 29; on the Polk family tree of 1849 Johanna Knox is mentioned as John's first wife and "Jugga Hugg" as his second.

[44] Smith left lands to each of his sons-in-law rather than daughters, but Johanna appears to have been separated from Hugg by 1727, so it appears that in her case he made the bequest to her son, then of age.

[45] Confusion over this marriage apparently led to the apocryphal Jugga, or Jugurtha, Hugg appearing in some Polk family histories.

[46] Robert is also said to be of age about 35 on 9 November 1742 in a land commission recorded in DOLR, Old #10, p. 157.

[47] Located along Clearbrook Creek between Seaford and Bridgeville DE.

78

important county official in Dorchester.[48] He was a Justice of the Peace for many years and appears very frequently as the approving official for land conveyances. He was also a tobacco inspection officer for Dorchester.[49]

Robert was married to Alice Covington[50] and had eight known children: Robert (Jun.), Daniel, John, Sarah, Betty, Ann, William, and Esther.[51] William is the individual later known as Colonel William Polk of Polk's Defense, the father of Trusten Laws Polk and great-grandfather of Governor/Senator Trusten Polk of Missouri. W. H. Polk considered him to be a son of Robert Polk Jun.,[52] but from the latter Robert's will (1727) we know that he had no such son. To the contrary, William is mentioned as a son in a deed of gift from Robert Polk (son of John), in 1768,[53] for the three properties, Loss and Gain, Long Delay, and Polks Double Purchase in the Clearbrook Creek area, then in Dorchester. In 1776 these same properties, which had by then become part of Sussex County, Delaware, were combined with additional adjacent lands and vacancies to form the new tract, Polk's Defense, patented in the name of Colonel William Polk.[54]

John Polk, the other son of John and Johanna Polk, first appears on record in the household of Thomas Hugg in the 1725 Nanticoke Hundred tax list. Hugg died in 1729, and in 1729-31 John appears as a taxable in the household of "Johanah Hugge, wido." Johanna is not mentioned in tax lists after that time, but John Polk is listed continuously as head of household in the subsequent tax records.[55] He was referred to as John Polk "of Little Creek" and had a great number of descendants. W. H. Polk incorrectly describes John of Little Creek as a son of

---

[48] PF&K, p. 672-3. W. H. Polk says that Robert Polk, the Colonial official and attorney of Dorchester, was son of Robert Polk Jun., but Robert Polk (III) was less than 14 years old in 1726 when Robert Jun. wrote his will. The age of Robert, the Dorchester official, is noted in several documents and indicates a birth in 1706-7. For example, his deposition in the commission on Little Goshen (James Pollock's land) gives his age as about 35 on 9 November 1742.
[49] See Dorchester Tobacco Inspection Records, 1748-1775, MD Archives.
[50] According to W. H. Polk, Alice's maiden name was Nutter (PF&K, p. 673), but it is more likely that she was the daughter of Abraham Covington and Sarah Langrell. Covington's will refers to his daughter Alice Polk. See MDW 28:534.
[51] Robert's will (MDW 38:213, 1771) mentions sons Daniel, John, and William; Robert (Jun.) died at almost the same time and is not mentioned. Robert (Jun.) apparently had no children but mentions two of his brothers, Daniel and John, in his will (1771). See MDW 38:309. To compound the confusion, Robert, the son of Joseph Polk, also died intestate in Dorchester in 1771.
[52] PF&K, p. 672.
[53] DOLR Old #12:337.
[54] SXLR P2:86, P3:40.
[55] No probate records have been located for Johanna (Polk) Hugg, but she was probably still alive in 1740 when a deed for the tract Good Luck, from Patrick Caldwell to John Polk of Little Creek, describes the property as being on Rossaketoms Branch "about a mile below Johanna Hugg's."

Ephraim Polk,[56] but Ephraim never had a son named John.[57] This is not to say that the subsequent information in *Polk Family and Kinsmen* regarding the offspring of John of Little Creek is incorrect, only his paternity.

~~~~~~~~

In 1707 John Polk elected to relocate and sold Ballendrett for 15,000 pounds of tobacco and 5,000 nails. This was a substantial price considering land typically sold for 4000-5000 pounds of tobacco per hundred acres at the time, indicating the improvements that he had made and desirability of land in the Manokin area. At almost the same time he acquired two tracts totaling 500 acres, Kirkminster and Friends Denyall, from Matthew Wallace for 13,000 pounds of tobacco. These tracts were located on the Friends Denyall Branch, at the head of the Wicomico, near the northeastern corner of present-day Salisbury.

In the deed of conveyance Matthew Wallace is mentioned as being "now in Newcastle." It was apparently about this time that a nucleus of Scotch-Irish, notably members of the Wallace, Alexander and MacKnitt families, began a collective move from Somerset to Cecil County, Maryland, some fifteen miles inland from Newcastle, where they purchased lands in the Manor of New Munster. It is difficult to say whether their relocation was motivated purely by perceived economic advantages, or was in some way done in consort with Francis Makemie's missionary efforts. The first Presbytery in America was established at Newcastle under Makemie's leadership at this same time. A petition from some Presbyterians in Newcastle to the General Assembly of the Church of Scotland in February 1705/6 provides some insight:[58]

> We undersubscribers and the greatest number of us born and educated in
> Ireland under the ministry of Mr. William Traill presbiterian minister
> formerly at liford are by a Divine providence setled with our families at
> Newcastle and about it in the province of pensilvania and we have for
> present one Mr. John Wilson a scotsman who preacheth amongst us to
> whom belongeth[?] a few of different nations as we doe but they are
> neither capable to maintain a minister nor build a meeting house and so we
> are in feardayly to be cast desolate and to our great griefe we and our
> posterity left as a prey tosuperstition and heresies
> Therefore though it may be unusuall yet out of pure necessity and
> consideration of our souls circumstances we do most humbly address our
> selves to you as unto our mother church and to solicit your advice in this
> our uncertain condition and if there canbe any supply granted for our small

---

[56] PF&K, p. 491.

[57] Ephraim's children are listed in the SOJR, 1723-25:.272. See also section on Ephraim Polk.

[58] Scottish Record Office CH 1/2/28 fol. 4; see also Public Record Office of Northern Ireland, T3762; provided to author by R. K. McMaster.

congregation which is the custom of otherpersuasions to doe for them of their way

Your Supplicants Shall Ever pray ~

Newcastle Feb 11th 1705/6

Ninian Dunlap	*Abraham Emott*
John Stall [Steele?]	*Adam [?] Wallis*
James Wallace	*John Bolard*
Matthew Wallace	*Thomas Wallace*
David Miller	*Joseph Hook [Shook?]*
John Garner	*James Wallis*
Robert Walis	*Cornelius [?] Cooke*
Andrew Miller	*David Wallis*
William Wallace	*Thomas Southerland*
Morgan Pattan	*John Emott*

In any case it is clear that there was a residual connection maintained by these Scotch-Irish families with their kinsmen still in Ulster and Scotland, and this may have proved a deciding factor when the main flow of Scotch-Irish immigration to America commenced a decade later and Newcastle became a leading port of entry.

~~~~~~~~

John Polk died intestate in 1708, the year after his move to the Friends Denyall area. His son William inherited his lands, including those in Damned Quarter that John had apparently inherited on Robert Polke's death in 1703. Shortly before his death, John made a dying request to his brother William to look after the two surviving children, William and Anne, of his first wife, Jane Knox. This is noted in the Somerset Court records of June 1708 where William petitions for their custody:

To the Worhipfull the Justices of Somerset County now in Court sitting Wm. Polk humby showeth that when your petitioner's brother John Polk late of this county dec'd left two children behind him, to wit Wm and Anne Polk who upon his deathbed he requested that your petitioner and his wife to take care of them to see them educated and brought up Christian like and also to bring up the boy to learn a trade which your petitioner humbly craves that he may have the children ordered under him as your worships shall in your prudence and discretion think fit to be done (reasonably) for the orphans and petitioner as in duty bound shall ever pray.

This petition was granted with a security bond of £10 on William Polk to

do his best to prepare what parts is delivered to him of their
portions left by their deceased father till of age and then to return
their increase if any and do take care to learn the said William Polk
a trade and to read and write and do allow the said William and
Anne Polk all necessary and convenient till they come of age.

In fact, William became a blacksmith and remained in the Friends Denyall area for about fifteen years after his father's death, when he sold his father's lands and moved to Dorchester. Anne married her cousin Edward Roberts and moved to Damned Quarter.

~~~~~~~~

William, son of John and Jean (Knox) Polk, was for a long time considered by family historians to have been the William Polk of Cumberland County, Pennsylvania, ("near Carlisle") who was the progenitor of the principal line of Polks of North Carolina and Tennessee. This is the lineage that appears in the family tree published in 1849 and in Mary Winder Garrett's articles of 1896-99. It is also the supposition found in most of the papers and correspondence of W. H. Polk while he was preparing *Polk Family and Kinsmen*. This assumption was not based on any certain knowledge; it was just a reasonable conclusion based on the firm tradition that William Polk of Cumberland had originally come from Maryland. Since the only known Maryland Polks when the family history was first being compiled were those of Somerset, it was natural to assume a connecting link with those Polks, and William, son of John, was an obvious candidate. He was known to have sold his father's lands on Friends Denyall Creek in 1723 and departed the area. The presumption was that he headed for Pennsylvania and this understanding became the accepted version of family history until 1908 when Earle B. Polk of Somerset discovered the will of William Polk recorded in Dorchester County in 1726.

In December 1722, perhaps as part of the family relocation scheme, or perhaps because of the problems with Thomas Hugg, William Polk purchased the tract Colliers Adventure in Dorchester on the west side of the Nanticoke.[59] This new property was adjacent to the land of his cousin John Pollitt, as noted in William's will and a land commission in 1751. William must have moved there directly, since he is not found in the Somerset tax lists for 1723. In January 1723/4 he sold Kirkminster and Friends Denyall. His half-brother Robert Polk also moved to Dorchester about this time and may have in fact lived with William for several years until he acquired his own land. He is on the tax list for Wicomico Hundred in Somerset in 1723 and 1724, but not thereafter. There are no extant tax lists for Dorchester, but we find Robert as one of the witnesses on William's will signed in November 1726, so it appears they were close.

---

[59] DOLR Old #2:167.

William died in December 1726 or January 1727, barely in his thirties, leaving a will probated in Dorchester County. The will mentions three children, John, Jane, and Ann. John inherited the dwelling plantation, Colliers Adventure, and sold this to William Turpin in 1750.[60] The deed identifies him as John Polk of the "Territories of Pennsylvania." This probably refers to the three lower counties of Pennsylvania which later became the state of Delaware. Nothing further is known by the author of the fate of this John Polk.

Jane and Ann inherited the lands in Damned Quarter that William had himself inherited from his father (parts of Polkes Folly, Forlorn Hope, and Polkes Lot). One may wonder how William came to possess these lands since they were supposed to have been bequeathed to his father's brother, David, according to the terms of Robert Polke's will. The fact that they had instead descended to William through his father, John, the oldest of Robert's sons, is evidence that David Polk had in fact predeceased his father and had no heirs. Curiously, in a somewhat belated and circuitous fulfillment of the provision in Robert's will that David provide for his youngest brother, Joseph, Jane must have conveyed these lands to the latter at some point, for in 1748 Joseph included them in the sale of the residual Damned Quarter Polk lands to John and William Shores.[61]

<center>~~~~~~~~</center>

The children of John Polk (son of Robert and Magdalen) by his second wife, Johanna, were not included in his brother William's request for custody. Since they were Johanna's natural children she had clear right and responsibility for their care, so there was no basis for William to make a request to be appointed their guardian. These children, Robert and John Polk, (and perhaps daughters for which no record has been found) were accordingly brought up in the household of Johanna and her second husband, Thomas Hugg.

The relationship between Thomas Hugg and widow Johanna Polk was clearly a difficult one. Hugg was hauled into Somerset Court for a long string of debtor suits beginning in 1712, losing in almost all cases, some very substantial. These culminated in 1717 when the Sheriff reported Hugg as *non est inventus* (no longer in the County),[62] and in 1722 his goods were attached by James Adams to collect against an earlier judgment.[63] Hugg appears to have recovered somewhat from this low point and later returned to the county, but matters did not improve much. In 1723 Thomas and Johanna Hugg sold her dower rights to the tracts Kirkminster and Friends Denial originally purchased by John Polk when her stepson William Polk sold his portion of those lands and moved to Dorchester County. Then in 1725 Thomas Hugg was charged with adultery with "a certain Ann Bullingall" and brought in for trial. Although he was acquitted in this case, we can safely infer

---

[60] DOLR Old #14:480.
[61] SOLR 22 (A):4,5.
[62] SOJR 1715-17:377: 399.
[63] SOJR 1722:25.

some serious conjugal discord behind the scenes. Since no husband is mentioned for Bullingal, as would be expected if there were one, it is unlikely that she was married and probable that the charges had been pressed by Johanna herself. Beginning in 1727 Thomas Hugg disappears from the tax lists and Johanna is listed as the head of household with her son John Polk the single taxable. Thomas Hugg was still in the area however, for he appeared in other court cases and made a deposition to a commission on Friends Denial and Kirkminster in 1728. He died by May 1729 when his will, written in February 1726/7, was probated. In it he provides for "my well beloved wife Johana" and children William, Jane, and Mary.

~~~~~~~

Hugg family appearances in Somerset tax lists:

Before 1722	No tax lists survive	
1723	Thos. Hugg, Robt. Polk	Wicomico Hundred
1724	Thomas Hugg, Robert Polk	Nanticoke Hundred
1725	Thos Hugg, Robt Friggs, John Polk	Nanticoke Hundred
1726	No extant tax list for Somerset	
1727	Joanah Hug, Jnº. Polk (one taxable)	Nanticoke Hundred
1728	Att Joannah Hugs, John Polk(one taxable)	Nanticoke Hundred
1729	Widow Hugg, John Polk (one taxable)	Nanticoke Hundred
1730	Joanah Hugg, John Polk	Nanticoke Hundred
1731	Johanah Hugg Widow, John Polk	Nanticoke Hundred
1732	No extant tax list for Somerset	Nanticoke Hundred
1733	John Polk	Nanticoke Hundred
1734	James Cooper, John Polke	Nanticoke Hundred
1735	James Cooper, John Polk	Nanticoke Hundred
1736	John Polke	Nanticoke Hundred
1737	John Polk	Nanticoke Hundred
1738	John Poke	Nanticoke Hundred
1739	John Polk	Nanticoke Hundred
1740	John Polk—Little Creek	Nanticoke Hundred

The last entry is important since it identifies this John Polk as John Polk of Little Creek who married Sarah Vaughan and died in 1788. He is also referred to as John Polk of Little Creek in later tax records for Nanticoke, and his will filed in Sussex County explicitly identifies him as John of Little Creek. There is another John Polk appearing in Nanticoke tax lists throughout the same period, a cousin, John, son of James. The two can be readily distinguished from each other by the way the tax lists are organized into localities.[64] John of Little Creek, for instance, is consistently listed closely adjacent to a certain James Cooper, in fact he is in

---

[64] See SOTL and Russo.

Cooper's household in 1734 and 1735, whereas John of James lived in the area of Johns Neck and is consistently juxtaposed in the tax list with his brother James, cousins Charles and Ephraim Polk, Robert and Samuel Owens, and Manuel Manlove, all of whom lived in the same area.

~~~~~~~~~

There are a great many descendants of John and Johanna Polk through their sons Robert Polk of Dorchester and John Polk of Little Creek. This has never been recognized because of the confusion about their genealogy in the earlier family histories. There is much information about Robert and John's progeny in *Polk Family and Kinsmen*, but their own parentage is incorrectly attributed to other sons of Robert and Magdalen. See Appendix I for what the author believes is the correct four generation tree of the family, beginning with Robert and Magdalen.

3.3 Margaret Polk (1670-1734+)

Born: Ireland, most likely at Monyn, Ballendrait, Donegal
Probate: no records located
Spouses:
(1) Thomas Pollitt (1640-1708), married 27 Dec 1687 by Rev. Thomas Wilson
(2) Richard Tull (d.1711); m. after 1708
(3) Charles Williams (c.1650, d.1734); m. between 1711 and 1717
Children by Thomas Pollitt:
(1) John (1688-1749), m. Mary Polk(?)
(2) Thomas (1690-1743), m. Sarah Miles
(3) William (1690-1742/3). m. Alice (N)
(4) Richard (1694-?)
(5) Margaret (1700-after 1742)
(6) Isabel (1702-)
Children by Richard Tull: none known
Children by Charles Williams:
(7) possibly John Williams (b.c.1712, d.1760)

****

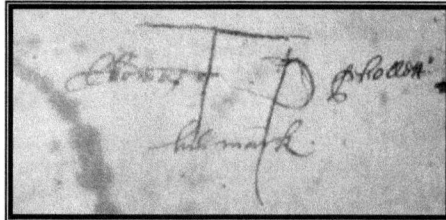

Mark of Thomas Pollitt, first husband of Margaret Polk, from his will
****

MARGARET, like Anne, was not mentioned by Robert Polke in his will or any other primary source document, but the indirect evidence establishing her as his daughter is compelling. Somerset Liber IKL (p. 213) records the marriage of Thomas Pollett in 1687 to a woman named Margaret whose surname is not given, but W. H. Polk cites family tradition to identify Margaret as the daughter of Robert and Magdalen Polke.[65] The Polk family tree of 1849 and Mary Winder Garrett's articles on the Polk family in the *American Historical Magazine* also list Margaret as one of the children of Robert and Magdalen, and wife of Thomas Pollitt. Without further evidence, Margaret Pollitt's filial relation to Robert and Magdalen would be somewhat questionable, but a close family association between the Polks and Pollitts is corroborated by numerous records. Pollitts are witnesses to the wills of James Polk and Magdalen Polke. John Pollitt and William (son of John) Polk moved to adjacent properties in Dorchester, and William bequeathed a parcel of his land to John Pollitt in 1727. The Somerset court record of

---

[65] PF&K, p.40, 92-3.

November 1710 states that Thomas Pollitt and John Polk (both deceased by then) were the bondsmen along with Anne (Polk) Roberts for the estate of Francis Roberts, and in their name a suit was brought to protect the inheritance of Anne's son, Edward Roberts. Also, William Polk and Thomas Pollitt (Jun.) jointly applied for patent of the tract Come by Chance in 1734 and joint ownership was quite unusual at that time. This Polk and Pollitt association continued over several generations in both Somerset and Dorchester. In fact, in his notes on Polk family history, Josiah F. Polk refers to "old Mr. Thomas Pollitt who knows more of the family history than any other person."[66] Since there is no other direct marital relationship with the Pollitts to explain their close association in this early period, it seems only reasonable to accept the strong family tradition that Margaret, wife of Thomas Pollitt, was the daughter of Robert and Magdalen Polke.

The fact that Robert's will does not specifically mention Margaret is explained by her being already well provided for as the wife of Thomas Pollitt. Her sister Anne was similarly omitted from Robert's will, and there is no question of Anne being his daughter. She was certainly well-off as the wife of Francis Roberts, so Robert presumably felt no need to make any bequests, either to her or to Margaret. In contrast, his unmarried daughter Martha is mentioned as recipient of one third of his goods and chattels, which is another indication of Robert's intent to provide for all his children in the most even-handed manner possible, considering their individual needs and situations.

This other daughter, Martha, is referred to twice in the will of Robert Polke; first, specifically as his daughter in the original will of 1699, and second as "Martha Poock" in the codicil of 1702 in which he adds a provision to let her cattle "run on the plantacon until she gets plantacon." This is clearly not a person already married to Thomas Pollitt, but W. H. Polk thought this was just a misspelling of "Margaret"[67] and that they were one and the same person. He was not aware of the 1687 date of Thomas and Margaret Pollitt's marriage recorded in Somerset Liber IKL. In fact, he thought Martha/Margaret Pollitt was born about 1679.[68]

~~~~~~~

Margaret's approximate birth year is known from her age, stated as sixty in a deposition she made (then as Margaret Williams) on 27 August 1730 concerning the tract David's Destiny.[69] This places her birth in 1669-70, consistent with her known first marriage occurring at the age of eighteen, quite typical for young women at that time. Her date of death is not known, but in 1734 her then husband Charles Williams mentioned his wife in his will without stating her name. Presumably this was Margaret since Williams was already over eighty at the time, and a remarriage after 1730 would have been highly unlikely had Margaret died

---

[66] See Josiah F. Polk notes, Appendix II.
[67] PF&K, p.92.
[68] PF&K, p.93.
[69] SOJR 1730-33:8

in the interim.

The known children of Margaret Polk and Thomas Pollitt are:
  John Pollitt, b. 18 Jan. 1688(NS), Somerset; d. Aug 1749, Dorchester
  Thomas Pollitt, b. 28 Sep. 1690, Somerset; d. before 26 Jan 1743, Somerset
  William Pollitt, b. c.1692, Somerset; d. c. Mar. 1743(NS), Dorchester
  Richard Pollitt, b. 17 June 1694, Somerset; probably died young
  Margaret Pollitt b. 31 Mar. 1700, Somerset
  Isabel Pollitt, b. 15 Apr., 1702, Somerset

These birth dates are found in Somerset land records, Liber IKL, and Somerset Parish Records,[70] except that of William, which is an estimate. Nothing is known of the subsequent life of Richard Pollitt; this citation of his birth is the only known record mentioning him. Since Thomas Pollitt provided for his other three sons in his will without mentioning Richard it seems likely that Richard died young.

~~~~~~

Margaret's second and third marriages are confirmed from the probate accounts of Thomas Pollitt Sen.,[71] which refers (1711) to "Margaret Tull, relict of Richard Tull, Admx of Thomas Pollitt, deceased," and of Richard Tull[72] which mentions (1717) "Charles Williams et ux Margaret adm. estate of Richard Tull." She is also referred to as the wife of Charles Williams and administratrix of Thomas Tull in Somerset Judicials 1715-17:125. Her third husband Charles Williams was also the father of her two sisters-in-law, Elizabeth, the wife of Ephraim Polk, and Anne, the wife of James. In his will, probated in 1734, Charles Williams mentions his daughters Anney Polk and Elizabeth Laws (widow of Ephraim Polk, remarried to John Laws).

The date of Margaret's marriage to Charles Williams is not known, but had to occur before October 1716 when Thomas Dashiell made a claim against Charles Williams citing his wife as the administratrix of Richard Tull's estate. Charles Williams had a son, John, who was born about 1712, as indicated by his first appearance on the Monie tax list in 1728. It is therefore possible that Margaret was John's mother, assuming the marriage had taken place in 1711-12;[73] however, without a record of the marriage date, or of the death of Charles Williams' previous wife, this remains uncertain.

~~~~~~

Thomas and Margaret Pollitt acquired their plantation known as Pollitts Choice (Pholletts Choyce), a parcel of Shipways Choice, in the neck of land between the

---

[70] Barnes, *Somerset Parish Records.*
[71] MDIA 32B:256.
[72] MDA 1:435.
[73] Richard Tull had died by August 1710; MDIA 32B: 98.

Manokin River and Shipways Branch just to the northeast of present-day Princess Anne in 1699. This was in close proximity to the tract Golden Quarter which Margaret's brother William Polk purchased two years earlier—another addition to the Polk/Gullett/Owens/Knox community that took up much of this area. Where they lived in the twelve years prior to that is not clear—perhaps in Damned Quarter, but there is no record of their presence there.

When Thomas Pollitt died in 1708, he bequeathed his Manokin property, Pollitts Choice, to his eldest son John and his other property, Prestine, near Salisbury, to his sons, Thomas Jun. and William. By some means, for which there is no record, John conveyed Pollitts Choice to Thomas Jun., who remained there permanently. He died in 1743 mentioning five sons and five daughters in his will. Both John and William Pollitt chose to join the Polk migration to the Nanticoke area, in fact John slightly preceded it. He purchased the property Welshman's Kindness (400 acres) from Thomas Taylor in November 1718. This was then in Dorchester, but now in Delaware, on the north side of the Nanticoke about five miles downstream from Seaford. He was followed not long after by William, son of John Polk, who purchased the adjacent tract Colliers Adventure (250 acres) from Matthew Harmanson in December 1722. Harmanson gave John Pollitt power of attorney to sign on his behalf in this transaction. When William Polk wrote his will in 1726 he made a provision bequeathing to John Pollitt "a parcel of land from my upper fence now belonging to the manor plantation, that is to say if the said John Pollet doth secure to my heirs conveniency such a quantity of land." William's widow Priscilla seemed to have been a bit dubious about this provision and shortly after his death petitioned the Court to have a £200 bond placed on John Pollitt to protect against any encroachment of her land.[74] The confusion about ownership appears to have persisted nonetheless since Margaret Pollitt (presumably John's daughter) requested a commission to enquire into the boundaries in June 1751, six months after William and Priscilla's son John sold Colliers Adventure.[75]

---

[74] DOLR Old #8:254.
[75] DOLR Old #14:552.

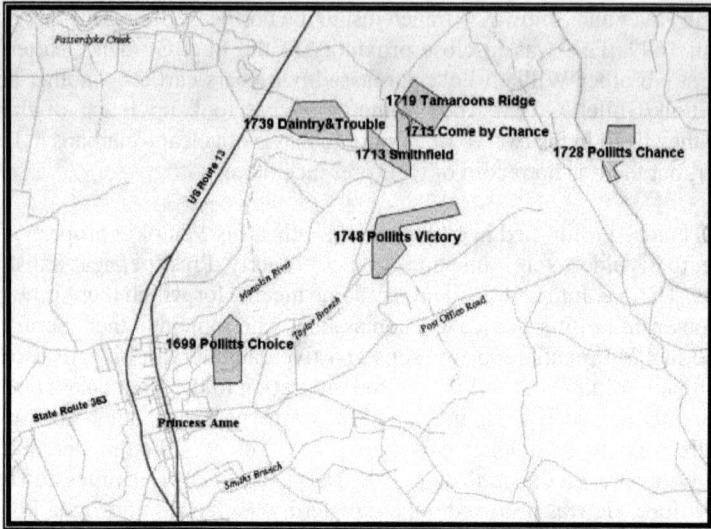

Figure 11. Pollitt land tracts in Manokin area. (Date shown is the year acquired. Pollitts Choice (Pholletts Choice) was formed from subparcels of two other tracts, Shipways Choice and Deep, purchased by Thomas Pollitt Sen. The other tracts were acquired by Thomas Pollitt Jun.)

John Pollitt was married to a woman named Mary, possibly the daughter of James Polk. James' will was witnessed by a John and Mary Pollitt, and since Thomas Pollitt (Sen.) had no daughter named Mary the surname Pollitt was her married, not maiden, name, and these two probably signed as husband and wife. Mary also appears as the administratrix for John's estate as noted on his inventory[76] filed in Dorchester County in 1749.

William Pollitt followed to Dorchester somewhat later, purchasing the tract Bensons Adventure from Henry Benson in 1731. He had been living in the household of his mother and stepfather Charles Williams at Roberts Lott until 1728, when he was listed as head of a separate household in Damned Quarter. This is his last appearance in the Somerset tax lists and he presumably joined the final phase of family move to Nanticoke after the passing of the family matriarch, Magdalen, whose will he witnessed. In 1741 he added another 50 acres with the survey of a tract that he called Pollitts Alley adjacent to Bensons Adventure.[77]

~~~~~~~

The following entries for Charles and John Williams appear in the tax lists for Monie Hundred:

Before 1722   No tax lists survive

---

[76] MDI 40:309.
[77] MDLP BC&GS #01:408c & TI #4:086p; also Dorchester Land Records 15:494.

1723	Charles Williams, William Pollitt, James Betsworth
1724	Charles Williams, William Pollitt
1725	Charles Williams, William Pollitt
1726	No list
1727	Charles Williams, William Pollet
1728	Charles Williams, John Williams
	William Pullet (separate household)
1729	No extant list
1730	Charles Williams removed from tax list; 80 years old [78]
	John Williams – in household of John Miller,
1731	John Williams – in household of John Lawes
1732	No list
1733	No entry for John Williams
1734+	John Williams appears regularly as head of household; single
	Taxable

Charles Williams died in 1734, so presumably John Williams took ownership of the plantation at this time. John had an only child, Charles, born c.1736, who inherited the property when John died in 1751. The latter Charles petitioned for a commission to investigate the boundaries of Roberts Lott in March 1758; the petition contains references to his grandfather, the first Charles Williams, and to the Polk, Renshaw, Wallace, and Pollitt families.[79]

Thomas Pollitt, Jun., appears in the extant tax lists for the Wicomico Hundred more or less continuously throughout the period 1723-1740. His son Thomas (III) begins to appear in 1731 and son William in 1738. His brothers John and William had moved to Dorchester (John in 1718 and William by 1731) and do not appear in Somerset tax lists.

---

[78] SOJR 1730-3:2.
[79] SOJR 1757-60:140.

3.4 William Polk (1673-1739)

Born: Ireland, most likely at Monyn, Ballendrait, Donegal
Occupation: cooper
Probate: will written 23 January 1740(NS); probated 24 February 1740(NS); no
 inventory or administration account on record
Spouse: Anne Knox, widow of William Owens (d.1698); married 1698-99
Children:
(1) James (1700-1771), m. Betty Cottman (possibly first married Mary Cottman)
(2) Jane (c.1703-1775), m. James Strawbridge
(3) David (1705-1778), m. Elizabeth Gillis
(4) Elizabeth (c.1710-1775). m. John Williams
Property: Golden Quarter (150A, 1697); Widows Choice (250A, 1713); Come
 by Chance (10A, 1714); Roxborough (210A, 1715); Tamaroons Ridge
 (120A, 1718); Harthberry (50A, leased from William Smith); Denegall
 (100A, 1725); Ramas (100A, 1725); Moneen (100A; 1725); Williams
 Adventure (64A, 1727); Smiths Hope (100A, 1727); Rich Land (200A,
 1728)

****

Signature of William Polk from will of William Porter, 6 December 1695

****

WILLIAM was an industrious and prescient man who raised children of strong
character. After the early death of his brother John in 1708 he became the family
leader whose vision guided the relocation from Damned Quarter to the upper
Nanticoke. His legacy was the foundation he prepared for the next generation to
build on.

~~~~~~~~~

The year of William's birth was 1672 or 1673, as known from four separate
depositions in which he stated his age.[80] Tradition places him as the second son,
both as shown in the Polk family tree of 1849 and in the notes of Josiah F. Polk,
and the land records of Somerset show that he was the second of Robert's sons to
acquire his own plantation. The family histories by W. H. Polk and Mary Winder

---

[80] SOJR, 1730-33:8; 1733-35:186; 1738-40:184, 202. These give his age as 58 on 7 Aug
1730, 61 on 10 June 1734, 66 on 11 Aug 1739 and 66 on 27 Nov 1739, respectively.

Garrett also place William as the second son.[81]

As already described, William and older brother John learned the cooper's trade from George Parks around 1690 by paying for lessons and learning on the job. John soon left Damned Quarter to settle in Manokin, and we might suppose that William accompanied him at that time, for they formed a partnership and worked together as coopers. We cannot be sure how well they did overall, but one indication of success was that in February 1702/3 William was able to order "*a sound lusty negro woman fitt for service between fifteen & five & twenty years of age*" to be purchased and brought to him by merchants Nicholas Evans of Somerset and Jeffery Gray of Boston. The price is not indicated, but when Evans and Gray failed to make delivery, William went to court and obtained a judgment against them for the substantial amount of £50, equivalent to 12,000 pounds of tobacco at the standard rate of one penny per pound. William later proceeded against Evans a second time to attach his goods and chattels.[82]

William did not acquire land at the same time as John, but by 1697 he was in a position to buy Golden Quarter, a tract of 150 acres, from William Goldsmith for 6000 pounds of tobacco, a better bargain than John had extracted from Captain Henry Smith for Ballendrett. This was a well-chosen location on the main branch of the Manokin River, about a mile upstream and to the west of Princess Anne. The town did not exist at that time, but the head of the Manokin had been the location of a trading post with the Indians from before the county was established. When Worcester County was split off from Somerset in 1742, Princess Anne became the county seat of the residual Somerset and continued to grow. It was also the site of the Manokin Presbyterian Church, first served by Rev. Thomas Wilson and active to this day. William Polk's descendants were prominent citizens in this area for many generations.

In 1702 William took Captain Henry Smith to court for payment of 1600 pounds of tobacco due since 1697 to the estate of William Owens, his wife Anne's first husband. Smith, who was in considerable financial difficulties by this time, did not show up to plead his case and the court ordered his goods and chattels forfeit. Whether William and Anne were able to collect is not known; there was already a line of creditors trying to collect from Smith at this time.[83]

~~~~~~~~~~

---

[81] PF&K, pp. 203-4 and Garrett, AHM, Vol. III, No. 3, July 1898, p. 263.
[82] SOJR 1705-06:50, 226.
[83] Smith was an influential person and one of the early Justices of Somerset but seems to have been a rather unsavory character. Torrence is kind to Smith in *Old Somerset* but others have written rather scathing accounts of the man. He certainly overextended himself in business, was frequently brought into Court, and eventually left Maryland to end his days in Sussex County, Delaware. His first marriage in Virginia was one of the few of that era to end in an officially recorded divorce.

For some reason William's brother and partner, John, decided to leave Manokin in 1707. Perhaps he decided that land values had appreciated to the extent that it was time to cash in. He did indeed acquire substantially more land along the Friends Denyall Branch in the northeast section of what is now Salisbury for the price of the land he sold in Manokin. His partnership with William must have dissolved at this time, but when John died a year later there was still a residual commitment between them which led William to bring suit against his sister-in-law, Johanna Polk. In August 1709 he presented the following account in court:

The estate of John Polk late of Monocan deceased
<u>Contra</u>

1698
Tobco: due to me upon partnership of coopers working 2400
To: 4¾ gallon of Molasses at 3 shillings p/gallon £ 0-14-3
To 1 ¼ gallon Rum for his body & funeral 0-08-9
To: 1 gallon molasses & ½ bushel salt 0-06-0
To: 300 staves lent ~
—————
01-09-0

True acc't errors excepted Wm Polk

<u>Dr</u>

By 2 gallons molasses returned 00-06-00
By 300 pipestaves returned ~ 1707
Memo that this day being the 22th of Febry
came Wm Polke & made oath on the Holy
Evangelists that the above acc't of 2400 pds
of tbco & twenty three shillings in money is
due & that he hath received no part or
Parcel thereof
Testes Thos Dashiell

Johanna did not contest the claim:

And the Defendant comes into Court in her proper person & confesseth judgment wherefore considered by the Court here that the Plt Wm Polke recover of the estate of John Polke deceased 2400 pds of Tobco & twenty three shillings in money as also two hundred forty three pounds of Tobco for his cost & charges laid out & expended by means of retaining sd debt and the Deft in Mercy

<div align="center">~~~~~~~~</div>

William remained permanently in Manokin, and as he prospered he increased his property holdings, not just in Manokin, but also in the upper Nanticoke area. Curiously, his first transaction was a land swap with his stepsons, John and William Owens, in which William (Polk) gave Golden Quarter to John and

94

arranged for Charles Philips to convey Smiths Hope to William. This was in exchange for their deeding him the tract Widow's Choice, which they had inherited from their father, William Owens, in 1698. William had most likely resided on the Owens property ever since his marriage to Anne, and when John and William came of age it made more sense for them to relocate to new dwelling places than for William and the rest of the family to do so.

Altogether, William amassed over 1400 acres of land in Manokin and Nanticoke in his own name. His other land acquisitions in Manokin included half of a twenty-acre parcel of Come by Chance in 1714 (shared with Thomas Pollitt Jun.), Roxborough (210 acres, 1715), Tameroons Ridge (150 acres, 1718), Williams Adventure (64 acres, 1727), and Smiths Hope (100 acres, 1727). There was also an arrangement with Capt. Henry Smith for leasing Harthberry. (There are no records for such lease arrangements, but the Proprietary Rent Rolls and Debt Books list him as responsible for the ground rent.) All of these properties were clustered to the east and northeast of present-day Princess Anne. See Figure 12.

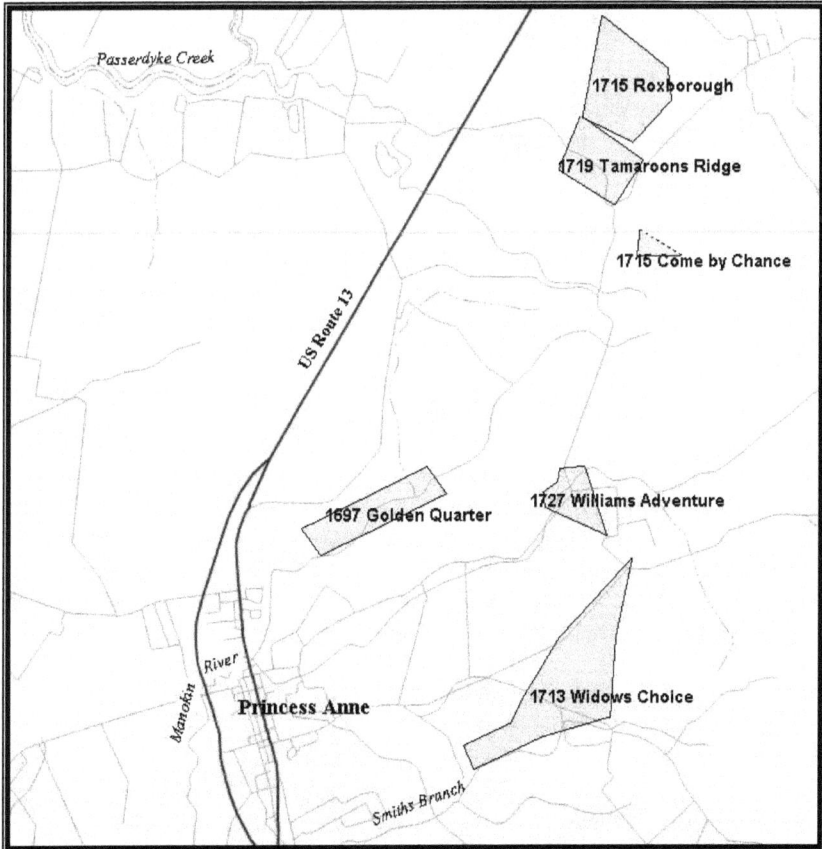

Figure 12. William Polk's lands in Manokin (Princess Anne) area. Year shown is date of acquisition.

William's interest in the Nanticoke area was motivated more by his vision for establishing his extended family there than for his own needs, but he did acquire property there for himself. As already noted, he took out warrants totaling 700 acres in 1720-1721 for the use of his stepchildren Samuel, Robert, and William Owens, and nephew Charles Polk (son of Ephraim). He retained 300 acres for himself, and these were used as warrants in the surveys of Moanen, Ramas, and Denigall. In 1724 he obtained a warrant for another 200 acres which he later used for the survey of Rich Land. These properties are all located in the area known as Johns Neck to the northeast of Bridgeville, Delaware.

~~~~~~~

It has been stated in Polk family histories that William Polk inherited the family home White Hall from Robert Polke, the immigrant, and passed it on to his son David, but this is not the case. There was no such home in Robert or William's time. White Hall was actually patented much later, in 1795, by David's son, Judge William Polk, as a resurvey of land first acquired by David in 1741 along the Wicomico River just above Cuttmaptico Creek.

Judge William's residence was a graceful mansion located at this site and was the dwelling known as White Hall in family history.[84] The property was sold by Judge William's son James Polk to cousins in the Harcum family in 1822, who retained them until quite recent times. The original mansion burned down in the late nineteenth century and was replaced by a farmhouse of conventional design. The antiquity of this estate was exaggerated in later accounts of the family, such as the memoirs of Esther Winder Polk, wife of Governor Enoch Louis Lowe, and this tradition has generally been accepted since then, but the records do not support it. Robert and Magdalen lived out their days in Damned Quarter on the land where they first settled.[85]

~~~~~~~

William raised strong-minded children. Fractious might be an even more apt description for them, if the notes of Josiah F. Polk are any indication. He had two sons, James born in 1700 and David in 1706, and two daughters, Jane who married James Strawbridge, and Elizabeth who married John Williams. Both sons were very active and respected members of the Somerset community, appearing many times in the records as county officials, jurors, attorneys, and litigants.

James was closely associated with the Presbyterian Church at Manokin; his house in Princess Anne, located just across the river from the present church, was mentioned as the site of church services in 1747.[86]

---

[84] Esther Winder Polk Lowe, "Memories." She was very familiar with the residence itself, but had an incorrect understanding of its early history.
[85] A more complete history of White Hall appears in Chapter 5.
[86] SOJR 1747-49:22.

*Whereas the Reverend Mr. Charles Tennent, a Presbiterian Minister,
personally appeared here in his Lordship's, the Right Honourable the Lord
Proprietary of Maryland, his County Court of Somerset, and did then and
there before his said Lordship's Justices, in court individually sitting, take
the Oaths appointed by an Act of parliament made in the first year of King
William and Queen Mary, and repeated the declaration, directed by an act
of parliament made in the thirtyeth year of Charles the Second, and
subscribed the same, and declared his approbation to the Articles of faith in
the Church of England, and subscribed to the same (except those articles
and part of an article as is disallowed of by such discenting ministers).*

*I desire that you will register the Severall places within mentioned for
publick Service and preaching of the Gosple of Jesus Christ, the places are
as followeth: at the meeting house at Rockawakin on the head of
Wickamoco River, and at the meeting house at Olliphant's, and also at
Broad Creek Bridge, and also at the dwelling house of Joshua
Caldwell, and also at Wilson Rider's, and also at the house of James Polk's
in Princess Anne Town on his Lot No. 2. Sep 23ʳᵈ 1747.   Charles Tennent.*

While his Presbyterian beliefs may have formed his character, the Ulster Scot heritage in James had its contentious side, for he was brought before the court and convicted and fined for assault or contempt on at least four occasions. One gets the distinct impression from the records that he considered the money well spent.

The earliest incident occurred in 1725 when William Stoughton, Esq., one of the Somerset Justices complained that "*a certaine James Polke of Somerset County Planter had abused him, and said he did not do him Justice and that he owed him a spite or else he would not have done as he did.*" Polke appeared but "*had nothing in his defence to offer that was materiall.*" Several witnesses supported Stoughton; the court found James guilty and fined him 500 pounds of tobacco. He chose instead to pay £5 sterling, far more than required, no doubt intended as a show of contempt for Stoughton and the proceeding. The court in turn placed him under an unusually high bond of £40 for his good behavior.

Another case occurred in 1733 when James was brought into court for shooting the dog of William Gray. James claimed the dog had been harassing his own animals, had warned Gray, and clearly felt that the dog deserved what it got. The jury agreed with him, but the court seemed to have its own opinion about James at this point, and did not accept the jury's verdict. The case was remanded and resurfaced several times in later sessions, until Gray finally failed to show and was fined for his "false clamour."

James did not mellow with age. In fact, he appears to have become more rather than less contentious and was convicted in court for assault three times after reaching the age of sixty. In March 1761 he was tried under an indictment stating that he "*with force and arms in and upon a certain William Hailey ... then and there ... an assault did make and him the said William then and there did beat wound and evilly treat so that of his life it was much despaired.*"[87] He did not contest the charge and was fined ten shillings, which he paid in Court. This behavior repeated itself with regularity—in June 1765 and June 1769 he was tried on similar charges with similar results in the cases of William Addams and Rachel Robertson.[88]

One contemporary who clearly did not have a high opinion of James Polk and said so publicly was William Heath, which led Polk to sue Heath for defamation in 1765. Josiah Polk, James' nephew, acting as his attorney, extolled James' character as

> "*an honest subject of our Lord the King that now is, and as a good, true and honest and liege subject...and from his nativity hitherto...hath behaved and governed from all perjury ... unspotted and unsuspected all the time ... much good will and friendship of all his neighbours and others...*"

and went on to accuse Heath of

> "*plotting and maliciously intending the said James of his good name, fame, credit and reputation to deprive and him into public contempt and ignominy to bring ... on [date unsaid] 1767 at the County afsd falsely and malitiously spoake, published and pronounced with a loud voice these false, feigned, scandalous, malitious and approbrious words following, to wit: "You [to him the said James Polk speaking and him meaning] old perjured son of a bitch, you old foresworn dog, if you had sworn the truth yesterday I [the said William himself meaning] would have had that red-headed dog [meaning a certain Benjamin Polk] bound to his good behaviour" by which...words the said James in his good name (is) much hurt and vilifyed ... to the damage of the said James one hundred and thirty pounds current money of Maryland and thereof he brings this suit.*

The Court found in James' favor, but may have shared some of Heath's sentiments, awarding only a nominal sum of six shillings for damages.[89]

~~~~~~~~

A few comments on James' children are in order to clarify some inaccuracies in W. H. Polk and Mary Winder Garrett's accounts of them. Both authors state that James Polk had two wives, Mary and Betty Cottman, daughters of Benjamin Cottman.[90] They further indicate that Mary was the mother of five of James' children, Virginia, Benjamin, Priscilla, Nancy, and William (in that order), and

---

[87] SOJR 1760-63:73.
[88] SOJR 1763-65:232; 1769-72:45.
[89] SOJR 1767-69:132.
[90] PF&K, p. 215; Garrett, AHM, Vol. 4, No. 1, p. 46.

that Betty was the mother of two daughters, Leah and Mary. Neither author identifies a source for this information, and they are probably incorrect as regards the maternity of the children. Somerset probate records certainly confirm James' marriage to Betty Cottman, for Benjamin Cottman mentions Betty Polk as a daughter in his will (1748), and James Polk appoints his wife, Betty, as executrix in his will (1771).[91] But it should also be noted that when Betty Polk wrote her own will (1779), she made bequests to William and Benjamin, referring to them as her sons, and to Nancy, Leah, and Mary Polk, and Priscilla Whittington as her daughters, all in very equal measure.[92] She also refers to William's son, James, as her grandson. This strongly indicates that Betty was actually the mother of all these children. Furthermore, in his will Benjamin Cottman left his dwelling place to son Joseph, daughter Betty Polk, and Mary Stockwell, wife of Thomas Stockwell. While not explicit, the language surely implies that the latter Mary was Cottman's daughter, and clearly not the wife of James Polk.

It is of course possible that James Polk had a previous wife, before marrying Betty Cottman. Her oldest child, William, was born about 1730 when James was himself aged 30, so an earlier marriage was possible.[93] An intriguing factor in this regard is that an individual named John Polk, otherwise unaccounted for, appears in the Somerset tax lists in a time frame appropriate to have been a son of James from an earlier marriage. The tax, land, and probate records show that this person had a strong connection with the Polks of the Manokin area, but they do not reveal a specific relationship. In the author's opinion it is quite probable, though unproven, that this John Polk was James' eldest son, born about 1727-8. From later records it is known that he departed Somerset for "Carolina" in 1756, which could explain why he is not mentioned in James' will. A more complete discussion of this individual is given in Section 4.3, John Polk of Manokin.

James and Betty Polk also had a son Joshua who was born about 1740. Although he is not mentioned in James' will, James deeded the two tracts Donegal and Moneen to son Joshua "for natural love and affection and five shillings" in 1768,[94] and Betty makes several bequests to him in her will (1780). Joshua died in 1790 leaving a substantial inheritance to his wife Mary (Brown?), but with no mention of any children in his will. Mary died a few years later and a subsequent petition in Sussex County asks for partition of Joshua's lands among his brothers and sisters.[95]

Another correction to the previous family histories is that William, not Benjamin, was James' oldest son. For one thing, he is mentioned first in both James and Betty's wills and received a far more substantial inheritance than Benjamin, to

---

[91] MDW 25:578, SORW, EB1:135.
[92] Neither will mentions daughter Virginia, so she presumably died young.
[93] W. H. Polk says that Virginia was the oldest child, born in 1734, but as noted in subsequent paragraph, William was born c.1730.
[94] WOLR G:400.
[95] Sussex Orphans Court, Case Files for Joshua Polk, 1795, 1805.

include the family dwelling place. Even more to the point, William appears in the tax lists for Manokin Hundred in 1747, six years before Benjamin's first appearance (1753). In the 1760-63 Somerset Court records, William's age is entered as thirty in May 1761, and thirty-two in November 1761. While these are slightly inconsistent, they both indicate that William was born c.1730, not 1744 as stated in *Polk Family and Kinsmen.*

~~~~~~~~

David Polk, William's second son, was active as a surveyor early in life and laid out some of the Somerset county roads. Later he served frequently as a juror, both on the grand and petit juries; so frequently in fact, that he acquired the skills to represent others as an attorney in court and in due course was appointed a judge in Somerset. His son William followed this lead as a profession and ultimately became the first Justice from the Lower Eastern Shore to the Maryland Court of Appeals when it was formed after the Revolution.[96]

David Polk was known as an ardent Whig, even though he was seventy years of age at the start of the Revolution. The following account of his rather fearless temperament is offered by his grandson Josiah F. Polk:

> *He looked upon the church tax as a thing too nefarious to be endured, and suffered himself, before the Revolution, to be thrown into prison, rather than pay it. .....*
> *Their sons paid the tax, but those of David Polk durst not let him know what they had done, certain that if they did he would never forgive them and would disinherit all who had any hand in it. It was with difficulty that he could be induced to leave the prison. This was a short time before the Revolution and had a great effect in Somerset. He commanded a Militia Company during the Revolution. Judge Done told me, as a fact of his own knowledge, that David Polk by some means discovered a band of Tories—40 or more—secreted in a house in the suburbs of Princess Anne town, whose object was to plunder and burn the town, that he went to them, without the aid of a solitary being, and literally chased them as fast as they could run, over and a considerable distance beyond the bridge near the Presbyterian Meeting House.*

~~~~~~~~

James' and David's sister, Jane Strawbridge, was made of similar cloth. Like her brothers, she appeared frequently as a litigant in the Somerset Court in her later years. This she did when it suited her litigious purposes, but had little use for the

---

[96] Judge William Polk's portrait was painted by Charles Willson Peale, as mentioned in Peale's autobiography (Peale, Vol. 5, p. 189).

court when it did not. Although her husband James Strawbridge's will is on file, in which he leaves his entire estate to Jane, there are no subsequent probate records to be found, even though he was certainly well-off and the estate presumably sizable. Neither do any probate records appear for Jane herself, or her son William. These doubtlessly deliberate omissions later gave rise to a long and complicated case disposing of the Strawbridge property when Jane's granddaughter and sole legatee died intestate at a young age.

The following account of Jane was left to us by Josiah F. Polk:

> *Jane Strawbridge, sister of James and David Polk, was a remarkable woman. She was masculine in her mind and manners. Like her brother David she cherished the strongest abhorrence of the Church Tax and even let her resentment extend to all the ministers of the English Church. She was an uncompromising Whig and even before the Revolution began, poured out the bitterest denunciations of Church and State oppression, whenever she would meet with a respectable Tory. On one occasion, disputing with Parson Bell—he made some personal remark, being an irascible man—which greatly offended her, when, raising a chair in great rage, she aimed a blow at his head, and being a powerful woman, would have beaten out his brains in an instant, had it not been arrested by a third person. She once fell out with her preacher and would go no more to hear him, but, hearing that another parson was to preach on a certain day, she went to church. She had ascended half way up the aisle, when the voice of her old preacher—for he was reading in the pulpit—fell upon her ear. She stopped suddenly, raised her eyes, and fixed them on the preacher, at the same time taking an enormous pinch of snuff. Then clenching her fist and extending it toward him in a threatening manner, exclaimed in a voice that startled the whole congregation, and an emphasis that withered the parson, "Why, is it you?" And turning round marched out with the stateliness of a Queen Bess herself.*

William Polk's other daughter, Elizabeth, was probably the youngest of his children. Although we do not know the date of her birth, a reasonable estimate would be 1710-15, based on the date of her marriage to John Williams which occurred on 10 April 1733. Williams was a shipwright and the son of Thomas and Frances Williams of Annemessex. A good account of the Williams family can be found in *The Boston Family of Maryland*,[97] which may be consulted for further details.

Elizabeth was actually the third wife of John Williams, who was born in 1692,

---

[97] Wise, p. 438-41.

and considerably older than she. They had five known children: Priscilla (b.1734), who married Samuel Curtis; Mary (b.1736), who married her cousin, William Polk (son of James); Capt. John Williams (b.1739); Josiah (b.1742); and Benjamin (b.1747). A note in *Boston Family of Maryland* states that Josiah and Benjamin went to North Carolina, but there is no further explanation for this. Elizabeth mentions them in her will as though they were still in Somerset at the time she wrote it (1775). This may be confusion with the sons of Job Williams of Worcester County who moved to Old Dobbs County, North Carolina. [98]

~~~~~~~~~

The earlier Polk family histories (Josiah F. Polk, Mary Winder Garrett, Mary Polk Branch) had presumed that William, son of Robert and Magdalen's eldest son John, was the William Polk who settled in the Cumberland Valley, or Carlisle, Pennsylvania, area in the 1730s and was progenitor of the southern branch of the family. This belief had its origin in the firm tradition of the North Carolina Polks that William of Carlisle had originally come from Maryland. Since William, son of John, was known to have left Somerset in the 1720s, he was deemed the logical candidate and was accepted as such until his will was found by Earle B. Polk about 1908 [99] and shared with W. H. Polk then finalizing his work on *Polk Family and Kinsmen*. In light of this, the lineage of the southern Polks back to John Polk could no longer be sustained. Up to that point there was never a suggestion that the southern line descended from William Polk of Manokin, or that William had any other sons besides James and David. In fact, Josiah F. Polk, who was a grandson of David Polk, is quite definite that William had only the two sons and two daughters as described above.[100]

The claim that William Polk of Carlisle was a son of William Polk of Somerset was first made in *Polk Family and Kinsmen*. W. H. Polk cites no authority for this, but simply states that "the weight of the evidence indicates that William Polk who married Margaret Taylor, was a son of William Polk Sr., second son of the immigrants."[101] In addition, concerning Charles Polke the Indian Trader of Hancock, Maryland, he states[102] that "judging from the data procured concerning him, (he) was one of the two eldest sons of William Polk Sr., (second son of Robert and Magdalen Polke) .... Another son of William Polk Sr. by the same wife, as the proof adduced indicates, was that William Polk who went from Maryland to Carlisle, where he married Margaret Taylor and moved thence to North Carolina about 1750..." What the "data procured concerning him" or "proof adduced" might be, is not revealed. It is, in fact, nothing more than speculation.

There are a lot of problems with these assertions. There are many citations of

---

[98] Peden; p. 172.
[99] PF&K, p. 33.
[100] Josiah F. Polk notes, Appendix II.
[101] PF&K, p. 34.
[102] PF&K, p. 265.

102

William Polk (son of Robert and Magdalen) and his family in the Somerset records, but not one that hints at the existence of sons named William and Charles. Nor do the prior accounts of the family history make any such claim. Clearly James was the oldest son of William and Anne Knox, since he was born in January 1700(NS),[103] and William and Anne were only recently married at that time—Anne's first husband, William Owens, died in April 1698. James' brother David was born in 1705-6, as known from various depositions he made, and both of these sons appear, as would be expected, as taxables in the household of William Polk in the Manokin Hundred beginning with the tax list of 1723, the first such list extant. The supposed other sons, William and Charles, are not found in these tax lists,[104] nor are they mentioned in William's will (1739) or any other Somerset record the author has located. W. H. Polk suggests that they had been given some portion of their inheritance in advance so that they might seek their fortunes elsewhere, but this is just speculation and not very plausible. There was little need for them to have taken such a course since William had prospered, and was vesting not only his own sons, James and David, but also his young nephews and stepsons, with lands in Manokin and Nanticoke, as we have already seen. He surely would have done no less for other sons. All of his known children and his Owens family stepsons remained in Somerset or Dorchester, and there seems very little reason to suppose that other sons, if there were such, would have headed for a distant and hostile frontier to seek better prospects.

In any case the issue has been definitively resolved using Y chromosome DNA testing. A Polk/Pollock DNA project has been organized and as of this writing has test results from nearly a hundred donors. These are currently accessible on line (http://www.worldfamilies.net/surnames/polk) at the *WorldFamilies Polk/Pollock Project* website. Two major lineage groups will be seen in the Y-Results chart at the website in addition to a number of smaller ones. The two major ones are Haplogroup R1b1b2, Lineage Group 1, and Haplogroup I2b, Lineage Group 1. Several known descendants (including the author) of William Polk who married Margaret Taylor ("William of Carlisle") belong to the former group and a known descendant (P-51, A. S. Polk) of Robert and Magdalen Polk belongs to the latter. Since these are different haplogroups there is no chance that members of the two different groups share a common male-line ancestor for many generations (thousands of years) back. That is, William Polk of Carlisle (and his descendants) and Robert Polke of Somerset (and his descendants) do not have similar Y chromosome DNA and therefore do not have a common male-line Polk ancestor within a genealogically meaningful time frame.

DNA test results also show that Charles Polke, "the Indian Trader," is not genetically connected through male Polk/Pollock ancestry to either Robert Polke of Somerset or to William Polk of Carlisle. Two persons in the Polk/Pollock Y-Results chart, P-73, D Polk, and P-74, H J Polk, are proven descendants of Charles

---

[103] Barnes, *Somerset Parish Records*, p. 196.
[104] See SOTL; also Russo.

Polke's son Edmund, but as the results show, their Y chromosome DNA is quite different from that of the two lineage groups associated with Robert Polke and William Polk.

~~~~~~~~~

Following are the entries for William Polk, his sons, and household in the Manokin Hundred tax lists. Entries for Allen Gray have been included since he was mentioned in William's will and W. H. Polk inferred from this, incorrectly, that William Polk had taken Allen's mother as a second wife and Allen as a stepson.[105]

Prior to 1723	No tax lists survive
1723	William Polk, Abra---, James Polk (list damaged)
1724	William Polk, James Polk, David Polk, 3 Negros (unnamed)
1725	William Polk, James, Polk, David Polk, Negros Mumodah, Oteen, Hannah
1726	No list
1727	William Polk Sen,[106] David Polk, Negros Abner, Oteen, Hannah
	James Polk (separate household; crossed out but counted)
	John Gray Jun., Allen Gray, Negro Lenda (separate household)
1728	List badly damaged, no Polk entries found
1729	William Polk, Reverend John Robertson, 4 Negro taxables
	John Gray Jun., Alan Gray, Negro taxable (separate household)
	List damaged, no James Polk entry
1730	William Polk, David Polk, Negros Owen, Abner, Hanne
	James Polk (hereafter as a separate household)
	Allen Grey in household of Hugh Nelson, Pocomoke Hundred
1731	William Polk, David Polk, Negros Owen, Abner, Haner
	James Polk (separate household)
	Allen Gray in separate household, next to Hugh Nelson in Pocomoke
1732	No list
1733	William Polk, David Polk, Alen Gray,[107] Negros Totan, Abner, Hannah
	James Polk (separate household)
1734	Wm. Poak, Allan Grey, Negros Outten, Obur, Hannah
	James Polk (separate household)

---

[105] PF&K, p. 204.

[106] Possibly to differentiate him from William Pollock who appears in household of John Waller in Monie Hundred in 1727-28. See Chapter 4.

[107] In prior years Allen Gray was in household of his father, John Gray Jun., who continues to appear in the tax lists until his death in 1748. W. H. Polk speculated that William Polk had married the Allen Gray's mother, believing her to be a widow, but this was clearly not the case. William did mention Allan Gray in his will, but that was probably only a token of gratitude and regard for his service to William during 1733-39.

	David Polk (in Wicomico Hundred in this and subsequent years)
1735	Wm. Polk, Allen Gray, 3 Negros
	James Polk (separate household)
	David Polk (separate household)
1736	William Polk, Allen Gray, Negros, Olan, Hannay, Abner
	James Polk, Negro Ogy (separate household)
	David Pollock (separate household)
1737	Manokin part of tax list did not survive
	David Polk, Slave Thamor (separate household)
1738	Wm. Polk, Allen Gray, Negros Outten, Abner, Hanah
	James Polk, Slave Ogg (separate household)
	David Polk, Slave Tamor (separate household)
1739	Wm. Polk, Allen Gray, Negros Oleon, Abner, Hannah, Pleasant
	James Polk, Negro Ogg (separate household)
	David Polk, Negro Tamer (separate household)
1740	James Polk, Negros Peter, Ogy, Pleasant
	David Polk, Negros Otern, Abner, Hannah, Tahmer (separate household)

William died in late 1739, and does not appear in the 1740 tax list or thereafter.

~~~~~~~~

The will of William Polk:

In the name of God, Amen. I William Polk of the County of Somerset and Province of Maryland being sick and weak of body but of perfect mind and memory (Blessed be God) do make ordain and constitute this my Last Will and Testament (revoking all other Wills by me heretofore made) and in manner and form following.

Imp's: First I bequeath my soul into the hands of Almighty God that gave it, my Body to the Earth from whence it was taken, there to be Buried with a Decent-like Burial at the Discretion of my Executor hereinafter named.

Item. I will that all my just debts be justly paid.

Item. I give and bequeath unto my Son David two negroes the one named Oteen and the other named Hannah together with eight Barrels of Pork that is now killed in my house and eight Barrows not under a year old and the advantage and likewise five Sows and Piggs and the bay Mare and Colt and my Gray Horse and Feather Bed and Furniture belonging to it (curtains only excepted) one large Pewter dish one Iron Pot about eight Gallons and one small Iron Kettle and the one half part of the Still now standing on my Plantation together with five Sheep, three Cows one with her yearling the other two with her two year old Steers, one Curb'd Bridle of Wilks make, six and a half yards of Linnen it being the half of a Remnant left in the House at the Decease of my Wife, and Ten Pounds in Paper money and seven Yards of Linnen which was made in the house last Summer, a Waistcoat of Kersey for Oteen all to the proper use and behoof of him the said David Polk his heirs and assigns for ever together with the one half part of my Coopers Tools.

Item, I give and bequeath unto my Daughter Elizabeth Williams one Negro Woman named Amy, three cows with their yearlings, Eight Barrows, Five Sows and Piggs, one Red Rugg, one hundred Acres of Land called or known by the name of Ramoth, situate, lying and being in the County aforesaid together with five barrels of Pork all to the Proper use and behoof of her the said Elizabeth Williams her Heirs and Assigns for ever, with one Iron Pott about eight gallons.

Item, I give and bequeath unto my Daughter Jane Strawbridge ten Shillings Sterling to the only proper use and behoof of her the said Jane her heirs and assigns for ever.

Item, I give and bequeath unto my Grandson William Polk, son of James Polk, one Negro Woman named Pleasant, my Gray Riding Mare Bridle and Saddle, one Gun, the Stock being broke, one Feather Bed with sheets, Blankets and Quilts together with curtains and Vallians belonging to it to the only proper use and behoof of him the said William Polk his Heirs and Assigns for ever.

Item, I give and bequeath unto Allan Gray one little black Mare and one little black Cow and her Calf to the only proper use of him the said Allan Gray his Heirs and Assigns for ever.

Item, I give and bequeath the Rest and Residue of my Estate both Real and personal unto my Son James Polk whom I appoint Executor of this my Last Will and Testament for the same performed. In witness whereof I have hereunto put my hand and Seal the twenty third Day of January Anno Dom 1739/40.

Signed sealed published and declared as my Last Will and Testament in presence of

Abraham Heath   his
Matthew Heath   William P Polk   ¤
Chas King   mark   seal

February the 24th 1739/40 Came Abraham Heath, Matthew Heath and Charles King subscribing witnesses to the will——

3.5 Ephraim Polk (c.1675-1718)

Born: Ireland, possibly at Clonmel, County Tipperary
Occupation: planter
Probate: died intestate; admin bond issued 19 March 1718(NS), Somerset
  County; inventory appraised at £191/15/0, 30 July 1719
Spouse: Elizabeth Williams (1681-1735+), daughter of Charles and Mary
  Williams
Children:
(1) Magdalene (c.1702-1770), m. 1. Samuel Owens, m. 2. Emmanuel Manlove
(2) Charles (1704-1784), m. (1736) Patience Manlove
(3) Elizabeth (c.1706-)
(4) Priscilla (c.1708-)
(5) Ann (c.1710-)
(6) Mary (c.1712-) m. John Waller(?)
(7) Joseph (c.1715-1812), m. Sarah Coverdale
(8) Ephraim (1718-1791), m. Mary Manlove
Property: Clonmell (100A, 1702); Long Delay (274A, 1707); Golden Quarter
  (150A, 1710); Polks Chance (Dorchester, 200A, 1715); Locust Hummock
  (125A, 1716)

****

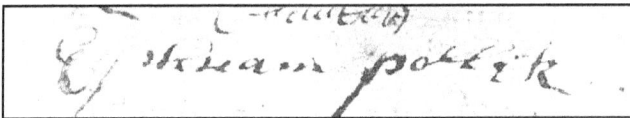

**Signature of Ephraim Polk on assignment of warrant rights
to James Polk, 14 May 1716**

****

EPHRAIM was described by his descendant W. H. Polk as an "enterprising man"
and the records bear this out. He died rather young, but provided well for himself
and his children in his forty-plus years.

He was no doubt born in Ireland and made the harrowing transatlantic crossing as
a young lad not quite in his teens, to be immediately plunged into the struggle
which the family faced in its first years in Somerset. There is no special trade or
profession recorded for Ephraim other than planter, which all landowners were by
default, but on that he concentrated his energies. By necessity, he must have
learned well and first-hand the skills needed to clear and develop land from its
virgin state into a productive plantation. In time he became active in land
acquisition and development, at first in Damned Quarter and afterwards farther
north along the Nanticoke, to which area he and brother James were the first of

the family to venture.

Until his early twenties Ephraim probably worked on his father's lands, for his name does not appear in any land records prior to 1700. However, he must have done rather well in this as he was in a position to lend £25 sterling to William Carlisle sometime before July of 1699 as specified in a later claim against Carlisle's estate.[108] This was a substantial sum of money, certainly enough to have purchased a respectably sized plantation at the time. The fact that Ephraim had disposable funds of this magnitude and was willing to lend them out is a strong indication that the family was on solid financial footing by this time. It is also significant that this action was taken by Ephraim, and not his father, who would have had much to say about transactions involving the family's monetary assets. This is a clear sign that Robert was successfully establishing his sons as independent and responsible citizens in their own right, something no doubt on his mind as he drew up his will.

It was in May of 1700, a year after Robert wrote his will, that Ephraim and younger brother Robert Jun. acquired their own properties in the Damned Quarter area. Both were assigned rights from a warrant issued to William Whittington for 623 acres by the Provincial Land Office.[109] In September, Ephraim surveyed Clonmell, a 100-acre tract in Damned Quarter, obtaining the formal patent in April 1702. The description indicates that this was situated on the east side of the path from Monie to Damned Quarter. It was also configured and oriented very similarly to Polkes Folly, and although the latter is not specifically mentioned in the tract description, it is safe to assume they were nearly contiguous.[110] Robert Jun. obtained his 200 acre tract, Ballyhack, in the Pigeon House area at the same time.

The choice of the names Clonmell and Ballyhack is intriguing. Tract names were sometimes selected to honor an immigrant's place of origin, such as "Ballendrett" used by John Polke and "Ballyshannon" used by William Owens. Clonmell is a town in County Tipperary Ireland on the River Suir, quite removed from Donegal, and a town named Ballyhack is found near Waterford, perhaps thirty miles downriver from Clonmell. This area was notable as the home to a large dissenter population including a contingent of Huguenot refugees fleeing from persecution on the continent, and there was a natural association between them and the

---

[108] SOJR 1701-02:115.

[109] Whittington was probably not a close associate of the Polks, but was Deputy Surveyor for Somerset and took out warrants in sizable quantities for parceling out to interested persons—one of the perquisites of this office.

[110] Determining the exact location of colonial land tracts is not a simple matter. The descriptions in the survey certificates are not deterministic, typically referring to a marked tree along a certain creek as the point of beginning, with few, if any references to adjacent properties or landmarks. Tracts were surveyed on a random, one at a time basis and no general plat maps were ever drawn up in colonial times to control and organize the process.

Presbyterians of Ulster.[111] These tract names seems to hint at an episode in the family's past associated with this area, but there is nothing else in the records to explain this connection.

It is not clear why Ephraim and Robert selected these lands, for even in those times they were described as swamps.[112] Possibly this was urged by their father as he drew up his will, intent on providing for the future of each of his sons and also bringing the remaining lands around Pigeon House Creek under the family's control. As it turned out, neither Ephraim nor Robert Jun. appears to have actually settled on these properties, but the transaction seemed to have been something of an object lesson for Ephraim that he turned to his advantage several years later. On 15 March 1705(NS) he applied directly to the Land Office for a warrant in his own name, and was issued one for 871 acres. The use of this warrant marks the emergence of Ephraim as family leader in the Damned Quarter area following Robert's death. It was used to survey the following properties for the family:

Long Delay, 274 acres, Ephraim Polk, 26 March 1705
Charles Adventure, 140 acres, Charles Williams, 28 March 1705
Edwards Lott, 220 acres, Ann Roberts, 29 March 1705
Marvells Chance, 27 acres, John Marvell, 1 April 1705
James Meadow (Poalkes Meadow), 200 acres, James Polk, 1 June 1705

The assignment of rights to John Marvell is intriguing since all the other assignees are known members of the family. Moreover, Marvels Chance adjoins the tract Locust Hummock, which was patented by John Polkey in 1682, on its north end. Polkey had died not long before, in 1703, inexplicably bequeathing his property to a William Kent, about whom little is known. Kent sold it back to Ephraim Polk in 1716 and the Somerset Rent Rolls list the property as being in the care of Francis Graydon (Craden) on behalf of the relict and orphans of Polkey. All of this hints strongly at both a family connection with Marvell and a close relationship between John Polkey and the family of Robert Polke, but the exact connections remain unclear. It seems reasonable to suppose that Marvell was married to a daughter of John Polkey.

The surveys of Ballyhack, Clonmell, and Poalkes Meadow more or less completed the partitioning of land around Pigeon House Creek, so Ephraim had to look elsewhere to find additional lands. There were opportunities not far away at the end of the Damned Quarter peninsula, adjacent to the head of Devil (Deal) Island. He surveyed the tract Long Delay (274 acres) here in 1705, and afterward purchased Golden Quarter (150 acres) from Willoughby Allerton (1710). It may be presumed that this area became the permanent "dwelling place," where his young family grew up, where ties with the Laws family of Devil Island were formed, and where Ephraim remained until his rather early death in 1718.

---

[111] The Presbytery of the Laggan sent two ministers, William Cox and William Liston, to Clonmel and Waterford in 1673. See Reid, Vol. 2, p. 336; see also Butler, pp. 81-101, and Lee.

[112] See e.g. 1739 deed of sale for Clonmell, "a tract of swamp;" SOLR MF:109.

In 1709 Ephraim and his brother James jointly obtained another warrant for 600 acres, but this time in a wholly new direction—Dorchester. James used his 300 acre share almost immediately to survey a tract to which he gave the name Hazard, located near an Indian village at the lower end of the Marshyhope River (northwest branch of the Nanticoke). For whatever reason this remained unpatented, but it is the first recorded step that the family took towards the Nanticoke area. Ephraim held on to his 300 acre share of the warrant until 1716, when he assigned the rights to James, but obtained a special warrant in the interim for the survey of Polks Chance (200 acres) on the west side of Fishing Bay.[113] This, too, was never patented.

~~~~~~~

Ephraim married Elizabeth Williams (b. 1681), the daughter of Charles Williams, owner of Roberts Lott and Charles Adventure in Damned Quarter. She was the older sister of Anne Williams, who married Ephraim's brother James. The marriage is not recorded in Liber IKL[114] or other existing Somerset documents, but probably took place around 1700 when Ephraim began acquiring land and Elizabeth was eighteen or nineteen years old. The will of Charles Williams in 1734 mentions his daughter as Elizabeth Laws, for she was by then married to her second husband, John Laws. Elizabeth was multiply related to the Polks—in addition to sister Anne's marriage to James, her father Charles married Ephraim's older sister Margaret as his second wife.

Ephraim and Elizabeth had eight children: Magdalen, Charles, Elizabeth, Priscilla, Ann, Mary, Joseph, and Ephraim. This is recorded in Somerset court on 16 March 1725(NS) when a bond of £254/16 is placed on John Laws, John Jones, and William Turpin on behalf of the orphans. From this we know that John Polk of Little Creek (now located in Sussex County, [115] Delaware) was not a son of Ephraim, as has been claimed in previous histories.[116] The birth years for Ephraim's children probably ranged from about 1702 for Magdalen, the oldest, to 1717 for Ephraim Jun., the youngest. The birth date for Charles, the second child, is stated as 16 March 1704(NS), by both Mary Winder Garrett and W. H. Polk, although they give no source; possibly this came from records of the Manlove family.[117] (Charles married Patience Manlove, and Magdalen married Manuel Manlove.)

~~~~~~~

---

[113] A special warrant was needed for patenting land that had been previously claimed but abandoned and escheated.

[114] A large number of Somerset marriages and births are recorded in this volume, interspersed among the land records.

[115] SOJR 1723-25:272; 16 March 1725(NS).

[116] PF&K, pp. 450, 491; Garrett, AHM, Vol. 4, p. 127. From other records it is now clear that John Polk of Little Creek was actually the son of Robert and Magdalen's oldest son John. This was discussed in Section 3.2 above.

[117] See Bendler, pp. 13-16, for more detail on the Polk-Manlove family relationship.

After Ephraim's death Elizabeth married John Laws, sometime between November 1720, when she is listed on the court docket as Elizabeth Polk,[118] and April 1724, when she filed the probate account as "Elizabeth Laws."[119] Laws lived on Devil Island, only a short distance from Ephraim's plantation at Long Delay and Golden Quarter, but separated by a water passage known as Law's Thoroughfare. Whether the family moved to the house of their new stepfather or remained at their own father's dwelling place is not known, but in either case they joined the family exodus to the Nanticoke when the time came. Probably Magdalen, the eldest, went first as the wife of Samuel Owens who settled there in 1721. Charles, the first son, remained in Damned Quarter through 1725 listed as a taxable in the household of John Laws, but in 1727 he is listed as a head of household in the Nanticoke Hundred next to Samuel Owens. This was the nucleus for a group of closely allied families—Owens, Knox, Manlove, Laws, Nutter, and Polk—that settled and populated the area known as John's Neck on the eastern side of the Nanticoke northeast of Bridgeville, Delaware. All of this may be seen as the natural outcome of the family bonds initially forged with the marriages of John Polk to Jean Knox, and William Polk to Anne (Knox) Owens. As the family relocated to the Nanticoke, these ties were soon extended to the Laws family, who followed the Polks, the Manloves who came there independently from Annemessex, and the Nutters who had been in the area from its first settlement.

~~~~~~~~~~

The deposition of Ephraim Polk (II) recorded in the Proceedings of the Council of Maryland, 1753-1761, was already quoted in part. The full text tells us more about his early years:

> *The Deposition of Ephraim Polke of the County afsd Yeoman aged Forty One Years or thereabouts taken at Lewis in the said County this Nineteenth day of May in the year of our Lord One Thousand Seven Hundred and Fifty Nine. This deponent being solemnly sworn on the Holy Evangelists did depose & say that he was born in the County of Somerset in the Province of Maryland at the Lower end thereof: but that when he was about Eight years of age, his Brother Charles Polke (who had the care of him) became a Settler at the upper end of the said County of Somerset, now called Worcester County; and the Deponent further saith that the Place his aforesaid Brother settled on at his Removal as aforesaid[120] (being now about Thirty two years Past) was Reputed to be on the Borders between Somerset County as it was then called and the County of Sussex aforesaid but then more Generally called by the People of the Province of Maryland Whorekill County, The Deponent further saith that he lived with his aforesaid Brother Charles at his*

---

[118] SOJR 1719-22:81
[119] MDA 5: 426.
[120] The tract Charles Purchase surveyed for Charles Polke on 21 October 1721.

Settlement on the aforesaid Reputed Borders, until he was upwards
of Twenty Years of age; he then married and went to Settle on an
Improvement made by a certain George Bishop under a warrant of
Survey from the Land Office of the Government of Maryland the
Certificate of which Warrant had Some time before been Assigned
over to the Deponent, by the said George Bishop who had Had (by
Virtue of the said Warrant) a Survey made for him the said George:
the which Improvement is Scituate on the North Side of a Branch
called by the Name of Maple Marsh Branch, and lyeth
Northeastward from the Plantation of his Brother Charles Polk
about two miles, the Deponent further saith that in about two or
three Years after that he had went to live on the Improvement
aforesaid he sold his Right therein to a certain Richard Coverdale
Jun, and then came to settle in the Forest Part of Ceedar Creek
Hundred in Sussex County Afsd and in which Hundred he has ever
since Dwelt, the Deponent Likewise saith, that on the said Maple
Marsh Branch on the Same Northern or rather Northwestern Part
of it a Certain Edward Cary now dec'd had made an Improvement
under a Pennsylvania Right (as it was then Commonly called)
which Lay within about a Mile of the Improvement so as aforesaid
assigned over to him the Deponent by George Bishop aforesaid and
Near upon three Miles Northeastward of the Plantation and
Settlement of his aforesaid Brother Charles Polke: He further saith
that the Improvement of the aforesaid Edward Carey is now quietly
held and possessed by a certain Joseph Polke,[121] *Cousin to this*
Deponent, and under the Right of the Government of the Counties
of Delaware and was so held by the aforesaid Edward Carey in his
life time Peaceably and without any Maryland Claim being made
thereto to the best of the Deponents belief and knowledge, he
having never heard of any such claim, The Deponent further Saith
that the Plantation whereon John Wiley (now a Prisoner at Lewis)
lately dwelt, was formerly his Property and that it is scituated in a
Part of Ceedar Creek Hundred in Sussex aforesaid commonly
called the Upper Part of the Great Neck: the which Property he
held under a Warrant from the Land Office of the Honourable the
Proprietarys of the Province of Pennsylvania and Counties of
Delaware; nor doth he know, nor did he ever hear either before or
at the Time of the Survey made for him of any Claim having been
made to that Part of the Great Neck aforesaid by the Government of
Maryland; but that the same hath been constantly reputed and
esteemed to be within the Limits and boundaries of Ceedar Creek
Hundred aforesaid, and further this Deponent saith not.
Jurat Coram Me   *Ephraim Polke*

---

[121] SXLR Vol. 7(G): 307; conveyance to Joseph "Pollock" in 1751. Presumably this is
Ephraim's uncle, Joseph, son of Robert and Magdalen.

This requires a word of explanation. Ephraim's deposition was taken during an extensive and complicated jurisdictional dispute arising from the murder of an under-sheriff, William Outten of Worcester County, by John Wiley of Cedar Creek. Wiley was taken into custody by Delaware authorities, but the crime occurred at a location that Maryland believed to be within its limits. This raised the practical question of who would have the privilege of hanging Wiley, but more important to the authorities was the implied confirmation of the inter-provincial boundary. There are a great many pages of testimony recorded in the proceedings concerning this episode which provide a revealing glimpse into the uncertainty regularly faced by the inhabitants of the area about which province they owed allegiance to. No doubt they would have preferred to belong to neither when it came to paying taxes and could be expected to exploit the situation as long as they could to avoid doing so.

These problems continued to be a source of confusion even after Mason and Dixon laid out the North-South division lines between Delaware and Maryland in 1764. It was well into the next decade before Delaware gained effective administrative control of western Sussex County. The complex jurisdictional history of this region is clearly illustrated in Figure 13 which shows the areas that were administered at different times by different counties. The contested zone in the central area is the region where both Maryland and Delaware claimed jurisdiction, i.e. issued survey certificates, prior to the border settlement of 1760. Before that almost two-thirds of Sussex County was fully under control of Maryland authorities. The extent of this region has only recently become apparent due to the work of John Lyon and Mike Hitch in mapping the colonial era land tracts of this area, as mentioned in the Acknowledgements.

Somerset tax list entries for Ephraim's children and in-laws:

Monie –

1723	John Laws, Charles Polk; Negros Ceasar, Duna, Prince
1724	John Laws, Charles Polke; Negros Prince, Ceasar, Duner
1725	John Laws, Charles Polk; Negros Duner, Prince, Ceasar
1726	No list
1727	John Laws; Negros Duna, Princess, Cesar
1728	John Laws; Prince, Cesar, Duney
1729	No list
1730	John Laws, William Wallace; Negros Prince, Ceasar, Dunah
1731	John Laws, John Williams, William Wallace; Negros Prince, Duen, Secar
1732	No list
1733	John Laws, Sam'l Rose; Negros Prince, Lunea, Ceasar
1734	John Laws; Negros Prince, Cesar, Dooniar
1735	John Laws; Negros Prince, Juner, Caesar
1736	John Laws; Negros Prince, Ceasar
1737	John Laws; Negros Prince, Cesar

1738	John Laws; Negros Prince, Ceesar
1739	John Laws; Negros Caesar, Prince
1740	John Laws, John Laws, Jun; Negros Prince, Ceasar
1741	No list
1742	No list
1743	John Laws, John Laws, Jun; Negros Prince, Ceasar
1744	John Laws, Sen., John Laws, Jun; Negros Prince, Cesar

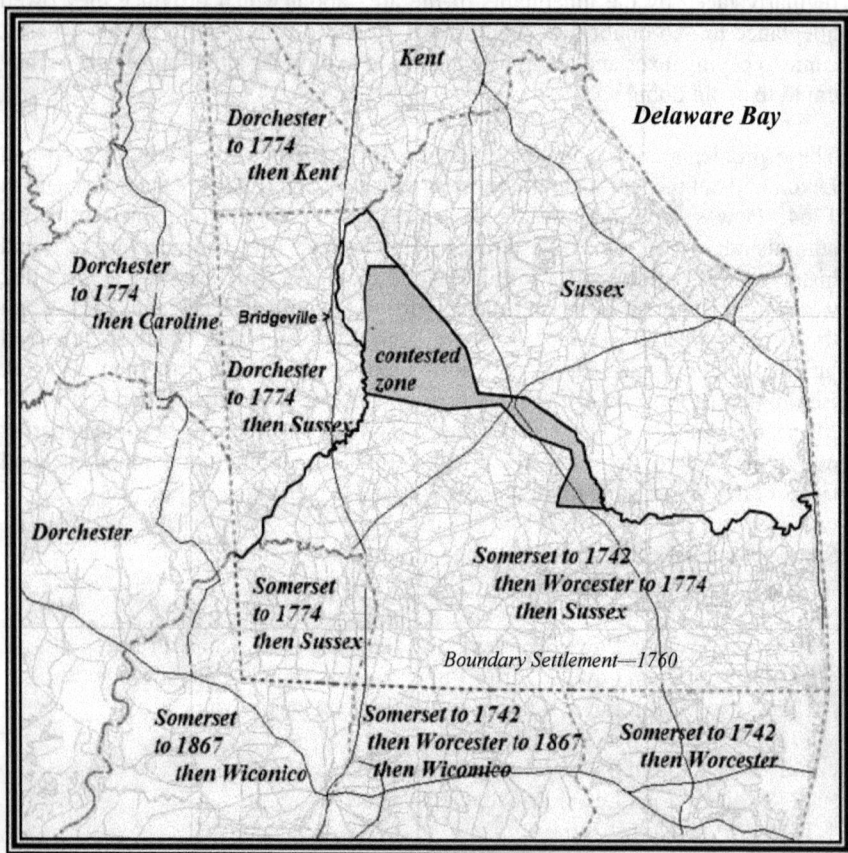

Figure 13. Historical jurisdictions of Sussex County region. (Map courtesy John C. Lyon.)

Nanticoke –

1723	Samuel Owens, Robert Owens
1724	Samuel Owens, Robert Owens
1725	Samuel Owens, Robert Owens
1726	No list
1727	Charles Polk
	Samuel Owens, Robert Owens; Negros Quako, Nell
1728	List badly damaged
1729	Robert Owens; Negro Quaco
	Samuel Owens; Negro Cate
1730	Charles Polk
	Robert Owens; Negro Cate
	Manuel Manlove; Negros Quako, Nell
1731	Charles Polk
	Manuel Manlove; Negro Ned
	Robert Owens; Negro Tom
1732	No list
1733	Charles Polk
	Manuel Manlove; Negro Quoco
	Robert Owens; Negro Cate
1734	Charles Polk
	Manuel Manlove
	Robert Owens, John Nocks (Knox); Negro Cate
1735	Charles Polk, Ephraim Polk
	Manuel Manlove; Negro Quaco
	Robert Owens; Negro Cate
1736	Charles Polk, Ephraim Polk
	Manuel Manlove; Negro Quaco
	Robert Owens; Negro Cate
1737	Charles Polk, Ephraim Polk, William Coapes
	Manuel Manlove; Negro Quaco
	Robert Owens; Negro Cattey
1738	Charles Polke, Ephraim Polke
	Manuel Manlove; Negro Quaco
	Robert Owens, John Knox; Negro Kate
1739	Charles Polk, Ephraim Polk
	Emmanuel Manlove; Negro Quaco
	Robert Owens; Negro Atte
1734	Charles Polk
	Ephraim Polk
	Manuel Manlove; Negro Quako
	Robert Owens; Negro Katt
1741	No list
1742—	Upper Nanticoke taken into Worcester County; no tax lists

~~~~~~~~

In time, the move to Nanticoke proved a wise one for Ephraim's children, for they prospered and had many descendants. Samuel Owens died in 1730-31, leaving Magdalen with three children. She afterwards married Manuel (Emanuel) Manlove, a neighbor from nearby Sussex. Magdalen and Manuel had seven known children before he died in 1743. She survived him by almost three decades and died in 1770. Both left wills probated in Sussex County. Charles Polk married Manuel's sister, Patience Manlove, in 1736 and they had at least six children. Among Charles' descendants were two Governors of Delaware, Charles Polk and John Hall, and numerous other descendants who moved and settled in the Ohio Valley after the Revolution.

Joseph, Ephraim's second son, also moved to the Nanticoke, probably as a youth, before or at the same time (1727) that his younger brother Ephraim (II) accompanied Charles to the area. However, Joseph went farther to the northeast settling in the Cedar Creek and Slaughter Neck Hundred, which was always regarded as part of Delaware even before the Calvert-Penn settlement. He never appears in Maryland records, but is found in Delaware tax lists for Cedar Creek Hundred and had many descendants. See Figure 14 for lands acquired by Ephraim's children at the head of the Nanticoke.

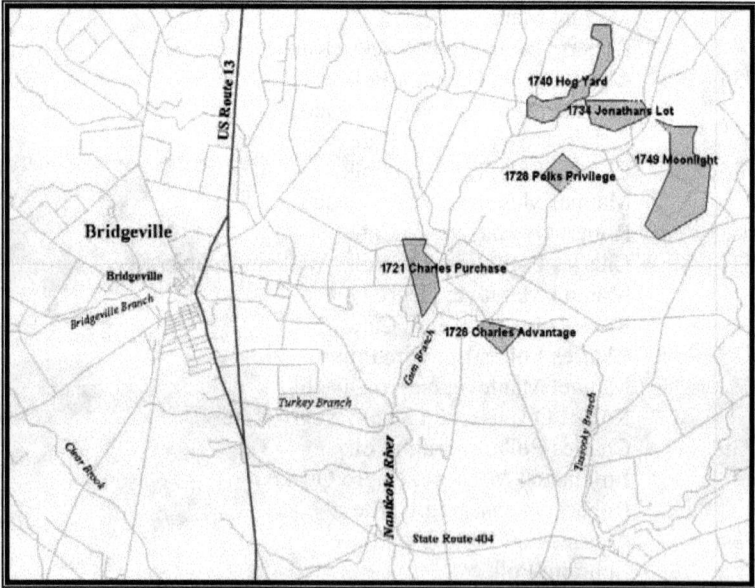

Figure 14. Land tracts of Ephraim Polk's children at Head of Nanticoke.

One of Ephraim and Elizabeth's daughters, Mary, did not leave the Damned Quarter area at the same time as the others, but married John Waller in 1734 as recorded in the Somerset Parish Records[122] and most likely lived on his tract Marvels Choice. The connection with the Waller family was a close one and continued beyond Damned Quarter to the Nanticoke area where other members of the Waller family are found. What became of Ephraim's other daughters, Elizabeth, Priscilla, and Ann is not known at this time. It is reasonable to suppose that they, too, moved from Damned Quarter to the Nanticoke, but this remains an open question. It is always difficult to trace female lines in the colonial records. Elizabeth and John Laws remained in Damned Quarter, or on Laws' plantation on Devil Island, for the balance of their lives as far as can be determined, although other members of the Laws' family made the move to Nanticoke. The Laws family is well represented in Sussex County records, and there were intermarriages with the Polks.

W. H. Polk descended from Ephraim II, and much information about Ephraim's line may be found in *Polk Family and Kinsmen.* [123]

~~~~~~~~

Ephraim died intestate. Following is the inventory made at the time of his death:

An Inventory of the goods and chattels of Ephraim Polk late of Somerset County dec'd taken by us the Subscribers this 30th day of July Anno Dom 1719 and appraised in current money of Maryland -

	£ S D
To a parcel of cash in all weight	*030.00.00*
To two negro men and one Mollatto Girl at	*073.00.00*
To four Feather Beds and furniture all at	*015.00.00*
To a parcel of Books all at	*001.04.06*
To forty five pounds of Pewter and 1 Brass Kettle	*003.12.00*
To twenty four head of Cattle young and old at	*027.10.00*
To one old Horse and one young Ditto at	*007.10.00*
To eight head of Sheep at	*002.08.00*
To twenty head of Hoggs young and old at	*005.00.00*
To one Hand mill and frame and 1 Grindstome	*001.17.00*
To 150 lbs of Pot iron @3d pr lb	*001.17.06*
To 65 lbs of old iron and 37 lbs of steel at	*000.15.07*
To 1 Smiths Anvill and Vice, 2 hammers and tongs	*004.01.00*
To 45 lbs of new nails at 4d pr lb	*000.15.00*
To a parcel of Carpenters and Turners Tools at	*003.04.08*
To one Cam and Geer at	*002.02.00*
To 2 old Gunns and one set of Wedges all at	*001.02.06*
To one pair of Fire tongs and 6 old hoes all at	*000.06.00*

---

[122] Barnes, *Somerset Parish Records*, p. 196.
[123] PF&K, p. 510.

To 1 pair of small Stilliards and 1 Flash Fork	000.06.06
To three hides of Tanned Leather at	001.00.00
To 1 Hackle one Boxiron and Heaters at	000.06.00
To 6 small Chests 1 Table 1 Box Gold Chains	002.03.00
To a parcel of Goods and Table Linnen at	002.05.00
To a set of Harrow teeth and 2 Frying Pans	000.10.00
To 2 Linnen Wheels and 2 Woolen Ditto and Cards	002.07.00
To a small Looking glass and 4 Sifters at	000.05.09
To 6 Cyder Casks and other Lumber at	001.06.00
	£191.15.00

Approved pr us, next of Kin   *John Jones*
James Polek, Joseph Polek   *John Laws*

Memorandum That this day viz the first day of March 1719 Came before me one Eliza Polke Ad'x of Ephraim Polke deceased and made oath upon the Holy Evangelists that the within Inventory was a just and true and perfect Inventory of the deceaseds whole Estate that by any means or ways whatever hath come to her hands or knowledge and that she doth not believe or suspect that there is any more other part thereof that is unappraised or wilfully concealed & in case she shall hereafter know thereof she will Exhibit in Additional Inventory of what shall or may come to her hands or possession.
Exhibited the day above written   *Sam Hopkins Dept Comnr*

The value of Ephraim's goods and chattels was thus appraised considerably higher than that of either his father or older brother John. The most significant factor making the difference is the value of the three Negro slaves possessed by Ephraim. In addition to this moveable property, Ephraim also left nearly one thousand acres of land, probably worth between one and two hundred pounds sterling at the time.

3.6 James Polk (c.1677-1727)

Born: in Ireland, most likely at Monyn, Ballendrait, Donegal
Occupation: shipwright, carpenter
Probate: will written 8 Nov 1726, probated 11 May 1727, Somerset County; inventory appraised at £446/9/6 on 23 May 1727
Spouse: Anne Williams (1683-1735+), daughter of Charles and Mary Williams
Children:
(1) David (1704-1773), m. Elizabeth Turpin
(2) Mary (c.1706-), m. John Pollitt(?)
(3) Henry (1708-1757)
(4) John (1709-1779), m. Mary (N)
(5) Sarah (c.1711-)
(6) Margaret (c.1712-)
(7) Elizabeth (c.1715-)
(8) James (c.1718-1772), m. Sarah Henderson
(9) Magdalen (c.1720—)
(10) Jane (c.1722-)
(11) Anne (c.1724-)
(12) Unnamed (Roger Tasker Polk?) (c.1727-1777)
Property: James Meadow (200A, 1707); Hazard (300A, 1709, Dorchester, unpatented); Lott (200A, 1715); Polks Lott (125A, 1716; Nanticoke, unpatented); Contention (100A, 1716); Salem (800A, 1721); Dublin (100A, 1722); Green Pasture (200A, 1728); White Oak Swamp (100A, 1730)

****

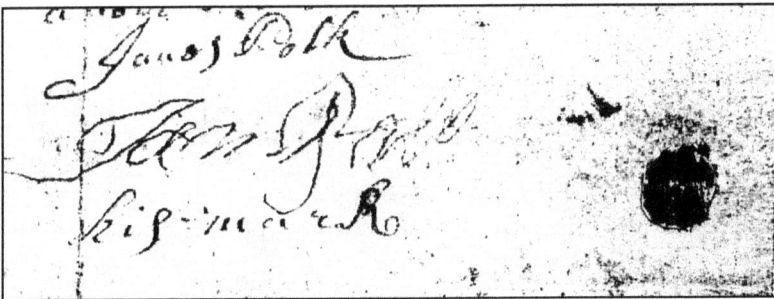

James Polk's signature (middle line) and seal on his will
8 November 1726

****

JAMES was the most successful of Robert and Magdalen's children, both in terms of wealth and number of descendants. At his death he possessed nearly three square miles of real property in both Somerset and Dorchester, and the inventory of his goods and chattels, appraised at £446/9/6, was the largest for any of Robert's children. Eleven children are mentioned in his will.

His name was almost always spelled in the records as "Polk" but curiously his sons appeared to prefer the spelling "Pollock", particularly David and Henry.

~~~~~~~

James' success came by hard work. His occupation, as mentioned in his will and elsewhere, was that of ships carpenter or shipwright, and it was no doubt this trade which led in time to his gradual accumulation of wealth. Just how he learned this trade is not known, but it was certainly built on a foundation of basic skills. Earlier in life he was described more modestly as a "sawyer." In a deposition made for a land commission in 1720,[124] he mentions that he had worked mauling logs for his brother-in-law Francis Roberts some years earlier, which would have been before 1703 since Roberts died that year. He also described himself as a sawyer in a 1703 court case against the estate of William Carlisle. One can imagine what a sawyer's life entailed on a colonial frontier. A glimpse of this comes to us from a suit James brought in 1716 against John Navarr, an innholder of Annapolis, for non-payment of 4,920 pounds of tobacco, the balance due from an original purchase of 6,140 feet of "inch planck" at a pound of tobacco per foot of planking. Probably by this time James was hiring others to produce the lumber so he could concentrate on more lucrative shipbuilding activities. "Inch planck" was a basic commodity produced the hard way in those times—by sawing tree stems lengthwise into one-inch thick boards using a ripsaw. Usually this was done by a two man team, one working above and the other below a tree stem supported horizontally above a sawing pit.[125]

~~~~~~~

James turned to land acquisition somewhat later than his brothers Ephraim and Robert, perhaps because he was fully occupied before then with the demands of his principal trade. His first patented tract was James Meadow, later called Polks Meadow, surveyed in 1705, using warrant rights of 200 acres assigned to him by Ephraim. This tract was located between Pigeon House and Damned Quarter and took up most of the remaining unclaimed land in that area. He probably lived at the western end on this tract where it bordered on Damned Quarter or Williamsons Creek. It was left to his eldest son David as the first item in his will.

James' second venture, four years later, was in Dorchester near the mouth of the northwest fork of the Nanticoke now known as Marshyhope. This was actually situated on or adjacent to lands of the principal Nanticoke Indian settlement on the west side of the Marshyhope, known and frequently documented as the

---

[124] SOLC 1717-21: 123
[125] Sloane, p.70-71.

Chicone Reservation.[126] The description of the tract surveyed there for James, called Hazard, states that it was at the northeast corner of "Indian fields that was formerly called Rocason Towne." This tract was never patented and probably never cultivated. Possibly James wanted it for the value of its timber—it is referred to in his will as "land lying on or near the black walnut landing at the Norwest Fork." No further record has been found which tells its later history. It is not listed in the Proprietor's Debt Books for Dorchester, which begin in 1734, as a tract from which annual ground rent was collected or expected.

In the period 1715-16 James took out three additional patents for what appears to have mostly been marshlands: Contention, White Oak Swamp, and Lott, all in Monie. Green Pasture, near Locust Hummock in Damned Quarter, was a similar acquisition in 1722. Here again, we might surmise that he acquired these lands principally to secure the rights for whatever timber they contained and supply the basic commodity needed for his shipbuilding business.

~~~~~~

In 1708 James had an encounter with the Somerset authorities, recorded as follows:[127]

> *Her Majesty vs James Polk~ per recog ~ For words spoken by the said James of the Burgesses which he at that time could not prove his other living out of the county. Wherefore considered by the court here that the said James be bound for good behavior and to give security therefore, at which day came Ephraim Polk and became his security per recog ~ the principal in £10 and his security in five pounds sterling mony due to be levied on his or their goods and chattels lands and tenements for theuse of Somerset County // The condition of wch recog. Is that if the said James Polke be of his good behaviour and good abearance to all her Ma'tys liege people of this province & especially the Burgesses of Somerset County then this recog. To be null and void otherwise to be and remain in full power force and virtue in the law*
> *~ taken in open Court This 16th day of October 1708*

This seems to have been a misunderstanding since he was exonerated in the March Court following:[128]

> *This day James Polk having produced a certificate under the hand of John Keene, one of her Majesty's Justices that Matthew Travers made oath before him that Mr. John Browne of Patuxent told him that sum of Somerset County Burgesses informed the Gov'r what was spoken in March. Ordered the said James Polk be released of his bond.*

---

[126] Rountree, p. 109.
[127] SOJR 1707-11:164.
[128] SOJR 1707-11:172.

The wording of this action is a little opaque and curious in that it suggests that James was living outside the county, but there is nothing further to explain the passage. He was living in Damned Quarter as far as other records show, including the survey and patent of James Meadow in 1705-07, frequent court appearances in 1708-09, and appointment as Constable of Monie in 1710.

~~~~~~~~

James was no stranger to the Somerset Court and probably made more appearances there than any of his siblings. In general, these were not due to transgressions on his part, but simply the result of business and other matters that came his way more frequently than to the others. We already noted the conflict James ran into with his stepbrother-in-law, John Roberts, over a stolen piece of beef. In that case James was involved only by virtue of his being Constable for Monie at the time, but it was not the first encounter between the two found in the court records. James had also become embroiled in the conflict over ownership of Elliotts Choice by chopping down the first bounder of the tract while mauling logs for Francis Roberts. Although a cedar post was erected as a replacement there was a fundamental issue over the correct location of this bounder which was investigated by land commissions formed in 1720 and 1730. One part of the testimony from the 1730 commission has already been quoted. (See section on Anne Polk.) Following is a second excerpt:

> *Henry Ballard aged thirty years or thereabouts being sworn on the Holy Evangelists of Almighty God saith that he was in Company with the Land Commissioners and was on a tract of land called Elliotts Choice belonging to Edward Roberts which was Maj Charles Ballard, Capt John Tunstall, Mr. Ephraim Wilson and Mr. John Caldwell and that they went to a pine stump standing near a marsh side about two hundred and fifty yards South from the house of Edward Roberts where he then lived and there examined James Poalke on his oath and he said he was employed by Francis Roberts to maule some logs and that he went to the aforesaid place where the afsd mentioned stump now is and that he went to falling some logg lumber and sometime after Francis Roberts came to the said James Polke and told him he had fell the bounder of Elliotts Choice and that James Polk asked him whether it was the first bounder of Elliotts Choice and that Roberts said it was and there was Patrick Quatermus and some others as declared near the same relating to the same bounder and that the aforesaid Commissioners allowed that to be the bounder of Elliotts Choice and further the said Deponent saith that he knew of no other bounder of Elliotts Choice and further saith not.   Henry Ballard*

Besides these, James appeared in court in connection with various legal cases. The longest running was a suit he brought against George Hutchins for an unpaid debt of £6/6/6. Although he initially received a favorable decision, James faced a long series of challenges from Hutchins who took the matter to the Provincial Court and dragged the case out for several years.

122

James' most important property acquisition in the Nanticoke area, and a cornerstone of the next generation's prosperity, was the tract Salem, nominally 800 acres, in Johns Neck on the Somerset side. He bought this from Thomas Layfield on August 1721 "for sixty pounds, one half in silver & gold & the other half in beefs porke & tobacco." He added to this the following year with the purchase of the adjacent property, Dublin (100 acres), from Richard Layton for £16 sterling. As already noted, he made these purchases in concert with his brother William's strategy to shift the family from Damned Quarter to the upper Nanticoke. William set up his nephew Charles Polk, son of Ephraim, and his stepsons Robert and Samuel Owens in this same area at exactly the same time. Together, these actions were the crucial first steps in implementing the strategy. In the succeeding decades, the third generation Polks/Pollocks together with the allied families of Owens, Laws, and Manlove took ownership of large pieces of the Northwest Fork and Nanticoke Hundreds of what is now Sussex County, Delaware.

Once again, the details of the exodus from Damned Quarter are revealed by the Somerset tax lists. The following entries for James Polk and his family appear in the lists for Monie Hundred:

Prior to 1723	No tax lists survive
1723	James Polk, David Polk; Negros Roger,[129] Samboe
1724	James Polk, David Polk, Henry Polk; Negros Roger, Samboe
1725	James Polk, David Polk, Henry Polk, John Polk; Negros Roger, Sambo
1726	No list
1727	David Polk, Henry Polk, John Polk; Negros Roger, Sambo, Sib
1728	David Polk, Henry Polk; Negros Sambo, Rodger, Sibb
1729	No list
1730	David Polk; Negros Rodger, Sambo
1731	Widdow Polk; Negros Roger, Sambo
1732	No list
1733	No entry for this family

Much can be gleaned from these few entries. The inclusion of David in 1723 means he was already of age (sixteen) by that year, and the first appearances of Henry and John in 1724 and 1725 tell us that they turned sixteen sometime during the preceding years. The omission of James in the 1727 list is of course due to his death by May of that year, whereas the disappearance of Henry and John between

---

[129] Roger was brought into court by James Polk, August 1709, adjudged to be 12 years of age; SOJR 1707-11:234

1728 and 1730 indicates that they probably departed for the Nanticoke during that period. The departure of David occurred soon after, leaving James' widow (Anne Williams) as the head of household in 1731. She apparently also left Damned Quarter at that point, following her children to Nanticoke, as she no longer appears on the Monie tax list after 1731; but was still alive since she is mentioned in her father's (Charles Williams) administration account in 1735.

Although they did not live there, David, James, and John Polk continued to pay annual land rent on their inherited land in Damned Quarter[130] until they sold it to their cousin Edward Roberts in 1743.

~~~~~~

James bequeathed Salem to sons Henry, John, and James, but only John and James actually settled on it. James' son John first appears in the Nanticoke tax list in 1730; he may have also been in the 1728 and 1729 lists, but these are badly damaged and some entries are obliterated or illegible. The youngest brother, James, is listed in John's household in 1735 and as head of a separate household starting in 1737. (Some care is needed to extract these entries since another John Polk, son of John and Johanna Polk, also resided in Nanticoke, but the two can be distinguished by their position in the tax lists relative to their respective neighbors, which is consistent from year to year.) Following is the full set of entries from Nanticoke Hundred pertaining to them through 1740:

1728	List badly damaged
1729	List difficult to read
1730	John Polk
1731	John Polk
1732	No list
1733	John Polk
1734	John Polke; Negro Atty
1735	John Polk, James Polk; Negro Atto
1736	John Polk, James Polk; Negros Sib, Atte
1737	John Polk; Negros Sib, Att
	James Polk (separate household)
1738	John Polk; Negros Attee; Sib
1739	John Polk; Negros Atte, Sip
	James Polk
1740	John Polk; Negros Atte, Sib
	James Polk

There are no Somerset tax lists for 1741 or 1742. In 1742 Worcester County was split off from Somerset, taking John, James and others in the upper Nanticoke with it, and the tax lists for Worcester from the subsequent years do not survive. Those for the lower Nanticoke area, including Little Creek and Broad Creek,

---

[130] See Proprietary Debt Books for Somerset County.

which remained in Somerset, do survive but do not mention the sons of James Polk since they had become citizens of Worcester.

～～～～～

James' oldest son David, who had inherited the largest share of the Dames Quarter land, did not inherit any of his lands on the upper Nanticoke, but soon decided to follow his brothers to that area. Based on the tax lists, he probably moved in 1731. He eventually acquired very substantial holdings, almost 2,000 acres along Clearbrook Creek, which is on the Dorchester side of the Nanticoke northeast fork rather than on the Somerset side where his father's plantation Salem was located. For this reason, David no longer appeared in the Somerset tax lists after 1731 but can be found in the Debt Books for Dorchester. The Debt Books are somewhat different from the tax lists—they only provide a roster of property owners and the rents due on their lands, rather than an enumeration of taxable individuals.

David's first patents were Addition (200 acres) and Maidens Blush (50 acres) both surveyed in November 1731 and located along Deep Gulley or Deep Valley, which feeds into Clearbrook Creek. At the same time, he petitioned the Provincial Land Office for a special warrant to survey 250 acres of land "adjoining to tract Venture belonging to your Petitioner, partly cultivated".[131] The special warrant was granted and David used it to survey Plymouth/Plimouth in June 1732, incorporating an additional forty acres of vacancy for a total of 290 acres. The mention of Venture is curious since there is no record of his owning or acquiring such a property. This probably refers to the tract of that name first owned by his uncle, Robert Polk Jun., and bequeathed to Robert's son Thomas in 1727. The land was adjacent to Robert Polk's other property, Hazard, which was never patented, but which David Pollock also took over through a special warrant and incorporated into the patent for Davids Hope in 1741.[132] See below section on Robert Polk Jun. for more about this.

～～～～～

Henry Pollock, James' second son, was the only one to take up his father's occupation as a shipwright.[133] This may be the reason he did not settle in Nanticoke like his brothers but moved to an area now in Caroline County, but then in Queen Anne's County, north of Dorchester and west of the upper Nanticoke. This location had more direct access to the Chesapeake, so was better situated for a shipbuilder. He may have made this move directly from Damned Quarter since, unlike his brothers David, John, and James, he no longer appears in the tax lists of Somerset, either in Monie or Nanticoke after 1727. It is also possible that he lived for a time in Dorchester with his brother David, but in any case his next

---

[131] Maryland Land Office Petitions, MSA S26-7, Dorchester #65.
[132] Maryland Land Office Warrants, MSA S23-13, Liber LG#A:285.
[133] The deed for Colne Rectified identifies Henry as a shipwright; Queen Anne's County land records RT#C:218.

appearance in Maryland records is with the purchase of the tract Colne Rectified in Queen Anne's County from Richard Bennett in 1747. This is located at the mouth of Piney Branch on the east side of Tuckahoe Creek off the Choptank River, and not that distant from the upper Nanticoke area where his brothers lived, perhaps twenty miles by straight line. Henry died intestate in 1757, and the probate records mention Nathaniel Knotts as the administrator, rather than his widow as would be the usual practice, so if Henry married his wife must have predeceased him. The only record of any descendants that has come to light is the subsequent entry of a John Pollock as the owner of Colne Rectified in the Debt Books for Queen Anne's County in the 1760s. It seems likely that this was Henry's son. John Pollock died in 1773 and the probate records show Rachel Pollock, presumably his wife, appointed as administrator.[134] No children are mentioned.

~~~~~~~~~

James' sons John and James took up life as planters on the tracts Salem and Dublin that he left to them on the Somerset, later Worcester, side of the Nanticoke. They must have reached an accommodation with older brother Henry about his share of these properties, for he never appears in the records for Worcester. John would have come of age at about the time they moved to this area, while James was still a minor, about twelve years old. We can estimate the latter's year of birth as 1719 since he first appears as a taxable in Nanticoke in 1735. In 1737 James was listed as a head of household, so had moved to a separate residence by that time, but this was probably also on the tract Salem since there are no other records of James patenting or purchasing any new properties. He appears not to have become a landowner in his own right until John conveyed 400 acres of Salem to him in 1761 for the rather nominal price of £30. By this time John had acquired additional lands, all of which were resurveyed in 1753 into a single property called Polks Conclusion containing 1,372 acres.

James died intestate in 1772. His probate account was filed in Worcester[135] and indicates that he had nine children but mentions only two by name, John and Sarah. His wife Sarah was probably the daughter of John and Sarah Henderson of Worcester County.[136]

The properties which James and his sons acquired in the Nanticoke area are shown in Figure 15. As is obvious in the map, they fall into two groups. The northern one, to the east of Bridgeville, is clustered around Salem which James purchased in 1721. This is where his sons John and James (Jun.) settled. The southern group is clustered around the tract Plymouth. All of these tracts were purchased or patented by David Pollock.

---

[134] MDTP 45:204, 46:122, 47:64.
[135] Rather surprising since the Nanticoke area had been ceded to Delaware in the boundary settlement of 1760, so the probate should have been filed in Sussex—an indication of how slowly the new jurisdictions were taking hold.
[136] MDW 23:92; WOLR A:20.

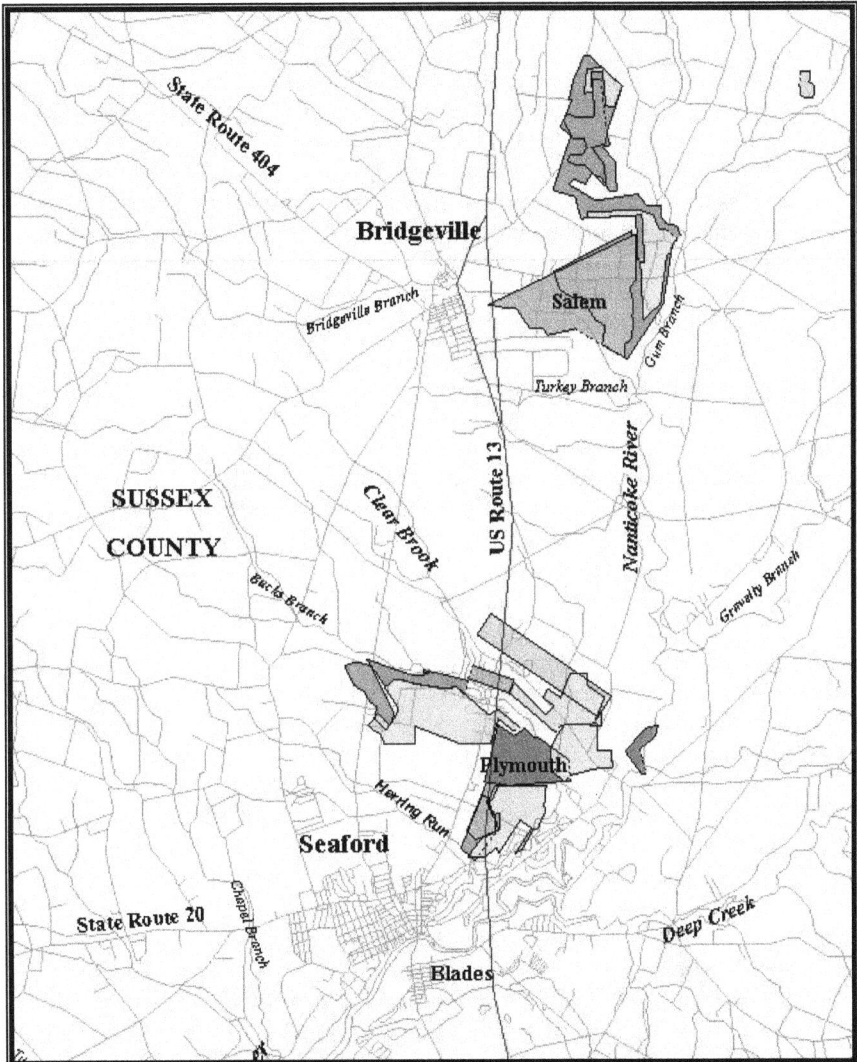

Figure 15. Land tracts of James Polk and his sons in Nanticoke area.

〜〜〜〜〜

John died in 1779 leaving a will filed in Sussex County which mentions one son, John, and four daughters, Jenny, Elinor, Nanny Maxwell, and Mary Williams. They were all listed in the text of the will under the name Polk, including John himself, but the signature is clearly "John Pollok". There are four witnesses: Joshua Polk, John Polk, John Pollock, and James Pollock—a good example of the variability in the spelling of the name even at that late date.

〜〜〜〜〜

In his will of 1727 James Polk mentioned an unborn child. It is not known if this child grew to maturity and can be identified with some individual appearing in later records, but a reasonable possibility is that this child was Roger Tasker Polk, whose place in the family tree is otherwise unknown. Roger Tasker Polk is named as an interim administrator in the probate records of Priscilla, wife of David Pollock Jun. (who died shortly after David), reflecting a close tie with them. If Roger Tasker was indeed the son of James, then David Polk (Sen.) would have been his much older brother and in effect a foster father. This would explain a close, fraternal relationship with David's own son, David Jun. And the very name, Roger Tasker, seems a deliberate choice to highlight a direct connection with Magdalen Polke, especially as middle names were very uncommon in the colonial period. If Roger Tasker Polk was actually James' posthumous child, then he would have been Magdalen's grandson with a birth coinciding almost exactly with her death, so the name may have been chosen to honor her and her father's memory. While this is speculative, no other record has been found which discloses Roger Tasker Polk's parentage. He died intestate in 1777 and his probate, recorded in Sussex County, Delaware, mentions a wife Nancy. It lists no children of his own but includes the children of David Pollock Jun. as legatees.

The last will and testament of James Polk

> *In the name of God Amen. The eight day of November in the year anno dom 1726 I James Polk of Somerset County in the province of Maryland ship carpenter being very sick and weak of body but of perfect mind & memory thanks be given therefore unto God, therefore calling to mind the mortality of the body and knowing that it is appointed once for all men to dye I do make and ordain this my last will and testament, that is to say principally & first of all I recommend my soul (to) the hands of almighty God that gave it & for my body I recommend it to the earth to be buryed in a Christian like & decent manner at the discretion of my Executors nothing doubting but at the resurrection the same to receive again by the mighty power of god, & for such worldly estate as it hath pleased god to bless in this life I give devise & dispose of in the following manner & form. Item I give my son David my now dwelling plantation to him & his heirs for ever. Item I give to my son David the one half of all that land & marsh that I have on pidgeon house. Item I give unto my sons John & James the other half of the aforsd land and marsh on pidgeon house. Likewise I give a warrant for one hundred acres of land which my cousen Charles is to make over both which land and warrant I give and bequith unto my son David one half of both land and warrant and the other half I give my sons John & James to them & to their heirs forever. Likewise I have two hundred acres of marsh lying on Samuel Joneses illand one hundred acres thereof I give and bequith unto my son Henry & the other hundred acres of the aforesd marsh I give and bequith unto my cousan Edward Roberts and to his heirs forever on the proviso my cousan Edward do deliver up the bond that I past to him. Item I give unto my sons Henry, John & James that land I purchast of*

Thomas Layfield & likewise all that land I purchased of Richard Laton both tracts of land lying on the head of Nanticoke in a Neck called Johns Neck to them my sons and their heirs forever to be equally divided among them and likewise I give and bequith unto my sons Henry John and James all that parcel and tract of land lying on or near the black walnut landing at the mouth of the norwest fork to them and to their heirs forever to be equally divided among them. Item I give and bequith unto my daughters Mary & Sarah Margaret & Elizabeth & Magdalen & Jane & Anne tenn pound to each of them. Likewise I give & bequith unto the child my wife is now with tenn pounds if please god it lives, and likewise I will that my well beloved wife may have full privileges of my dwelling plantation and marshes during the time of her widowhood. And likewise I leave my sons David Henry & John to be my Executors in full and I do herby utterly disanul all other wills or testaments and legases by me in any wise before this time named ratifying and alowing and confirming this and no other to be my last will & testament in wittnes whereof I have hereunto set my hand and seal the day and year first above written ~
Signed sealed
and delivered
In the presents of

William Polke   **James Polk ¤**
John Pollet   *his mark*
Mary Pollet

129

3.7 Robert Polk, Jun. (c.1679-1727)

Born: Ireland, possibly Ballyhack, County Wexford
Occupation: planter
Probate: will written 25 February 1726(NS), probated 10 May 1727, Dorchester
County; inventory appraised at £83/18/10, 27 July 1727
Spouse: Grace Gullett (1682/3—?), marriage c.1700
Children:
(1) Thomas (b. 29 Dec 1703, d. 21 May 1781, Colleton County, SC)
(2) Robert (c.1713-)
(3) Daughter (b.<1710)
(4) Daughter, possibly Susan (b.<1710)
(5) Daughter (b.<1710)
(6) Grace (b.>1710)
(7) Mary (b.>1710)
Property: Ballyhack (200A, 1702); Long Ridge (50A, inherited in 1703);
Venture (Dorchester, 300A, 1719); Hazard (Dorchester, 200A, never
patented)

ROBERT was the first of the family to move to the upper Nanticoke. He died
only a few years afterward, and his children soon departed the lower Chesapeake
region altogether. Their fate and eventual destinations are still uncertain.

Robert's year of birth is estimated as 1679. There are no depositions on record in
which his age is stated, but this date is consistent with the known ages of several
of his siblings and the traditional placement of Robert as one of the younger
sons.[137] More concretely, his father is cited as "Robert Polk Sen." in the Somerset

---

[137] The author has been given Family Group Record (FGR) sheets for the family of
Robert Polk Jun., by a Polk family researcher, Mrs. Myrtle Polk Hilton, of South
Carolina, now deceased. This record sheet cites the Quaker Monthly Meeting, West
Nantmeal Township, Chester PA, Society of Friends, 1698-1774, (GS Film 50330, Pts 1-
4), as a source attributed to the genealogist, Mr. Charles H. Starr. As already noted in
Section 2.1, the author has tried to locate this record, both in the LDS catalog and at the
Swarthmore College Library, the acknowledged primary repository for American Quaker
records, but no such source was found either as an original document or on microfilm.
The authorities at Swarthmore stated that the West Nantmeal MM did not keep its own
records, but would have entered them at the Goshen MM, later transferred to the
Uwchlan MM. In any case, no relevant Polk records from any Quaker MM were located
in the Swarthmore holdings. The Family Group Record cited here is certainly incorrect
with respect to the wife of Robert Polk (III) being Alice Nutter, something also claimed
in *Polk Family and Kinsmen*. In fact, the Robert Polk having a wife and widow named
Alice was Robert Polk, the Dorchester official, son of John Polk (P12), not the son of
Robert Polk Jun.; furthermore, Alice's maiden name was Covington, not Nutter, as noted
in Section 3.2 on John Polk. The record is also wrong with respect to the birth date of
Robert (III) shown as November 1709. We know from Robert Jun.'s will (transcribed
below) that Robert (III) was certainly less than age fourteen when the will was written on
21 February 1726 (NS), so he was born no earlier than 1712.

court records beginning in November 1695, but not earlier.[138] This would indicate that Robert Jun. had reached sufficient age to require such a distinction at that time, i.e. he had at least reached taxable age (sixteen).

The wife of Robert Polk Jun., was Grace Gullett (Gillett) who is not mentioned by name in his will, but is identified as executrix in his inventory. The Gullett family had arrived early in Somerset and had settled in the Manokin area. Grace's father William Gullett patented the tracts Gulletts Advisement (100 acres) in 1675, Gulletts Assurance (100 acres) in 1685, and Gulletts Hope (50 acres) in 1683, and had married Susanna Mills on 1 November 1674 as recorded in Somerset Liber IKL. They had at least five children whose births are also recorded there—Mary (b.1675), William (b.1678), Susanna (b.1680), and twins, Elizabeth and Grace (b. 3 March 1683(NS)).

An association between brothers-in-law William Gullett Jun. and Robert Polk Jun. is found in their joint appearance in Court on 9 June 1708 to face charges of disturbing the peace: [139]

Her Majesty vers   *Somerset County ~*
Robert Polk and William Gullett,
The Jurors of our Sovereign Lady the Queen that now is in their oaths doe present for our sd Lady the Queen Robt Polke and Wm Gullet late of this County laborers for that they the sd Robert and William the fear of God before their eyes not having on or about the 11th day of October in the year of our Lord 1707 at Manny (Monie) in our said county with force of arms that is to say with knives dogs and guns on a certain tract of land and marsh belonging to John Panter of our said county then and there did hunt and three unmarked shoats did feloniously kill and carry away of the value two hundred pounds of tob'co contrary to the Peace and against the form of the Act of Assembly in that case made and provided //   Peter Dent Clerk To wch Indictmt they the said Robert and William pleads not guilty of any breach of her Ma't'ys laws and for tryall puts themselves on the country ~ Worthington for Deft. And the Queen also ~ Dent.

Wherefore command was given to the Sheriff of Somerset County that he cause to come here twelve good and lawful men of his Bailywick to trye the issue joyned between her Majesty Pltf & Robert Polk and William Gullett //

At which day came Capt. William Round, Richard Tull, Jun., William Stevenson, Henry Dolman, Robert Wattson, Peter Surman, Afrodocia Johnson, Nathanial Cottman, Edward Martin, Capt. Nicholas Evans, Alexander Carlisle, Henry Bishop, who being duly elected and all sworn

---

[138] SOJR 1695-97: 68, 129, 134; 1696-98:194.
[139] SOJR 1705-08:104.

*and the evidences sworn and deliberately heard and the charges given
return with this verdict Wee the jury do find the deft guilty of hunting upon
Mr. Pantters land after being forewarned. William Round foreman.*

*The verdict being not full (unanimous) the Clerk of Indictments humbly
prayed the court that the said jury may be recommended to their room who
after some space return with the same verdict as aforesaid. Whereupon they
were recommended and return with the same verdict. Recommended the
third time and return immediately with the same verdict aforesaid.
Recommended the fourth time and after some space return with this verdict
Wee of the jury find the defendant not guilty. Wm Round foreman ~
Ordered the verdict be entered. Considered by the court here that the said
Robert Polk and William Gullet be acquitted of this indictment paying their
fees become due according to law and to give bonds for their good
behavior.*

Three days later Robert Polk posted bond for £10 with William Smith his security
on condition that he "*be of good behavior to all her majesties liege people of this
province and especially to John Pannther.*" He apparently came out of this brush
with the law untarnished, for he was appointed Constable for the Monie Hundred
later in the year (1708).[140] It is curious that Robert is described as a laborer in this
passage rather than as a planter since he was certainly a landowner having
patented Ballyhack in 1700 and inherited part of Forlorne Hope in 1703. This may
indicate a lack of status or success with his holdings.

~~~~~~

Robert was the only one of Robert and Magdalen's children to move to the
Nanticoke area, other than Joseph who made the move much later, as the final
step in the family's exodus from Damned Quarter. Robert moved to Dorchester
County on the west side of the Nanticoke, probably about 1719 when his purchase
of the tract Venture from Samuel Jackson was recorded.[141] His time there was
short, for he died in 1727 leaving a family of two sons and five daughters. Within
a few years his children appear to have departed the area, possibly for Cecil
County, Maryland, and eventually to the Carolinas, but the full story of their
eventual destinations has yet to be unraveled.

~~~~~~

Robert Jun. had two sons named Thomas and Robert, Thomas being the elder.
When Robert Jun. wrote his will in February 1726(NS), Robert (III) was not yet
fourteen since the will provided that he was to be made a freeman when he

---

[140] SOJR 1705-08:152.
[141] Surprisingly this transaction is recorded in Somerset Land Records, SOLR 1719:15,
(appended to the 1719 Somerset Judicials), although the tract was located on the west
side of the Nanticoke, in Dorchester.

attained that age. By implication, Thomas had already reached that age since a similar provision was not made for him. There is also a citation of Robert (and Thomas) in the 1729 tax list for Nanticoke Hundred, so Robert (III) was sixteen by that point and therefore born about 1712-13.

In *Polk Family and Kinsmen* W. H. Polk claimed that Robert Polk (III) was the individual of that name who became a Dorchester official.[142] This is incorrect. Robert Polk, the Justice of the Peace and a tobacco inspection officer in Dorchester, was actually the son of John Polk, eldest son of Robert and Magdalen. See *ante,* Section 3.2. W. H. Polk also listed Colonel William Polk of Delaware, husband of Mary (Vaughan) Woodgate, as a son of Robert Polk Jun., born about 1705, but there was no such son as is clear from the aforementioned will. Colonel William Polk was in fact the son of the Robert Polk, the Dorchester official.

~~~~~~~~~

Robert Polk Jun.'s will provided, as its first item, that Thomas was to receive "my now dwelling plantation called Venture" and as the second item that Robert would receive the tract Hazard. The latter tract has a history which leaves an intriguing hint about the subsequent fate of Robert (III), of whom there is almost nothing known other than that he departed Dorchester within a few years after his father's death. The Maryland land office records show that Hazard, Robert Polk's second Dorchester tract, was surveyed in 1723,[143] citing a warrant for 200 acres issued to his brother Joseph three months earlier but was never patented. Years later in 1741, a petition of David Pollock, son of James, concerning the warrant first cited by Robert appears in Maryland Patents Liber LG#C, folio 97:

> *To the Hon'ble Levin Gale Esq, the Lord Proprietary's Chief*
> *Judge in Land affairs within this Province, the petition of David*
> *Pollock of Dorchester County humbly sheweth—That Joseph*
> *Pollock of Somerset County had on the tenth day of January 1722*
> *granted unto him a warrant for two hundred acres of land in*
> *common form and that by virtue thereof a Certif't had been*
> *returned into his Ldshp's Land Office for and in the name of*
> *Robert Pollock for that qty said to be by assignment from the said*
> *Joseph as per the said Certif't dated 29th March 1723 app'rs, but*
> *no such assignment appearing in the office in patent has hitherto*
> *issued so that the said Cert so returned in the name of Robert Polk*
> *remains still in the Office postponed **and the said Robert has for a***
> ***considerable time absented himself and gone to parts unknown***
> *and your petn'r having for a valuable consideration purchased the*
> *sd warrant from Joseph Pollock to whom the same was first*
> *granted and never no such ass'n (assignment) as in the afsd Cert is*

---

[142] PF&K, p. 673.
[143] MDLS, Dorchester 549, Unpatented.

*mentioned or any other by such means this sd Cert can be of no
effect. Your Petn'r therefore humbly prays that as he has hereto
produce(d) as ass'n under the hand & seal of the affores'd Joseph
Pollock bearing date the 8th day of Aug't 1739 that Robert
Pollock's Cert so returned as afs'd may be vacated on record and
that the warrant retn'd in name of your petn'r in common form.
And as in Duty bound, he'll pray, etc.*

[In separate hand] *To the Chief of the Land Office April 18, 1741
Let the Certif't be vacated on Record and new warrant issue as
prayed. Levin Gale*

It was, of course, something of a stretch to say that Robert (Jun.) had gone to parts unknown since he had died on his plantation in Dorchester in 1727. David Pollock seems to have glossed over this point, which may have been too fine a distinction to make with the Provincial Land Office fourteen years afterwards and must have actually been referring to Robert Polk (III), the inheritor of the land. Robert (III) had himself taken some action towards patenting the land since the survey certificate is annotated "examined and passed, J. Ross Examiner" on 1 January 1730(NS), but for some reason the patent was never issued. David's petition was granted and he afterwards cited this warrant to account for 200 of the 450 acres of the tract Davids Hope, which he surveyed in October 1741.

The location of Robert Polk's two tracts, Venture and Hazard, are shown in Figure 16. It should be noted that this is the same area, at the lower end of Clearbrook Creek, where David Pollock accumulated extensive lands as seen above in Figure 15.

The unanswered question posed by this record is why Robert (III) left for parts unknown without making any apparent settlement for his rightfully inherited land. It does not seem plausible that he just abandoned it, or that his relatives had taken it over without suitable compensation. One would expect Robert's older cousins, such as Robert (son of John) who witnessed Robert Jun.'s will, or his uncles William and Joseph, to look after the interests of the orphans. It can only be surmised that David or Joseph paid Robert for his rights but did not formally record the action since the land had never been patented. In due course, David exercised these rights through the above petition and acquiescence of Joseph.

What is known is that both Robert and Thomas appear, inexplicably, on the Nanticoke Hundred tax list for Somerset County in the single year 1729[144] adjacent in the list to their step-cousins Samuel and Robert Owens; and that

---

[144] Both are listed as single taxables. They do not appear on the 1727 list, or in what remains of the 1728 list, or in any years after 1729.

Thomas sold 100 acres of his land, Venture, to Charles Hopkins in 1734. By that point, the children of Robert Jun. seem to have left the area. The author has not identified any further appearances of either Robert or Thomas in the records of Somerset or Dorchester after this time.

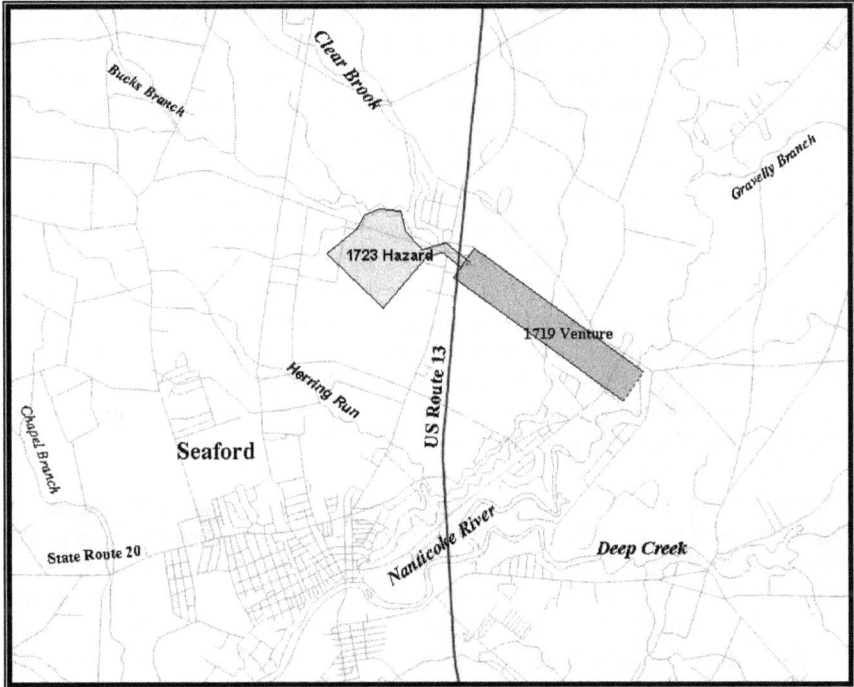

Figure 16. Location of Robert Polk's tracts, Venture and Hazard, near present-day Seaford, Delaware.

In some published and unpublished family histories[145] it is asserted that Thomas moved north and joined with the Welsh Baptists who had settled in an area known as the Welsh Tract along the border between Cecil County, Maryland, and Newcastle County, Delaware, and afterwards migrated with them to the Peedee River area of South Carolina. The author has located no records to establish his presence in the Welsh area of Cecil and Newcastle Counties, but there is indeed a record of a Thomas Polk obtaining a warrant for land in South Carolina in 1737,[146] when the Welsh moved there from Maryland and Pennsylvania under encouragement from the South Carolina government. The following excerpt is taken from "Petitions From the South Carolina Council Journals, Vol. 1, 1734/5-1748", p. 114, for the meeting of Friday, 3 March 1738(NS):

---

[145] Comfort, Part V, p. 234-245.
[146] See Petitions for Land, South Carolina Councils Journal, Vol. 1, 1734/5-1748, p. 114.

Read the Petition of Tho's Polk praying a warrant for two hundred and fifty acres and a lott in Queensborough of the Welch Tract. Order'd that a warrant do issue for the Township of Queensborough.

The survey of these 250 acres was not performed until 28 March 1749. This Thomas Polk, whether the son of Robert Jun. of Dorchester or someone else, was the progenitor of a large number of Polks in South Carolina whose descendants migrated into other areas of the south. He died in 1781 and was buried in the Broxson Family Cemetery, Colleton County, South Carolina.[147] There are a number of genealogical discussions of this line, some having very specific detail about the births and deaths of Robert Polk Jun.'s family and later offspring. The primary reference cited by these accounts is the minutes of the Quaker Monthly Meeting of West Nantmeal Township, already mentioned above, but as already noted, no such record could be located either in the LDS catalog or the Swarthmore College Library.[148] They are, therefore, not included here. On the other hand, Y chromosome DNA testing has been done on several descendants of Thomas Polk of South Carolina and results compared with the modal values for the lineage group of Robert Polk (the original immigrant to Somerset County) with positive results. On this basis it appears likely that Thomas Polk of South Carolina was indeed the son of Robert Polk Jun.

Another factor that would be consistent with Thomas' joining the Welsh settlers of the Cecil and Newcastle counties area would be one of his sisters having moved to the same area at that time. Such a claim has been made in histories of the Reese family of North Carolina, but cannot be regarded as certain since it is based mainly on family tradition rather than documented records. The wife of David Reese of Wales, who arrived in this area about 1725 and afterwards moved to the Cumberland County area of Pennsylvania, and then to Mecklenburg County, North Carolina, is identified as Susan Ruth Polk in some Reese family histories[149] and in membership papers filed in DAR records. It is claimed that she married David Reese in Cecil County on 23 December 1738. Moreover, in these histories

---

[147] The author has a copy of tombstone inscriptions from this cemetery, said to have been recorded by Charles E. Lowther, along with those of other South Carolina and Georgia cemeteries, during the period 1880-1916, and sent to the Mormon Church for recording in the 1930s. Apparently these were lost, but some were later discovered by Mrs. Vivian Lowther, wife of a grandson of Charles Lowther. According to these records, Thomas Polk died 21 May 1781, aged 77 years, 4 months and 23 days, and his wife, Priscilla Dunn, died 16 October 1789, aged 63-7-18. The graveyard itself no longer exists.

[148] Per the genealogist, Charles H. Starr, these are found on LDS microfilm GS 50330, but as noted, no such microfilm or related records could be located either in the LDS catalog or the Swarthmore College Library.

[149] *Genealogy of the Reese Family*, Mary E. Reese, Richmond, VA, 1903; *Lives and Times of the 27 Signers of the Mecklenburg Declaration of Independence,* Victor C. King, Charlotte NC, 1956; *Hope for a Better Age, From Wales to America with the Descendants of David Reese*, Jon O. Reese & Cynthia Jones Reese, Wichita Falls, TX, 1987; *The Genealogical Study of David Reese and Related Families*, Cynthia Jones Reese, Wichita Falls, TX, 1990.

three of David and Susan's children are said to be named David <u>Tasker</u> Reese, Charles <u>Gullett</u> Reese, and James <u>Polk</u> Reese. The choice of these particular middle names would certainly make their descent from Robert Polk Jun. and Grace Gullett seem credible, but the validity of the middle names is open to question. Their use, and the assertion that Susan Reese was daughter of Robert Polk Jun., both trace back to a work entitled *Genealogy of the Reese Family* by Mary E. Reese, published in 1903. Although Ms. Reese cites some sources in her work, they are not at all conclusive. A more recent and more carefully documented account of the Reese-Polk family connection will be found in *Fighting Charles Reese* by Mr. Parker Sams of Findlay, Ohio, with whom the author has corresponded on this matter.[150] Mr. Sams regards the family tradition that David Reese's wife was Susan Polk as strong and consistent, but also agrees that there is insufficient basis at present to either confirm or exclude Susan Reese as the daughter of Robert Polk Jun., and that there are no primary source records indicating that David Reese's children had ever actually used, or been given, the claimed middle names.[151]

We must therefore leave the eventual fate of the two sons, Thomas and Robert, and the five daughters of Robert Polk Jun. as an open question with some possible answers but no final resolution.

<hr />

The last will and testament of Robert Polk Jun.[152]

> *February the 21st Day 1725. In the name of God Amen. I Robert Polk of Dorchester County in the Province aforesaid, planter, being very sick and weak of body but of sound and perfect mind and memory praises therefore be given to Almighty God do make & ordain this my last Will & Testament—in the manner and form following that is to say First & principally I recommend my soul unto the hands of Almighty God hoping that through the Merits and Death & passion of my Saviour Jesus Christ to have full and free pardon of all my sins & to inherit Everlasting Life & my body I commit to the Earth to be buried at the discretion of my Executors & as touching the disposition of all such Temporal Estate as it hath pleased Almighty God to bestow upon me I give & bequeath as followeth First I will that my just Debts & Funeral Charges be paid & discharged. Item, I give unto my son Thomas my now dwelling plantation called Venture bounded & angling according to the pattent to him my afrsd son Thomas to him & to his Heirs for Ever*

[150] Sams, p. 64-7.
[151] Ibid, p. 76. Mr. Sams notes that in his will, David Reese refers to his wife specifically as "Ruth," not Susan Ruth. No other original source document has thus far been found that specifically identifies David Reese's wife as either Susan, or Susan Ruth.
[152] MDW 19:136.

only I reserve my well beloved wife her priveledge on the afrsd plantation during her widowhood—Item, I give & bequeath unto my son Robert a certain Tract of Land called Hazard joyning to the aforesaid Tract of Land called Venture bounded and running accordingly as shall appear on record to him the aforesaid Robert & to his Heirs for Ever— Item, I give and bequeath unto my Brother Joseph Polk part of Forlorn Hope on the northern End being a certain Tract of Land formerly surveyed for Augustin Stanford & likewise a Certain Tract of Land called Ballehack lying near the Head of a Creek called Pidgeon House Creek to him & to the heirs of his own Body for Ever— Item, I give unto my well beloved wife a Negro Man called Minggo during her natural Life only I will the said Negro shall labour & help to my two youngest daughters Grace & Mary—Item, I give unto my son Thomas one gun— Item, I give unto my son Robert one gun being the newest of the two—then as the rest of my moveable Estate I will that it be equally divided amongst my Five Daughters only sett apart my Wifes thirds. Likewise I will that my Five Daughters shall have a priveldge upon both of the aforesaid Tracts of Land for their Creatures Cattle Sheep & Hoggs or any other usefull Creature whatsoever till such Time as they are disposed in Marriage providing that the Girls do provide such food as is necesssary for their Creatures on their own cost & charge. Likewise I will that my son Robert shall be a Freeman at the age of fourteen or before he be of that age if my wife should marry & likewise I will that my Two Daughters Grace & Mary be free whenever their Mother marrys otherwise to remain with their Mother till the years of Sixteen as Witness I have hereunto set my hand & fixt my Seal
Signed Sealed & Delivered in the presence of
William Polk   *Robert* **X** *Polk*
Daniel Harrison   *his Mark*
Robert Polk

May the 10th 1727 Came Daniel Harrison & Robert Polk two of the Subscribing evidences to the Last Will & Testament of Robert Polk late of Dorchester County Deceased & made Oath upon the Holy Evangelists of Almighty God that they saw the within named Robert Polk sign & seal & heard him publish & declare the within Instrument of writing to be his Last Will & Testament & at the Time of his so doing he was to the best of their Apprehension in perfect Sense & Memory & that the other witness, vizt. William Polk was then & there present & signed with them
              John Pitt   Dept Com'r for Dorsett County

3.8 David Polk (c.1682-c.1702)

DAVID is known to us only from the mention made of him in his father's will (1699) in which he is named both as a legatee and as the co-executor with Magdalen.

In 1702 Robert Polke amended his will, making sons Ephraim and James co-executors. Although there were no changes in the terms of the will, the properties that David was supposed to inherit, Polkes Folly and part of Forlorne Hope, were inherited instead by his oldest brother, John. This is known from the will of John's son William, probated in Dorchester in 1728, which shows that William owned these properties at that time presumably by right of inheritance from John who had died intestate in 1708. There is no record of their conveyance by any other action. From this we conclude that David died between 1699 and 1702, and had no wife or children with prior claim over John to his estate.

The David Polk/Pollock who appears until 1730 in the tax lists of Monie Hundred, Somerset County, and in later land records of Dorchester County, and as a witness on Magdalen Polke's will, was the eldest son of James Polk/Pollock. See Section 3.6.

3.9 Martha Polk (c.1685-?)

MARTHA, like David, is known to us only through what is mentioned of her in the will of Robert Polke written in 1699—"*Another third of my goods and moveables I leave to my daughter Martha be it little or much to her and her heirs forever.*" An added stipulation was made in Robert's codicil of 1702 that "*Martha Poock may have liberty to let her cattle run on the plantation until she gets plantation*".

It is reasonable to suppose that Martha grew to maturity, married and had a family, but no other records from Somerset have been located that offer further information about this daughter of Robert and Magdalen. The name Martha was not uncommon at that time, but the population itself was not large, and there are only a limited number of possible married ladies named Martha to consider in the available records. While researching for this book the author looked for possible candidates. One such is Martha Rencher, wife of William Rencher, who lived in Monie just east of Damned Quarter. She appears as his cosigner on a deed for the sale of Covingtons Meadow and Comfort Adventure to Thomas Roberts in 1769. If this is Robert and Magdalen's daughter she would be very elderly, in her mid-eighties at that time. No other information has been found on her so this must remain as unconfirmed speculation for now. It is always more difficult to trace the female lines in the colonial era since they were rarely involved in the legal processes from which documents are recorded. Some church records are available, but only a fraction of all marriages can be found in them especially in the early periods. The other common source for such information is the mention of daughters' married names in the wills of their fathers, but unfortunately in this case that does not apply.

It might be noted that the Register of Derry Cathedral, Parish of Templemore, contains an entry for the baptism of Martha, daughter of a Robert Poke, on 16 April 1664. However, this is not the Martha later found in Somerset for the Register also records the burial of Martha Poke, daughter of Robert Poke, on 6 December 1672.

3.10 Joseph Pollock (1689-1752)

Born: Damned Quarter, Somerset County, Maryland
Occupation: planter
Probate: will written 12 Sept 1751; probated 10 June 1753, Dorchester County;
    inventory: appraised at £322/19/8 on 4 August 1752
Spouses:
(1) (N) Wright, daughter of Thomas Wright (d.1753) of Damned Quarter
(2) Lydia (N), probably from Dorchester
Children by (N) Wright:
(1) Ann (1737-1816), m. Daniel Morris, Jun.
(2) Robert (c.1738-1768), m. Betty— -
Children by Lydia (N):
(3) Zephaniah, m. Lucretia Causey
(4) Rebeccah
(5) Rhoda, m. William Masten
(6) James (d.1789), m. Lucilla— -
(7) Magdalen
Property:
Polks Lott (50A, after Magdalen's death); Polkes Folly (100A); Forlorne
    Hope/Lone Ridge (100A, 1727); Ballyhack (100A, 1727); Forlorne Hopes
    Addition (90A, 1738); Clonmell (100A, 1739); Little Goshen (Dorchester,
    300A, 1740; resurveyed to 550A, 1750); Dublin (Dorchester, 100A, 1743);
    Horseys Swamp (Dorchester 100A, 1749)

****

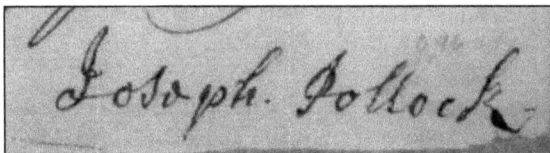

**Joseph Polk's signature on assignment of warrant rights, tract Jacobs
Forest, 1749**

****

JOSEPH was the youngest of Robert's children. He remained at Polks Folly with
Magdalen, the family matriarch, through her final years and eventually disposed
of the family lands in Damned Quarter.

This was a role that would probably have been filled by his older brother David
who was supposed to inherit Polks Folly and part of Forlorne Hope, but David
apparently predeceased his father and the responsibility passed to Joseph instead.
The fact that the ownership of this land reverted to Robert's oldest son John and

then to John's son William seems to have caused some friction in the family, and may explain Magdalen's devising her estate in Donegal to Joseph.

Joseph was only thirteen or fourteen and just learning the skills needed by a colonial planter when his father died.[153] His oldest brothers, John and William, had moved some time earlier to the Manokin area while his brothers Robert, James, and Ephraim were settling nearby on their own lands at Pigeon House Creek. Robert and Ephraim had already patented the tracts Ballyhack and Clonmell, while James was learning his trade as a shipwright and would soon patent the tract which he called James Meadow. Together these Polk properties would comprise the entire area from Pigeon House to Damned Quarter Creek, but a good portion of the land was probably of marginal value referred to as swamp or marshland even in documents of that era.

The reality of the long term prospects in Damned Quarter was no doubt clear to the family and, as already described, they seemed to have decided by 1720 on relocating to the upper Nanticoke. As the rest of the family moved ahead with this plan Joseph remained behind in the original settler's house with Magdalen while she was alive and afterwards with his own family, gradually accumulating the lands left by the others until he was the last of the name Polk remaining in Damned Quarter. By 1739 he possessed all of the tracts Polkes Folly, Forlorn Hope, Ballyhack, Clonmell, and Forlorne Hope's Addition. Perhaps the family strategy was intended to proceed this way from the outset, or it may have just evolved as events unfolded, but in either case it was a steady progression. When William's death in late 1739 left Joseph as the family patriarch, he took the final steps in the exodus. On 21 January 1740(NS), Joseph purchased a 300-acre tract called Little Goshen on the Dorchester side of the Nanticoke for £75 and took up residence there during the ensuing year. In 1740 his name appeared on the Monie Hundred tax list for the last time.

In 1748 Joseph conveyed all of the Polk lands in Damned Quarter, totaling 590 acres, to neighboring landowners William and John Shores for 4,000 pounds of tobacco and £37 sterling. This is a rather modest price on a per-acre basis, rather indicative of the large amount of unusable land contained in the property. By comparison, just three years later Joseph's nephew David Pollock (son of James) sold the 100-acre tract Contention located about a mile to the east on Little Creek in Monie to Joseph's father-in-law, Thomas Wright, and his son Henry, for 4,000 pounds of tobacco and £100.

~~~~~~~~

Joseph acquired several other properties in Dorchester, all located in the same area

---

[153] Joseph's age is recorded in two depositions; on 7 August 1730 it was stated as "aged about forty-one or thereabouts" in SOJR 1730-33:8; on 20 December 1750 it was stated as "aged about sixty years or thereabouts" in DOLR Old #14:498; forty-one being a more "exact" number than sixty, we use it as basis for his birth year being 1689.

as Little Goshen. In 1743 he purchased fifty 100 acres. Then in 1750 he petitioned for a resurvey of Little Goshen and almost doubled its size with the addition of 250 acres of vacancy.[154] Altogether his estate in Dorchester comprised 700 acres—a significant step up from the 590 acres of mostly marshland he had held in Damned Quarter. These tracts are shown in Figure 17.

The legacy of Joseph's presence persists to this day in the names Polk Road and Dublin Hill Road which may be found about two miles northwest of Bridgeville, Delaware.

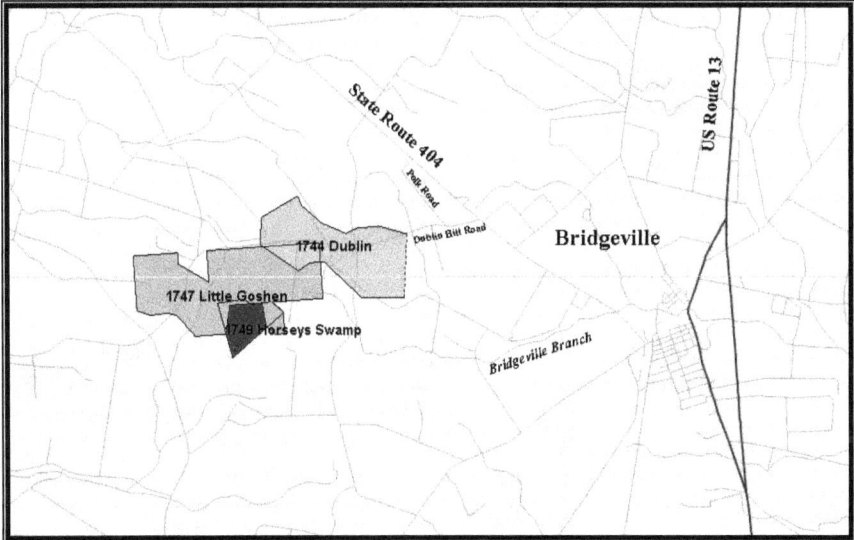

Figure 17. Joseph Polk's lands west of Bridgeville, Delaware.

One of the significant episodes in Joseph's early adult life was the rather bitter dispute with his sister Anne and her second husband John Renshaw over the disposition of the estate of Francis Roberts. This was already discussed in the earlier section on Anne Polk and, as mentioned, must have been the source of considerable contention within the family. It may even have been a factor in the decision to move to the upper Nanticoke. After the departure of the rest of the family it was Anne and her descendants that remained behind as the only enduring Polk presence in Damned Quarter, at least by blood, if not name.

---

[154] In the mid-18th century there were a great number of resurveys made in Maryland whose basic purpose was not to correct boundaries, though this may have indeed been needed, but to acquire adjacent "vacancies" which had not yet been claimed. The basic principal was that the "first discoverer" could take up any unclaimed lands contiguous to lands already possessed. This led to the patenting of some very bizarre shaped land tracts that would make "Gerrymandering" appear respectable by comparison.

It is curious that Joseph was the one who came to the fore as the "friend" to represent Francis Roberts' son Edward in the case. Although Joseph was an adult by this time, he was the youngest of the Polk brothers and only three years older than Edward himself. At twenty-three years he was only half his sister Anne's age. Why did William, Ephraim, James, or Robert not take on this role? One might see the hand of Magdalen was at work in this. She was the family matriarch presiding from the house in which Joseph was the only remaining child and nominal head of household. As a woman, she could not press the matter formally in court. If she felt that such action was needed, then she would turn to a male of legal standing for that purpose and Joseph was the convenient choice, if not the optimal one because of his relative youth. It still leaves the question of why a more senior brother did not step in—and this may reveal further friction going on within the family. Perhaps the others were not as convinced of the need or wisdom of such a course and preferred to stay out of it.

The rancor between the Polks and their Roberts and Renshaw in-laws also drew Joseph into the dispute over property boundaries. The 99-year lease of part of Elliotts Choice to John Roberts caused considerable confusion and led Edward Roberts to request a commission in 1730 in which Joseph made the following deposition:[155]

> *Joseph Polk aged about forty one years or thereabouts being sworn on the Holy Evangelists of Almighty God deposeth and saith that about twenty five years agoe he was in a peach orchard in company with one John Hillman and that the said Hillman told the deponent he would show him the bounder of Elliotts Choice as Samuel Jones told him and they went to a pine stump standing near a marsh side about two hundred and fifty yards from the dwelling home of Francis Roberts and about South from the said house. The deponent further saith that the said Hillman told him that a cedar post standing by the said stump was put up by Samuel Jones and the said Jones told the said Hillman that it was first bounder of Elliotts Choice and that Samuel Jones took severall young people and told them that the afsd bounder was the first bounder of Elliotts Choice. The deponent saith that John Roberts interrupted James Polk on his oath and then Richard Wallis Sen standing by said that John Roberts was a liar for the afsd pine stump was the first bounder of Elliotts Choice. Likewise John White said John Roberts was a rogue for the pine stump aforesaid was the first bounder of Elliotts Choice and further saith not. Joseph Polk.*

It is this record that allows us to determine the year of Joseph's birth.

～～～～～

[155] SOJR 1730-33:8; 7 August 1730.

Tax list appearances of Joseph Polk/Pollock in Monie Hundred

Prior to 1723   No tax lists extant
1723   Joseph Polk
1724   Joseph Polke
1725   Joseph Polk
1726   No list
1727   Joseph Pollock
1728   Joseph Polke
1729   No list
1730   Joseph Pollock, John Neal
1731   Joseph Pollock, John Neall
1732   No List
1733   Joseph Pollock, John Oneal, Owen Macdaniel
1734   Joseph Pollock, John Neall, John Makdaniel
1735   Joseph Polk, John Neial, Owen McDonald
1736   Joseph Pollock, Owen Macdaniel
1737   Joseph Pollock, Owen Macdannell
1738   Joseph Polke
1739   Joseph Pollock, Charles Bazwell, Jnº Neill
1740   Joseph Pollock, Charles Bazwell
After 1740   No further appearance

From this it would appear that Joseph was moderately well-off. He owned no slaves at this time, for none were listed in any of these entries, but had some hired help in his employ—whether indentured servants, apprentices or just paid workers. The individual John Neal listed here as a taxable followed Joseph to Dorchester where he became a land owner in his own right and was one of the witnesses on Joseph's will written in 1751. He was married to Margaret White, daughter and legatee of John White of Damned Quarter.

Joseph probably was not married during the time that Magdalen was alive and living at Polkes Folly, but he eventually married twice and had seven known children. His first wife was the daughter of Thomas Wright of Damned Quarter, but her given name does not appear on record. By this first wife Joseph had daughter Ann, born c.1737, and son Robert, born c.1738. These two children are mentioned as grandchildren in the will of Thomas Wright (written 1754) and bequeathed one shilling each by him, a legal formality to prevent any further claim on his estate. Probably Thomas Wright, who died a year after Joseph,[156] felt that they were adequately provided for and had no need of additional considerations. Joseph's first wife appears to have died about the time he left Damned Quarter. Her death may have hastened his move since he no longer felt constrained to remain near her family.

---

[156] MDW 28:442.

There is a great deal known about Joseph's daughter Ann, who married Daniel Morris Jun. in 1754 and had many descendants. This is covered in *Polk Family and Kinsmen*[157] and will not be repeated here, except to note that they left Delaware in 1793 and moved to the area of Fayette County, Kentucky. Her year of birth can be judged from the probate account of Joseph Pollock which notes her as a minor in May 1753 and as "of age" in October of the same year.

Joseph's son Robert married Elizabeth, or Betty, Polk, the daughter of his cousin Robert Polk, son of John Polk, and had one child by her, a son named Clement. After Robert's death in 1771, Clement was made a ward of Betty's second husband, Emanuel Manlove, but had a rather brief life dying unmarried and under thirty in 1784. He left a will which was rather unusual in the explicit instructions it gave for the construction of his grave—specifying that it should be a brick walled structure eight feet by fifteen feet and four feet deep.

~~~~~~

The second wife of Joseph was a Lydia of unknown surname who outlived him by a great number of years, at least until 1787 when she last appears on the tax list for Northwest Fork Hundred, Sussex County. It seems probable that Joseph remarried shortly after he relocated to upper Nanticoke and that Lydia belonged to a family from that area. In any case, she became the mother of the five other children, Zephaniah, Rebecca, Rhoda, James, and Magdalen, mentioned as minors in the May 1753 probate account for Joseph's estate.[158] If any of these had also been children of Joseph's first wife, then they would have been mentioned in Thomas Wright's will along with Ann and Robert.

~~~~~~

In *Polk Family and Kinsmen* W. H. Polk speculated that Joseph returned to Ireland to claim and sell the estate Moneen bequeathed to him by Magdalen. In unpublished notes among his papers at the University of Kentucky, W. H. Polk seems to have changed his mind several times on this question. Although no information has appeared to settle the matter conclusively, it seems unlikely.[159] There is no obvious gap in the records during which Joseph was absent from

---

[157] See Chapters LXI, LVII and LVIII.

[158] See MDA 34:118.

[159] W. H. Polk prepared a draft manuscript on Joseph Polk that will be found in Box 10, Folder 3, of his papers at the University of Kentucky Library. He suggests in this that Joseph took his children with him to Ireland and gave some of "Moneen" to one or more of his sons. He goes on to speculate about William Polk "of Carlisle," who married Margaret Taylor, being one of those sons and proceeds to conclude that this was in fact the case, but all of the discussion is speculative and no evidence is introduced to support it. In any case, he dropped this theory at some point and, as already discussed, in *Polk Family and Kinsmen* asserted instead that William "of Carlisle" was the son of Robert and Magdalen's second son, William, for which there also was no evidence.

Somerset or Dorchester for a matter of years. His presence is seen in the tax lists and land and judicial records rather continuously through the balance of his life, not to mention his two marriages and the fathering of seven children. One possibility would be a fairly short trip to settle matters in Ireland during the year following Magdalen's death, 1729, but this is simply speculation. The author attempted to find some evidence of a land transaction for the sale of Moneen in Ireland, but this has been unsuccessful—no local land records from that period have survived.

~~~~~~~~

The last will and testament of Joseph Pollock

In the Name of God Amen. This twelfth day of September Anno Domini one Thousand Seven Hundred and fifty one I Joseph Pollock of Dorchester County and Province of Maryland Planter being sick and week of Body but of perfect Mind and Memory and knowing it is appointed for all Men to Die do make and Ordain this my last Will and Testament. First I Commend my soul to Almight God that gave it and my Body to be buried in a Christian like manner at the Discretion of my Executors here after Named as touching Such Worldly Estate Wherewith it hath pleased God to bless me with in this world I give Devise and Dispose of the Same in manner and form following—

Imprimis I Give and Bequeath to my well Beloved Son Robert Pollock the Westermost End of a Tract of Land Called Little Goshan and Likewise a Tract of Land Called Horsays Swamp containing one hundred Acres to him and his Heirs forever and in Case he Dies without heir then to fall to my Youngest Son James Pollock and his Heirs forever upon the Condition of him the Said James Pollock paying my Daughter Ann Pollock the Sum of fifty Pounds Currant Money of Maryland in lieu of the Land when he Shall arrive at the age of twenty Eight Years of Age I Likewise Give and Bequeath to my Son Robert Pollock a Young Negro Boy Called Sam being in full for his part of my Estate

Item I Give and Bequeath to my well Beloved Son Zephaniah Pollock the Eastermost End of a Tract of Land Called Little Goshan to him and his Heirs Forever and in Case he Dies without Heirs then to fall to my Youngest Son James Pollock and his Heirs forever Likewise my Will and Desire is that the Tract of Land Called Little Goshan be Equally Divided between my two Sons Robert and Zephaniah Pollock at the Discretion of my Friend John Pollock Son of James Pollock and in Case the Said Eastermost End of Goshan Should be lost by means of a Suit of Law then in Lieu thereof I Give unto him a Young Negro Girl Named Fender but in Case he Obtains the Land then the Said Negro Fender to be Equally Divided among my Other Children I Likewise Give and Bequeath to my Son Zephaniah Pollock a Gun in full for his part on my Estate

Item I give and Bequeath to my Eldest Daughter Ann Pollock a Young

Negro Girl Named Rose in full for her part of my Estate

Item my Will and Desire is that my trusty friend John Pollock after my Death may prosecute the Suit of Law now Depending Between my Self and Christopher Nutter and the Charges thereof to be Defrayed out of my Estate

Item I Give and Bequeath to my Son James Pollock all my Smiths tools and the Remainder of my Estate to be Equally Divided among my Other Children

Item I Likewise Leave my well Beloved Wife full and whole Executrix of this my last Will and Testament and my Will and Desire is that my Son Robert Pollock may Dwell with his Mother in Law till he arrive at the Age of Eighteen Years or till the Day of her Marriage and I do hereby Utterly Disanull and make Void all the Other Wills and Testaments before this by me in any Wise Named Ratifying and Confirming This and no Other to be my last Will and Testament in Witness I have hereunto Set my hand and Seal the Day and Year above Written

Joseph Pollock ¤

Signed Sealed pronounced and Declared
By the Said Joseph Pollock to be his
last Will and Testament in presence of us
    Charles Rawlins
    Jacob Layton
    John Neal

Chapter 4. Other Polks of Somerset

The preceding chapters have been concerned with the family of Robert and Magdalen Polke. In this chapter we turn to several other members of the Polk/Pollock family of Somerset who have not been adequately reported or understood in previous family histories. The most important of these was John Pelke [*sic*] who registered a cattle earmark in 1680. As it turns out, he was not a son of Robert and Madgdalen as previously believed. In addition, several other Polks appearing in Somerset records are not easy to place in the family tree of Robert and Magdalen Polke.

4.1 John Polkey of Locust Hummock (1651-1703)

Much confusion exists about this individual because he has not been recognized as a separate person from John, the oldest son of Robert and Magdalen. If for nothing else, he would be of interest simply for the number of spelling variations with which his name appears in the records. Here is a sampling:

1680	Cattle Earmarks: Pelke	
1682	Patent of Locust Hummock: Pelkee	
1697	Patent of Front of Locust Hummock: Pellkey, Pellikey	
1702	Somerset Judicials (1701-2): 208: Polkey	
1703	Inventory: Polkey	
1703	Will: Poalkey, Polkey	
1716	Sale of Locust Hummock & Front of Locust Hummock: Polke	
1734	Rent Rolls: Pelky, Pelliky	

We use the form "Polkey" here since despite all the variations the contemporary records seem to indicate rather consistently that the name was pronounced in that form, i.e. with a second syllable, assuming at least a rudimentary connection between the recorded spelling of the name and the phonetics of its pronunciation.

Whatever form of the name used, the essential point is that there were two distinct John Polks that appear in the records of Damned Quarter—one the eldest son of Robert and Magdalen, the other being John Polkey of Locust Hummock already present when Robert and Magdalen Polke of Donegal arrived in 1686-1687. They may have been related in some way, and the occurrence of such similar names in such a sparsely settled area along with other associating factors is hard to dismiss as pure coincidence, but there is no direct evidence to prove a relationship between them.

The existence of two distinct individuals, rather than one, only becomes apparent

149

when the full collection of Somerset records is taken into account which were not available to W. H. Polk while he was writing *Polk Family and Kinsmen*. This is clear both in the book itself and in some of his correspondence with R. C. Ballard Thruston.[1] We now know that these two were distinct from the Somerset probate records which show that John Polkey died with inventory dated 24 July 1703 and will probated on 24 May 1703 with wife Elizabeth as administratrix, while John Polke, son of Robert and Magdalen, died intestate in 1708 with an inventory dated 2 September 1708 and widow Johanna as administratrix.

The first certain appearance of John Polkey of Locust Hummock is found in 1680 when he recorded his cattle earmark in the Somerset land records:[2]

John Pelke his mark vizt Cropt of the Left ear recorded the 5th day of September Anno Dom 1680

However, as noted in Chapter 1, he may have also been one of the persons listed in Maryland Land Office records as accompanying Francis Roberts from Virginia to Somerset in 1672 and assigned a fifty-acre headright.[3] The record actually mentions a "John Pelton" but this is a 1726 transcription of the original document, now lost, and errors in transcribing were not unusual given the vagaries in clerks' handwriting. More to the point, there are factors which strongly support the identification of John "Pelton" with John Polkey, in particular the subsequent connections between John Polkey and the Francis Roberts group and the lack of any further mention of a John "Pelton" in the land, court, or probate records of Somerset. There is a record of "John Pelkee" in the Order Books of Northumberland County, Virginia, as an indentured servant adjudged to be aged fifteen in 1668.[4] Another connection is the jointly conducted surveys made by Francis Roberts and John "Pelkee" of nearly adjacent tracts in the southwest part of Damned Quarter on the same day, 10 September 1682, and entered together in the Maryland Land Office records.[5] Then there is the juxtaposition of Christopher Little's entry in the above-cited Somerset cattle earmark register immediately preceding that of John Pelke on the same date. Little was the only other male transportee listed with "Pelton" in the headrights registered by Francis Roberts in 1672. Finally, John Polkey, Christopher Little, and Francis Roberts all had specific connections with Robert and Magdalen Polke: Roberts married their daughter Anne, as recounted in Chapter 3; Christopher Little's orphan son, of the same name, was apprenticed to Robert and mentioned in his will; and John

---

[1] See, for example, letters of 28 Nov. 1874 and 7 Aug 1898, W. H. Polk Papers, Box 1, folder 1.

[2] SOLR B1:32.

[3] MDLP 17:33.

[4] Northumberland County Order Book, 1666-78, p. 40. In the transcription by Ruth and Sam Sparacio (The Antient Press, 1995), this is spelled "Pelker," but examination of the original document indicates the spelling could just have well have been "Pelkee."

[5] MDLP 22:79; tracts Jesimon and Roberts Recovery were surveyed for Roberts, and Locust Hummock for Pelkee.

Polkey's land was eventually conveyed to Ephraim Polk through William Kent. Taken together these connections seem more that coincidental and provide a fairly convincing case for identifying John Polkey of Damned Quarter with John Pelton, the transportee from Northumberland.

There is relatively little information about Polkey and his family. If he was the individual mentioned in the Northumberland records, then he was born c.1651. From Somerset probate records we know that he died in 1703 leaving a very modest estate and was married to a woman named Elizabeth. His will mentions his wife without naming her, but no children, although both the Rent Rolls and Somerset debt books refer to his property as held "by Francis Cradon in the right of the relict of Pelky and orphans."[6] The name of his wife, Elizabeth, is mentioned in the Testamentary Proceedings of the Maryland Prerogative Court, where his will was forwarded for recording.[7] There is no record of the number or names of his children, but it seems reasonable that one of them was a William Polk/Pollock of Damned Quarter, who will be further discussed below.

John Polkey's dwelling place, Locust Hummock, was located on the south side of the Damned Quarter peninsula and appears to have been almost an island to itself, surrounded by marshland as the name implies. A faint trace of this tract may still be seen in present-day topographic maps.[8] It was surveyed on 10 September 1692, beginning at a "marked stooping white oak standing on a humocke of woodland in marshes on waterside," and nominally containing fifty acres. The patent was issued in 1685 to "John Pelkee." About fifteen years later he added the tract, Front of Locust Hummock (seventy-five acres), which was located nearby but probably not contiguous with his first property. The record of ownership and care of Polkey's lands after his death is rather confusing since different persons are mentioned in the various records. His will leaves "the land to my wife [for] her life," but goes on to bequeath "Locust Hamock and the marsh facing to itt unto Wm. Kent and if he should die without issue then falling unto Lewis Jones and if he should [die] without issue then falling unto Eliz~ Moore". From the Somerset land records we know that William Kent sold the two properties to Ephraim Polk in 1716 and that Ephraim's oldest son, Charles, inherited them two years later, eventually selling them in 1764.[9] These transactions notwithstanding, it will also be noted that the Proprietary Rent Rolls (which were compiled in 1734 from older records) mention that Francis Craden held Locust Hummock in right of the "Relict of Pelky and Orphants," and that Front of Locust Hummock was "in the Poss'n of John Marvil." The Somerset Debt Book for 1738 mentions that Locust Hummock was held by Francis Craden "for Polk's orphans." These apparently conflicting citations may be referring to the interim period between Polkey's death and the conveyance to Ephraim Polk in 1716.

---

[6] MDRR 9:23; SODB 1738, p.24.
[7] MDTP 19a:210; 20:65. Elizabeth Polkey also appears in Somerset Court, 25 September, 1702; SOJR 1701-2: 208.
[8] Approximate location 38°9.9'N, 75°54.5'W.
[9] SOLR EF:20, C:230.

Polkey's only real neighbor was Charles Williams, who lived a bit to the north at Roberts Lot, a tract originally patented by Francis Roberts but sold to Williams in 1682. This was a long, north-south oriented property running between the upper and lower parts of the Damned Quarter peninsula. In the years that followed, this property and Williams himself proved to be a unifying connection between John Polkey and Robert and Magdalen Polke. Williams arrived in Maryland from Virginia at the same time as John Polkey and the Francis Roberts' group.[10] His daughters, Elizabeth and Ann, married two of Robert and Magdalen's sons, Ephraim and James, and he himself took their daughter, Margaret, by then twice widowed, as his own third wife, so his family connections with the Polks were close and multifaceted. These connections all coalesce in the warrant issued to Ephraim Polk on 15 March 1705(NS) for 871 acres, subsequently allocated among the following properties:

> Edwards Lott, 220 acres, surveyed for Anne (Polk) Roberts, 19 March 1704/5
> Charles Adventure, 140 acres, surveyed for Charles Williams, 28 March 1705
> Long Delay, 274 acres, surveyed for Ephraim Polk, 26 March 1705
> Marvells Chance, 27 acres, surveyed for John Marvell, 2 April 1705
> James Meadow, 200 acres, surveyed for James Polk, 1 June 1705

The noteworthy feature in this list is the assignment of twenty-seven acres to John Marvell for the survey Marvells Chance. This tract surrounds the top end of John Polkey's tract, Locust Hummock, and links it with Roberts Lot and other Damned Quarter tracts. The appearance of John Marvel in this list and the location of his property make it probable that he was related to Polkey by marriage, particularly in light of the mention in the Rent Rolls that Locust Hummock and Front of Locust Hummock was for a time in Marvel's possession. The later history and eventual fate of John Marvell is unknown to the author. It appears that he either died or left Somerset by the 1720s since he is not mentioned in the tax lists or land records.[11] Charles Polk is listed as the responsible rent payer for Marvells Chance in the 1734 and 1735 Somerset Debt Books, although there is no record that he ever purchased the tract.

Inventory of John Polkey [12]
An Inventory of the Goods and chattels of John Polkey late of Somerset County deceased taken this 24th of July Anno 1703 ~~

Imprs
26 head of cattle young and old all at ~~~~~~~~ *26.10.00*
12 head of Hoggs at ~~~~~~~ ~~~~~~~~~~~~ *03.00.00*

---

[10] Headrights for Charles Williams were asserted by William Jones of Monie, 12 May 1672; MDLP 17:30.
[11] See also Batchelder, p. 177; this suggests that John Marvell may have connected with the later Marvels of Georgetown DE.
[12] SORW EB14:293.

1 Feather Bed with Covering and 1 flock ditto ~ ~ ~ ~ ~	04.10.00
62 pounds of pot iron at 3d per lb ~ ~ ~ ~ ~ ~ ~ ~ ~ ~ ~	00.15.06
2 Pewter Dishes & 4 spoons & a parcel of earthen ware ~	00.10.00
1 Frying Pan and old Iron and other Lumber ~ ~ ~ ~ ~ ~	01.04.06
2 old Chests and one Gun all at ~ ~ ~ ~ ~ ~ ~ ~ ~ ~ ~ ~ ~	01.04.06
1 Box Iron and Heaters and 1 old sword ~ ~ ~ ~ ~ ~ ~ ~	00.07.06
	£38.01.06

John Jones (seal)
John Panter (seal)

Will of John Poalkey[13]

*IN THE NAME OF GOD AMEN I John Poalkey of Somerset County in the
Province of Maryland being sick and weak of body but of sound and perfect
sense and memory praised be God doe make this my last will and testament
in manner and form following ~ first I give and bequeath my Immortall soul
unto God that gave it, trusting through my blessed Lord and Saviour Jesus
Christ his merrits death and passion to obtain remission and absolution for
all my sins.*

*Item ~ I give my body to the earth from whence it came to be decently buried
according to the discretion of my Executor hereafter mentioned.*

*Item ~ as to my worldly goods which it has pleased the Lord to bestow upon
me I give as followeth after my funeral right and charges and all debts and
bequests paid likeways I give the land to my wife (for) her life. Item ~ I give
and bequeath unto Wm. Kent my plantation now dwelling upon called Locust
Hamock and the marsh facing to itt and if he should die without issue then
falling unto Lewis Jones and if he should (die) without issue then falling unto
Eliz~ Moore ~~*

Item ~ I give unto Elizabeth Moore two cowes and two cowes heffers

*Item ~ I give and bequeath unto Lewis Jones my guns. In witness where of I
doe hereof put my hand and (seal) this 20th day of December 1702*

	his
Signed sealed and delivered	*Jno **P** Poalky*
In presence of us	*Mark*
Jno White	
Jno Miller	*On the back side of the afsd will was this*
Geo Hutchins	*written (vizt)*
John Laws	*Md that this 24th day of May 1703*
	The within will proved by the oaths of
	JnoMiller George Hutchins and John Laws before me
	Peter Dent Depty Clerk

---

13 MDW 11:345.

4.2 Francis Roberts (1636-1703), Husband of Anne Polk

The travails of Francis Roberts have already been mentioned in Sections 1.3 and 3.1 and will not be repeated here. He was, of course, not a Polk himself but did marry Robert and Magdalen's oldest child, Anne, under a special arrangement that is recorded in the Somerset land records. This section is included mainly to catalog the many earlier actions relating to him in the records of Northumberland County, Virginia, and his land dealings in Somerset.

The following cases involving Francis Roberts are recorded in the Northumberland Order Books:

21 Jul 1662: Judgment for John Hughlet against Roberts for 2000 lbs/tbco; Roberts did not appear.

10 Dec 1663: Judgment for William Taylor against Roberts for 570 lbs/tbco, or a cow and calfe.

8 Mar 1664(NS): Suit of Richard Fielding against Roberts for 1134 lbs/tbco; Roberts acknowledges debt.

20 Apr 1664: Suit of Richard Flynt against Francis Roberts for 805 lbs/tbco; Roberts acknowledges debt.

20 Jan 1665(NS): Judgment for Lt. Colonel Samuel Smith against Roberts for 1100 lbs/tbco.

10 May 1666: Case of Francis Roberts against William Brereton dismissed; Roberts to pay 50 lbs/tbco for damages.

20 Jun 1666: *Whereas the Grand Jury have presented Mr. William Brereton for abusing Francis Roberts by saying that he bee a hogstealing rogue & could not prove it, it is ordered that the said Mr. William Brereton in open court declare that he hath done him wrong & is sorry for it & pay costs...*
Whereas the Grand Jury have presented Francis Roberts for committing a trespasse in hunting upon the lands of Capt. Thomas Brereton without license: it is ordered that the said Roberts make present satisfaction according to Act.

Dec 1667: *Whereas Elizabeth Tydwell by her Petition hath informed the Court that Francis Roberts hath gott her with child & turned her out of doors, it is ordered that Hugh Fouch shall bee satisfyed for his trouble in entertayninge of her until the next Court by the said Roberts, or Elizabeth, as the Court shall then think fitt.*

17 Feb 1668(NS): *Whereas Alice Arnold servant to Francis Roberts hath had a bastard childe in the time of her servitude it is ordered that she make her sd. Mistress satisfaccon by service according to Act.*

10 Mar 1669(NS): Suit of Mr. William Lloyd against Francis Roberts for 3000 lbs/tbco; Roberts acknowledges debt.

20 Feb 1670(NS): Suit of Francis Roberts against Daniel Holland for 1000 lbs/tbco; Court finds for Roberts; attachment given to Sheriff returnable at next court.

25 Jan 1671(NS): Judgment granted William Morgan, assignee of William

Keynes, against Francis Roberts for payment of 379 lbs/tbco plus costs.

24 Feb 1671(NS): Judgment granted James Austen against Fr. Roberts for 1000 lbs/tbco for payment of bill dated 18 May 1669.

19 Jul 1671: *Whereas on 7 October last it was ordered that Joseph Fielding should not entertayne the wife of Francis Roberts & yet notwithstanding in contempt of the sd order he hath the wife of the sd Roberts above one night (without the consent of her Husband), that he pay the Fine of 2000 lbs/tbco & caske. And if hereafter it shall appear that Fran. Roberts doth unlawfully beat or abuse his sd. Wife it is ordered that he also pay the fine of two thousand pounds of tobacco & caske.*
Whereas Eliz. The wife of Joseph Fielding hath carried herself contemptuously & uncivilly towards the Cort & openly did declare that she would not yield obedience to their order it is ordered that the Sheriffe forthwith take the sd,. Elizabeth & convey her to Prison, there to be kept without Bayle or Main Prise until Order for her release be sent under the hands of at least three of his Majesties Justices of the peace for this County.

15 Nov 1671: Judgment for Richard Austen against Roberts in amount of 350 lbs/tbco, plus costs, payment to Austen for teaching Roberts' children.

15 Nov 1671: Judgment for Thomas Humphreys against Roberts for 400 lbs/tbco plus costs.

20 Dec 1671: *Ordered that Elinor, the bastard Childe of Francis Roberts, serve Edw. Jones or his assignees until she be eighteen yeares of age."*

16 Sept 1672: *Certificate is granted Fran. Roberts for the taking up the run away Servants belonging to Capt. Lightfoot, according to Act.*

20 Feb 1673(NS): *Whereas Joseph Fielding obteyned Judgmnt. against John Read for two hundred eight and two pounds of tobaccoe and caske with costs, being the value of some clothes belonging to Jno. Winser & by ye sd. Fielding attached into the hands the sd. Read & by him delivered unto Francis Roberts who engaged to save the sd. Read harmelesse. An Attachmt. is awarded the sd. Read against the estate of the sd. Roberts for the summe retorneable at the next Cort.*

21 May 1673: *Whereas it appears to this Court that Fran. Roberts standeth indebted unto Mr. James Gaylard the summe of five hundred pounds of tobaccoe & caske, & is departed this Colony, an attachmt. is awarded the sd. Mr. Gaylard against the estate of the sd. Roberts for the sd. Summe with costs retorneable to the next Court.*

Note in the next to last item that the attachment was made against the "estate" of Roberts. Of course, Roberts had not died but had simply fled the Province as the final entry makes clear.

Turning to Somerset, as already mentioned, Francis Roberts engaged in extensive land dealings in his new county of residence, principally in Damned Quarter. The following is a compilation of his Somerset land transactions prior to the arrival of Robert and Magdalen Polke:

29 Sep 1668	Taunton Deane (300A), purchased from William Thorne, price not listed
11 Mar 1672(NS)	Davids Destiny (350A), purchased from Thomas Kendall, 3500 lbs/tbco
20 June 1671	Taunton Deane (300A), sold to Benjamin Cottman
6 June 1672	Headrights for 550 acres, proven on record at land office
13 Aug 1672	Headrights for 300 acres, assigned to William Keine
18 Nov 1673	Davids Destiny (50A), sold to Alexander Draper, 8000 lbs/tbco
18 Dec 1673	Lott (1000A), purchased from William Thorne, 14,000 lbs/tbco
24 Mar 1674(NS)	Second Purchase (250A), surveyed for Roberts
9 Jun 1674	Lotts Wife (108A parcel of Lott), sold to William Wright, 5000 lbs/tbco
28 Aug 1675	The Downs (100A), surveyed for Roberts
18 Apr 1676	Elliotts Choice (200A), purchased from Alexander Draper, 8000 lbs/tbco
18 Apr 1676	Davids Destiny (350A), purchased from Alexander Draper, 9000 lbs/tbco
1 Feb 1679(NS)	Lott (892A parcel), sold to Edward Gibb, 30,000 lbs/tbco
1 Feb 1679(NS)	Second Purchase (250A), sold to Edward Gibb 10,000 lbs/tbco
27 Aug 1679	Roberts Lot (100A), surveyed for Roberts, assigned to Charles Williams
9 Mar 1683(NS)	Lott (892A parcel), purchased from Edward Gibb, 30,000 lbs/tbco
10 Sep 1682	Jeshimon (150A), surveyed for Roberts
10 Sep 1682	Roberts Recovery (100A), surveyed for Roberts
17 Nov 1683	Biters Bit (100A parcel of Davids Destiny), sold to Christopher Little, 3000 lbs/tbco
17 Nov 1683	Rowland Ridge (100A parcel of Elliotts Choice), sold to Samuel Jones 2000 lbs/tbco
17 Nov 1683	Lott (892A parcel), sold to William Harris Jr. (grandson), 5000 lbs/tbco
26 Apr 1684	The Downs (100A), sold to Henry Leaton, 2000 lbs/tbco

At some point Francis Roberts took up residence permanently at Elliotts Choice alongside Williamsons Creek, as we know from later land commission records,[14] and lived in a dwelling later referred to as a "Fort House." His wife Rosamond must have died shortly after their arrival since she is not mentioned in the sale of Davids Destiny in November 1673 or any of Francis Roberts' other land sales. (The usual practice in land conveyances at this time was to include the grantor's wife in the deed to ensure the property was not encumbered with residual dower rights. Wives were not mentioned in purchases. Rosamond Roberts was mentioned, for example, as the wife of Francis Roberts in the sale of Taunton

---

[14] SOLC 1717-21: 123, and SOJR 1730-33:8.

Deane in 1671, but not in its 1668 purchase.) Some accounts claim that Francis Roberts took Rachel Grandee as a second wife at this time,[15] but there is really no basis for claiming that they were formally married. If they had been, Rachel would have been mentioned as his wife in at least some of the seven land sales that Francis Roberts transacted between 1673 and 1684. In fact, Rachel was brought into September Court 1676 for bastardy as appears in the following record:[16]

> *In y Lord Prop^{ty} Sute ag^t: Rachell Grounde for bearing a Bastard Childe ~*
> *The Said Rachell Ground appeares before y board & acknowledgeth her*
> *fact:*
> *And thereupon this Co^{rt}: orders that for her fact the said Rachell Grounde*
> *Shall give in Sufficient Security for an able man with meat & Drinck to pay*
> *twenty five Days work in makeing of a bridge over y Deviding Creeke*
> *William Stevens planter appeares before y board & ingageth to See y Same*
> *prformed ~ ~ ~ ~ ~ ~ ~ ~ ~ ~*

There is no mention of Francis Roberts as father in this case but there was undeniably a son born of the couple during this period who was given the name John. There are many records of him to be found in later tax, land, and probate records of Somerset, but his dubious status is apparent in the ambivalent use of the surname Roberts and Grandee/Grundy to identify him. This ambiguity persisted even to the next generation where as late as 1773 John's son Rencher refers to himself in his own will as "Roberts alias Grandee."[17] His widow is identified in his inventory as "Mary Roberd Grande."

When Roberts died he left an estate which was inventoried rather modestly at £79/4/0. The principal items of value were a servant boy, five feather beds, twenty head of cattle, and twelve hogs.[18]

4.3 John Polk/Pollock of Manokin (c.1723—?)

This individual, whom we shall refer to as John Polk of Manokin, had a strong association with the family of William Polk, second son of Robert and Magdalen, but there is no clear proof of a specific relationship. In the author's opinion, it is most likely that he was a son of William Polk's oldest son, James, although there is no record that James had a son of that name. In particular, there is no son John mentioned in James Polk's will written in 1771. By that time, John Polk of Manokin had long since departed the Somerset area for the Carolinas and may well have left with an understanding that he would have no future inheritance in

---

[15] Batchelder, p. 221; also Roberts.
[16] SOJR 1675-77:54.
[17] MDW 39:522. Rencher Roberts' name was taken from his mother Mary Rencher, daughter of John Rencher Sen. (d. 1711).
[18] MDIA 24:97.

Somerset. Or he may have simply predeceased his father without issue. In any case, we must leave his exact connection and ultimate fate as open questions for now.

It might also be conjectured that John Polk of Manokin was a son of David, the second son of William Polk, but this is less likely based on the account of David Polk's family and descendants written by his grandson, Josiah F. Polk (see Appendix II). Josiah's account is very specific about the children of David Polk, and if there were a son John among them he would have been Josiah's uncle, so Josiah would certainly have been aware of him. Although Josiah also describes James Polk's family without mentioning a son named John, his knowledge of James's descendants is far less authoritative. In fact, he only mentions three of James's children, although there were at least eight, so we may safely assume his knowledge of that line was imperfect.

The appearances of John Polk of Manokin in the tax lists of Somerset are as follows:

1740	Not listed	
1741	No tax lists	
1742	No tax lists	
1743	Annemessex	Dependent, household of Thomas Lister
1744	Annemessex	Dependant, household of Thomas Lister
1745	Not listed	
1746	Not listed	
1747	Annemessex	Head of household, no dependents
1748	Annemessex	Head of household, no dependents
1749	Manokin	Head of household, no dependents
1750	Manokin	Head of household, dependent Edmund Willis
1751	Manokin	Head of household, dependents Edmund Willis, George Scott
1752	Manokin	Head of household, dependents Edmund Willis, Bailey Matthews
1753	Manokin	Head of household, dependents Edmund Willis, Bailey Matthews
1754	Manokin	Head of household, dependent Bailey Matthews
1755	No tax lists	
1756	Not listed	
1757	No tax lists	
1758	No tax lists	
1759+	Not listed	

Bailey Matthews was an orphan who was bound to John Polk in 1751 as an apprentice to learn the trade of a wheelwright.[19] This record specifically identifies

_____

[19] SOJR 1750-53:51.

John Polk as a wheelwright, which is also confirmed in the Somerset Debt Books.[20]

The appearances of John Polk in the Annemessex Hundred place him in close proximity to the household of Capt. John Williams, who was the husband of James Polk's sister, Elizabeth. Williams lived in the northeast corner of Annemessex, about five miles south of Princess Anne where James Polk lived. If John were a son of James Polk as we conjecture, this may have been an arrangement for him to learn a wheelwright's trade from Thomas Lister who lived nearby. Benjamin Cottman, father of James' wife, Elizabeth, also maintained a residence in that area in addition to his property on Wicomico Creek in Manokin; his appearances on the Somerset tax lists alternated between the two hundreds.

When John Polk relocated to the Manokin Hundred in 1749, it most likely coincided with his marriage to Ellen (Erin/Ella) Gray, the widow of John McGrain, which occurred at about that same time.[21] Ellen was the daughter of John Gray and sister of Allen Gray, who lived for some years in the household of William Polk (d.1739).[22] She was bequeathed a tract Come by Chance (150 acres) in her father's will, written 25 December 25 1748 and probated a month later.[23] This tract was located just northeast of Princess Anne. John Polk (Pollock) resurveyed and expanded the tract in July 1750 under the name Labour in Vain, so clearly he and Ellen had married in the interim.[24] Their marriage probably occurred at Manokin Presbyterian Church, but the church records for that era no longer exist so we do not have a more exact date.

John Polk of Manokin appeared frequently in the Somerset Courts during the period 1750 -1756, mostly as a member of the grand or petit jury. His conjectural father and uncle, James and David Polk, had similar appearances often on the same juries. His last citation in the court records was as a defendant in a defamation of character suit brought against him by a Rebecca Whittingham in June 1756, which he lost and was made to pay £4 in damages. Whether because of this, or for entirely unrelated reasons, John Polk/Pollock departed the area soon afterwards. By October 1756, John "Pollock" and wife Ella were said to be "now of Carolina" in their deed conveying Labour in Vain to John Done.[25] This is the last mention of either that the author has located in Maryland records.

---

[20] SODB, 1755:131.
[21] See MDI 28:442 and MDA 20:372 for inventory and account of John McGrain, 1744.
[22] Allen Gray was cited in William Polk's will, leading W. H. Polk to conclude that William had taken Allen's mother, presumed to be a widow, as a second wife. This is clearly incorrect since Allen's father outlived William Polk.
[23] MDW 25:523; MDI 41:412. John Gray's inventory was valued at £597/11/7½, approved by Allen Gray and John Pollock on 3 October 1749.
[24] MDLP BS&GY#4:60.
[25] SOLR Liber B:143. John Done married a granddaughter of David Polk and became a judge of the Circuit Court.

4.4 William Polk/Pollock of Damned Quarter (c.1690—?)

****

Signature of William Polk from will of Samuel Jones, 1719

****

From Somerset records, it is clear that there was an individual named William Polk or Pollock, not a son of Robert and Magdalen, who lived in Damned Quarter, was an adult by about 1715, if not earlier, and appears in the Monie Hundred tax lists records during 1725-1728. No further record of him has been found after that date. In the author's opinion, he was probably the son of John Polkey of Locust Hummock discussed in Section 4.1 above, but this is by no means certain.

The first unambiguous record of this individual is as a witness or testator to the will of Samuel Jones of Damned Quarter, written in October 1719.[26] His signature is bold and well-formed in comparison with many other signatures found in contemporary records and is distinctly different from that of William Polk of Manokin, second son of Robert and Magdalen.[27] This same individual signed as a witness to the will of James Polk, son of Robert and Magdalen, in November 1726; the handscript of the signature is definitely the same as that appearing on Samuel Jones's will. It is these two signatures and the appearance of William Polk/Pollock on the Monie Hundred tax lists of 1725-28 that clearly establish this person as an inhabitant of Damned Quarter.

Beyond these, the factual evidence relating to William Polk of Damned Quarter is very sparse. Only four other citations in Somerset records have been located which might be identified with him and which are somewhat questionable since they could be referring to William Polk of Manokin, second son of Robert and Magdalen. The first of these is in William Kent's sale of the tracts Locust Hummock and Front of Locust Hummock, which he inherited from John Polkey, to Ephraim Polk.[28] Kent, described as being from St. Jones (now Kent) County,

---

[26] MDW 15:321.

[27] The author has found five separate examples of the signature of William Polk of Manokin in documents at MSA; they are consistently written, and distinctly different from that of the William Polk discussed in this section. The documents are the wills of William Porter (1695) and William Owens (1698), and assignments of property rights for tracts Goshen (1721), Charles Purchase (1721), and 64 acres on Shipways Branch (1723). His original will also is on file, but that was written shortly before his death and only a mark, not his signature, is inscribed.

[28] SOLR EF:19.

in the territories of Pennsylvania (Delaware), appointed "my good friend William Polke" as his attorney for this sale. This power of attorney was witnessed by "William Polke" and "Joseph Polke." We cannot be certain which of the two William Polks of Somerset was the one designated here by Kent, since only the recorded text in the land records exists, not the original deed, and there is no way to distinguish between the two based on the signature.

The second citation is in the Proprietary Rent Rolls entry for Long Delay, the tract originally patented by Ephraim Pollock in 1705.[29] Long Delay is located at the far end of the Damned Quarter peninsula adjacent to Ephraim Polk's other tract Golden Quarter. The Rent Roll record states that the property was possessed by "Wm. Pollock to whom it was assigned." Since the tract was later (1739) sold by Ephraim's oldest son Charles Pollock, it appears that the term "possession" here does not mean ownership, but stewardship, probably for an interim period after Ephraim's death when Charles was still a minor.

Finally, William Pollock also appears in the Somerset Debt Books in connection with the tract Long Delay, both in 1733 (the first existing Debt Book) and in 1738 where the annotation "denied" is entered. The tract was sold in 1739 by Charles Polk.

All of these records pertain to properties in Damned Quarter, so it seems more probable that they refer to William Polk of Damned Quarter rather than Manokin. Moreover, the intersecting relationship between Ephraim and William Polk exhibited in these two records seems to echo Ephraim's 1705 warrant for 781 acres, part of which was used to survey Long Delay and part of which was assigned to John Marvel to survey the lands surrounding the north end of John Polkey's Locust Hummock. In this light, it would be quite consistent to suppose that William was a son of John Polkey, and John Marvel was related to them by marriage as already suggested in Section 4.1. This is admittedly speculative and unproven, but the recurring connections between John Polkey, William Polke, and Ephraim Polk in the miniscule community of Damned Quarter seem to betoken more than simple coincidence. It is unfortunate that no further records have been located to help clarify their formal relationships.

Little more can be said of William Polk at this time. His final appearance in Somerset or Maryland records known to the author was as a taxable in the household of John Waller of Monie in 1728. There are no known probate records from Somerset or the Maryland Prerogative Court that can be associated with this William Polk. It is possible that he simply died in Somerset around 1728-29, leaving no legatees or probate records. It might be conjectured that he was the same William Pollock who purchased the tract Moyn in Cecil County in 1727 and that we have described as progenitor of the North Carolina Polk family, but there seems little reason for a person purchasing land in Cecil County in 1727 to be

---

[29] MDRR 9:212.

carried as a taxable in a Somerset household in 1727 and 1728.

4.5 Miscellaneous

The following individuals appear in Somerset records as indicated, but have no known connection to the other members of the Polk/Pollock family already described. In most cases these can probably be explained simply as an error in the entry made by the recording clerk.

~~~~~~~

Rosanna Polke -- listed in cattle earmark registry, 24 December 1709; Somerset Land Records Vol. 11 (IKL). This is probably a misspelling for Rosanna Pope, who was listed in the same volume as daughter of Robert Pope, born on 30 June 1678. It might also be a misspelling for Johanna, widow of John Polk.

~~~~~~~

King Poke -- listed in cattle earmark registry, 5 March 1712 (NS); Somerset Land Records Vol. 11 (IKL). Most likely this should be King Poole, who was listed in the same volume as the son of Thomas and Elizabeth Poole, born on 3 November 1678.

~~~~~~~

Matthew Polk -- listed among persons making payments to the estate of Francis Roberts, 12 July 1712. This individual appears in no other record located by the author. It is suspected that this entry is simply a mistake for Matthew Wallace who lived in the area. Otherwise it would seem likely that Matthew Polk is one of the unnamed children mentioned in the probate records of John Pelkey.[30]

~~~~~~~

Dicklo Poack -- appears as defendant in court case brought by Seamore More; Somerset Judicials 1713-15:143. There is no other known appearance of this individual.

~~~~~~~

Edward Polk -- gives evidence concerning tracts Elliotts Choice et al., date not recorded, but sometime in 1720; Somerset Land Commissions, 1717-21:124. The author suspects this was actually Edward Roberts, son of Francis Roberts and

---

[30] MDIA 33A:220; 16 July 1712.

Anne Polk. Several other Polks gave evidence in the same case.

~~~~~~~~~~

Henry Polk -- Henry Polk listed as a surety on account of Thomas Tull, 1760. Somerset Judicials, 1760-63:47. This could not have been Henry Polk, son of James Polk, since that individual died in Queen Anne's County in 1757.

5. The Polk Ancestral Home, White Hall

"My ancestor, Robert Bruce Pollock, came from the North of Ireland about the year 1660 and settled in Somerset County on the Eastern Shore of Maryland having received a grant of land from the King of England. From some cause or other the place was known as "Polk's Folly". Why it was so called no one seems to know—perhaps they went to unnecessary expense for those times when the stability of government was insecure owing to various causes, notably the constant threat of Indian outrages in that section, the Nanticokes just there being a most savage tribe. Robert Bruce Pollock moved from these lands, which were situated upon the Manokin River—beautiful tributary of the Chesapeake Bay to lands purchased by him on the Wicomico River—another beautiful stream, arm of the Chesapeake Bay. This place was named "White Hall", and it was there that Judge David Polk, grandson of Robert Bruce Pollock, and grandfather of my Father, and my great grandfather, was born, lived and died."

"Memories", 1913, Esther Winder Polk Lowe (1824-1918) [1]

The Polk ancestral home "White Hall" is thus permanently recorded in the memoirs of one of Robert Polke's more prominent descendants, Esther Winder Polk, the wife of Governor Enoch Louis Lowe of Maryland. It is also frequently referenced as the family "ancestral home" in standard histories of the Polk family by Mary Winder Garrett, William H. Polk, and Mrs. Frank M. Angellotti, as well as other sources.[2]

But where is White Hall? One would expect that the ancestral home of the Polk family in America would be well known and recognized. Surprisingly this is not the case and the answer to this simple question is not at all straightforward. There has been considerable confusion and misunderstanding about its location and authenticity. White Hall is in fact something of a myth. Not that it did not exist—in fact there have been two Polk Houses of that name, which only adds to the confusion. The myth is in the claimed antiquity—that it dates back to the time of Robert and Magdalen Polke. In this Esther Lowe and others were quite mistaken, as the Somerset County land records conclusively show. The tradition of White Hall as the original home of the Polk family began in later generations and was

---

[1] A handwritten transciprtion of Esther Winder Polk Lowe's memoirs, entitled "Memories," and identified as MS 1949, is archived in the Special Collections of the Maryland Historical Society in Baltimore. The author's transcription of the full text is included in Appendix IV of this work.

[2] With the publication of Mary Winder Garrett's articles in 1896-99 Robert Polke became known as Captain Robert Bruce Pollock, but there is nothing in colonial era records to support either the title or the middle name. As noted in Chapter 2, Robert is cited nearly fifty times in the Somerset colonial records, the great majority with the spelling "Polke". The title "Captain" and the middle name "Bruce" never occur.

accepted as fact in the principal Polk family histories, whose authors did not have such ready access to the land records as we do today.

5.1 The Tradition of White Hall

The tradition of White Hall as the family ancestral home is firmly asserted in the three standard references on Polk family history: Mary Winder Garrett's articles that appeared in *The American Historical Magazine*, 1896-99; W.H. Polk's *Polk Family and Kinsmen* (1912); and Mrs. Frank Angellotti's "The Polks of North Carolina and Tennessee," (1923-4), a series of articles appearing in the *New England Historical and Genealogical Register*, now published in book form.

Mary Winder Garrett's work was the earliest of these three references and was used by the others. She mentions White Hall a number of times, as in Vol. I, No. 3, p. 263, "William Polk, the second son of Robert Bruce Polk, or Pollok, and Magdaline his wife, inherited 'White Hall,' the home place in Somerset County, Maryland ....William Polk had two sons, David Polk and James Polk. David Polk inherited 'White Hall' from his father .... Judge William Polk, son of Judge David Polk, married the widow of Henry Dennis ... their son was Col. James Polk who .... inherited the family estate 'White Hall.'" (Col. James was the father of Esther Lowe quoted above.) This account is repeated again in Volume II, No. 3. Miss Garrett, who was not actually a Polk descendant and did not live in Maryland, got her information about White Hall from Winder family relatives in Somerset. Apparently the antiquity of the house had been enhanced somewhat in the family lore over the years, and the memory of its actual age lost.

In *Polk Family and Kinsmen* W. H. Polk states (p. 204) that "under the then existing law of primogeniture, and being the oldest son of Magdalen at her death in 1727, William inherited the manor plantation 'White Hall,' making it thereafter his regular abiding place, and at his death in 1740 it descended to his eldest son, Judge David Polk." He further states (p. 58) "Magdalen Polk is said to have lived to be over ninety years old, dying at her home place 'White Hall,' in Somerset County."

Mrs. Angellotti, whose work is an excellent source of information on the Polk family in the South, relied entirely on these earlier works for the Somerset portion of her history. Concerning White Hall, in "The Polks of North Carolina and Tennessee" she states that William Polk, son of Robert the immigrant "lived at the old family home, 'White Hall,' on the Eastern Shore of Maryland" and further, that William's son David "lived at 'White Hall,' the old homestead of his father and grandfather."

In what follows, the actual history of White Hall and its antecedents will be retraced, working in reverse chronology. Although White Hall was a significant home of the Polk family in Somerset (now Wicomico) County, Maryland, with an important early history of its own, the record will clearly show that it did not trace back to Robert and Magdalen Polke.

5.2 The 1794 Patent for White Hall

On 18 November 1795 Judge William Polk was granted a patent by the Land Office of the State of Maryland for the 897 acre tract "White Hall"[3] lying alongside the Wicomico River in then Somerset, now Wicomico County. See Figure 18. The patent was actually a resurvey comprising seven existing tracts that William, his brother Josiah, and father David Polk had acquired over a period of years beginning in 1741; these were Fortune, Hoggs Down, Come by Chance, Uniack's Chance, Addition, Buttocking Ridge, and Crusty. Of these, Fortune was the most important as it was the seminal purchase by David Polk, lay alongside the Wicomico, and was the actual site of his dwelling place that came to be known as White Hall. This tract had earlier passed from David to his eldest son, Josiah, who died without issue in 1784 and bequeathed it to William along with his other holdings in the area.

To tidy up the records and acquire some remaining vacant land William decided to combine all his holdings into a single tract. A resurvey of this property was carried out and formally recorded by the Somerset County Surveyor, his brother James Polk, on 14 March 1794 using the name White Hall. Just why William chose this name and whether it was a carryover from earlier usage is not known at this time, but it was the first occurrence of the name White Hall in the Somerset records as far as the author is aware. In any case, it is certainly the White Hall that William's granddaughter, Esther Lowe, described in her memoirs, for its pedigree is clear originating as Fortune with Judge David Polk, passing to his son Josiah, to Josiah's brother William, and in 1812 to William's son James, when he was only eighteen. James Polk (later Colonel James Polk, naval officer of the port of Baltimore) married Anna Maria Stuart in 1817, and they soon decided to move to Princess Anne where for a while he was Register of Wills. Esther was born to them in 1824 and grew up in Princess Anne but her memoirs indicate that she was frequently at White Hall and knew it well. Clearly, the tradition of White Hall as the Polk ancestral home was strongly established in her generation which included her cousin Colonel William Winder, one of the primary sources of W. H. Polk's information about Polk family history in Somerset County, as explained in his introduction. Miss Garrett obtained much of her information on the Polk family from the Colonel Winder's papers and other contact with the family. With the publication of her work and W. H. Polk's book, the White Hall tradition became the accepted account of the family history.

---

[3] MDLP IC#K: 410

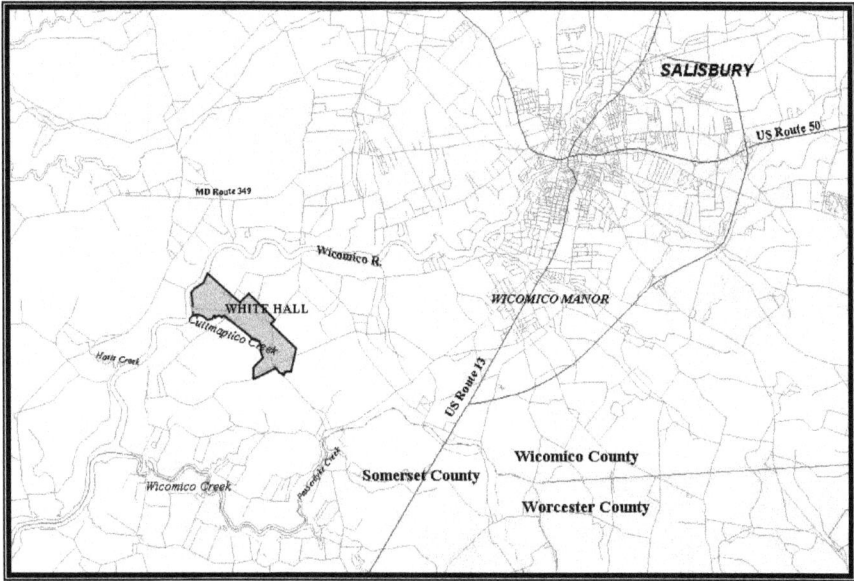

Figure 18. Location of the White Hall tract surveyed in 1794.

White Hall was sold by James Polk to his second cousin Samuel Polk and Lee Harcum in 1822. The major part of the lands passed on to the Harcum family which owned it for many years until quite recent times. Their family burial plot is prominently marked by a small grove of cedars along the entrance road. Lee Harcum was married to Samuel Polk's sister Elizabeth, so the land was actually still in the Polk family, but it became known as the Harcum Farm and its earlier identification as White Hall was largely forgotten. At some point the original colonial house of David Polk burned down and was afterwards replaced by a farm house of conventional 19th century architecture. See Figure 19.

Figure 19. Harcum family farm, site of White Hall (courtesy of Mrs. Jane Bailey).

5.3 David Polk and the 1744 Patent for Fortune

David Polk (c.1705-1778) was the second son of William Polk, the second son of Robert and Magdalen. As a youth David lived with his father in the Manokin Hundred to the northeast of present-day Princess Anne, learned the management of a plantation, and was active as a surveyor. Beginning in 1734 he is no longer listed as a taxable in the house of his father in the Manokin Hundred, but appears as head of a separate household in the Wicomico Hundred.[4] There were no records of any land purchases by him at this time and it may be presumed that he took up residence somewhere on his father's land tracts Roxborough, Tameroons Ridge, and Come by Chance, which were formally conveyed to him in a deed recorded in 1738. These tracts are not far from William's dwelling plantation to the east of Princess Anne, but were in the Wicomico, not Manokin, Hundred. As far as the subsequent tax lists reflect, David remained in the Wicomico Hundred for the balance of his life. His move to the later site of White Hall did not take him into a different Hundred.

---

[4] Russo.

On 1 June 1741, David purchased 75 acres of land at the north end of the tract Little Belean,[5] along the Wicomico at the mouth of Cuttmaptico Creek, from the daughters of John Watts, the son-in-law and legatee of John Winder Jr. This acquisition was a shrewd move for it provided the basis for a resurvey that he immediately filed to obtain patent for a larger tract, which he called Fortune, which incorporated 230 acres of adjacent vacant (unclaimed) land between the tracts Little Belean to the south and Hoggs Down to the north. Perhaps David had realized the actual configuration of these adjacent land tracts from his surveying activities and perceived the opportunity to obtain some unclaimed lands. The request for resurvey was challenged in court by Thomas Goslee, owner of the adjacent tract Hoggs Down, who apparently thought his lower boundary at Southerns Gutt was actually located at Cuttmaptico Creek. The suit was heard and rejected in the March Court of 1743 [6] and patent for Fortune was granted to David Polk on 1 June 1744—the first and largest piece of what would in due course become White Hall. He apparently moved there and established Fortune as his dwelling place by March 1743/4 when a line in the Somerset Judicials speaks of David Polk's plantation in Manokin as land "that he used to live on." [7]

In the 1740s and 1750s David Polk was very active in the Somerset court, appearing many times as a juror, frequently as foreman. By 1763 his stature in the community was such that he was appointed one of the Somerset Justices and served in the position through August 1765. All of this courthouse experience gave him enough on-the-job training to parlay the activity into a profession and he was formally recognized as an attorney-at-law by the Somerset court in the November 1770 session.[8] He died in 1778 and left Fortune and several other land tracts to his bachelor son Josiah Polk, a practicing attorney.

5.4 Earlier History of Fortune

When Somerset County was created in 1666, its first inhabitants were mostly disgruntled settlers from nearby Accomac County, Virginia, who had frequent quarrels with the Virginia government. The Act of Religious Toleration passed by the Maryland Assembly in 1649 strongly appealed to members of non-conforming faiths such as the Quakers of Accomac. After the restoration of the monarchy in 1660 the establishment church in Virginia began enforcing oppressive religious policies which alienated the Quakers, and they gladly responded to Lord Baltimore's invitation in 1661 to resettle in his lands immediately to their north. This gave him exactly what he needed most—loyal subjects to establish clear ownership of the lands at the boundaries of his Province. They arrived already well motivated to defend the border from any incursions by the Royal colony to

---

[5] SOLR MF: 235.
[6] SOJR 1742-45:83. See Appendix 4.
[7] SOJR 1742-45:203.
[8] SOJR 1769-72:167.

the South from which they had just departed.

Besides these Quakers there was a smattering of other pioneers attracted to Lord Baltimore's province looking as always for cheap and fertile land. John Winder, originally of Nansemond County, Virginia, was one of the earliest arrivals to Somerset and one of its founding fathers. He was among the Commissioners of the Peace to whom the Charter establishing Somerset as a county in August 1666 was directed, and he continued to serve actively throughout his life as a commissioner, magistrate and as an officer in the militia. In 1687 a major treaty meeting with the "Great Men of the Nanticoke Indians" was held at John Winder's house with Colonel William Stevens representing the Provincial government.[9] Clearly he was recognized as one of the preeminent leaders of the county.

John Winder acquired two land tracts in 1666, Winders Choice (200 acres) on Back Creek off the Manokin and Kickotans Choice (300 acres) on the north side of Wicomico River across from what is now Cuttmaptico Creek. He appears to have settled on the Wicomico property and acquired the two adjacent tracts, Wittys Invention and Whittys Later Invention from Richard Whitty in 1672. In 1694 he acquired 1000 acres of the tract Little Belean on the directly opposite (south) side of the Wicomico but afterwards sold off most of this tract, retaining the 75-acre parcel of Little Belean lying on the north side of Cuttmaptico Creek. Apparently this was of special importance to him and his residence was in this area; as Torrence says, he "settled on a plantation on the South side of the Wicomico River and north Side of Cuttymoctico Creek. This .... continued to be Winder's home through the remainder of his life."[10] It was willed to his son John Winder Jr after Winder's death in 1698 and later passed to John Watts, the son-in-law and legatee of John Winder Jr.

5.5 William Polk

It was not long after Robert Polke had established himself in Damned Quarter that his oldest sons moved to their own plantations. John purchased a 150-acre parcel of Smiths Recovery in 1692 and gave it the name Ballindret. William purchased a tract called Golden Quarter in 1697 located "back in the woods" from the head of the Manokin River, about two miles northeast of present-day Princess Anne, about 15 miles by direct line from his father's lands in the "Damned Quarter," a considerable distance in those days. William was a cooper as already noted and in time prospered sufficiently that he acquired numerous additional tracts of land in this area as already recorded in Chapter 3. He was well established at the time of his father's death in 1703 and remained at his Manokin home for the balance of his life. It has been said that William Polk inherited White Hall but Robert Polke in fact bequeathed nothing more than "twelve pence" to his sons William

---

[9] Torrence, p. 332.
[10] Op. cit.

and John exactly because they were well established. Robert left his "now dwelling place" to wife Magdalen. This was a standard phrase in wills of that time and should not be taken to imply that he had moved from elsewhere. Magdalen Polk later appears in the Somerset Rent Rolls and Debt Books as owner of Polks Folly and Polks Lott. There is no mention of anything called "White Hall" either in Robert's will or afterwards in Magdalen's or any of his children's possessions This is of course because there was no such tract.

5.6 The Polk Burial Site

White Hall was well located along the east side of the Wicomico just above Cuttmaptico Creek with a lovely westward view of the broad meandering river and marshland on the opposite side. Immediately on the north side of the point of confluence about 100 yards from the home site there is a unique feature, a small, slightly elevated and wooded knoll in an otherwise flat topography. This knoll is basically an aggregation of sand, and its formation might be the long-term result of depositions from wind currents as they are redirected by the large bend of the river occurring at that location. In any case, with a strategic view of the river in an otherwise uniform landscape it was apparently considered by the native Nanticoke Indians as a special site and used by them as a meeting place. In the Harcum family, which lived here in more recent times, there was a long-standing belief that this was an Indian burial site. Actually the Indians normally did not bury their dead but left the remains in above ground repose, sometimes in *quiocosin* huts. [11]

On the other hand, this site may well be a burial ground for the Polks who lived here in the eighteenth and early nineteenth century, including its first owner David Polk. Such a site certainly existed, for notes of Mr. George B. Fitzgerald, late of Princess Anne, comprised of entries from Polk bibles and other sources includes the information that Euphemia Ann Polk and Littleton Purnell Dennis Polk, two of the children of James and Annemarie Polk that died in infancy (in 1818 and 1821), are "buried in the family burying ground at White Hall." [12] The shaded knoll that overlooks the juncture of the Wicomico and Cuttmaptico would seem a natural location for this in the otherwise mostly cultivated area.

This is further confirmed by unpublished notes about the Polk family written by Elmer F. Rouark, former Mayor of Salisbury, in which the following remark is made: [13] "An elevation on the bank of the river is said to be the site of the old Polk family burying ground where Judge (William) Polk is buried. However, no tombstones mark the graves and it is impossible to determine what members of

[11] Rountree, p. :134.
[12] Provided to the author by Mr. Richard H. Pollock, former President of Clan Pollock, from his private correspondence with Mr. Fitzgerald.
[13] Obtained by the author from the Nabb Research Center for Delmarva History and Culture, Salisbury, Maryland.

the family are buried there."

About 1980 a summer house was constructed in this location by Mr. Wilson Davis Jr. In private communications, Mr. Wilson has stated that considerable care was taken when doing the initial excavations to look for evidence of burial remains or Indian artifacts at the building site, but that nothing was found. The concern was more for the possibility of Indian remains, rather than for the Polk family which they were not aware of at the time. The house was subsequently sold to Mr. Stephen Pusey and has been considerably enlarged.

5.7 Portrait of Judge William Polk by Charles Willson Peale

In September 1791 the colonial artist Charles Willson Peale[14] passed through Princess Anne on his way from Accomac County to Philadelphia. He was commissioned by Judge William Polk to paint his portrait and invited to stay at the Judge's residence to do so. Peale recorded the episode in his autobiography as follows (written in the third person):

> *Sep 4th. They leave this agreeable family but only get as far as Coll. Done's that evening. Mrs. Peale[15] being in want of some articles to make work and thereby fill up her time while he is employed on his Portraits, they go to Princess Anne to purchase them and as there was to be an election to choose a senator, he expected to see Mr. Polk there and waited until near dinner time without seeing him. They then return to Coll. Done's and* (on the following day*) in the afternoon go to Mr. Polks 9 miles further* [16]*, and begin the portrait of Mr. Shields*[17] *that evening and the next morning one of Mr. Polk.*

> *It is an old saying,* love me love my dog. *Peale's beautiful little greyhound mentioned in a former part of this history, had now become lame, for passing by the side of the horse on the road, the horses hoof cut and striped off some of the skin of the fore leg of the dog. The beautiful Italian grey hound had been a Pett with several gentlemen previous to his belonging to Peale, and been allowed many indulgences. This poor lame dog was resting himself on a chair, when a principal of the family cruilly threw him on the floor with violence. This*

---

[14] Peale's sister, Elizabeth Digby Peale, married Robert Polk, a Chesapeake shipmaster, later a privateer killed in a naval engagement in 1777. There is no known direct family connection between this Robert Polk and the Polks of Somerset. Y chromosome DNA test results on their descendants have, however, shown that there is a genetic relationship tying them together at some earlier generation.

[15] His wife; Peale refers to himself in the third person in his autobiography.

[16] Judge's Polk's residence on the Wicomico; it is not known if this was called White Hall at the time.

[17] John Dashiell.

inhumane act so offended Peale that he determined to make all the dispatch he possibly could to finish his portraits, in order to leave a house where his dog was not welcome to rest, and he does not remember to have painted with more expidition since he practiced the art, being only 5 days in finishing two portraits of ¾ size, yet he believes they were faithful portraits and not slightly executed, and done with great deligence. And in the afternoon of the 13ᵗʰ they left Coll. Winders and crossed the Nanticoke at Viana, and went to Capt. Waters and spent the day there.

Clearly Peale left White Hall with less than fond memories of the place.

5.8 The Other White Hall

An additional source of confusion in the White Hall tradition is a different Polk house, still standing and quite well known, which in the twentieth century came to be known as White Hall. This house was built by David's older brother, James Polk (c.1700-1771), about 1760 and is located along Wicomico Creek, off Polks Road in the Mount Vernon area of Somerset County. The land on which it is located originally belonged to the Cottman family, two of whose daughters James married in succession. It is a lovely colonial home, with its own history and well maintained through a long succession of owners. The name White Hall was only acquired fairly recently, around 1950, when a couple from Tennessee purchased it and applied the name from their previous home in Tennessee, a simple coincidence, but the unfortunate source of a lot of confusion. The house is described in several architectural publications[18] and was featured in an article in the *Baltimore Sun Sunday Magazine* in 1974. In some references this house has been identified as the ancestral home of the Polk family, but this is incorrect. According to the present owners the place had been previously known as Somerset Farms.

A large amount of land in this vicinity was acquired by James Polk and his son William (1744-1806) and passed down through the family. Colonel William Thomas Gillis Polk, grandson of William and Register of Wills in Somerset County, owned a large mansion, situated on Wicomico Creek a little downstream of the James Polk house, which burned down about 1863 as mentioned in *Polk Family and Kinsmen*, p. 50. The location of W.T.G. Polk's property is shown in the Mount Vernon section of the 1876 centennial map for Somerset which corresponds to the recent development known as Melody Acres. Because of the extensive Polk holdings along Wicomico Creek, the inland road running east-west through this area came to be known as Polks Road.

---

[18] Touart, p. 223.

5.9 The Polk Ancestral Home

From the foregoing it is clear that the true ancestral home of the Polk family in America was not White Hall, as first stated by Mary Winder Garrett, but rather the crude settler's cabin in Damned Quarter that was built by Robert Polk and his sons on the tract called Polkes Folly. The land where it was situated at the head of Pigeon House Creek has subsided and eroded in the intervening three hundred years and is now a nearly pristine wetland formally designated by the State of Maryland as the Deal Island Wildlife Management Area. There is nothing left to identify the exact location of the original structure or the final resting place of Robert and Magdalen Polke.

Afterword - The Polk Clock

In the Foreword to this work a remark by W. H. Polk from *Polk Family and Kinsmen* was quoted in which he mentions a clock brought from Ireland by Robert and Magdalen, and reflects on the time consumed in writing his book. Further on, he transcribes a letter received in 1874 from Colonel William T. G. Polk of Princess Anne, which recounts the history of the clock as follows:

".... I will also state in this connection that there are three articles of personal property, two of them, at least, in our current possession, which were brought from Europe by our family. [Mention is made of a family bible and of a large case with 15 square glass bottles.] .....

"The third article is a large brass clock, which in the case stands eight or nine feet high, with great leaden weights of ten or twelve pounds each. In addition to keeping the hours of the day, it keeps the day of the month and the phases of the moon, and is a repeater. A string may be attached to a lever inside the clock and carried to the foot of your bed. At any hour of the night, if the string is pulled, she will repeat the last stroke, unless it is within a half hour of the next strike. So you can know within a half hour the time, without rising from your bed. Seventy years ago it was given by my grandfather [William Polk] to my father [Samuel Polk], with the old homestead. When he took possession of them he found the old clock in a lumber room covered with dust. Supposing it to have finished its work, he proposed to a clockmaker to trade it in part payment for a new clock, if there was any value in it. It was sent, and when my father saw the clock-man, the latter told him that no man need want a better clock. He cleaned it up for a few dollars. I left it thirty years ago on a farm which has been in my immediate family one hundred and nine years, with some servants, and although it has not been cleaned in that time, when I have occasion to spend some days on the farm, or when I send mechanics to repair or build houses, if she is wound up, she will run eight or nine days and keep excellent time. My father laid aside the old case and had a new one of mahogany made. This clock was made, I suppose by "W. Nicholson, White Haven," which is inscribed on a plate screwed to the face and there is an inscription, also on the face – "*Tempus Edax Rerum*," and I find it true in reference to our family, for Time has consumed almost everything relating to its early history."

When I first read these words they made me wonder about this ancient family heirloom, what it looked like, whether it still existed, and where it was. The answer to these questions were a long time in coming and, as it turned out, the clock itself had made quite an odyssey in the intervening years before reaching its present home a long way from Princess Anne. By good luck I found a typewritten account of the later history of the clock in the local history files of the public library in Princess Anne. The clock had passed by a rather circuitous path to W.T.G. Polk's grandson, Brigadier General (BG) James Brittingham about 1966. BG Brittingham was an artillery officer who had a distinguished career in the U.S. Army, serving in World Wars I and II and the Korean War, and retired near Fort Sill, Oklahoma. He took his stewardship of the clock very seriously and had it appraised and carefully restored by an horologist, Mr. Marshall Dull, of Wilmington, Delaware, in 1972. He also wrote a history of the clock, and sent a copy with related documents to Princess Anne where I later found it.

BG Brittingham passed away in 1983 and left the clock to his daughter, Mary Polk "Polly" Brittingham who was married to Colonel Jack Lee, also an artillery officer, as I found out when I obtained a copy of BG Brittingham's obituary. When I tried to contact Polly Lee I found out that she had died in 1992, but I was able to speak with Colonel Lee and ask about the clock. He told me that they had decided to donate the clock to Colorado College in Colorado Springs because both of their daughters had attended college there. When Colonel Lee died several years later the clock was bequeathed to the college as planned and given a nice home there in Alumni Hall. I had an opportunity to visit the campus in 2008 and see the clock for myself, bringing my long quest to an end. It was a special experience to touch something that goes so far back in the history of our family. The clock itself is a truly beautiful piece of furniture that would grace any home. See Figure 20. I am gratified to know that it will be well cared for and is available to be seen by all.

Those who wish to see the full history of the clock as written by BG Brittingham, and the related correspondence, can contact the Princess Anne Library or the author. The history contains details of Colonel W.T.G. Polk's family history which are not needed here. What is important are the conclusions reached by Mr. Dull after examining it. He wrote the following in his letter to BG Brittingham dated Sept 1972:

1- There is no evidence that any part of this clock was in existence in the 1600s. The case is appraised as American Provincial (possibly Maryland) of date between 1790 and 1830. It is believed that the original works was English, 30 hour, Time and Strike, Single Weight & Rope, with Brass Dial, (the "square weight" would appear to be original).

2- The works-switch to Seth Thomas is believed to have been long before the Washington, D.C. episode, and at a time when the "Eight-Day" works were coming into vogue. The mid-section of the case widely departs from the design (crotch veneer & inlays) of the Hood and the Base.

Figure 20. The Polk Clock, now located at Alumni Hall, Colorado College.

3- The most satisfying and authentic change that can be made is to return to the "Works" described in 1-, above, reusing your old dial and weight. I have located a source of three from which an appropriate assembly should be possible.

(a) The only way I could perform the complete task of works-exchange would be for me to have access to the complete clock, here in my shop.

(b) I can provide you a complete works of the original type, making use of your dial and "square" weight and you can employ some local clock man to make the adapting fit.

(c) My membership directory (for the National Association of Watch and Clock Collectors, Inc.) list eight (8) clock enthusiasts in Lawton, who, either directly, OR through reference could help you get the necessary, nearby skilled help. Their names & addresses follow:

....

4- My only way to be of further service to you is in the acquisition of an appropriate works-mechanism. I do good business with a nearby importer of English Grandfather Clocks and have access to their "inner sanctum". I will need some "Works-Mount Dimensional Information" and I supply herewith a sketch with the needed dimensions identified by letters. I can provide a firm quote, following receipt of the dimensions.

BG Brittingham had the clock shipped to Mr. Dull in Wilmington who restored it as proposed, and returned to Fort Sill where BG Brittingham lived in retirement. Eventually it was given to Colorado College as already described, and now permanently resides in a stately setting at Alumni Hall, on the campus. It has, however, left us with a bit of an enigma as to its true origin. Colonel W.T.G. Polk related that it was brought from Ireland by Robert and Magdalen Polke, but this could not have been the case, and neither the original works nor the case has survived. It was most likely originally purchased by W.T.G. Polk's grandfather, William Polk (c.1730-1806), but probably at an earlier date than 1790 as suggested by Mr. Dull, for it hardly would have been consigned to a "lumber room covered with dust" supposedly having "finished its work" so soon after its acquisition.

All we can say for sure is that the provenance of the clock is older than any of its parts. Truly *Tempus Edax Rerum* (time consumes all things).

Figure 21. Face of the Polk Clock.

Appendix I

Descendants of Robert and Magdalen Polk
A Four Generation Family Tree

The genealogical tree of the Polk family of the Maryland Eastern Shore and Delaware presented here was developed from primary source records available at the Maryland Hall of Records at Annapolis, and at the Delaware State Archives at Dover. All available county and provincial probate, land, judicial and tax records were consulted. It cannot, of course, be claimed that this tree is comprehensive since there may have been children and marriages for which no record was found, especially on the female side.

In a number of cases the information shown here does not agree with assertions made in *Polk Family and Kinsmen* (PF&K) by W.H. Polk, published in 1912, one of the standard references for Polk family history. It should be recognized that that work was based in large part on secondary sources obtained in correspondence from Polk's home in Lexington, Kentucky. He had little access to primary sources so it is not surprising that some errors would occur, especially with respect to the colonial period. In a few cases, limited to the fourth generation, the present tree has incorporated information taken from *Polk Family and Kinsmen* which could not be otherwise confirmed.

A simple indexing system is introduced to identify each descendant and spouse. A single digit is used for the first generation, and an additional digit added for each subsequent generation. Thus P1 is the immigrant and progenitor, Robert Polk. In the second generation P15, for example, denotes Robert's fifth child (Ephraim), and P152 is the second child (Charles) of Ephraim, etc. Wives and husbands are indicated by adding a ".w "or ".h" to the spouse's index.

First generation:
P1   Robert Polk (d.1703)
P1.w   Magdalen (Tasker) Polk (d.1728)

Second generation:
   P11   Anne Polk
   P12   John Polk
   P13   Margaret Polk
   P14   William Polk
   P15   Ephraim Pollock
   P16   James Pollock
   P17   Robert Polk (Jun.)
   P1d   David Polk (died young)

P18   Martha Polk
P19   Joseph Pollock

Notation

(N) — an unknown name
b.   — born
c.   — circa
d.   — died.
m.   — married
>   — no earlier than
<   — no later than

Family of P11—Anne Polk

P11   **Anne Polk** b.1665-6 m1.1690 m2.1710 d.c.1732
P11.h1 Francis Roberts b.c.1628 m3.1690 d.1703
P11.h2 John Renshaw   m.1710 d.1721
   P111   Edward Roberts b.1691-3 d.1774
   P111.w Ann Polk (P122) b. 1698/1/27
        P1111   William Roberts b.1729 d.1794
        P1111.w Mary Jones d.1825
        P1112   Edward Roberts unm. d.1762
        P1113   Francis Roberts b.1732 d.c.1775
        P1113.w Elizabeth Pollock (P1612) d.>1775
        P1114   Priscilla Roberts m.>1754 d.1773
        P1114.h   David Pollock, Jun. (P1611) d.1770
        P1115   Mary Roberts d.1754
        P1115.h (N) Williams d.<1754
   P112   Priscilla Roberts b.1694 m1.? m2.1729-30 d.1768
        P112.h1 William Polk (P121) b.1695 m.? d.1726
        P112.h2 Patrick Quatermus m.1729-30
        P1121   Jean Polk
        P1122   Ann Polk
        P1123   John Polk
        P1123.w Elizabeth (N)

181

Family of P12—John Polk

P12   **John Polk**, cooper, b.c.1668 m1.c.1692 m2.<1706, d.1708
P12.w1 Jane Knox m.ca 1692 d. 1700/10/28
P12.w2 Joanna (N) (possibly Smith) m.<1706, d.>1731
    P121   **William Polk** b.1695/7/11 d.1726
    P121.w Priscilla Roberts (P112) b.1694 d.1768
        P1211   Jean Polk
        P1212   Ann Polk
        P1213   John Polk d.1775
        P1213.w Elizabeth (N)
    P122   **Anne Polk** b.1698/1/27
    P122.h Edward Roberts (P111) b. 1692 d.1774
        P1221   William Roberts b. 1728   d.1794
        P1221.w Mary Jones d.1825
        P1222   Edward Roberts d.1762
        P1223   Francis Roberts b.1732 d.1775
        P1223.w Elizabeth Pollock (P1612) d.>1775
        P1224   Priscilla Roberts m. >1754 d.1773
        P1224.h David Pollock, Jun. (P1611) d.1770
        P1225   Mary Roberts d.1754
        P1225.h (N) Williams d.<1754
    P123   **John Polk** b. 1700/10/22 d.1700/10/29
    P124   **Robert Polk** b.c.1706 d.1771
    P124.w Alice Covington d.1773
        P1241   Col. William Polk b.c.1724 m1.c.1744 d.1788
        P1241.w1 Sarah Laws m.c.1744
        P1241.w2 Eleanor (N)
        P1241.w3 Mary Vaughan Woodgate m.<1782 d.1789
        P1242   Robert Polk, Jun. d.1771
        P1243   Daniel Polk b.1750 m.1775 d.1796
        P1243.w Margaret Nutter White b.1758 m.1775 d.1796
        P1244   John Polk d.1774
        P1245   Sarah Polk d. by 1770
        P1245.h Christopher Nutter d. by Feb 1773
        P1246   Betty Polk
        P1246.h1 Robert Polk (P192) b.c.1734 d.1768
        P1246.h2 Manuel Manlove (P1515) m.c.1770 d.1773
        P1246.h3 Levin Crapper m.c.1774 d.1775
        P1246.h4 Rev. Sydenham Thorn d.c.1793
        P1247   Ann Polk
        P1247.h John Laws, Jun. d.c.1788
        P1248   Esther Polk
        P1248.h1 Winlock Russum d.1774
        P1248.h2 Richard Stanfield m.c.1775
    P125   **John Polk (of Little Creek)** c.1708 m.<1743 d.1788

```
P125.w  Sarah Vaughan  b.c.1715-20  m.<1743  d.1783
    P1251     William Polk  d.1791
    P1251.w1  Rachel Bell
    P1251.w2  Leah Marshall  d.1797
    P12512    Ann Polk
    P1252     John Polk, Jun  d.1782
    P1252.w1  Betty Moore
    P1252.w2  Polly Dolbee
    P1252.w3  Mary (N) Houston  m.>1775  d.> 1790
    P1253     Levin Polk  unm.
    P1254     Eunice (Nicey) Jane Polk  b.1743  m.1767  d.1809
    P1254.h   Capt John Scroggin  b.1743/11/13  m.1767  d.1812/12/14
    P1255     Elizabeth Polk  d.>1789
    P1255.h   Lowder Sirman  b.1737  d.1789
    P1256     Sarah Polk
    P1256.h   John Bacon
```

Family of P13—Margaret Polk

```
P13     Margaret Polk  b.1670   d.>1734
P13.h1  Thomas Pollitt/Pollett (Phollett)  m.1687  d.1708
P13.h2  Richard Tull  m.c.1709  d.1710
P13.h3  Charles Williams  b.1650  m.<1716  d.1734
  P131    John Pollitt  b.1689  d.1749
  P131.w  Mary (N) (poss. dau of James Polk (P16))  d.>1749
      P1311     John Pollitt, Jun.  b. 1728, d.1808
      P1311.w   Mary Dennis, widow of Samuel Handy
      P1312     Margaret
  P132    Thomas Pollitt  b.1690  d.1743
  P132.w  Sarah Williams  d.1771 (m2.Christopher. Dowdel)
      P1321     Thomas Pollitt  b.1715, d.1786
      P1322     William Pollitt  b.1721, d.1772
      P1323     George Pollitt  b.1719, d.>1774
      P1324     Jonthan Pollitt  b.1722, d.1806
      P1325     John Pollitt  d.>1771
      P1326     Mary Pollitt  d.>1771
      P1326.h   Michael Disharoon, blacksmith  d.1756
      P1327     Margaret Pollitt  d.>1771
      P1327.h   William Stevens  d.1770
      P1328     Elizabeth Pollitt  d.>1771
      P1239     Sarah Pollitt  d.>1753-4
      P123a     Priscilla Pollitt  d.1754
  P133    William Pollitt  b.c.1692  d.1743
  P133.w  Alice (N)  d.>1743
      P1331     Margaret Pollitt
```

P1332   Richard Pollitt d.1743
P1333   Magdalen Pollitt
P1334   Sarah Pollitt
P1335   Mary Pollitt
P134   **Richard Pollitt** b.1694 d.<1708
P135   **Margaret Pollitt** b.1700/3/31
P136   **Isabel Pollitt** b.1702/4/15

Family of P14—William Polk

P14   **William Polk**, cooper b.1673, m.1699 d.1739
P14.w Ann/Nancy (Knox) Owens, b.c.1670, m2.1699, d.<1739
    P141   **James Polk** b.1700, m.?, d.1771
    P141.w Betty Cottman, d.1780
          P1411   John Polk/Pollock b.c.1727; left for Carolinas by 1756
                            (Appears in tax lists; not mentioned in James's will, but
                            nowhere else to place him)
          P1411.w Ellen Gray, dau. of John Gray (d.1748)
          P1412   Virginia Polk (per PF&K, but no other record)
          P1412.h Unknown
          P1413   William Polk, b.c.1730 d.1806
          P1413.w Mary Williams
          P1414   Benjamin Polk, b.1738 d.1796
          P1414.w Sarah Whittington, d.>1804
          P1415   Priscilla Polk, b.1740, m.c.1760 d.1834
          P1415.h Col. William Whittington, b.c.1740, m.c.1760, d.1818
          P1416   Joshua Polk, b. 1740, d.1790
          P1416.w Mary (Brown?), d.1797
          P1417   Nancy Polk, unm.
          P1418   Leah Polk, b.c.1746
          P1418.h (N) Weatherly
          P1419   Mary Polk
          P1419.h1 James Bratton, d.<1797
          P1419.h2 Mr. Anderton
          P141a   Elizabeth (Betty) Polk
          P141a.h (N) Morrow
    P142   **Jane Polk** b.c.1703 d.>1766
    P142.h James Strawbridge b.1680 m2.c.1719 d.<1743
          P1421   Mary Strawbridge b.c.1721 m.c.1739 d.c.1788
          P1421.h Jacob Williams b.1718 m.c.1739 d.<1778
          P1422   William Strawbridge b.c.1723 m.1788
          P1422.w Mary Jane Whittington c.1770 m.1788
    P143   **David Polk** b.1705 d.1778
    P143.w Elizabeth Gillis
          P1431   Josiah Polk b.1736 unm. d.1782

P1432   Sinah Polk b.c.1741 d.1803
P1432.h   Esme Bayley d.1801
P1433   Gilliss Polk b.1742 d.1793
P1433.w Hannah Dunlop
P1434   James Polk b.1750 m.1774 d.1795
P1434.w Nancy Henry b.1755 m.1774 d.1809
P1435   David Polk d.1773-78
P1436   William Polk b.1752 d.1812
P1436.w1 Esther (Hetty) Winder b.1751 m.1775 d.1790
P1436.w2 Nancy (Purnell) Dennis d.1794
P1436.w3 Mary Hubbell m.1806

P144   Elizabeth Polk b.c.1710 m.1733 d.<1775
P144.h John Williams b.1692 m.1733 d.<1760/12
P1441   Priscilla Williams b.1733 m.1762
P1441.h Samuel Curtis
P1442   Mary Williams 1736/1/25
P1442.h William Polk (P1412) b.1731 d.1806
P1443   Capt John Williams b.1739 m.1767 d.1797
P1443.w Elizabeth (Betsey) Jones m.1767
P1444   Josiah Williams b.1742
P1445   Benjamin Williams b.1747

Family of P15—Ephraim Polk

P15 Ephraim Pollock, planter b.c.1675 m.1700 d.1718
P15.w   Elizabeth Williams b.1681 m.c.1700 d.>1751
P151   Magdalen Polk b.c.1702 d.1770
P151.h1 Samuel Owens d.1731
P151.h2 Manuel Manlove m.1732 d.1743
P1511   James Owens b.<1724 d.1760-2
P1511.w Keziah (Kisia) Evans
P1512   Ann Owens
P1512.h (N) Burroughs
P1513   Elizabeth Owens m.<1740
P1513.h John Burroughs m.<1740
P1514   Jonathan Manlove d.1785
P1515   Manuel Manlove (Jun.) m.c.1770 d.1773
P1515.w Betty Polk (P1246) m.c.1770
P1516   Boaz Manlove
P1516.w (N)
P1517   Elizabeth Manlove
P1518   Ann Manlove
P1519   George Manlove d.1787
P1519.w Sally (N)
P151a   Sarah Manlove

P151a.h (N) Manlove
P152 Charles Polk b.1704 m.1736 d.1784
P152.w Patience Manlove b.1711 m.1736 d.1776
    P1521 Mary Magdalen Polk b.1739 m.1760
    P1521.h1 Henry Bowman m.1760 d.1762
    P1521.h2 Robert Minors b.1737 m.1763
    P1522 Charles Polk (Jun.) b.1740 m.1786 d.17958
    P1522.w Mary Manlove (a cousin) m.1786 d.>1795
    P1523 Priscilla Polk b.1742 d.1818
    P1523.h1 Richard Hayes m.1766
    P1523.h2 Pemberton Carlyle
    P1524 Anna (Nancy) Polk b.1744
    P1525 George Polk b.1746 d.1795/12
    P1525.w Peggy Williams (or Ms. Ryan?) m.< 1776
    P1526 John Polk b.1748 d.1782
P153 Elizabeth Pollock b.c.1706
P154 Priscilla Polk b.c.1708
P154.h1 John Willey d.1742
P154.h2 Warren Burroughs m.by 1747
P155 Ann Polk b.c.1710
P156 Mary Polk b.c.1712
P157 Joseph Polk b.c.1715   d.1812
P157.w Sarah Coverdale
    P1571 Isaac Polk b.1751 unm. d.1824
    P1572 Lt. John Polk b.1754 m.1776 d.1814
    P1572.w Amelia Hurst m.1776
    P1573 Joseph Polk (Jun) b.1758 d.1823
    P1573.w1 m1. Miss Layton b.1762 d.1784
    P1573.w2 m2. Margaret Neal m.c.1786
    P1574 Jesse Polk b.1761
    P1575 Priscilla Polk b.1763
    P1576 Ann Polk b.1765
P158 Ephraim Polk II b.1718 m.c.1738 d.1791
P158.w Mary Manlove m.c.1738
    P1581 Elizabeth Polk b.1739 unm. d.<1799
    P1582 Emmanuel Polk b.c.1742 unm. d.1797
    P1583 Joseph Polk b.c.1744 d.1796
    P1583.w m. Elizabeth Hayes
    P1584 Jehosephat Polk b.c.1746 d.1801
    P1584.w Hannah (N) d.>1801
    P1585 Joab Polk b.c.1748 d.>1799
    P1586 Mary Polk b.c.1750
    P1587 Esther Polk b.c.1752
    P1587.h (N) Owens
    P1588 Nancy Polk b.c.1756
    P1589 Ephraim Polk (III) b.1758 m.1792 d.1814

P1589.w   Rhoda Morris (P191a) b.1773 m.1792 d.1839

Family of P16—James Pollock

P16 James Pollock, ships carpenter b.c.1678 m.c.1700 d.1727
P16.w   Anne Williams b.1683 m.c.1700 d.>1734
    P161   **David Pollock (I)** b.1704 d.1773
    P161.w Elizabeth Turpin (?)
        P1611   David Pollock (II) d.1770
        P1611.w Priscilla Roberts (P1114)
        P1612   Elizabeth Pollock d.<1775
        P1612.h Francis Roberts b.1732 d.1775
        P1613   Mary Pollock
        P1613.h Wm. Jewett (Duett) d.1783
        P1613.h Jesse Griffith
        P1614   Love Pollock
        P1614.h1 John Collins
        P1614.h2 Alexander Polk d.1807
        P1614.h3 Alexander Laws
        P1615   Emelia Pollock
        P1615.h Alexander Laws d.1789
    P162   **Mary Pollock** b.c.1706
    P162.h John Pollitt (?) (P131) b.1689 d.1749
    P163   **Henry Pollock** b.c.1708 d.1757
    P164   **John Pollock** b.1709 d.1779
    P164.w Mary (N)
        P1641   John Polk (of John) d.1796
        P1641.w Susan (N) d.<1805
        P1642   Elinor (Nelly) Polk unm. d.1789
        P1643   Jenny (Jane) Polk
        P1643.h1 William Polk m.<1790 d.<1797
        P1643.h2 (N) Owens m.<1797
        P1644   Nancy Polk m.<1779 d.>1797
        P1644.h (N) Maxwell m.<1779 d.>1797
        P1645   Mary Polk m.<1779
        P1645.h Edward Williams m.<1779 d.>1797
    P165   **Sarah Pollock** b.c.1711
    P166   **Margaret Pollock** b.c.1712
    P167   **Elizabeth Pollock** b.c.1715
    P168   **James Pollock** b.c.1718 m.c.1742 d.1772
    P168.w Sarah Henderson m.c.1743 d.1775
        P1681   James Polk d.1789
        P1681.w Lucilla (N)
        P1682   Sarah Pollock
        P1683   John Pollock

          P1684   Avery Polk (?)
          P1685   Leah Polk (?)
          P1686   Edward Polk (?)
          P1687   (N)
          P1688   (N)
          P1689   (N)
P169   Magdalen Pollock b.c.1722
P169.h   William Pollitt (?) b.1691
P16a   Jane Pollock b.c..1722
P16b   Anna Pollock b.c.1724
P16c   Unnamed child Pollock (possibly Roger Tasker Polk) b.1727
d.1778
P16b.w   Nancy Roberts (dau. of P1113)
          P16b1   Roger Tasker Polk, Jun

Family of P17—Robert Polk (II)

P17   Robert Polk (II) b.c.1679/80 d.1727
P17.w   Grace Guillett b.1682/3/3
     P171   Thomas Polk b.c.1705
     (From secondary sources, not validated)
          P171.w1   Lurvinah (Vier) Johns
          P171.w2   Priscilla Dunn
          P1711   Daniel Polk
          P1711.w   Nancy (N)
          P1712   Thomas Polk, Jun.
          P1713   John Polk
          P1714   Luke Polk
          P1715   Robert Polk
     P172   Robert Polk (III) b.c.1713
     (Note – on p.673-4 of PF&K Robert Polk the Dorchester County official is
     discussed and referred to as Robert Polk, 3rd. This is incorrect. That Robert
     Polk was actually P124, son of John Polk. Robert (P172), the son of Robert
     Polk Jun., actually left Maryland for "parts unknown" and is untraced. See
     Section 3.7.
     P173   (N) (daughter) Polk
     P174   Susan(?) Polk b.1717 m.1738 d.1800
     P174.h   David Reese(?) b.1709 m.1738 d.1787
     (This has not been validated; it derives from the 1903 genealogy of the
     Reese family by Mary Reese who cites no sources and has been questioned
     by later researchers)
     P175   (N) (daughter) Polk
     P176   Grace Polk
     P177   Mary Polk

P1d David Polk died c.1701, unmarried

P18 Martha Polk, untraced

Family of P19—Joseph Pollock

P19 Joseph Pollock b.1689 d.1752
P19.w1 (N) Wright d.<1740
P19.w2 Lydia (N) m.c.1740 d.>1783
  P191 Ann Polk b.1732 m.1754 d.1816
  (Following taken from *Polk Family and Kinsmen*)
  P191.h Daniel Morris Jun. m.1754
      P1911   Daniel Morris b.1755 d.1806
      P1912   Curtis Morris b.1755 d.1804
      P1912.w (N) Wright
      P1913   Rebecca Morris b.1759 unm.
      P1914   Robert Morris b.1761 unm.
      P1915   Brinkley Morris b.1763 d.>1830
      P1916   Mary (Polly) Morris b.1765
      P1916.h John Hopkins
         P19161   John Hopkins
         P19162   Robert Hopkins
         P19163   Betsy Hopkins
      P1917   Ann Morris b.1767 unm.
      P1918   John Morris b.1769 d.1817
      P1918.w (N) Loflin
         P19181   William Morris
         P19182   Thomas Morris
         P19183   Daniel Morris
      P1919   William Morris b.1772
      P1919.w (N) Beauchamp
         P19191   John Morris
         P19192   William Morris
         P19193   Jesse Morris
      P191a   Rhoda Morris b.1773 m.1792 d.1839
      P191a.h Ephraim Polk (III) (P1589) b.1758 m.1792 d.1814
      P191b   Sarah Morris b.1775
      P191b.h William Beauchamp
      P191c   Daniel Morris
      P191c.w Hannah Risque b.1779
  P192 Robert Polk b.c.1734   d.1768
  P192.w Betty Polk (P1246) d.>1787
      P1921   Clement Polk b.>1746 unm. d.1784

P193   **Zephaniah Polk** m.1775
P193.w Lucretia Causey m.1775
P194   **Rebeccah Polk**
P195   **Rhoda Polk** m.1791
P195.h William Masten m.1791
P196   **James Polk** b.c.1738
P197   **Magdalen Polk**

Appendix II

The Letters of Josiah F. Polk, 1848-9

Josiah F. Polk was a great-great-grandson of Robert and Magdalen Polke. His line of decent was Robert > William > David > Gilliss > Josiah. His actual middle name was LaFayette but he used "F" rather than "L" as his middle initial. At some point he moved to Washington D.C. where he served as Chief Clerk in the Office of 2nd Auditor of Treasury.

During the administration of President James K. Polk, Josiah became actively involved with the President, Bishop Leonidas Polk, and William H. Winder in developing a Polk family history. They carried on an active correspondence and some of the letters written by Josiah were later obtained by William Harrison Polk (WHP), in transcribed form, as he was preparing his family history eventually published as *Polk Family and Kinsmen*. These transcriptions have been preserved in the W. H. Polk Collection, Margaret I. King Library, University of Kentucky. In particular, transcriptions of the following letters are contained in Box 8 of the collection:

1. Letter to William H. Winder, 5 October 1848
2. Letter to William H. Winder, Undated
3. Letter to Gov. Charles Polk of Delaware, 2 February 1849
4. Letter to Gov. Charles Polk of Delaware, 22 February 1849

The transcriptions are dated 5 July 1876 and contain W. H. Polk's personal annotations in the side margins. These are re-transcribed here for reference. W. H. Polk's annotations are shown in italics. Some explanatory footnotes have been added by the present author.

Letter No.1: Josiah F. Polk to William H. Winder

Washington
October 5th, 1848

My Dear Sir,

I will give you a traditional anecdote respecting the original name and first change of the Polk name. It is said that on some great occasion a King of Scotland was marching at the head of an immense procession when an oak tree—of what size you can guess as well as I can—appeared directly in front of His Majesty, threatening to turn him and the whole procession from the direct line of march. But, just as His Majesty was on the point of making an oblique step, one of his attendants named Muirhead, a man of great physical strength, sprang forward, seized the tree and with a Sampsonian effort, tore it up by the roots and bore it out of the way, to the great admiration of King and people. The King ordered a halt, and on the spot knighted Muirhead, and changed his name to Pulloak, which in the course of time became corrupted into Pollock.

They tell another story about the same man, to this effect: An enormous and vicious wild boar infested a region of the country and deterred all persons from passing in that direction. A reward was offered by the King to anyone who should slay the dangerous beast. Pulloak determined to attempt it single handed. Armed only with a bow and arrows, he left his village, bent on the dangerous adventure. One story is that when the boar attacked him he climbed an oak tree, from the branches of which he shot and killed him. Another story is that he fled into a church which was hard by, sprang through a window, and running quickly to the door—the boar having entered in pursuit—closed it upon him and returned home. The people of the town were surprised at his safe return and at their enquiries and expressions of astonishment he affected equal surprise and at length said "truly a bit of a pig" had the hardihood to run at him, but he took it by the tail and threw it into the church where he could show it to them, if they would go with him. At first they were unwilling to venture having no idea that the boar was captured. At length, however, he persuaded some of the most courageous, and their astonishment was unbounded when they discovered that the "bit of a pig", of which he told them, was no more nor less than the dreaded and terrific wild boar himself. Thence some argued he was more than a Sampson, while others believed he must have had supernatural aid. He shot the boar to death from a window and for a long time kept the people in ignorance of the real means by which he got the beast into the church.

Yours Truly,

J. F. Polk

Wm. H. Winder, Esq.

Letter No. 2 : Josiah F. Polk to William H. Winder, Undated

My Dear Sir,

I return herewith the genealogical papers, having filed up some of the blanks. [WHP Note: *The rest of this letter relates to Michael Fox who desires a place at Mr Winders disposal and that has no reference to the genealogy of the family. W. H. Polk*]

J. F. Polk

Wm. H. Winder, Esq.

Attachment to Letter No. 2

Descendants of Robert Polk and Magdalen Tasker. She is said to have been an heiress and possessed an estate in the North of Ireland; also that she was the widow of a Col. Porter when Robert Polk married her. The family is said to be of Scotch origin; that the name was Pollock; and that to this day, in the North of Ireland it is written and called in both ways. The public records of Somerset County Md. Would seem to prove this tradition. Tradition says that Robert Polk and Magdalen, his wife, came to this country immediately after the siege of Londonderry, about the time of the expulsion of James the Second—say about the year 1688. [WHP Note: *The first grants to Robt. by Lord Baltimore were 2 tracts "Polks Lott", 50 acres, and "Polks Folly", 100 acres, on March 7, 1687. Therefore they came before 1688.*] In religion they were Presbyterians. The Bible which, it is said, one of the family would read while another kept a lookout for Papist spies, together with a very good clock they brought with them. [WHP Note: *A mahogany liquor case, square, and containing 15 bottles holding 2½ gallons each, was also brought with them and is now in the possession of the son of Col. Wm. T. G. Polk who died at Princess Anne.*] The Bible was destroyed in 1848 or '47 in the conflagration of the house of Littleton Polk. The Clock is still in use and is owned by Col. Wm. T. G. Polk, the Clerk of Somerset County Court. There is no record evidence that Robert Polk ever came to this country. [WHP Note: *There is such record evidence but J. F. Polk had not discovered it.*] It is certain that if he did that he never possessed any real estate here; and the probability is that he died soon after their arrival. That his wife Magdalen lived some time in Somerset there can be no doubt, as her will is recorded in the office of the Register of Wills of that County and bearing the date of 1723 [WHP Note: *April 7, 1726 is the date of her will; probated March 20, 1727.*] in which her name is called Pollock, as well as that of her son Joseph to whom she gives her estate in Ireland; but her name is signed Polk. The oldest public record evidence of the family is a deed from Henry Smith to John Polk,[1] dated March 1692, which was about 3 or 4 years after the arrival of the family. They all settled in what is now Somerset County Maryland. It is said that one of

---

[1] Smiths Resolve; the 150-acre parcel purchased by John Polk was renamed Ballindret.

their sons died just before they left Ireland, or on the passage here. His name I never learned; probably he was an infant.[2]

The children of Robert and Magdalen Polk were John, William, Ephraim, James, Robert, Joseph, Margaret and Anne [Note: *the name "Margaret" was struck through by WHP and overwritten with "Martha"*].[3] John married Jane (or Joanna) Knox. His second wife was Jugy (or Jugurtha) Hugg. [WHP Note: *John Polk's <u>widow</u> was called "the widow Joanna Polk" and hence was his last and not his first wife (See records of Somerset County). At his death he left his children, William and Nancy, to the guardianship of his brother William, which would seem to indicate that Joanna was not their mother, but stepmother. For the benefit of his children he conveyed property to Wm. Cent, or Kent, of Pa. who in turn conveyed it to Ephraim Polk, another uncle of Wm. and Nancy—this probably in trust for the children. It is possible that John Polk's first wife may have been Jugurtha Hugg and that she was mother of Wm. And Nancy.*][4] [5]It is believed he had no children by this second marriage. [WHP Note: *See letter of Josiah F. Polk to Wm H. Winder. Feb 15, 1847, where he makes another correction and from which it is affirmed that John had a 2nd son named John.*][6] The children of John Polk and Joanna Knox were William and Nancy. [WHP Note, 4 Nov. 1909: *The Somerset records show that Joanna was John's widow in 1708 and that his brother William took William and Nancy, children of John, to raise and educate. Joanna was evidently not the mother of William and Nancy*

---

[2] Possibly David, a son not known to Josiah F. Polk, but who is named as co-executor with Magdalen in Robert Polk's will written in 1699. In the codicil of 1702 Robert redesignates his executors as Ephraim and James. David presumably had died in the interim period—he does not appear in any other records of colonial Somerset.

[3] Josiah F. Polk had never seen Robert's will which was not discovered until years later, as W. H. Polk notes on page 64 of *Polk Family and Kinsmen*. This listing of Robert and Magdalen children indicates what was known, or not know, of them at the time (1848) Josiah was writing. He was not aware of either David or Martha, who are mentioned in the will, but did know of daughters Margaret and Ann who are not mentioned in the will, but who were already married and well provided for at the time that Robert wrote his will—and therefore not mentioned.

[4] John's first wife was Jean Knox and his second was her sister Joanna. William Knox (Nox) refers to his "two brothers James Nox and John Polk" in his will of 1695. Jean died in October 1700 a week after giving birth to a son John, who also died at that time. This is recorded in the Somerset Parish (Old Monie Church) records as noted by W. H. Polk (see PF&K, p. 34). John died in 1708 and Joanna subsequently married Thomas Hugg (d. 1728). She apparently died between 1731 and 1733 when her name stopped appearing in the Nanticoke Hundred of the Somerset tax lists.

[5] The tracts Locust Hummock and Front of Locust Hummock were not left in trust for the children of John Polk as far as the subsequent records show. They were held by William Kent until he sold them to Ephraim Polk in 1717 and inherited by Ephraim's eldest son, Charles, who retained possession until 1764.

[6] Actually John Polk had at least two children by his second wife Joanna. Their sons Robert and John Polk begin appearing in the Somerset tax lists for 1723 and 1725 respectively, after reaching the age of 16. They are listed as taxables in the household of Joanna's second husband, Thomas Hugg.

or she would not have consented in 1708 to her husband's brother taking William and Nancy to raise and educate.] William married Priscilla Roberts and his sister married Edward Roberts, his wife's brother. John settled in what is now Dorchester County[7], but then I believe forming a part of Somerset. His son William, soon after his father's death, sold in 1723, the land he inherited lying near Salisbury and removed with his family to Carlisle in Pennsylvania. [WHP Note, 14 Nov. 1909: *This since found to be a mistake. His will is dated 1726 and probated 1727. His widow Priscilla married Thomas Hugg and had issue by him[8]. The William who went to Carlisle married Margaret Taylor and about 1750 moved to N. C., dying shortly afterward.*] We were unable to trace this family any further till we met with the late Col. William Polk of Raleigh NC in 1828.[9] Old Mr. Thomas Pollitt[10] who knows more of the family history than any other person knew that this family left Carlisle after living there some 7 years, but thought they went to the West. He knew that a branch of the family went to North Carolina, but he thought that of Robert, which proved to be an error.[11] At the inauguration of President Jackson we saw Col. William Polk of Raleigh who stated that all he could say of his family was that they went from Maryland to Carlisle, in Pennsylvania, and thence to Mecklenburg County N. C.; that his grandfather's name was William and that he had understood they came to this country about the year 1722, which is about the time we have ascertained that they went from Maryland to Carlisle.[12]

---

[7] John sold his plantation Ballendrait in Manokin, to SW of Princess Anne, and purchased the tracts Friends Denyall and Kirkminster from Matthew Wallis in 1707. The latter are located on NE of present-day Salisbury, Maryland, and are not in Dorchester. His son William who inherited these sold them in 1723 and acquired the tract Colliers Adventure in Dorchester, where he died in 1727.

[8] William's widow actually married a Mr. Quatermus (Patrick or Isaac), not Thomas Hugg. See remarks on Priscilla in Chapter 3; also deposition by Priscilla Quatermus in Somerset Judicials, SOJR1730-33:8.

[9] A telling remark. It is clear that prior to 1828 the Polks of Somerset did not know of any connections to the Polks of North Carolina and vice versa. The Polks of North Carolina did know their patriarch, William of Carlisle, had come from Maryland so it was very natural to conclude that William Polk, son of Robert and Magdalen's eldest son John, who had sold his Somerset land in 1723 and was presumed to have left the area, was the same person. It was not until the 1900s that the will of the latter William, probated 1726 in Dorchester County, came to light and ruled out this connection.

[10] This reference to Thomas Pollitt provides further evidence for the inter-relationship of Polks and Pollitts.

[11] Actually old Mr. Thomas Pollitt was right—Robert Polk Jr's children did appear to move to the Carolinas sometime after his death in 1727. His elder son Thomas and wife Lurvinah sold his inherited plantation, Venture, in 1734 and later moved to South Carolina with the Welsh Baptists of Cecil County. His younger son, Robert (III) is untraced after after appearing on the 1729 tax list.

[12] William Polk, son of John, left Somerset for neighboring Dorchester County, not Carlisle, in 1722-3. The connection between William of Carlisle and the Polks of Somerset seems to have been taken for granted from this initial meeting of Colonel William Polk of Raleigh and Maryland Polks in Washington in 1828—the first step leading to the Polk Family Tree of 1848 and, in due course, to *Polk Family and Kinsmen*

The children of William, the son of John, as I learned from Col. William Polk were Thomas and Ezekiel. Thomas was Colonel of Mecklenburg when the Revolution began and originated the first Declaration of Independence by commanding the officers of his Regiment to call out their companies at a designated day, to choose delegates at Charlotte—the seat of Justice for the County—for the purpose of declaring Independence. The order was promptly obeyed, the delegates met accordingly and declared Independence the 20th day of May, 1775. If he had told me that there were any more than Thomas and Ezekiel, it has escaped my recollection. The children of Thomas—I am not informed as to any except William. He was a Colonel in the Revolutionary Army and behaved with great bravery. He was in several battles and was severely wounded, as I have heard Gov. Iredell remark, "he was covered with scars which attested his valor in the field." He received a Major's commission when he was but a youth, and Gen. Jackson once told me that it was seeing him, so young wounded and bleeding, his arm hanging uselessly by his side, bareheaded and covered with dust and blood and urging the citizens of a small town to arm and rush with him then to sustain the worsted friends who were slowly retreating—it was the fire and patriotism, he said, of that youth in such a plight that fired his breast and made him pant for honors in the field. He then— but fourteen years of age—seized a weapon and flew with that young man to battle. He attached himself to him "and from that moment", said he, "for fifty years we have been as David and Jonathan."

The children of Col. Wm. Polk of Raleigh, as well as I can recollect, are Thomas, George Washington, Alexander Hamilton, Andrew Jackson, Lucius, Leonidas (now Bishop of Louisiana). He had some daughters, but their names I cannot recollect. One married Judge Badger, now of the U. S. Senate and another married the Hon. Kenneth Rayner, late a member of Congress. Col Wm. Polk had, I think, three wives.[13] One was a Miss Hawkins.

The children of Ezekiel Polk, second son of William, who was the son of John, the son of Robert and Magdalen, were Samuel, William, I think, and Edward.[14] If there were any daughters I never heard of them. Ezekiel was a member of the Mecklenburg Convention that declared Independence in May 1775 and

---

in 1912. This connection seemed very plausible since the Polks of North Carolina and Tennessee knew that their predecessor William of Carlisle had earlier come from Maryland and the only Maryland Polks they knew of were from Somerset. The possibility of a connection to another Maryland, e. g. Cecil County, was never considered. However, the key point in Colonel William Polk's statement is that his forbearers arrived into this country in 1722, which is quite consistent with the account of Nathaniel Ewing in *Correspondence of James K. Polk, Vol. 8,* saying they arrived from Ireland to Cecil County in 1727. The Cecil County land records do in fact show that William Pollock purchased land there in 1727 and, with wife Margaret (Taylor), sold it 1736.

[13] Col William Polk had two wives. Griselda Gilchrist (1768-1799) and Sarah Hawkins (1784-1843). See Angelotti, *The Polks of North Carolina and Tennessee*, p. 14.

[14] Angellotti lists 12 children for Ezekiel, including six sons, by three wives. Op. Cit., p. 8-13.

commanded a Company of Whig Rangers from S. Carolina. The children of Samuel, the son of Ezekiel, were James Knox Polk, now President of the United States, one whose name I do not now recollect but I think it was John, William H. and Samuel.[15] There were some daughters, but how many and what were their names I do not know. I know that one of them is Mrs. Walker, of Columbia Tenn.

The children of William Polk, the second son of Robert and Magdalen, and of Nancy Knox, his wife, who was the widow Owens when he married her, were— James, David, Jane and Betsy.[16] William Polk died probably somewhere about 1730; [WHP Note: *Wm. Polk died in 1739/40. See his will.*] certainly not earlier than the 17th of August 1727, for that is the date of a deed to him from William Owens and wife.

James, the son of William, the son of Robert and Magdalen, married Nancy Cottman. Their children were William, Benjamin, Nancy and another daughter [WHP Note; *Priscilla*] whose name I do not recollect, but she married a Whittington. Nancy never married.[17]

The children of William [P1411], the first son of James, the son of William, the son of Robert and Magdalen, were Dr. John [WHP Note: *Dr. John Polk of Laurel*], Josiah, Betsy, Nancy and Samuel. John last named was a very skillful physician and settled in Laurel Delaware. He married Jane Polk, a relative, but her genealogy I cannot trace. Their children were Harriett, Clarissa, Margaret and William. Margaret married Mr. Stewart and is now living. I do not know that she has any children. Her brother William married his cousin, Miss Harcum

---

[15] Angellotti lists 10 children for Samuel Polk, six sons and four daughters. Op. Cit., p. 32-34.

[16] Note the significant omission here of any sons William or Charles, confirming that there were no such sons. In earlier family histories it was surmised that William Polk of Carlisle was the son of John Polk, oldest son of Robert and Magdalen. However, when the 1726 Dorchester will of William Polk, son of John, was discovered, it ruled out this connection. In its place, in *Polk Family and Kinsmen* (p. 34, 355) W. H. Polk rather arbitrarily, and with little explanation, assigned the paternity of the Pennsylvania Polks, William of Carlisle and Charles the Indian Trader, to John's brother, William, of Somerset. This was accepted by Mrs. Angellotti and has generally been accepted as the standard lineage for the Polks of North Carolina and Tennessee ever since. Unfortunately, there is really nothing in the records to support this linkage. The tax lists of Somerset, extant from 1723, show James and David as taxables in the household of William, but no William or Charles. If there were such sons they would have been younger than James who was born 6 January 1699/1700, since William's wife was previously married to William Owens who died April 1698.

[17] W. H. Polk lists eight children of James Polk, by two wives, Nancy and Mary Cottman, who were sisters. Five of these are cited in his will, and an additional one, Joshua, is mentioned in Betty Cottman Polk's will. Joshua also appears in the 1768 deed of gift from James for the tracts Moanin and Donegall, originally purchased by William Polk in 1725. See also PF&K pp. 215-6.

and is dead. He left some children but I know not who they are or where they are. [WHP Note: *Henry and another son.*] Harriett and Clarice have not married. Josiah, the brother of John last named, died an old bachelor. His sisters, Nancy and Betsy, married two brothers of Westmoreland Co. Va. They had children, but how many and of what name I know not. Samuel, the youngest son of William (and brother of John and Josiah) last named, married Sally Gilliss. Their children were Wm. T. G. (who is now Clerk of Somerset County Court), Joseph, Caroline, Littleton, Elizabeth and two or three more girls whose names I do not recollect. They are all living now in Somerset, Md. and some have intermarried with the Wolford family. Joseph married Miss Gillman of Washington D.C. Benjamin the brother of William and son of James last named married Sarah Whittington. [Note—name of Sarah Whittington is crossed out by WHP and following note added: *Benjamin born 6 October 1730 and Sarah Whittington is daughter of Southey Whittington and Mary Forsett Whittington.*] Their children were Benjamin, Whittington, Isaac, Southey, James, and another one or two, Polly, Nelly and three or four more girls. Most of them married but left very few children.

David Polk, the second son of William, who was also the second son of Robert and Magdalen, married Betty Gilliss. Their children were Josiah, Sinah, David, Gilliss, James, David and William.

Josiah was an eminent lawyer and was a member of the first Governors Council after the overthrow of the Proprietary Government. He was a contemporary with Leuther Martin when they commenced the practice of law. They practiced in the same courts on the Eastern Shore of Maryland and were intimate friends. Mr. Martin had a high regard for his talents and many virtues. He died of the gout— unmarried at forty-eight years of age, in the midst of his fame.

Sinah married Esme Bayley, of the Eastern Shore of Virginia, but they lived on the Wicomico in Somerset, Md. He was Register of Wills for the County for many years and died of consumption of many years standing. Their children were: Betsy, Patience, Josiah, James, Thomas, Henry and Margaret. Their mother was a woman of tremendous energy and firmness of character, as well as of great good sense. She brought her children up well and taught them to respect while they loved her. Esme Bayley, her husband, was a very good lawyer and practiced with success before he married her. Betsy, their oldest daughter, married Ezekiel Haynie. He was a scientific and skillful physician and had the best practice of any physician in that part of the country. Their children were: Esme, Henrietta, Charlotte and Hampden. Esme died when but 16 years old. He possessed a wonderful intellect, and was capable of grasping the most difficult sciences, though a boy only. He was very studious and he seemed to acquire anything without effort. He seldom joined his schoolmates in any of their sports excepting in the use of the bow and arrows, in which he greatly excelled all the rest, and consequently the boys called him "Indian". His countenance was grave, but had an agreeable expression. He was very mild in his disposition and kind in his deportment. His person was spare and his constitution delicate. Judge Fromentine, who was a learned man and knew him well and had often examined him, was heard to say that but few men of the best intellect who had been close students till forty years old knew so much as Esme Haynie at fifteen or sixteen years of age. He had read late one night and went to bed without closing his window—it rained during the night and the rain beat upon him while he slept. A bad cold was the consequence and a rapid consumption ensued, which in a very short time carried him off.

His sister Henrietta, a very superior woman adorned with every grace and excellence, still lives unmarried. Charlotte married Mr. Done. They are both dead, but have left several children, viz. Henrietta, John and William. Hampden Haynie died unmarried, at twenty eight years of age. He was a young man of extraordinary ability.

Patience, the second daughter of Sinah, married John Done, who was afterwards a Judge of the Circuit Court. Her children were: Betsy, Juliette, Leah and Anne. Betsy married John Morton and is dead. Leah married Mr. Briscoe of Baltimore where she now lives. Juliette and Anne are yet unmarried.

Josiah, the oldest son of Sinah was a lawyer of great celebrity in the State. For some years he was Attorney General of Maryland. Being a prudent man, he made a handsome fortune for his family by his practice. He was twice married. He had one child by the first marriage, William. He is dead. By the second marriage his children, all living, are Josiah, Alexander Hamilton, and Ann, all married.

Thomas, Sinah's second son, was a man of fine talents and an excellent lawyer. He died an old bachelor.

James, the third son, died before he finished his studies. He was said to be a young man of great merit. Henry, the fourth son, married Miss Rogers, near Baltimore. Their children were Sarah and Araminta. Sarah died young and unmarried. Araminta married Mr. Sidney Winder, the youngest son of Gov. Levin Winder of Maryland. They are both dead.

Margaret, the youngest child of Sinah, married Thomas Lockerman of Cambridge, Dorchester County, MD. Their children were: Elizabeth, Charlotte, Henrietta, Mary and Thomas. Elizabeth married Edward Leuckerman. Charlotte married Dr. Stewart of Cambridge. Returning from Florida to their native place, they, with their child were lost in the explosion of the steamer Priloski. She was a lovely child, and is said to have been equally lovely when a woman. Henrietta married Mr. Brown, a Scotchman, and they live in Florida. Mary has been twice married. Her first husband was Capt Chandler of the Army. They had one child, a daughter. Her second husband is Dr. Taylor, originally of Baltimore. They reside in Tallahaseee Fla. Thomas also resides in Florida and is unmarried.

Gilliss Polk, the second son of David, who was the second son William, the second of Robert and Magdalen was a farmer and planter and Justice of the Peace. A short time before his death he became the presiding or Chief Justice of the County Court of Somerset, as first organized after the Revolution. He married Hannah Dunlop, the only child of Capt. Dunlop of Pennsylvania, who owned a fine farm in Worcester County, but lost it through disasters at sea, as well as his own life. Their children were Gilliss (whose middle name was Washington Morris Round and was commonly called Morris), Anne, Elizabeth, Josiah, Sarah (middle name Cochrane, after her mother's relatives), Catherine (or Katy as they often called her, her middle name Wallace after her mother's mother) and Josiah Lafayette (or as generally called Fayette; hence the F in his name).

Gilliss was Assistant Surgeon in the Navy and went on a voyage with Commodore Rogers in the ship Maryland. He graduated in Philadelphia, and wishing to go to sea on account of an affliction of the liver, was so highly recommended by Dr. Rush, that the appointment of Surgeon was tendered him without hesitation, which he declined on account of his youth and want of experience, preferring the place of Assistant Surgeon with Surgeon Warfield. He was exceedingly handsome and exceedingly prepossessing in his deportment. He gave great promise of excellence in his profession and performed successfully astonishing surgical operations. He married Hetty Sittler of Baltimore who persuaded him to abandon his profession for mercantile pursuits, in the course of which he ruptured a blood vessel in the lungs, of which, in a short time he was dead, in the 26th year of his age. His children were Gillis and Virginia. Gilliss is yet unmarried. Virginia has been twice married. Her first marriage with Isaac Williams of Somerset was unfortunate and she procured a divorce from him of the Legislature. She had two children by that marriage, both girls, and both died in childhood. The oldest, however, had attained her 12th or 13th year and whilst a Chancery suit was pending for the possession of her person. Williams had died previously. Virginia's second Husband is Worthington G. Suethen, a lawyer, and son of a celebrated Methodist preacher. They have had two children. The first died in infancy, the second is living; his name is Worthington.

Anne, Sarah, Catherine and Josiah Lafayette are living but neither of them has been married and unless they take the step soon, it will probably not be worth taking at all. The three sisters and brother now keep house together in the City of Washington. He is the Chief Clerk of the Office of the Second Auditor of the Treasury and the writer of this sketch. Elizabeth died of consumption in 1825 unmarried and the first Josiah died in childhood.

Let us mention in connection here that the paternal grandmother of Hannah Dunlop, wife of Gilliss Polk, was a Cochrane and descended from the same family of the old Earl of Dundonald of Scotland, and her mother was the daughter of Thomas Wallace of Scotland who claimed a common origin with the great Sir William Wallace. The fact that her father's mother had a common origin with the Earl of Dundonald is shown by a genealogical tree in the family of the late General Cochrane of Cochranesville in Pa., who was cousin germaine of my maternal grandfather, Capt Dunlop.

Gilliss Polk, son of David died of gout in the fifty first year of his age. It should have been stated that his sister, Sinah, died also of the same disease when she was about 62 or 63 years of age. Their father, David, died of the same.

James Polk, the third son of David Polk and Betsy Gilliss, married Nancy Henry. He died at the age of forty five of gout, leaving no issue.

David, the fourth son died unmarried and when quite a young man. He was celebrated for activity and physical strength. They were all large and powerful men—James the least so.

William, the fifth (son) and youngest child was a sound lawyer. He rose to be Chief Justice of the supreme court of Maryland, called there the Court of Appeals. He was a man of remarkable good humor, wit and anecdotes. His colloquial talents were of the highest order, and his company was eagerly sought by young and old. He was fond of reading and the works which he seemed to take most delight in were Shakespeare's and Kotzebue's plays, and the works of Voltaire in general. The wit of the latter enchanted him, but there was no work that he considered so perfectly original, and over which he laughed so heartily, as Sterne's Tristram Shandy. He considered it one of the few works which a person who could appreciate it would ever read with undiminished delight. He was born in 1752, and was three times married. He died of gout in 1812, aged about sixty years. His first wife was Hetty Handy, a widow. Her maiden name was Winder, a daughter of Capt. William Winder and sister of Levin Winder, a Colonel of good conduct in the Revolutionary Army, and afterwards Governor of the State of Maryland during the War of 1812. William and Hetty were distantly related, his mother being her mother's aunt. His second wife was a widow Dennis. Her maiden name was Purnell. His third wife was Mary Hubble, a blooming, beautiful young girl from Connecticut. His children by the first marriage were Betty, Hetty, Gertrude, Josiah and William.[18] The issue by the second marriage was one son—James. The issue of the third and last marriage was one daughter—Anne.

Betsy married Elegius Fromentine, a French gentleman educated for the priesthood and narrowly escaped from Paris during the slaughter of the clergy in the Revolution. He thought no more of his clerical office after arriving in this country, but became a lawyer, and was successively Senator of the U. S. for Louisiana and Judge of the Territory of Florida. They both died without children.

---

[18] W. H. Polk also mentions Charlotte as a daughter of William. Op. Cit., p. 10.

Hetty married Major Nehemiah King first. Her second husband was Charles Winder (son of Capt. William Winder) who was a brother of Governor Levin Winder, above named. Her third and last husband was Major Alexander Stewart. He held a commission in the Army during the War of 1812.[19] She had no children by the last two marriages. By the first she had one son, Henry. He has already been married two or three times, and has had several children, but their names I do not know. His first wife was a daughter of Richard Handy, a lawyer, and son of Hetty (or Esther) Winder, by her first husband. Thus Henry King's first wife's father was his mother's half brother. His second wife was Miss Handy, daughter of Col. George Handy who commanded a troop of horse under Col. William Washington in the Revolution.

Gertrude, the third daughter of William and Esther, married William H. Winder, a son of Capt. William Winder, above named, and nephew of Gov. Levin Winder. He settled in Baltimore, became one of the most eminent lawyers in the U. States, and was a Brig. Gen'l in the War of 1812. He was a man of the most polished manners, chivalrous bearing and unbounded benevolence. Their children were John, Charles, Aurelia, Gertrude and ---. John is now a Major in the Army. He has been twice married. His first wife was ---. [WHP Note: *Elizabeth Shepard of Wingate (?) Va.*] The second a widow Eagan (?). His children by the first marriage were William., --- . By the second marriage are ---, ---, ---. Charles married Miss Sterrett of Baltimore. William is yet unmarried. Aurelia married ---- Townsend who resided at Oyster Bay L. I. Her children are ---, ---. [Nothing entered]

Josiah Polk, son of William and Hetty, married Rebecca Troup. Their children were Henry, John, William and Mary. Josiah, their father died at the early age of thirty. His oldest son, Henry, went to Texas about the time of their Revolution, and has not since been heard of. John and William are, I believe, married, but as I am ignorant of their families I leave a blank to be filled up by yourself, if you are acquainted with the facts.

Mary married Dr. Daniel Carr (Corr?) of S. Carolina, a man of science and literature. He died in 1847. Their children were Elizabeth and Charles. Elizabeth married a Mr. Brown of New York, early in August 1848. Charles is not yet grown.

William Polk, second son of William and Esther, married Miss Alma Townsend, of Oyster Bay, New York. Their children were Mary, William, Margaret, James and Louisa. Mary married Victor Monroe, a lawyer of Kentucky. [WHP Note: *Frankfort, Ky*] They have two children whose names I do not recollect. The others are all unmarried as yet.

James, the third son of William, the son of David, the fruit of the second

---

[19] Major Stewart was a surgeon in the Revolutionary War. See Lowe, *"Memories."*

marriage [of William], married Anna Stewart. Their children were Esther, William, Mary, Ariana, James, Lucius and Josiah. Esther married E. Louis Lowe, a lawyer in Frederick Md. They have two or three small children whose names I have not learned. [WHP Note: *Mr. Lowe was afterwards Governor of Maryland, now residing in N Y City*][20] Mary married a Mr. Gorter of Baltimore. They have one child, a few months old at this present time—Sept 1848. The rest of the children of James are unmarried.

Anne, the last child of William, the son of David Polk and Betsy Gilliss, and the fruit of his third marriage, married Herschel V. Johnson of Georgia, a lawyer of eminence, and at this time a Senator of the U. States from that State. Their children are Emmett and four or five more whose names I have forgotten. I have gone too fast—Anne was previously married to a Mr. Walker, of Georgia, by whom she had one son, William, a very estimable young man, now at Princeton College.

In closing here the line of David, the second son of William, the second son of Robert Polk and Magdalen Tasker, it may not be amiss to add that David Polk was, in some respects, an extraordinary man. He was rather hasty in his temper, fearless and ardent. He was uncompromisingly hostile to any form of oppression and injustice. He looked upon the church tax as a thing too nefarious to be endured, and suffered himself, before the Revolution, to be thrown into prison, rather than pay it. This example was followed by Ephraim King, grandfather of ex-Gov. Carroll. Their sons paid the tax, but those of David Polk durst not let him know what they had done, certain that if they did he would never forgive them and would disinherit all who had any hand in it. It was with difficulty that he could be induced to leave the prison. This was a short time before the Revolution and had a great effect in Somerset. He commanded a Militia Company during the Revolution. Judge Done told me, as a fact of his own knowledge, that David Polk by some means discovered a band of Tories—40 or more—secreted in a house in the suburbs of Princess Anne town, whose object was to plunder and burn the town, that he went to them, without the aid of a solitary being, and literally chased them as fast as they could run, over and a considerable distance beyond the bridge near the Presbyterian Meeting House.

At another time a large number of armed Tories, some 40 or 50, made their appearance before his house and demanded a quantity of salt which he possessed, threatening, if he refused, to take it by force and destroy all the rest of his property and put the whole family to death. But in the most indignant and peremptory manner he rejected the most favorable terms they proposed and assembling his five sons, all young, stout and determined, he made such a formidable preparation for defense that the Tories, knowing with whom they had

---

[20] Esther Winder Polk Lowe left a poignant record of her life in a manuscript entitled "Memories" which may be found in the Maryland Historical Society Library, identified as MS 1949. A transcript by the author is available at the Nabb Research Center for Delmarva History and Culture, Salisbury University, Maryland.

to deal, abandoned the enterprise without striking a blow. I have heard other anecdotes, illustrations of his hatred of Tories and British oppression and his fearless disposition.

I have now carried as far as I can the genealogies of John and William, the first and second sons of Robert and Magdalen. I forgot to observe, in connection with the genealogy of John, that many of the descendants of his daughter Nancy who married Edward Roberts, may be found at this day in Somerset County, about Dame Quarter, the very place where Magdalen and her children first set foot on shore in the New World. I know but little of her (Nancy's) descendants, but I can learn something definite, perhaps.

Jane Polk, the oldest Daughter of William, the second son of Robert and Magdalen, married Mr. Strawbridge. They had one child—William—who became a respectable physician. Dr. William Strawbridge, Jane's son, married Polly Whittington. They had but one child—Jane—who was killed while a small girl, by the kick of a horse, and so that branch of the family became extinct.

Betsy, the sister of Jane and last daughter of William, the second son of Robert, died in childhood.[21]

Jane Strawbridge, sister of James and David Polk, was a remarkable woman. She was masculine in her mind and manners. Like her brother David she cherished the strongest abhorrence of the Church Tax and even let her resentment extend to all the ministers of the English Church. She was an uncompromising Whig and even before the Revolution began, poured out the bitterest denunciations of Church and State oppression, whenever she could meet with a respectable Tory. On one occasion, disputing with Parson Bell—he made some personal remark, being an irascible man—which greatly offended her, when, raising a chair in great rage, she aimed a blow at his head, and being a powerful woman, would have beaten out his brains in an instant, had it not been arrested by a third person. She once fell out with her preacher and would go no more to hear him, but, hearing that another person was to preach on a certain day, she went to church. She had ascended half way up the aisle, when the voice of her old preacher—for he was reading in the pulpit—fell upon her ear. She stopped suddenly, raised her eyes, and fixed them on the preacher, at the same time taking an enormous pinch of snuff. Then clenching her fist and extending it toward him in a threatening manner, exclaimed in a voice that startled the whole congregation, and an emphasis that withered the parson, "Why, is it you?" And turning round marched out with the stateliness of a Queen Bess herself.

James and Ephraim, the third and fourth sons of Robert and Magdalen, married

---

[21] This is incorrect. Elizabeth (Betsy) Polk married John Williams and had five children. She is mentioned in William Polk's will, 1739, and lived at least until 1775. See Wise, p. 439.

two sisters, Misses Williams. [WHP Note: *Ephraim married Elizabeth Williams.*] They settled in Delaware as did also the children of John (the first son of Robert) by his second wife Juggy (or Jugurtha Hugg).[22] The late most estimable, universally loved John Polk of Laurel, not the Doctor, but the merchant was a descendant of the latter of John and Juggy Hugg. [WHP Note: *This statement that John Polk, the merchant of Laurel, was a son of John Polk, Sr by Jugurtha Hugg is contradicted in another letter of Josiah's, in which he lists the merchant John as a son of John (& Polly Dolbee), son of John (& Sarah Vaughan), 2nd son of Ephraim,1st, & Eliz. Williams.*][23] His brother Josiah died an old and rather intemperate bachelor. His brother William married in Philadelphia and had a son living whose name is Southey I knew them all. John also died an old bachelor about two years ago and about 70 years of age. I cannot trace their connection with the original stock but I will write Southey and get all he knows of the matter. The late Governor Charles Polk of Delaware, deceased, I supposed to have been a descendant of James or Ephraim. I shall probably be able to learn something in relation to those families from Mr. Robert Polk, a highly respectable citizen of Delaware City, whom I intend to apply. I once stayed a day or two at the house of Gov. Charles Polk at St. Johnstown and with him attended the funeral of a relative of his, also Charles Polk, who was killed in being thrown from a sleigh.

Robert, the 5th son of Robert and Magdalen, married Miss Guilette, what issue they left I have not yet been able to learn, excepting a son Robert who married Miss Peale, sister of the founder of the Peale Museum.[24] He was a naval officer and was killed, it is said, in a desperate engagement in which he greatly

---

[22] Per earlier note, John's second wife was Joanna (or Johanna) Knox, who later married Thomas Hugg.

[23] Records now available show that Josiah F. Polk was correct and W. H. Polk wrong on this point. Ephraim Polk did not have a son named John. The Somerset Court Records, SOJR 1723-5:272, lists his children as Magdalene, Charles, Elizabeth, Priscilla, Ann, Mary, Joseph and Ephraim. The John who W. H. Polk believes to be a son of Ephraim (See PF&K, p. 491) is actually the son of John Polk and Joanna Knox, who was known as John Polk of Little Creek. He can be traced through the Somerset tax lists where he first appears in 1725 as a taxable in household of Thomas Hugg, and later of Widow Hugg, and finally as John Polk of Little Creek, head of household, following Joanna's death. See Russo, *Tax Lists of Somerset County, 1730-40*. John of Little Creek was married to Sarah Vaughan and grandfather of John Polk, the merchant of Laurel. His will was probated in Sussex County Delaware, 1788.

[24] Robert Polk, Jr. mentioned two sons, Thomas and Robert, in his will probated 1727 in Dorchester. Capt. Robert Polk (1734-1777) was not his son, as claimed here, but the son of James Pollock of Hopewell Township, Cumberland County, Pennsylvania, who died in 1773. The life of Robert Polk III, who is mentioned as under 14 in the will of Robert Polk Jr., has not been traced. He is not Robert Polk, the lawyer and colonial official of Dorchester County, as stated in *Polk Family and Kinsmen*, p. 673, since that Robert was older (aged 35 in 1742, according to deposition in Dorchester Land Records, Old #1:157) and could not have been under 14 in 1727. That Robert was actually Robert (P124), son of John Polk. See Sections 3.2 and 3.7.

signalized himself, but whether in the French War or our Revolution I have not been able to learn. I am inclined to believe it was the former.[25] Robert the Naval Officer, and Miss Peale left a son Charles. (If there were other children I am not informed.) Charles Peale Polk was three times married and had 13 children, but I do not know who were his wives, or the names of his children, excepting Robert and David. Charles lived for a number of years in the city of Washington and with his son Robert was employed in the public service. One of them was Chief Clerk in the Treasury Department. They probably came with the Government from Philadelphia. He possessed a portrait of his father Robert, taken in uniform and his last wife took it with her to Fredericksburg, Virginia, after his death, where she went to reside.

Robert the oldest son of Charles married Penelope Maury of Virginia. Their issue was Robert Isaac Watts, and two daughters whose names I have not. They were all married and were, not long since, living, one of the daughters in the West and one in Philadelphia. The son, Robert I. W., lives in Winchester Virginia, has two children—Mary Elizabeth and Penelope Maury—after his mother. He is a silversmith, bears an excellent character and is very highly esteemed at Winchester. He has a fine taste for music and is a good organist. He writes an excellent letter in a fine hand and would make a first rate clerk, but his occupation is hurrying him to the grave. His youngest child four months ago was seventeen years old. There may be more by this time.

David, son of Charles Peale Polk, was an officer in the Army or Navy. He, as well as his brother, has been dead some fifteen or twenty years. I do not know who he married. I think it was Miss (Letitia) Stewart of Baltimore. He left a son, William Stewart, an exceedingly interesting young man, very amiable and genteel in deportment, very sensible and very handsome. He is a clerk in a wholesale and retail dry goods store in Baltimore. He has two or three sisters younger than himself in, I think, Philadelphia. I am told they are beautiful girls.

As to Joseph, youngest son of Robert and Magdalen, I can only suppose he went to Ireland and remained on the estate left him by his mother. [WHP Note, Lexington Ky, 28 May 1903: *Some say that Joseph went to Ireland and sold his estate to his Aunt Barbara, wife of Capt. John Keyes and returned to America. Old "Broomfield Castle" fell into decay. Capt Keyes built a new Castle since known as "Castle Keys" and Moneen was added to the estate.*]
[WHP Note No. 2 (Nov 14, 1909): *It now appears from the fact that the name of Joseph disappears from the Maryland Records after the filing of his mother's will in 1727 that he must have gone back to Ireland and stayed there. The*

---

[25] Capt. Robert Polk commanded a privateer called the *Black Joke* and died in a voyage to the West Indies in September 1777. No naval or newspaper records confirming the engagement in which he was said to have been killed have been located. The logbook from his final voyage is in the British Public Records Office; document number HCA32/28/20. It makes no mention of any incident or the fate of Robert, but the ship was commanded by Levin Trippe on its return voyage from Martinique.

Joseph who was born about 1770 (sic), and who is of record was the son of Ephraim Polk. So Josiah Polk's supposition seems to have been correct as to Joseph, son of Robert and Magdalen.]

[WHP Note No. 3: *Still further——shows that Joseph Polk must have come back from Ireland about 1740, for in that year we find that he purchased "Little Goshen", a tract of land in Dorchester County, Maryland and died there. See his will of 1751-52, mentioning his children Robert, Ann, Zephaniah and James. The first two were doubtless by his first wife, Miss Wright, and the last two were by a second wife who was alive at the time of his death, as will shows.*][26]

Letter No. 3: Josiah F. Polk to Governor Charles Polk of Delaware

Washington Feb 2, 1849

My dear Sir,

As ready as you may be to afford any information you possess respecting the genealogy of the Polk family I fear you will find me a troublesome customer.

In making a synopsis for Mr. Winder from the statement received from you, it is not stated to whom the following named persons were married, viz. your grandfather—your father—your uncle George, Manlove Hayes (son of Priscilla Polk & Rich. Hayes)—nor do you name any children of your aunt Anna who married Mathew Morain.

If you can with convenience supply those answers at an early day I will be much obliged to you.

Your mothers genealogy must be quite a curiosity, running back so far, as well as forming a most interesting piece of family history—There is a chart also of my mother's family among some of the Cochranes of Pa. It was in the possession of the late Gen'l Sam'l Cochrane of Cochranesville, Chester Co. Pa. I never saw it—but two of my sisters saw it when they were on a visit at Genl Cochrane's. He was a cousin of my mother whose father was a Dunlap—a Scotch Irishman who claimed to have descended in his maternal line from the family of Sir William Wallace, but of this I know nothing. It is certain however, according to the genealogical tree of Gen'l Cochrane, that my mother's mother

---

[26] It is highly unlikely that Joseph ever went to Ireland. He appears regularly in the Maryland records throughout this period, was married to the daughter of Thomas Wright and had children c.1732 and after, relocating to near Bridgeville, Delaware, then in Dorchester County, no later than 1740. Possibly land records in Ireland could settle this question, if they can be found.

was descended from the Earl of Dundonald who was saved from execution in the time of James 2 by his daughter Grizella robbing the mail of the death warrant which afforded time for the interposition of friends to procure his pardon ~

With great respect & esteem -

Yr ob't Srt -

Josiah F. Polk

Chas Polk, Esqr

Letter No. 4: Josiah F. Polk to Governor Charles Polk of Delaware

Washington Feb 22d 1849

My dear Sir,

I have received and read with great interest & pleasure your letter of 10th inst; but, owing to Mr. Winder's engagements—endeavoring to arrange with Congress for the rent of an immense fire-proof building of his in this City, for public offices—I have not had an opportunity to show him that letter. I understand that the lithographing is in progress, in Philadelphia, by a first rate artist. Mr. Winder was very anxious to have it completed before the President leaves, but in this he will probably fail; but, it has in all probability proceeded too far for some additions and corrections I would be glad to have inserted. This, however, is the first edition, and cannot be expected to be perfect. A work of this kind requires a good deal of time and patient enquiry. I shall pursue my researches & not cease until I have obtained all the information that can be got from all parts of the country; and, if I live, I will then compile as perfect a history as the materials will afford. I will endeavor to make it sufficiently interesting to the various members of the family to justify its publication.

I have received a letter from Wm. C. Polk of Bridgeville. It is very satisfactory—as far as it goes. But he goes no further back than Wm. his great grandfather,[27] who had a brother Daniel, of whom I have heard before. This is in addition to those named by you—Robert, David & Wm.[28] I have now to find out

---

[27] Col. William Polk (P1241) of Dorchester (a part now in Delaware) whose descendants are described on PF&K, p. 675-96. He owned Polks Defense near present-day Bridgeville Delaware, which was a 1776 resurvey of land he acquired or inherited from his father Robert Polk (P124), the Dorchester colonial official.

[28] There is probably some confusion here. There is no other record this writer has found of Robert Polk (P124), the father of these individuals, having a son David; there was a fourth brother John (P1244) who died as a minor in 1773, two years after his father.

who was the father of those four brothers. I conjecture, now, that it was Robert, the 5th son of Robt & Magdalen agreeing with a supposition expressed in one of your letters for Wm. C. Polk says he has in his possession some land patents of Robt. Polk of Dorchester Co. Md. dated 1753.[29] I shall have the records of Dorchester searched, and doubt not some important facts will be elicited. The Robt, who, as you suppose, left no children, may turn out to be a son of Robt, the 5th son of the immigrants.[30] If so, he was the one that went to Phil, married a sister of Peale, the founder of the Museum, became a Naval Officer and died of a wound rec'd in an engagement, an account of part of whose descendants I have procured.[31] I suppose that Mrs. Jane Polk was sister of Edward of whom you gave me an account & had written to Miss Harriet, a daughter of hers now living in Somerset, to learn the truth; but I have as yet rec'd no reply. It was on her business that I made my visit to you; but Joshua Polk was brother of her husband, Dr. John Polk, of Laurel.[32] I learn from the records of Somerset that your great grandfather, Chas Polk, of Ephraim, was the oldest son. I had supposed him to be the 2d. In more than one place he is styled the son and heir at law of Ephraim. He lived at one time in Worcester County.

One thing is a little mysterious; you say that Robt Polk of Delaware City & Uncle of Charles T. Polk, of Cantwell's Bridge, was of a family who came some time after our ancestors. Now, Chas T. gives from the old family Bible, the names of Ephraim's three sons—Chas, Jno & Joseph & says that Joseph, from whom his family are descended, was born about 1720 & speaks of the family being thrown on the Delaware side of the line between Penn & Baltimore.[33] His uncle Robt, he says was the youngest of his father's brothers. Pray is this Robt

---

Probate records for John are found both in Dorchester, Maryland and Sussex, Delaware records.

[29] Robert Polk II (P17), son of Robert and Magdalen, died in 1727. As mentioned, the Robert Polk who was father of these brothers was actually Robert (P124), son of John Polk and his second wife Johanna. W. H. Polk believed him to be the son of Robert II, but the latter was too old to have been the son mentioned as under 14 in Robert Jr's 1725 will. This Robert (P124) actually appeared on that same will as a witness.

[30] This is probably Robert (P1242), second of the four sons of Robert (P124), who died at almost the same time as his father, 1771. He was apparently unmarried; his will, probated in Dorchester, leaves his estate to his brothers Daniel and John; no wife or children are mentioned, neither is his brother William.

[31] Captain Robert Polk was actually the son of James Pollock of Carlisle, Pennsylvania, not the colonial official of Dorchester and wife Alice, as asserted in *Polk Family and Kinsmen*, p. 709. His actual father lived in Cumberland County, Pennsylvania. Robert inherited a tract of land located along North Mountain in Hopewell Township him and made provision for it it in his own will. See *Selected Papers of Charles Wilson Peale, Vol. 1*, p. 332.

[32] Dr. John Polk of Laurel, Delaware, had a brother named Josiah, not Joshua; they were sons of William Polk (P1413). See his will (Somerset Wills, EB23:98). William had a brother named Joshua (P1416).

[33] The judicial records of Somerset County list the children of Ephraim as Magdalen, Charles, Elizabeth, Priscilla, Ann, Mary and Ephraim. (See SOJR 1723-5:272.) Ephraim died in 1718; Joseph was more likely born c.1715.

and the one at Delaware City the same? Magdalen, the Mother of the immigrants, gave by will to her youngest son, Joseph, her estate in Ireland. I have not been able to learn whether or not he went to Ireland to possess it, and if so, whether or not he returned. The Joseph Polk of whom you speak as coming after the rest, may have been this same heir of Magdalen. But I think I have some evidence that he was in Somerset from 1735 to 1755. Magdalen's will is dated 1723. The earliest recorded evidence of the family is 1690. [W. H. Polk Note: *Later records found say 1672. The first grant to Capt Robt Bruce Polk was in Mar 1687 & would had been ---(?) his son John before that time*] Our family tradition is that they came in the same year in which the siege of Londonderry was raised by Wm. the 3rd and Jas II was expelled (from) the Throne and Kingdom, which was I believe in 1688.[34]

Gen[35] Taylor is to make his entry in this city this evening. The weather being bad, I fear you will not make the journey for the 4th of March. It is not settled; I believe, that Mr. Clayton to be Sec. of State. I should be delighted if the Legislature would fill the vacancy in the Senate with yourself. As long as Mr. Clayton has. [*W. H. Polk note: The rest of this letter is lost or in the possession of John P. Polk, Clerk State Dept Wash DC, who owns the portion here copied*]

---

[34] Robert and Magdalen Polk were in Somerset by 1687 when Robert's name first appears in the Maryland land records. The certificate is in the name of Robert Polke. The title Captain and middle name Bruce were never used in any of the Maryland records citing Robert Polke. The siege of Derry lasted from April to August 1689.
[35] President Elect General Zachary Taylor.

Appendix III

Early Correspondence Relating to Polk Genealogy

1. Letter of Nathaniel Ewing to Presidential Candidate James Knox Polk, 3 September 1844

2. Letter of John Pollock, Templemoyle, Londonderry, to James Knox Polk, 6 February 1846

3. Letter of Robert Pollock, Templemoyle, Londonderry, to James K. Polk, 4 March 1848

4. Letter of James K. Polk to William H. Winder, 20 September 1848

5. Letter of James K. Polk to Bishop Leonidas Polk, 30 October 1848

6. Letter of James K. Polk to William H. Winder, 30 October 1848

7. Letter of Leonidas Polk to President James K. Polk, 17 January 1849

8. Letter of Mrs. Smart to Bishop Leonidas Polk, 15 February 1849

9. Letter of Bishop Leonidas Polk to Wm. H. Winder, Esq., 19 July 1849

1. Letter of Nathaniel Ewing to Candidate James Knox Polk, 1844

This letter to James K. Polk from Nathaniel Ewing of Vincennes Indiana, originally from Cumberland County PA, was written after Polk's nomination as the Democratic candidate for President. It is found among the collected letters in JKP's correspondence (see Cutler, Correspondence of James K. Polk, Vol. 8, p.9). There is no evidence that JKP actually saw it or, if he did, that it was of more than a passing interest. It is not mentioned in his later correspondence with William H. Winder or Leonidas Polk when it would have been quite *apropos*, in light of the letter received from Robert Pollock of Templemoyle in 1848, which Polk took quite seriously.

~~~~~~~~~~

Vincennes I[ndiana]
Sept. 3d 1844

Dear Sir

A sketch of your biography happening to fall into my hands, I find that I am better acquainted with the early history of your family that perhaps any of your immediate relatives now alive.

Your forefathers and mine emigrated in the same ship from the North of Ireland in the year seventeen hundred and twenty seven, landed at Newcastle & settled together in the upper part of Cecil County adjoining the Pennsylvania Line and Lancaster County. [1,2]
There was a large colony composed principally of Ewings Porters Gillespies & Polks. Your great grandfather and two Grand Uncles[3] were of the number. Of your great grandfather and one of his brothers I have no recollection. They with some of my relatives of the names of Gillespie and Porter had removed to Cumberland County near Carlisle before my time. One of the brothers John Polk remained where he first settled until he died which was about the year seventeen

---

[1] The immigration of the Ewing family is well documented and their arrival in 1727 is said to have been aboard the ships Rising Sun and Eagle Wing. See Fife; also McMichael.

[2] Ewing is confusing the ancestor of James K. Polk, William Polk/Pollock, who lived on Christiana Creek in northeast corner of Cecil County, with the Poaks/Polks who lived next door to his Ewing family in Octoraro in northwestern Cecil County. See section on William Polk in Chapter 6. County land records show that William Pollock, cordwinder, acquired the 80-acre tract "Moyn" on Christiana Creek from David Alexander on 20 April 1727. He, and wife Margaret (Taylor), afterwards sold this to Walter Beatty of Ireland on 2 April 1736.

[3] One brother was John Polk as mentioned by Ewing. The others were most likely from the Poak family of Nottingham and Octoraro, actually six in all, as discussed in Chapter 6.

hundred and eighty three.[4] Him I well recollect as his land & my Grandfathers joined[5], and a constant intercourse always subsisted between the families, during their lives. On his land was the place selected by the emigrants on their first arrival for a burying ground[6] and in it is inter'd both my grandfathers and grandmothers my Father and Mother with Uncles Aunts & cousins without number. John Polk and his family also lie there.

In the year seventeen hundred & eighty eight I found living in Cripple Creek one of the head branches of New River a numerous band of my relatives descendants of those who had removed from Cumberland County Pa. and from the old settlement in Cecil Co. Md. I understood the Polks had settled further South in Carolina. In this tour I found my relatives scattered from Prince Edward Co. Va. through Bortitort Wythe Washington and down to Knoxville, all the descendants of the emigrants of seventeen hundred and twenty seven. I have this date from record. One of my aunts was born on sea on the passage to America & this is the recorded year of her birth. Here ends my knowledge of the family of the Polks except the grandsons of John Polk by his daughter Isabella who married Thomas Grubb.[7] With those I was raised and schooled three of whome are still alive all living in Pennsylvania one in Franklin Co. & two in Erie Co near the town of that name.[8] One of the latter Judge Grubb is a man of six feet four & half inches high of good proportions. About ten years ago I visited the ancient site of the Emigrants after and absence of more than forty years. I was much surprised to find so little alteration in the superficial appearance of the country. The lands were unaltered the woodland but little diminished the only and great change was in the improvement of the soil. The fields which I had left in the most decay state of poverty I found covered with luxuriant crops of clover and wheat. The tracts of land which were originally large I found divided into small ones not much exceeding one hundred acres on each of which were fine brick houses & barns and every convenience necessary for a neat farm.

---

[4] John Poak's will was written 20 December 1786 and probated on 13 September 1787 in Cecil County. He mentions sons James, John and William, daughters Frances, Martha and "three eldest", but unnamed, other daughters. See Cecil County Wills EE#5:152.

[5] John Polk acquired a tract called The Tomb, 196 acres, in northwest Cecil County along the Octoraro Creek where it crosses the Pennsylvania line. This was surveyed in 1767 and never patented by John, so it had to be patented by his son James in 1793. James's petition for a belated patent mentions that John had settled there earlier.

[6] This explains the apt choice of the name "The Tomb" for the tract. Sadly, the cemetery has been plowed under and a development now stands on this hallowed ground. The inscriptions from the tombstones do not seem to have ever been recorded.

[7] This marriage is recorded in Little Britain, Lancaster County, Pennsylvania; Little Britain Township is adjacent to Cecil County. In 1774 Thomas Grubb and wife Isabel sold two tracts, Cornwell and Cornwells Addition, totaling 300 acres, to John Poak who immediately resold them back to Thomas Grubb as some sort of legal formalism.

[8] David Poak, son of David Poak (d.1792), who lived adjacent to John Poak in the Octorara Creek area of Cecil County, also moved to Erie County, Pennsylvania, after selling his inherited land in 1799. In Erie his descendants used the name Pollock. See Craytor, *Descendants of David Pollock, 1755-1841.*

In the year seventeen hundred and seventy nine there was one of your family living near Natches, placed there by the state of Virginia as their agent to accept & pay the bills of Genl. Clark when carrying on his expedition against the British forts at Kaskaskia & Vincennes. Thus I have given you my recollections & traditions of your family from their first landing in America. Your family like mine were originally from Scotland & emigrated from that Country during the Protectorship of Cromwell. ...

[Ewing's letter continues for several more paragraphs but the remainder is concerned with his political views.]

2. Letter of John Pollock, Templemoyle, Londonderry, to James Knox Polk, 6 February 1846

This letter was provided in e-mail correspondence to the author by Prof. Wayne Cutler, University of Tennessee, Knoxville, editor of Correspondence of James K. Polk, with the following note: I've been going through our JKP files and found a letter from John Pollock of Templemoyle to JKP that may be of some help. The document is in the JKP papers at the LC ms division. Unfortunately, the filming of the letter is very light and difficult to read. Also the author of the letter wrote without regard to modern conventions of capitalization, punctuation, paragraphing, etc. The letter is almost a stream of consciousness. I have supplied spacing where I thought the sentences began/ended and have run the words together when I could not discern the syntax. So here's what I can make of the text:

~~~~~~~~~

Templemoyle
6 February 1846

Honoured Sir

As A Letter Wrote by Mr William Ross of Philadelphia to his friends in this Country fell into my hands A few weeks ago wherein was Stated that he had An interview With you Sometime Shortly previous to his writing And that you Seemed Somewhat Desirous to know Something of your Genealogy from Ireland   This Sir I think Can be easily obtained   I As A Near Relative of your Can Give you A Little intelligence on the Subject As I understand that your Grandfather was Ezekiel Polk. He and my grandfather were Brothers Children they were both borne in Templemoyle where I now reside. I frequently heard my father Speak of him As being A Stout Active man   he had A Sister Called Nancy was married to A man by the name of Maxwell   they had A Son named Ezekiel for his uncle whom I was perfectly Aquaint with from my infancy he is Dead Some twelve years Ago   my father is Dead upwards of this

214

thirty years   My uncle Samuel And uncle Robert are still Alive but neither of them Recolect Seeing your Grandfather   there is just the three families of us now liveing on the inheritance of our forefather And when I Give you A Short Sketch of our present Standing in Life you will no Doubt be Ready to Say with An old Aunt at the birth of my uncle Roberts youngest Daughter it would seem that the Good Old Name was About to Die Away As uncle Samuel has only one Son Alive And he and his wife have no children And I have neither Brothers nor Sisters And Am Just in the Same Standing As Robert so far As family is Concerned   uncle Robert has three fine Daughters And As the most of our Relatives have all Emigrated to America And are now become American families there uncle Samuel had four Sons went to America three of whom were married Each of Whom left four children they Are All Dead So that out of five Sons he has only one Alive they all Died under fifty So I think when you Are become As I may Say A Multitude you must Send Some of your Sons over to ireland that they may get married to uncle Roberts Daughters And Revive the Name once more   you will no Doubt be Surprised Sir When I tell you that I Can have our Genealogy back upwards of two hundred And forty years   I Can Assure you Sir that you And I Are Sprung from A good Staunch branch of Presbiterians   Our Ancestors Came from Scotland About the year 1600 (And were in high Estimation in their Native Land) And Settled in And About where we now reside   And As nothing in Life Could give me So much pleasure As to have A personal interview with So Near A Relative more Especialy When Raised to So High An Emminance in Life only the Distance is to great And my circumstances rather Limmited being An industrious farmer And Subject to A pretty high Rent So that the undertaking would be Rather Ardious for me to undergo but Should you And I Never have the pleasure of meeting in this world of trouble and trial I hope we Will meet At the Right hand of our God there to unite in that Happy Anthem of Moses And the Lamb throughout the Endless Ages of Eternity   As both high And Low must bear in mind that we Are only poor perishing mortals it is our incumbent Duty to Have our Lamp trimmed And our Lights burning So that When the voice of the Bridgegroom Cometh we may be Ready to Appear with him in glory And As it has been the good pleasure of your God to place you in the Chair of State for A time over So Large a Community I hope you will be Enabled to Rule to the glory of God And the good of your brethren of Mankind. And may you be Enabled to Set Such An Example As Did David And Solomon So that yourName may be imortalized to Sons yet unborn but me thinks I hear you Say Who is Sufficient for these things Listen to the words of our Saviour Jesus Christ to All his humble followers My grace is Sufficient for you And my Strength Shall be made perfect in your weakness   And in these Days of Light and Renewals we are taught to Look forward to that Ancient prophecy where it is predicted that Rulers become nursing fathers And their Queens nursing mothers to the true Church of the Liveing God   And may you be Enabled to Rule with A Single Eye to the happy amen of Malineal glory where one will not have to say to Another know ye the Lord, for all know him from the Least to the Greatest And With Such feelings And humble prayer I Subscribe myself your humble Servant And benevelent friend.

John Pollock

P.S. Sir When this Comes to hand if you think me worthy of your Notice
or my Letter worthy of your Reply I Certainly would find A Secret plesure in
Looking over And Reading A Letter from your hand   As God in his providence
has been pleased to place us in Distant Lands yet we ought to Rejoice that we
have the knowlege of Communicating our Ideas to Each other by Letter if So
Direct to John Pollock of Templemoyle Near Newtown Limavady County
Londonderry to the Care of John Hunter a merchant & [word illegible] You See
Sir there is A Little Difference in Spelling the name but the Substance is the
Same.

[cover]

Sir I Do not properly know your Address if I am in Error you will
please forgive me   Request you send it on.

To James K. Polk Washington
President of the United States of America

[cancelled by stamp]   Mar 31
[place of cancellation illegible]

3. Letter of Robert Pollock, Templemoyle, Londonderry, to James K. Polk; March 1848

The following is a transcription of a document found in the papers of W. H. Polk,
now in the Library of the University of Kentucky. It was his copy of a letter
originally sent to President James K. Polk relating to Polk family genealogy. This
copy was provided to him by Aurelia Winder Townsend, daughter of William H.
Winder, in 1875. Several side notes were written on the document by W. H. Polk,
and are included in this transcript.

~~~~~~~~~~~

Endorsement by W. H. Winder:

The original of the within letter was handed to W. H. Winder of
Philadelphia by the President Polk on the 20th day of Sept 1848, with the
request that he (W. H. W.) would answer it. He—W. H. W.—being then
engaged in making out for the President a genealogical tree of the Polk
family, which settled originally in Md. and W. H. W., being of the branch
(by his maternal line) which remained in Maryland, and had the best
knowledge of the origin of the family. On the envelope of the letter was

216

endorsed in the handwriting of the President what follows. He also addressed, at same time, a long letter to W. H. Winder relative to the family, making enquiries upon many points. The copy was made on 21st and this mem. was also made on the 21st by W. H. Winder, whose signature this is.

Endorsement by President Polk:

Robert Pollock of Ireland, Rec'd June 9th 1848. He represents that he is related to my family & makes enquiry on the subject. Referred to Bishop Polk of La. who is requested to furnish me with such information as he may possess on the subject. JKP

Copy of a copy of a letter written by Robert Pollock, Templemoyle Ireland to Jas. K. Polk and now (1876) in possession of Mrs. Townsend, Oyster Bay Long Island

Copy

To his Excellency, The President of the United States,

The undersigned Robt. Polk (alias Pollock) of Templemoyle County Londonderry, Ireland Testifieth

That subscriber is the son of Samuel Polk now 90 years old, that the said Samuel Polk declares he was born years after Ezekiel left this country to sail for the United States; that Ezekiel Polk, he has been led to believe, was grandfather to James K. Polk, the presiding president of the United States, that the said Ezekiel Polk and Samuel Polk were first cousins; that besides the subscriber and his father, there also resides in Templemoyle Robert Polk, Sr., brother of Samuel, and uncle to the subscriber.

That feeling pleased and honored that one bearing the name of Polk of Irish extraction, sprung from the same ancestry, occupied the highest situation in one of the first and most powerful nations on the Earth, subscriber could not resist the temptation (when an esteemed and excellent friend was to sail for America) of making known to President Polk, that in the land of his forefathers, and in the very house of his progenitors, there still lives in peace and independence a few descendants of that old family, who feel a disinterested pleasure in knowing that a near and worthy Kinsman has been advanced to honor.

The above particulars I will have transmitted, with every proof of their authenticity, should you at any time require it, and anything farther you may desire to know can be communicated verbally by Mr. Jas. K. Fisher, my young friend and the bearer of these lines,

With every feeling of respect,

believe me yours faithfully,
Robert Pollock
Templemoyle
4 March 1848

Notes by W. H. Polk (inscribed in margin):

As Bishop Polk wrote to James K. Polk, the writer of this letter was mistaken as to the degree of relationship and Ezekiel, grandfather of James K. was not born in Ireland. The letter shows, however, that there were Polks in Ireland in 1848. Were they descendants of Joseph Polk, devisee under his mother's will?

This statement, in March 1848, shows that there were Polks then in Ireland bearing the well know family names of Robert, Joseph. It is possible that they descended from Joseph, devisee of Magdalen. Col. Wm. T. G. (Polk) said the records indicated that Joseph was in Md. much later than the date of his mother's will of 1727. It is also possible that these Polks in Ireland may have descended from a brother of Capt. Robert Bruce Polk. The Joseph Polk who married Miss Wright and died in 1751 was not too old to have been Magdalen's devisee, and my opinion is that he went to Ireland, sold Moneen and returned to Md. about 1738.

4. Letter of James K. Polk to William H. Winder, 20 Sept 1848

The following is a transcription of a handwritten document in the papers of W. H. Polk, now in the Library of the University of Kentucky. It was his copy of a letter originally written by President James K. Polk relating to Polk genealogy. The same letter can also be found in the correspondence of James K. Polk in the form of a letter press copy made from the original and kept for White House records.

~~~~~~~~~~~~

Copy of a letter written by Jas. K. Polk to Wm. H. Winder of Philadelphia, son of Gen. William Winder and which is in possession of Mrs. Aurelia W. Townsend of Oyster Bay, Long Island.

      Washington City

      Sept 20th, 1848

Dear Sir:

I thank you for the information you have given me on the Polk, or Pollock,

218

family. As requested in your note, I have traced the issue of John Polk, the eldest son of Robt. and Magdalen Polk, and return to you herewith the headings of that branch of the family which you enclosed to me, with the information you desire. You will perceive that I have not given the names of the grandchildren of Ezekiel and their intermarriages, except those of my own immediate branch of his family, nor of his great-grandchildren and their intermarriages. I possess, I believe, as accurate knowledge of them as anyone now living, and if you desire it, will furnish you with their names, intermarriages and issue. I shall be under additional obligation to you, if you will furnish me with the "tree and short history or biography" which you inform me you are preparing. In one of your communications you inform me that a correspondence took place in the Spring of 1824 between Col. Wm. Polk of Raleigh NC and your father, the late Gen'l Wm. H. Winder, of Baltimore. If this correspondence has been preserved, I would be much gratified to have a copy of it. The synopsis which you give of Col. Wm. Polk's account of his family, and of their participation in the Revolution, I know from tradition and the history of the times to be correct. The fact which you state in one of your communications that, "Ezekiel was a member of the Mecklenburg Convention, which in May 1775, first proclaimed Independence, and he commanded a Company of Whig Rangers", I know also, from the same source, to be correct. His original commission as a Captain has been preserved and I have it now in my possession. I would be pleased to receive from you any additional information which may be in your possession, and upon which your statement is based. It appears from the genealogy of the family, which you have furnished, that I descend from John & you descend from William, who were brothers and the sons of Robert and Magdalen, and that we are the fifth generation from Robt. and Magdalen. I observe a remarkable circumstance in your account. It is that John, my ancestor, married Jane Knox, and from that marriage my family sprung, and that William, your ancestor, married Nancy Knox, and from that marriage your family sprung. Both John & William married wives named Knox. Did they marry sisters? If so, you and I are more nearly related than the degrees of descent would indicate. I remark further that Samuel (my father) married Jane Knox. Have you any trace of the Knox family? In looking at the coincidence of the names, it has occurred to me that my mother may be of the same family of her name, who were intermarried four generations before, with John and William (sons of Robert and Magdalen) and that the two families (the Polks and Knox's) may have removed from Carlisle to N Carolina about the same time. My mother—now quite an aged lady—is still living, and I will hereafter ascertain from her whether she can give any information on this point. I think it probable, too, that she may be able to give more minute and accurate information concerning some of the elder members of the family, descended from William Polk, of Carlisle, and their descendants, than I have done. I will take pleasure in furnishing you with any additional information which I may be able to obtain.

I fear, my dear Sir, that I may impose too much labor upon you by the request I make, but I know of no other source from which I can derive so much and such reliable information concerning our family, as from yourself. I desire to obtain and preserve all the information concerning the family which I can procure. It may be interesting to those of our family who may come after us. After you shall have completed the "Tree and History", which you are preparing, I would be pleased to see and converse with you on the subject.

With High Regard
I am most respectfully
Your ob't Serv't
James K. Polk

To William H. Winder, Esq.

5. Letter of James K. Polk to Bishop Leonidas Polk, 30 October 1848

Washington City
October 30th,
1848
My Dear Sir!

William H. Winder, Esqr. of Philadelphia who is the son of Gen'l Winder of Baltimore has (illegible) a correspondence with me, and has (spoken to?) me personally with a view to obtain information of the Polk family. He is preparing a genealogical tree of the family and informs me that he will have as many copies struck off as will take him to furnish a copy to each member of the family who may desire it. I have furnished him with all the information which I possessed, (---) such of my own immediate family—it is not full. Mr. Winder is a gentleman of large fortune and is well educated and intelligent. His mother was a Polk (--- --- ---) in the genealogy of the family. I have promised him to write to you and request from you such information as you may possess. (--- --- ---) a subject between your father and Gen'l Winder shortly before the death of the latter in 1824—but your father (--- ---) unfortunately (--- ---). You will probably know the names of the brothers and sisters of your Grandfather's issue and something of their descendants. Two of the brothers I have informed him I thought were named Charley and John & that they had numerous descendants. Did they not have a sister named Deborah who married Samuel McCleary & lived in (---)sburg? I have a distant recollection that there was such a person and my impression is she was sister.—

In Mr. Winder's last letter to me he says regarding some memoranda I had collected for the purpose of making a genealogical tree of the Polk family I gleaned(?) the following, to wit. "In 1830 resided near LaGrange Tennessee a William Polk aged at the time about 50 years. He had a married daughter, probably three children. He had a distillery. Can you give me information as to which branch of the family he belonged?" I have assured him that there was such a person as I had understood residing in that part of the country some years ago, but I was unable to inform him from whom he had descended. Can you give this information? From this inquiry you will perceive that he designs to make the genealogical tree very full and minute. I desire that you will furnish me with all the information that you may possess, that I may furnish it to him. I gave him your address some weeks(?) ago and he may have written to you himself.

I have received a letter from a Robert Polk of Ireland, a copy of which I have furnished him and he is in (-----) to have this con(---)tion. He has collected much information but I can not undertake to give it to you in a letter—I will only mention that the first immigrants to America were Robert and Magdalen Polk. They had seven (several?) sons. Magdalen became a widow. Indeed it is not positively certain whether her husband (Robert) died before or after she came to America. She landed and settled in Maryland in 1668 . She lived to a very advanced age & died in 1727—having a will which is recorded in one of the counties of Maryland. I have a copy of it. It is a remarkable and interesting document. From her the N. Carolina Branch of the family is very satisfactority (sic) traced by Mr. Winder from the information in his possession.

When I receive your (---) I will furnish Mr. Winder a copy of it, and will request him to forward to you a copy of the genealogical tree as soon as it is completed.

With kind regards to Mrs. Polk,

I am very faithfully
& truly your friend
James K. Polk

To the
>Rev. Leonidas Polk
>Bishop of Louisiana

6. Letter of James K. Polk to William H. Winder, 30 October 1848

Washington City
October 30th 1848

My Dear Sir!

I have Received your note enquiring what knowledge I may have of a William Polk who according to your memoranda(?) resided in 1830 near LaGrange Tennessee and was at that time about fifty years of age. I have heard of a person of that name residing in that part of the country. I never saw him personally but understand that he may be of the N. Carolina branch. He must be one of the descendants of Charles or John, who were the brothers of Thomas and Ezekiel. He removed some years ago to the State of Mississippi. I will make enquiry concerning him and will give you such information as I may obtain.

Mr. Bancroft has not yet transmitted to me a copy of the papers which he (---) to write in the British Archives, which confirms (--- ---) the fact of the Mecklenburg Declaration of Independence in May 1775. I expect to receive these papers soon and will furnish you with a copy of them.

I am very faithfully
Your friend & ob. Ser't
James K. Polk

To
      William H. Winder, Esq.
      Philadelphia

7. Letter of Leonidas Polk to President James K. Polk, 17 January 1849

The following is a partial transcript of Bishop Polk's letter. The remainder of the contents pertain only to the Polk family in North Carolina and Tennessee. See *Polk Family and Kinsmen*, p.191-5, for the complete text.

<div align="center">~~~~~~~~</div>

Thibodoux, La.
Jan.17 1849.

My Dear Sir:—In reply to your letter on the subject of our ancestors, I regret to say I have misplaced and cannot find a memorandum I made several years ago, which contained a good deal of the information which Col. Winder wants. It contained the names of the children of William (the son of John, the son of Robert Polk), of whom your grandfather and mine were two. That William was he who first emigrated from Maryland and settled in the county of Anson, out of which he and his descendants, and their associates, caused Mecklenburg County to be formed. I may yet find it; if so. I will transmit it to you or Mr. Winder.

As it is a matter of some importance to us, I have addressed a letter to old Mrs. Smart, an old relative of ours, who was a contemporary of my father, and who, I believe, still lives (under cover to Julius Alexander) requesting her to give give me the names of the children of William Polk, of Maryland, and to inform me what became of them. So soon as I shall hear from her I will forward you her letter. She was a well informed old lady, and if living will give us some interesting facts.

I have been much interested in the letter you have caused to be copied and sent me, from Ireland. I have not a doubt that the writer is of the same family, as well from the name of the locality, for that was the precise region from which I have always heard our ancestors came. He is, however, deceived in the degree of his relationship to us.

I can lay my hands on a single sheet, only, of the memorandum I have spoken of, and that contains an account of the relationship of the Polks and Alexanders.

222

From it I learn that William Polk (son of John, son of Robert) who removed from Maryland (our great-grandfather) married a Miss Taylor, who was the mother of our grandfathers. She was one of five sisters; one other of the five married a Mr. Ruse [Reese] and was the mother of Rev. David Ruse [Reese]. The other three married Alexanders, who were the progenitors of all those of that name in Mecklenburg. These grades of relationship I find on that sheet, but as it is aside from Mr. Winder's purpose, I say no more on it.

....

8. Letter of Mrs. Smart to Bishop Leonidas Polk, 15 February 1849

The following is a transcription of a document found in the papers of W. H. Polk, now in the Library of the University of Kentucky. This copy was apparently provided to him by William H. Winder in 1876.

~~~~~~~~~~

Copy of Mrs. Smart's letter to Bishop Leonidas Polk, enclosed by the latter in his letter of July 19th 1849, to Wm. H. Winder of Phil., original letter at this time (1876) in possession of Mrs. Aurelia Townsend of Oyster Bay, Long Island

Charlotte Feb 15th 1849

Dear Sir:

You letter, enclosed in one to Mr. Alexander, I have received, and will answer it as well as I can. I never saw your great grandfather—William Polk—but was informed by your grandfather, and my parents, that he died several years before, at least twenty five years before the Revolutionary War. His wife was a Taylor (Margaret) he married her in the North, in Penn, and removed to North Carolina, and settled west of the Yadkin, where he died. He left the following children, Thomas, your Grandfather; William, who was the oldest son, John, Charles, Ezekiel, who was the grandfather of the President; the following daughters, Susan, who married Benjamin Alexander, Debora, who married Samuel McCleary & died without issue; Margaret, who married Robert McCree leaving a large family, among whom is James P. McRee of Tennessee. Susan Alexander left a large family, many of whom now live in this county. She was the mother of William Alexander, a Captain, commonly called "Black Bill", a distinguished soldier in the Revolutionary Army. John Polk married Eleanor Shelby, the daughter of Col. Isaac [Gen. Evan] Shelby. He had three sons and one daughter. The sons by name, Charley, John and Taylor, the daughter, Eleanor. Those now living, belonging to the family, reside in the West. William married a woman whose name I do not remember. They removed to Tennessee many years ago and had many children. Charles married Polly Clark, a full cousin of your father,

223

on the Mother's side. They removed to the West, having a large family. Ezekiel married Nanny Wilson, the mother of Samuel Polk, and the grandmother of the President, and after her death was married twice; by his second wife he had no children that lived any time; by his third, whom he married in Tennessee, I am informed he had several children.

Your grandfather, Thomas Polk, who was the most distinguished man of the family, married Susan Spratt, my mother's sister. They had the following children: your father; Thomas who was killed at the battle of Eutaw, by the side of my brother, John Barnett; Ezekiel, who died at sea; James who married the daughter of Col. Moore; Charley, who married the daughter of Hezekiah Alexander, died leaving two children, one now living in Tennessee, Thomas I. Polk; Martha, the eldest daughter, married Dr. Ephraim Brevard, who had one daughter, Martha, who married Mr. Dickerson of South Carolina, leaving one son, the late Col. James Polk Dickerson who was killed in Mexico; Margaret, the second daughter, married Governor Nathaniel Alexander and died without children; Polly, the fourth, married Daniel Brown, a distinguished lawyer of South Carolina; they had three children who died young. The third daughter, Debora, died at the age of fourteen.

My Aunt Susan, who married your Grandfather, Gen. Thomas Polk, was the daughter of Thomas Spratt, who was an excellent man and died highly esteemed by everyone. Your father, with whom I was very intimate, was always proud of his Spratt blood and often boasted of it. Col. Thomas Neale of South Carolina married Jane Spratt, the daughter of Thomas Spratt, by whom he had several children, among others, Andrew, a Colonel in the Revolutionary Army, who resembled out father very much; he was killed at the Battle of Eutaw; and Thomas, a Major, who fell shortly after the battle of Eutaw.

I have mentioned your Grandmother—Susan Spratt—and her family, although you did not ask of them, which I think you should have done. I am now eighty seven years of age and although infirm in body, am yet able to visit my friends and converse with them and am now writing this letter at the house of Wm. J. Alexander who, with his wife, I consider among my best friends. This letter, of course, I am not able to write myself but have procured the services of Major Alexander's sister. I should be glad to hear from you and remain,

Yours respectfully,

Susan Smart

9. Letter of Bishop Leonidas Polk to Wm. H. Winder, Esq., 19 July 1849

The following is a transcription of a document found in the papers of W. H. Polk, now in the Library of the University of Kentucky. This copy was apparently provided to him by William H. Winder in 1876.

Copy of letter written by Bishop Leonidas Polk of Louisiana to Wm. H. Winder, Esq. and in possession of Mrs. Townsend at this time (1876)

Thibodeaux, La
July 14th, 1849

To
Wm. H. Winder, Esq.
Phil.

Dear Sir,

Just before leaving Washington my late lamented Kinsman Jas. K. Polk addressed me a letter informing me of his having hand an interview with you in regard to the Polk family, in which, after informing him of the fact that on the maternal side you were of that family & that your father, the late Gen'l Winder had corresponded with mine, Col. William Polk, of Raleigh N.C., in relation to it, you expressed a wish to procure material for a genealogical tree of the family with a view to its being printed & and its publication among the members of the family. The late president, at the same time requested me to furnish him such facts as I might have concerning our branch of the family, which he wished to place at your disposal. I accordingly made out a memo as full as my means of information would allow & sent it to him, as I did not have the pleasure of seeing him on his way through Louisiana & I have not since heard from him, I do not know whether it was ever received. I have a copy of the paper still in my possession, which I take the liberty of saying is at your service, should it be desired. In the meantime I herewith enclose an interesting letter from, as you will perceive, a very old lady still living in the County of Mecklenburg & town of Charlotte, the place to which my ancestors removed from Pennsylvania. She is, as you will perceive, a relation of the family, and writes in a style quite characteristic of her period. The paper you propose to have printed would be a compilation of great interest to the family & I presume we might without vanity believe, that its showing would not be otherwise than creditable to their integrity, their intelligence, their enterprise & their patriotism.

I am, Dear Sir
    Very Respectfully
        Your ob. Srv't   Leonidas Polk

Appendix IV

"Memories" – Esther Winder Polk Lowe

Esther Winder Polk was born in 1824 into the genteel ante-bellum world of the rural gentry in a quiet corner of the Eastern Shore of Maryland. In her early years she led an idyllic life of traditional values inhabited with colorful personalities, and in 1844 married Enoch Louis Lowe, an aspiring young lawyer from Frederick, Maryland. Mr. Lowe quickly moved up in political circles and was elected the youngest-ever Governor of Maryland in 1851, attaining the required age of thirty just before his inauguration.

With her husband as Governor, the departed President her kinsman, a burgeoning young family, a magnificent mansion astride the Chesapeake at Annapolis, and the pageantry of the new Naval Academy at her door, it is hard to imagine what more heaven could offer Esther Lowe, only twenty seven years old at the time. This surely was a perfect life. Yet somehow it was not one that left her unsuited for the hardships and the sharp reversal of fortune that was soon to follow with the maelstrom of the Civil War. Governor Lowe was a Southerner and his political views forced him to relocate to Virginia, and then to Georgia, for fear of retribution during the war. The years that followed surely tried the courage and character of this family, but did not find them wanting. As with many southern families, they lost all, and were reduced to the barest essentials, especially in the last winter of the war.

In the face of the post-war reconstruction Enoch Lowe decided to move to New York City and resume his legal career, believing the cosmopolitan environment to be more tolerant and hopeful than the devastated South. This proved a wise choice and in due course he met with success. Enoch and Esther Lowe lived out their days in Brooklyn, he dying in 1892 and she in 1918. The present memoirs were written very late in Esther Lowe's long life but with a clear and stately mind, and we are fortunate that they have survived. They are a poignant record of an aristocratic spirit living through a watershed era of American history.

The text of these memoirs, entitled by her as "Memories," is available in the form of a handwritten transcription from the original, identified as MS 1949 in the Special Collections of the Maryland Historical Society, whose permission to publish the present transcription, made by the author, is gratefully acknowledged.

~~~~~~~~~~

My dear Daughter: -

You ask my Memories. In a life well nigh spent, there is left but retrospect, and memory, clouded by age with its attendant infirmities, that will I trust appeal to your indulgence, should it fall short of expectation.

In the stream of life there are currents and countercurrents, some gliding smoothly, some in varied gradations slowly or rapidly wending their way until the end, whilst others rushing wild, foaming in maddened fury, leap over precipices and are lost in the vast ocean. My life is like the small stream rising in mountain fastness, slowly meandering its way, oftentimes calm, limpid, unobstructed, sometimes rippling and sometimes dashing against rocks and shoals, threatened to be swallowed by the whirlpool. And yet through all these changes of times and conditions, I have lived almost 89 years - surely a relic of the past.

It was on the 29th day of February, 1824, that I first saw the light, and traditions of the family were the only inheritance of which I can boast, and those interesting me were guarded as sacred.

My ancestor, Robert Bruce Pollock, came from the North of Ireland about the year 1660 and settled in Somerset County on the Eastern Shore of Maryland having received a grant of land from the King of England. From some cause or other the place was known as "Polk's Folly". Why it was so called no one seems to know - perhaps they went to unnecessary expense for those times when the stability of government was insecure owing to various causes, notably the constant threat of Indian outrages in that section, the Nanticokes just there being a most savage tribe. Robert Bruce Pollock moved from these lands, which were situated upon the Manokin River - beautiful tributary of the Chesapeake Bay to lands purchased by him on the Wicomico River - another beautiful stream, arm of the Chesapeake Bay. This place was named "White Hall", and it was there that Judge David Polk, grand son of Robert Bruce Pollock, and grandfather of my Father, and my great grandfather, was born, lived and died.

My grandfather, Judge William Polk, was Chief Justice of the Court of Appeals of Maryland, and I am proud to say he was appointed in those days when Judges were selected for high moral standing, superior talent, and knowledge of Jurisprudence, rather than by weight of dollars and cents or strong political following. My grandfather was married three times. His first wife was Esther Winder, who was a sister of Governor Winder. By that marriage there were three daughters, the oldest, Elizabeth, who married Mr. Fromentine, the first U. S. Senator after the purchase of Louisiana. The second daughter, Esther, married three times. By way of episode, I will mention that it was for this aunt I was named. The story goes that at my birth she said to my mother that if I should be called "Esther", after her, she would give me a fortune. My Mother, tempted by her promise, did so. I received the name, but not the fortune. My

227

Aunt Esther married Captain King, a man of high birth and fortune. Her second husband was Doctor Winder, her cousin, nephew of Governor Winder. A few years after his death she married Colonel Alexander Stuart - lawyer by profession and half brother of my mother. The third daughter, Gertrude, married General William H. Winder, her cousin, a distinguished member of the Baltimore Bar. These aunts of mine were women of talent, as were the Polks generally of that generation - men and women. My grandfather's second wife was Nancy Dennis, a widow - maiden name Purnell. Her husband was lost at sea. She had one child when she married my grandfather whose name was Littleton Purnell Dennis. He became a man of distinction in Maryland and died in Congress where his body now rests in the Capitol Cemetery. I remember him well, a kind man, Uncle Littleton! He never married, lived on a farm on the Wicomico River, which place was left by him to my Father, who was his half brother and the only child of the marriage of Nancy Dennis and Judge William Polk.

My grandfather when over 60 years of age, whilst attending a sitting of the court in Worcester County, met a beautiful young woman (whose name I cannot recall) and whom he afterwards married. He brought her to White Hall. She was the mother of Aunt Anne Johnson. After the death of my grandfather, she married Doctor Savage of Cambridge Maryland, and they emigrated to Augusta Georgia.

My Father was left motherless at the age of three years and was brought up by the three sisters above mentioned. They all seemed to live together happily at White Hall, but like all things human, changes took place and the home was broken up.

The marriage of my parents took place in 1817 - my Mother 17 years of age, my Father 21. They were married without the consent or knowledge of their brothers and sisters, having no parents to consult, both being orphans since early childhood and possessing adequate means to make the venture of matrimony. It was in the old home White Hall that they commenced their marital cares, and it was there the two first children were born and died. After that they moved to Princess Anne, a little village of about 900 inhabitants. My brother William was the first child born there - an extremely gentle, amiable boy. He grew to manhood; married in the state of Texas; enlisted in the Civil War; contracted disease and died. My sister, Mary, my companion by day and night, in doors and out of doors, in joy and in sadness - I say sadness because the next in our household was Elizabeth who died and although mere children, almost babies the death of that dear little sister is as fresh in memory as of yesterday. How mistaken those who say that the sorrow of children is not poignant. My sister, Ariana, came next. A sweet, black eyed child, now an old woman whose checkered life has been born with singular cheerfulness and resignation to the behests of fortune. After Ariana came Thomas Hampden, A beautiful boy - he died. Then dear James, my favorite brother - always kind, considerate of every

228

one, buoyant under the weight of unremitting misfortune. He died in the prime of life, beloved and regretted by all who knew him. Lucius and Josiah were the last, and when I married in 1844 were small children. Both of these brothers were affectionate and kind and I was much attached to them. Josiah died in 1901. Lucius is still alive.

It behooves the autobiographer to use freely the personal pronoun, a distasteful necessity, savoring as it does of conceit; but as it is one of those things subservient to usage and cannot be dispensed with, I hope, the writer will not be amenable to criticism.

One of my first recollections is the house wherein I was born - situated on the main street of the pretty little village. As all objects to the eye of a child are in proportion to physical capacity and limitation, so to mine that old home looked a magnificent structure, the columns supporting the piazza seemed gigantic - the very acme of architectural beauty. The grounds in the front were sodded and gloried in the possession of two magnificent trees - one sugar maple, the other a catalpa. Often under the shadow of those old trees my sister and I played doll house and the wealth of the Indies could not have given more pleasure in its wealth of ornamentation than did a little scrap of cotton tied around our home made rag babies. The garden back of the house, covering at least an acre of ground, was a beauty in its way, always plentifully supplied with luscious fruits and vegetables, and at the entrance were two beautiful arbors covered with sweet smelling woodbine, whose delicious blossoms, wet with morning dew, permeated the atmosphere with life giving odors. In a remote corner stood the cabin of old Aunt Hannah - our faithful old nurse - whose days for work had passed, her sole duty being to take charge of the children when mother was visiting. Aunt Hannah was a great prayer. Often have we stood at her door and listened to her fervent prayer. On Friday she fasted the entire day, a custom religiously observed throughout life. Why this self imposed penance I cannot imagine; certainly it was not the result of education or example since no one black or white ever followed that rule.

On the street back of our house was an Episcopal Church and quite an aristocratic congregation was there. About the time of the Oxford Movement headed by Doctor Pusey, an eminent divine of the Church of England, a change came over a certain portion of the Congregation who wished to join the Pusey Movement, whilst others, calling themselves low church, held fast to old rules and customs. No ornamentation of the alter had been spoken of, such a thing being considered rank heresy by some, or a tendency to Popery by others. Naturally there was great commotion among the faithful of high church and low church. John H. Stewart or J.H.S. as he often signed himself as vestryman, chief loud singer and Major Domo in all things pertaining to church matters, took the lead in the high church party, and had placed over the alter the letter J.H.S. (Jesu Salvator Hominum). Old Mrs. Betsy Pullett was leader of the low church party and jealous of John H. Stewart's authority, looked at the altar, saw the letters J.H.S. and exclaimed" What presumption! John H. Stewart to have the audacity to put his initials over the altar." There were exciting times with villagers whose isolation - results of the geographic situation of the Eastern Shore - made them more sensitive and than those in touch with the world. And now, whilst upon this subject, my memory goes back to the social conditions of those people 70 years ago. Isolation, although hampering them in regard to certain material advantages, has its full compensation in others. There were no steamboats, no railroads, and mails came but once a week, consequently following traditions of the old Country and thrown entirely upon their own resources for social entertainment literature was generally studied, and to be conversant with the highest standards of English Classics, was the ambition of all well bred persons. I have said there were no means of transport. Between Baltimore and the Eastern Shore small sail boats alone were used for conveying freight to and from those points. In order to get to Baltimore it was necessary to go in one of those little boats. Imagine the discomfort - a little bit of a cabin with four berths and sometimes it would take an entire week to make the Journey. Crossing the Atlantic was nothing in comparison to it. The traveler would be in consternation days before starting in apprehension of dangers to be encountered upon the waters of the Chesapeake. Sixty years ago, perhaps a little before, a steamboat came once a week to White Haven, a hamlet on the Wicomico River.

The sports of the old country, handed down from father to son, were religiously kept up -- considered a proud inheritance. Fox hunting, horse racing, card playing, and many other sports of country gentlemen were freely indulged in. Generally they were large land and slave holders. My grandfather had many slaves, and it is told of him that upon an occasion when the services of an extra cook or to assist was questioned by him was questioned as to her knowledge of cooking, she was asked, "Betty, can you make ice cream?" Her answer was "oh yes indeed Master." Then the question: "How do you do it?" To which she replied: "Well Master some fries it in butter, some in fats." As a result Betty's services were not required.

My grandfather died in 1814, so, of course, I never saw him, but to judge of his personal appearance in paintings made by Charles Wilson Peale, now in possession of my nephew, Judge James P. Garter, he was a man of fine presence, striking personality. My Aunt Esther lived in the country a few miles from Princess Anne. Her residence a large mansion built from brick brought from England, was one of the most elegant in the counties. I remember well her carriage, which as a child, I thought was so beautiful. It was yellow and quite a sorrow to me -- I was then six years old only -- that our coach was brown and not yellow. When my aunt came into town in that bright coach, drawn by two spanking gray horses and a footman opened the door and unfolded the steps that she might alight, I thought she looked like Queen Elizabeth, whose picture was in my spelling book. I had just begun to go to school, to a village school master. It was there that I commenced my education in ABC, and graduating in the primer, I was sent to a school kept by a relative -- a lady of superior *attainments, whose graceful form and dignified bearing were a practical lesson to her pupils. I can truly say that all I ever learned was at that simple school. Later when it was supposed that my mind was sufficiently developed to take advantage of a fashionable boarding school training, I was entered into what was styled a first class Young Ladies Academy. There were many girls from the adjacent counties -- also from the Eastern Shore of Virginia. My particular friend and classmate was Martha Denny from Talbot County -- afterwards married to Doctor Harrison, a man of literary acquirements. Martha was a congenial girl, happy and always ready for fun. She was the mother Mrs. Noble who lived near you in Baltimore. Two years ago she passed away. Another girl I remember was Rosa Williams. She was the star of the first magnitude whose superiority claimed the obeisance of the entire school, extending even to the Principle herself, who after Rosa's entrance, changed and made rules in accordance with those that Rosa followed in a boarding school in Philadelphia where she was supposed to have been at one time a pupil. She always wore demi-train, held up her head and walked like a queen. Recognition from her was an epoch from a girl and the condescension of a smile almost threw the fortunate recipient into fits. Well, Rosa married Lieutenant Inge of the US army who was stationed somewhere in a western fort. Major Arnold, whom I knew, was in command and lived there with his family. Mrs. Arnold, an amiable woman, of domestic habits, made her own preserves and pickles. One day when making preserves Rosa expressed the desire to see the process and looking intently at the boiling fruit said "Oh I perceive the sugar incorporates itself with the fruit and enters the interstices." This little incident was told me by the major himself who was greatly amused. It was at that period that the Mexican War commenced and Rosa's husband Lt. Inge was the first officer to loose his life in that conflict. I have never heard of her since, but suppose that like all my school mates and contemporaries has passed into the Unknown World.*

My Father and Mother loved to entertain. Hospitality was to them a sacred virtue and friend or wayfarer entering into their home was always sure of warm welcome, a generous supply of all things eatable and drinkable. Upon one occasion an old Methodist preacher from Devil's Island, which was distant about 20 miles from Princess Anne, was making his yearly visit to the town, as was the custom of the Islanders for the purchase of winter supply or provision, called to see my father. The old man was a well known character, uneducated, but original. All the Islanders knew my father and were fond of him. Upon one occasion, Mr. Joshua Thomas, such was his name, came to the village and my father asked him to dinner. After they had all finished the old man said: "Brother Polk, we will pray" and down they all knelt around the table. He said: "Oh Lord, bless brother Polk and his pretty little wife. He gave me not only the meats, but the sweets of his house also." Mr. Thomas had a canoe of extraordinary size, made by himself out of one pine tree, a boat that in the far South is called a dugout. It is said that always at the end of his prayer was:"Lord bless me and my Kuner" (canoe). These Islanders were people remote from civilization, knew nothing of the world and its doings. They lived upon the products of the water and in their simple lives enjoyed the bliss of ignorance.

Devil's Island is at the mouth of the Manokin River and it was upon that beautiful arm of the Bay that the sailboats which conveyed passengers to Baltimore anchored. To get to those boats it was necessary to go to the house of Colonel Arnold Jones, whose stately residence upon the silvery shore of the Manokin stood out a beacon light to seafaring people. Colonel Jones was one of my fathers intimate friends -- an aristocrat who loved those alluring sports of which has already been spoken. His home was called Elm Wood. Oh, how I loved that expansive water view and almost envy the fortunate owners of that grand old home situated upon a velvety lawn gently sloping to the rivers edge, whose shores of sparkling sand afforded delightful bathing. In minds eye now, I see the lavish style of entertaining in those country homes -- The grand old mahogany table groaning under weight of luscious viands -- the very acme of culinary skill. and with it "feast of reason and flow of soul" the embodiment of corporal, mental, and heart full hospitality. The Polk family, aristocratic by birth cultured and by nature genial were noted for their generous hospitality. My father partook largely of their characteristics. Just here I cannot omit to mention my mother whose claim to good breeding was quite equal to that of the Polks. She was the daughter of Doctor Alexander Stuart, conspicuous as Surgeon in the War of the Revolution and a particular friend of George Washington, on whose staff he served. It is through regard to the memory of my mother that I mention this and not for myself as I lay but little store in my family records beyond a certain point, agreeing with the poet that "rank is but the guinea's stamp, the man's the gold for a' that." My mother however, had different ideas and was proud of her Scotch ancestry. To go a little farther into her immediate family may be interesting to you. She had four brothers -- one was killed in a duel, as mentioned in Old Kent by George Hanson. Two were lawyers and one Consul to Manila under the administration of President Monroe. This last mentioned brother was killed in an insurrection of the natives. She had four sisters. The two elder ones married and lived to be very old. The third sister was thrown from a carriage and instantly killed. The fourth sister was the mother of Doctor Thomas Williams of Cambridge, Maryland, and of your two lovely cousins, Rebecca and Annie, who were brought up by my mother and were to me like sisters. You know they have both passed away. Rebecca died at our house in Frederick and rests in our lot in the Catholic cemetery. The grave marked by head and foot stone upon which is engraved simply her name and the beautiful words "Sursum Corda."

These little memories are I know fragmentary and disjointed, but dear child, you will have to take them as they come and go, irrespective of order -- so much by way of episode.

When I was about eight years old I had an experience never to be forgotten. For months, it seemed to be years, an inexpressible terror possessed me. There had been a rising of the Negroes in North Hampton Virginia, a butchery of the Whites rivaling that of San Domingo. The spirit of revolt spread throughout the Eastern Shore and in a county without police protection we were at the mercy of the slaves. The dread of massacre was at our door and the dread of terrible torture was maddening. This condition of fear was followed by months of unrest.

My father's mother was a native of Worcester County. Her name, Purnell, was the most prominent one there. A desire to visit my numerous relatives induced my parents to give consent. One summer I accompanied my cousin Hettie Purnell -- who was then at school in Princess Anne -- to her home to spend vacation. She was the daughter of Doctor George Purnell. He lived near the ocean; from his house could be heard the roaring of the great Atlantic. A favorite excursion was a walk to the beach, then only a long stretch of land, now the well known Summer resort, Ocean City. Upon one occasion my cousin and I together with a party of boys and girls set out for the bathing ground. We all donned bathing suits, such as they were, simple calico gowns. Mine happened to have been in use often and as the sequel proved, not seaworthy; however, there was no close examination for in the enthusiasm and buoyancy of youth anything sufficed for the moment. I was proud to be gallanted by a chivalrous youth who helped me to hold fast to the hulk of a old wrecked ship -- the only surety in case of danger. The waves rolled over me and my calico. I bore the brunt, but alas, my bathing dress succumbed and from the waste to foot was torn to tatters. Imagine my discomfiture. That was my first and last experience in surf bathing.

It was in 1843 that suffering from the effects of severe fever, my parents thought it necessary I should leave the low lands, hoping that bracing mountain air would restore me to health. A friend in the Virginia Valley had invited my sister and me to make her a visit. We did so, and a more genial, delightful family could not be found anywhere. They lived in a large stone house, beautifully situated in view of the Blue Ridge Mountains and surrounded by vast acres of fruitful land. Nothing particularly eventful or startling took place while there; one day passing pretty much as another -- mornings spent in exercise or reading and afternoons agreeably spent at the Jordan White Sulfur Springs which at that time was noted for the excellence of its waters. We stayed several weeks without friends and the efficacy of those waters was apparent in my complete restoration to health. To return to our home, it was necessary to pass the Frederick Junction of the B & O Road. We had a cousin in Frederick who had often invited us to visit her. Arriving at the Junction, we remembered and concluded to stop with her a few days. She was delighted to see us and nothing was left undone to make the time pass agreeably. A beautiful entertainment was given us to which were invited the best people of the town. Colonel Hanson mentioned the names of two or three eligible young men -- one in particular, a Mr. Lowe, recently from a college in England, and most enthusiastic in admiration ventured to say he hoped one of us would catch the prize. Mr. Lowe called. Not to be exact in detail

233

would be an unpardonable omission, therefore to pass the subject of that period of my life, so important and absorbing would be an injustice to the hero of my story. Your father's personal appearance to me, his charms were most striking. His was the form of an Apollo, slight and graceful; hair black, hanging upon his shoulders -- the supposed type of poetic temperament and to complete the comparison by his admirers, the prototype of Lord Byron -- even collar carelessly opened at the neck, according to Byronic style was so worn to accentuate more decidedly the similarity. Such was his appearance, and his physiognomy of classic mold in perfect harmony with the general personality was captivating in the extreme to young women -- even to those like myself not particularly blessed with romantic tendencies. To look back upon those days seems now a dream, and a pleasant one, although the sorrows and misfortunes of life would seemed to have effaced the memories of youthful pleasures. He looked to me grand -- distinguished, patrician. Entering the room, hat in hand, he made a sweeping bow of a style unknown to Eastern Shore people, something I thought particularly English as the Maryland style of bowing was rather short in comparison. He wore a Boston made coat which he considered a perfection of cut, and it did become his slight, graceful form. Several times he called to see us and books were discussed largely. I knew more about novels then than I do now, for to be considered "well-read" was quite a hobby with me. I was conversant with the works of Bulwer, Walter Scott and all the well-known authors of that day; also upon historical subjects my memory was fresh, and you may be sure, was not dormant, nor were the legitimate wiles of innocent finesse omitted upon that occasion. The question was quietly asked in the family which of the two sisters the handsome Mr. Lowe would fancy -- of course, if either one would be the lucky winner. An intuitive desire to marry a man of whom an ambitious young woman would be proud inclined in my most inmost heart the unworthy feeling of endeavor to look my best, even to the extent to surpass my sister, who was indeed handsomer than I, having the advantage of height and gracefulness of form, a charm that I had not; besides which she was endowed with grace of manner and readiness of wit which made her more magnetic than I could ever be. The advantage, and only one, with which nature had favored me was a fine, sympathetic voice, and the sequel proved it was not used in vain. We passed two weeks most delightfully in that pretty mountain village. The time came that we must go home and when leaving the door of our cousin, a messenger handed me a bouquet. Hidden in the leaves was a tiny, dainty little note saying that Mr. Lowe would go to Princess Anne soon. Imagine the agitation of hope uncertain. We left and reached Baltimore in good time, the next day taking the boat for home. I say the boat, because it was the only one; and such a boat -- two sails; a little bit of a cabin with two berths. I think it took about six days to reach the Manokin River where a canoe, rowed by one colored man, landed us on shore at the house of Mrs. Nancy Jones, widow of Colonel Arnold Jones, my father's friend of whom I have already spoken. Mrs. Jones according to the custom of the country gave us a hardy greeting and "Aunt Diana," the cook was told to tell "Uncle Simon" to take the canoe and go out into the river and bring in large oysters for dinner. How my memory goes back to those days of simple life when to ask a person to come for one week, or two weeks, or to name any particular length of time, was considered the greatest violation of hospitality. Come when you please, go when you please was the motto of the time. Mrs. Jones, seeing that we were anxious to go home -- remembering to welcome the coming and speed the parting guest -- ordered her coach and sent us home.

In the course of six weeks, the prophecy of the little note was fulfilled -- an epoch in the life of that little village. He remained a few days only. You wonder how he got there. A steamboat took passengers from Baltimore to Cambridge, thence by hired hacks, the only available public conveyances in those days. Six months afterwards we were married and I left the home of my childhood.

Since the Civil War, the Eastern Shore has taken on a new aspect. The gentlemen of estates, almost baronial, are no more, an influx of nondescripts have taken possession and no longer is seen the old coach with driver of ebony hue, or the gig made after English fashion, wending its quiet gait on those level roads, shaded by gigantic trees, on the way to visit Mrs. John Teackle or Miss Mary Gale; jogging along content with all the world; no thought of tomorrow or a rainy day since corn was plentiful and Negroes happy. How changed! Material advantages, so to speak, have superseded the primitive mode of that quiet, contented Eastern Shore, and with those innovations, so highly prized by present generations, the query comes, do they enjoy with their railroads and automobiles of lightning speed, the same sense of security and peace of mind as did our forefathers whose habits of life contributed to quiet thoughtfulness and culture of mind.

We were married on the twenty-ninth day of May 1844. My kinsman, James K. Polk, was just then nominated for the Presidency and the Democrats throughout the country were wild in excitement. It was on the first day of June that I arrived in Frederick and with timidity natural to youth, I approached my intended house with fear and trembling. How would I be received. What should I say; a thousand hopes and fears, rushing pell-mell into my brain -- and all for nothing. At the front door stood dear Aunt Victoire, face beaming with kindness. She kissed me and with the words: "Welcome, dear Child, welcome." Quietly handed me over to your grandmother who affectionately embraced me -- the wife of her adored son -- with the warmth of a mother's love. That scene is imprinted upon my heart never to be effaced. Looking back, and judging as I am now capable, those two women in superiority of mind and high moral qualities, were peerless. I lived with one of them seventeen years and with the other a few years less, and can truly say that apart from my own shortcomings -- those little inequalities of character generally found in youth -- no conflicting elements characterized our peaceful companionship. And how could it be otherwise when patience, so necessary to the tranquillity of family life, was ever the abiding principal and rule of action in that home.

Aunt Victoire in physique was regal -- of majestic bearing. At that period she had attained the age of 66 years, and although time had naturally made its impress, beauty of expression, of tenderness and sympathy were still in those eyes of loving kindness. She was angelic; I will never look upon her like again. Your grandmother perhaps was possessed of stronger mentality and somewhat of pride of intellect; but of unswerving principal and readiness to correct a wrong should she consider herself to have judged rashly. Self-sacrifice was their rule of life. They were most generous and appeal from any charity was never unheeded, unless it savored of Protestant progress, and in that they were stern as rocks. No compromise was the watchword and to give to the rearing of Protestant churches was considered by them as such. During the cholera, Aunt Victoire had tents erected just outside of Frederick where Irish laborers on the B&O road, then in the course of construction were cared for and nursed at her expense. Another interesting and notable example of her charity I must quote. These fact I have heard from a friend of the family; not directly from them, for they were not of the class to blazon to the world the works of the "right hand." Owing to the Insurrection of St. Domingo, people of vast wealth became impoverished. Obliged to flee the country, they sought refuge in the United States and elsewhere. Amongst them was a friend of Aunt Victoire who was wandering in the South with two grandchildren. Aunt Victoire heard of their pitiable condition and sent them to come to the Hermitage, and there they remained. They grew up to be charming women. One married and became the mother of three children. The two first were mutes, the third at the age of ten months, gave sign of being able to speak. The mother was overjoyed; but it was short-lived for she fell victim to that dreadful scourge, the cholera, before hearing him lisp the word "mother". The other daughter became a Sister of Charity. She went to New Orleans and there established a house for orphans where for twenty-five years she worked indefatigably and died the very day that the Union soldiers took possession of that city. Sister Francis Regis, a name well-known and revered by everyone in New Orleans. I hear that a monument would be erected to her memory. What became of the mother of these two children was a mystery. She deserted her children and no one knew why. Of course, there were whisperings. To continue this story as I heard it, one day Sister Regis, when upon a mission of charity, visiting a hospital was asked to see a dying woman there. She answered the call and in the course of conversation discovered that it was her mother.

It was in Annapolis in 1854 that Aunt Victoire met with the accident that caused her death a few weeks later. Your grandmother after a lingering illness, died on Good Friday in 1861. They both died as they had lived, the exemplar of all the virtues.

My life in Frederick after marriage was uneventful -- the same as in the course of human events characterizes every woman. Children came, and with maternity cares and responsibilities; but with all I managed to recreate myself by a visit now and then to Baltimore where my parents then resided. One visit in particular I remember which gave me great pleasure. It was about the year 1848 that Jenny Lind, the Swedish nightingale as she was called, was in Baltimore. Being the first famous singer since Mme. Malibran -- who many years before I was born had visited this country -- her coming created a perfect furor. In New York, boxes at the theater sold for fabulous prices -- notably one was bought by Knox the Hatter at an enormous price -- I think eleven hundred dollars. Of course it was an advertisement for his hats. Your father, grandmother Lowe and I went to hear her. I was disappointed but dared not say so, as the people were madly wild about her. Now, at liberty to express my opinions, I do say that I have heard others since that time whose vocalization pleased me more. There was some clap trap about her which took the crowd. Her voice was in a way phenomenal, possessing powers of ventriloquism which enabled her to perform vocal feats which no other singer had ever done before or since. For instance in the echo song she threw her voice so as to make a perfect, natural echo. Sister Mary and I called upon her. She was not pretty, nor was her manner either graceful or gracious. She was rather brusque, however public indulgence overlooked the superficial for those substantial qualities so nobly demonstrated in an unselfish desire to appropriate her talent to charity, as well as to her own personal profit. In every city she gave one concert for the poor. She sang only in concert. Her best and greatest number was "I know that my Redeemer liveth".

It was in 1850 that your father's ambition aroused, led him into a new career, that of politics. Up to that time, he had practiced law. Mr. John W. Baughman, his partner, was married the day before we were, and as companions for both your father and me were invited to live in our house as members of the family. We never regretted the companionship of these lifelong friends. Their first child, Victor was born three weeks before your sister Adelaide and the tie of friendship was knotted more tightly by those babies whose coming into a household without children shed light and cheerfulness where before a somber atmosphere had pervaded the house, inhabited as it had been by two women alone, whose tastes and habits were at variance with their surroundings. They were strictly religious Catholics and at that period there were few of such -- of their social standing -- in Frederick. The population was mostly German, and as may be supposed the teachings of Calvin and Luther, bitterly antagonistic to Catholicism, had taken so strong a hold on their prejudices as to control neighborly feelings. Naturally a cold, severe reserve gave a serious and sad coloring to the live of grandmother and Aunt Victoire. I remember how systematically once a year your grandmother called formally upon certain persons of her acquaintance -- how formal her demeanor, and a remark I once heard her make speaking of Mrs. T. "She is very sweet, but we are like two lambs upon the brink of a precipice -- a gulf between; we look across the gulf and smile at each other; but that impassable gulf is there." She seemed never able to throw off that feeling which seems to us strange now since the ingress of the foreign element has so changed social conditions as to make us forget the bitterness and bigotry of past generations.

237

When your Father was nominated for Governor he was not thirty years old, but attained the legal age before election. We had then four children, Adelaide, Anna, Paul, and Louis. On January first, after the election we went to Annapolis. Never can I forget our entrance into that grand old colonial mansion, once the abode of Governor Eden, the English Governor, who at the beginning of the Revolutionary War made his escape to England. His house was confiscated by the state -- a delightful residence situated upon Annapolis Bay, just where the beautiful Severn joins it. A broad expanse of water as far as the eye could reach was the view from the spacious back porch; only the outlines of Kent Island to interrupt it. The structure was built of English brick; a main building and at each end a wing -- one used as breakfast room, the other as library. A large hall of entrance separated dining and drawing rooms and at the end of the hall a large semi-circular room, extending the entire width of the building was used on special occasions -- such as state dinners held each week -- necessarily requiring a spacious room. The garden sloping gradually to the water was most attractive. Two immense fig trees, so large that children and even grown persons could sit in their branches. Bushels of figs were gathered from these trees and supplies sent to friends in Baltimore who like ourselves enjoyed the luscious fruit. Alas! Those beautiful trees were killed in the severe cold of the winter of 1863 or thereabouts. A few years ago the house was purchased by the U. S. Government and enclosed in the Navy Yard and has since been torn down -- upon its site has been erected a magnificent Armory.

Many a delightful hour have I passed in that delightful historic building; and again as "into each life some rain must fall" it was there that the first deep sorrow pierced my heart. One morning when all was bright and sunshine, I saw my little children playing in the garden and my little Louis, the elder boy, was wearing a wreath of morning glories upon his head. He looked the picture of health. That night a violent fever seized him and the next day at that same hour that I saw him running and playing in the garden, his little body lay in death. It was truly the first great grief of my life and for months the mention of his name was an arrow penetrating my very soul.

It was about that time my friend Mrs. Alexander Randall, daughter of the illustrious William Wirt, lost two of her children -- one a little boy of three years fell into a tub of boiling brine. How differently are all forms in this world, although doubtless possessed of equal depth of feeling. I thought she would be crushed, yet with a certain degree of Christianity or philosophy or whatever one may call it, she sat up in her chair and in her lap was held the seared body of that poor little boy -- posed for a photographer. She wrote me in her poetic style that "for sometime the Angel of Death has been hovering over our home." She was a very spiritual woman and highly gifted. I wondered how she could do and say all that she did. It only goes to prove that wise nature has created minds and hearts of varied forms and to put ourselves in judgment as to degree of feeling is truly presumption. Not long after I left Annapolis she died of cancer -- that lovely daughter of one of Maryland's most distinguished sons.

Our domestic contingent at the Government House consisted of cook, two butlers, housemaid, nurse and coachman. The butlers belonged to us. They were competent, honest, and self-respecting. Augustus particularly -- the first butler-- feeling superiority of his white blood, yielded to "no niggers" when it was a question of precedence, sustaining his right on the ground of aristocratic descent -- his father being an "Honorable Judge." There were many amusing things which happened among the "Colored ladies and gentlemen" of Annapolis. A marked feature of the Negro character was ambition to talk like educated people and in conversation to use words which they did not understand and naturally mispronounced. For instance, the servants of one of my friends gave a party. They seemed to be hilarious and she heard one of them say in loud voice "Mr. Johnsing exaggerate that waiter around upon your hyperbolia". What he meant was a mystery to be solved. One very important personage was Moses Lake, an aristocratic Black "gentleman" who enjoyed the distinction of professional barber. He was particularly distinguished having been valet of Chief Justice Buchanan during a tour of England and Ireland. It was in London, at a great function where guests were announced in loud voice, when Moses, unused to that custom, imagined that the Marquis of Wellesley, or some other grand dignitary, was receiving more honor than the Chief Justice, who was just approaching. Fearing he might not be noticed, Moses cried out in stentorian voice: "The Lord Chief Justice of America". The walls of Moses' barbershop were adorned with pictures of well-known places in England and Ireland. There was one labeled "Moses Lake in Westminster Abbey," another "Moses Lake at the Lakes of Killarney." Someone said to him, "Why Moses, I did not know that you were at the Lakes of Killarney," when with consequential air he answered: "oh yes, it was there I met the original family of the Lakes." Mrs. Lake, his wife, was as near in color to white as he was to coal black and quite as elegant, claiming right to highest regard, having been brought up in the aristocratic family of Commodore Porter. She was indeed a most dignified woman, and by general consent of everyone, white and colored, was called Mrs. Lake.

The gate of the Navy Yard was about twenty yards from our front door and I had many friends among the officers families, whom I prized highly. With pleasure I recall that of Professor Chauvenet, the light of the academy. He was Professor of Mathematics, applied to Astronomy, and to this was added the accomplishment of music. He gloried in the works of Beethoven and played on Sunday -- a great sin in those days of narrowness - even at the expense of giving scandal. That interesting family moved to St. Louis and most of them have joined the great majority. The Lockwoods were another family that I visited very intimately. They had one son who perished in one of those expeditions to the North Pole. Their daughter married Commodore Sigsbee who commanded the Maine when she was blown up on the coast of Cuba. Annapolis was a delightful old place; replete with historic associations. The massive buildings of St. John's College still stand intact -- vestige of ancient glory.

Six years ago I visited Robert at the academy and upon inquiry found that only one of my old friends was still there -- Mrs. Jessie Haversham, a grand-daughter of Francis Scott Key, author of the immortal "Star Spangled Banner." A queer history, recently come to light, is that of her granddaughter. It seems that a few years ago she became wildly enamored with the king of a band of gypsies, married him and left her luxurious home to wander around the world. Last year somewhere in the West, she died, leaving an infant. Her parents heard of it and sent for the child. A few weeks ago it died. Such was the fate of a descendent of the far-famed Francis Scott Key.

A favorite pastime with us was a sail in the "Rainbow" which the Commander of the Yard placed at our service. Upon one occasion a Midshipman, who was always ready to command the boat was our Captain. He was very much in love with my beautiful cousin, Rebecca Williams, whose charms captivated many of the officers. Our captain who was so much absorbed in conversation with her that he forgot the helm and allowed us to be almost run down by a schooner laden with wood -- one piece striking my cousin Annie on the head, so very near were we.

The Severn River, at that time only here and there dotted with a house, now has its shores lined with beautiful villas and land at that time ten dollars an acre now commands two hundred or more. The old home of Charles Carroll of Carrolltown, situated upon Spa Creek, an arm of the bay was directly in the rear. The Marchioness of Wellesley and Lady Stafford, granddaughter of Charles Carroll donated it to the Redemptorist Fathers; Father Rumfiler was Superior. He was a man of great learning but very eccentric. The first time he called at the Government House I naturally held out my hand to him. He shrank back saying; "I never shake hands with women." Your grandmother congratulated him upon his beautiful residence so situated upon the water as to afford them the delightful advantage of bathing. He replied gravely, "St. Francis Xavier, when upon the coast of China never bathed." Poor man, he lost his mind, became a raving maniac, was sent to Mount Hope and from there to some retreat in Germany.

Our position in Annapolis gave opportunity for acquaintanceship with many prominent and distinguished men and women. I remember Sir William Ously and Mrs. Ously, nee Van Ness. They were friends of the Randalls. Sir William Ously was at that time Ambassador to one of the South American republics. He sang well, and he and I sang duets, enjoying our old time English songs such as "I Know where the Woodbine Twineth". In those days that style of music was greatly admired; today perhaps such compositions would be ridiculed. The great Daniel Webster, eminent constitutional lawyer, the most celebrated this country ever produced, with Mrs. Webster dined with us. He was a man of remarkable personality and to give a pen picture of him is difficult. Imagine a ponderous physique, a figure grandly statuesque with features immobile. Under a forehead of projecting prominence were sunken eyes, deep,

240

dark, mysterious. He spoke but little -- it was multum in parva, but those few words uttered in slow, measured, sepulchral tones, given out in Delphic style evoked admiration not unmingled with shivering sensations of creeping coldness. Mrs. Webster was far from being a typical society woman. She was simple in manner, gentle and motherly. It was during the administration of Mr. Pierce that this visit occurred and in this connection, Mr. Pierce naturally comes to my mind. The contrast in style and manner between these two distinguished men was remarkable. Mr. Pierce was cordial and polished and in point of intellect might be compared to a sharpshooter; the other a Columbiad. It is impossible for me to remember all the persons of note that I meant during the administration of your Father. One I call to mind, as he visited Annapolis frequently. It was the honorable John G. Marcy, a member of President Pierce's Cabinet. A rather rough and tumble kind of man, with benevolent face and kind word for everybody. He was at the time Secretary of the Navy and his son Lt. Marcy was stationed at the Yard. Lt. Marcy, kind, good fellow, was one of the first victims of the Civil War. At the taking of Fort Sumpter he was struck by a cannon ball and instantly killed.

It was in the year 1852 that the President offered to your father the mission to China and to your grandfather Polk the Consulship in Bordeaux. Neither one accepted and as things happened they made a mistake, for soon the Civil War came on and the sad results we all know.

Amongst the many interesting and I may say amusing things that occurred in Annapolis, I note one in particular which was a source of amusement to us at that time. One day your father came from the State House and mentioned that a gentleman had called upon him that day, a man of fine presence and distinguished ancestry, no one more or less than Mr. Washington, grandnephew of General Washington and owner of Mt. Vernon where he then resided. He called upon Mr. and Mrs. O'Neil. Mr. O'Neil was Secretary of State. They were charmed and highly flattered at the attention. He showed Mrs. O'Neil the miniature of his sister in which she saw a striking resemblance to all of the pictures she had seen of the Washington family. His visit to Annapolis was short -- not more than two or three days; but in that time he was wined and dined and paid every consideration in honor of his great uncle. From Annapolis he went to Baltimore. Two days afterwards the papers were teeming with a great robbery. A man calling himself Washington had robbed the shops of two Jewelers, one of them a Mr. Brown and when the so-called Washington confronted Mr. Brown the former exclaimed; "Well, Mr. Brown, did I not do you up brown."

Another interesting occurrence mostly pathetic, I recall. With some friends I visited the Penitentiary in Baltimore, merely as a matter of curiosity. Passing through a hall, a young man sitting in one of the small rooms of the Prison attracted my attention. Unlike the class of criminals generally seen, I thought to myself that young man must have a history. He seemed to be

241

occupying himself in making pen and ink sketches and his work was very credible. He had the face of culture and refinement. Around him was negligently but tastefully entwined a sash of varied colors. Asking the Attendant particulars of his incarceration, was told that he was a stranger without friends in the City and had been convicted of stealing books. Good Heavens, I thought, poor, friendless, hungry for books, who like the poor steal a loaf of bread to sustain Corporal life, he may have hungered for mental sustenance and yielded to temptation. I knew that a report to your father would be heeded. I quickly gave it and with the desired effect. The case was investigated, the young man was pardoned and sent to his home in Canada.

In 1853 I made a short visit to my friend, Mrs. General Emory, then living in Washington. She was a great granddaughter of the illustrious Benjamin Franklin and a worthy descendant of her great ancestor. With her I called upon Mrs. Pierce at the White House and had a pleasant visit. She was not a handsome woman, pale, thin, with small attenuated features. Her manner was gentle, composed and marked with a tinge of melancholy, which one might well understand, coming as it must from the recent loss of her only child, a boy of eleven years, under circumstances most harrowing. The President, Mrs. Pierce, and the little boy were in a railroad car en route to Washington, the day before the Inauguration. A detached rail from the track pierced the car just where the little boy stood, struck him violently, causing instantaneous death. The stricken parents entered the City bowed down in sorrow. No flags were flying, no cannons booming on that day of interest to the Nation. A somber cloud overhung the City and acclamations due to the high honor bestowed upon the President was silenced. Alas! honors great and lofty are valueless to the heart yearning for that never-to-be-realized, never-to-return.

In looking over these scattered memories, I find that the history of the Vincendiere family as connected with their emigration to the United States. Of course it is interesting to you and such as I have heard will relate. They were refugees from San Domingo. Aunt Victoire told me that her uncle was one of the victims of the Insurrection, having been shot by a native whilst seated at the dinner table. Singular coincidence, my mother's brother, Andrew Stuart, Consul to Manila, was killed in a massacre of the English by the natives of that Island. To return to my subjects, your grandmother was Adelaide, said to have been beautiful and accomplished. She came to America when a child of four years. Helen, who married Mr. de Pitroy was an infant. Aunt Victoire was sixteen years old -- a charming young girl who gave up an engagement of marriage with a young nobleman to remain with her mother and devote her life to the education of her brothers and sisters. Aunt Emerentienne was next in age to Aunt Victoire -- a superior woman, but as I was told, without the charm of the other sisters. She married Captain Corbelay, an officer of the U.S. Army, who graduated at West Point in the same class as your grandfather, Bradley Lowe. Whilst endeavoring to find a record of Madame de Pitroy's marriage, that of your grandmother and Aunt Corbelay were found -- unfortunately there was no trace of that for which I was searching. There were in the family two sons. You have the sketches that were drawn by them. They both died of that dreadful Monocacy fever that was prevalent in Frederick at that time. Their graves are marked by a plain granite slab and by their side are the remains of your great-grandmother, Madame de la Vincendiere, and Chevalier de Pitroy -- the latter, I suppose of Louis de Pitroy. They were buried in the old churchyard and the church being torn down, were removed to a new cemetery where they now lie with our own dear ones. The lots are kept up in good condition. The Hermitage, their house was bought by the family and there they lived until the changes of time and conditions made it necessary to leave and move into the town. I have been told that their house was beautiful and an asylum for many a penniless exile from France and San Domingo. It was there that your father was born. They lived at the Hermitage several years after his birth. The family being reduced to three in number, they removed to Frederick where they built that old comfortable home which the cruel Civil War obliged us to leave. At the age of 13 your father was sent to Clongoes College, a Jesuit institution in Ireland and there remained until old enough to be admitted into Stonyhurst, in England. It was at the latter College that the President told a friend from America that there was a student there -- a young American -- "a diamond of the first order". At that College he was classmate and peer of Miles Gerald Kern, who was afterwards Colonial Secretary to Bermuda -- a man of brilliant parts! He took the silver medal for poetry and your father for philosophy. He and his wife visited us in Brooklyn; no one could ever forget his grand personality and the eloquence of his conversation. He had written many books; amongst them "Dion and the Sybils" which appeared in the Catholic Magazine and was treated by critics as a work of merit. The poor man contracted the terrible morphine habit and died in the prime of life. Another schoolmate of your father, I cannot forget, Judge Thomas Dwyer of Texas, a native of Kildare. He was a striking illustration of Irish wit and good manners. He came to America several years before I saw him, settled in Texas and was made Judge. It was a genuine pleasure to hear him and your father talk about schooldays and schoolfellows. The name of Lord Peter and another whose name is vague just now, were in imagination my familiar acquaintances. When I was young, I enjoyed the stories real and romantic of old Ireland. That famous country where at a certain spot "the Devil whipped his wife" and her moans and screams were heard ten miles away; and where a disease called shingles could only be cured by a drop of blood from a black cat's tail, or the blood of a man named Walsh; or again to enjoy, as in Seraphic dreams, the soothing notes of "The Harp that Once Through Tara's Hall". Now no more romance; cold realities have intervened to check the tide, and only dregs of youth's poetic musings are left to me.

In 1853 Kossuth, the Hungarian patriot, and his suite, visited Annapolis. He was charming! Although but a short time in the English speaking Countries, he spoke the language with an elegance rarely heard. It was said that he had taken the works of Shakespeare as his model. Madame Kossuth was a plain looking woman, unpretending. She spoke very little English. Count Polsky, next in rank, was rather insignificant in appearance and seemed to be a light-hearted cheerful person who enjoyed everything that came along -- particularly liver puddings and sausages, which he ate ravenously, for example three puddings and two links of sausages and when invoked to take a third helping, "Oh, no, I thank you, I never eat much". Those Hungarians were Hungrygarians, I assure you.

That winter was the coldest I ever felt. The Bay was entirely frozen over.

We left Annapolis in 1854. That year my Victoire was born. And my lovely Cousin Rebecca died at our house. For some time she had been engaged to be married to Bird Washington, great-nephew of the famous General Washington. Knowing that her disease was fatal, she broke the engagement and died two months after. She was one of those ideal women that we read of, but rarely see. Beautiful in form, angelic in nature, adored by friend, she died in her 28th year.

Soon after I returned to Frederick, Adelaide and Anna both small children, were sent to school at the Visitation Convent.

In 1861 rumors of war filled the air. Consternation and dread were everywhere felt. The Legislature of the State met in Frederick. All men of prominence, supposed to be sympathizers of the South were marked. Your father was amongst them and his intimate friend, Henry May, father of Mrs. John S. Gittings, was caught and imprisoned in Fort LaFayette. Your father, unduly excited, as you might suppose one of his mercurial organization would be, made his escape by crossing into Virginia, where we followed soon after. At that time I had eight children, Esther only five months old. Never can I forget the discomfort of that journey to Richmond, where your father was awaiting us. A few days in Richmond and we went to Ashland, a pretty little village a few miles away. There we remained several months with our little Maryland contingent, who were extremely congenial, notably the family of Admiral McBlair. Mrs. McBlair was bright and witty. I recall that upon one occasion a country woman of the peasant class called to see Mr. Cox, manager of the hotel. Her errand was selling eggs. The living room adjoined the office of Mr. Cox. One morning while we were all sitting and chatting in homelike style, the head of a woman covered with a countrymade hood was poked through a half-open door; "Is this the sitting room." Mrs. McBlair answered quickly: "Yes, this is the hens' sitting room and you will find the cocks next door."

My two daughters who were just old enough to enjoy society were pleased with their sojourn in Ashland, and I too enjoyed it until my darling little Stuart, that beautiful manly little fellow was taken to heaven. We left him in a vault in Richmond and after the war was over his remains were placed beside our dear ones in the St. John's Cemetery in Frederick.

Whilst in Ashland, we occupied one of the cozy little cottages on the grounds of the Ashland Hotel, the main building being crowded with persons, generally refugees like ourselves. We remained there until the following April - ten months - when the Union Army approaching Richmond, compelled us to leave. Where to go was the question. At last Georgia was decided upon, owing to the fact that both your father and I had relatives there. Admiral McBlair had been ordered to Mobile and upon the same day we all left together. When traveling the Blue Ridge Mountains in the extreme north of Georgia we halted for two or three days to rest which was necessary after a rough ride in a worn out car upon a most dilapidated road. Admiral McBlair remarked he had often heard the song "Old Virginny Never Tires" and he could now understand why, as nothing could go fast enough to tire. Such jogging along stopping everywhere and for everything was a wonder to us who had traveled on the B & O, however, we reached our destination at last. Perseverance gains its reward; but in that particular case it is hard to see where the reward comes in. The second stopping place was Marietta, a beautiful village and in it an excellent hotel. Amongst the guests I recall particularly a charming Jewish family named Levy, from Savannah. They were highly cultivated and belonged to that class of Jews who occupy a prominent social position in the South. It was at Marietta that we all separated; the McBlairs went to Alabama; Paul and Vivian were sent to the Jesuit College in Mobile. Victoire and Anna went to the Ursuline Convent in Columbia. The mention of that Convent revives memories dear and sacred. The following year I went to the Distribution there and to my surprise - it was all meant to give me such - Anna played upon the harp. I had no idea that she had taken lessons, so my wonderment and pleasure may be imagined. To continue this pilgrimage in the land, I may say of sorrow - for grim visaged war was at its height - the next place to be reached was Milledgeville where your Aunt Ariana lived with her husband Lucilius Briscoe, a lawyer well known as a brilliant orator. The following January you were born - a war baby. To relate all the trials, troubles and tribulations connected with your advent into this world at that epoch would be difficult. Suffice it to say that the back was fitted to the burden. Milledgeville was a sociable little place, the people somewhat rustic but very kind. Often we met Governor Brown and his wife - both genuine country people from the mountains of Georgia. Many stories were told of Mrs. Brown's awkward doings and sayings which must have been exaggerated - they were so very ridiculous. The Governor, a man of talent and much native dignity, had improved, so it was said, much more than his wife. My recollection of him is very vivid. It was he who sold your father Georgia bonds representing thousands of dollars which afterwards were repudiated by the State. It is not my intention to cast any reflection upon him, for if anything in the world could be considered safe, it was those bonds - the pledged honor of the State.

The summer of 1863 we left Milledgeville for a visit to Governor Johnson's family who lived on a plantation. Mrs. Johnson was nee Anne Polk. She was my father's half sister - the only child of my grandfather, Judge William Polk by his third marriage. With our kind Aunt and Uncle we spent six weeks;

then on to Augusta where in the hospitable home of Dr. Alexander Dugas, your father's cousin, we passed the remainder of the summer. In October we returned to Milledgeville hoping to find comfortable quarters for the winter. Just then, in the condition of the country, it was a difficult problem to solve - every nook and corner being taken up by refugees. Had we sought a house for two, three, or four persons, there might have been some difficulty; but a father, mother, and several children - think of it! Nobody wanted children. It looked to us like a hopeless case until a kind woman, whose expansive heart took pity, actually left her own house, which was situated in a little hamlet named Scottsborough, about three miles from Milledgeville, and went to live with her sister, Mrs. Carter, whose home was just across the road. Miss Maria Macdonald and Mrs. Carter were daughters of Governor Macdonald. They were that type of woman so often described in the English novels, quietly elegant, dignified, and cultured. They were very rich in land and negroes, even at that time, for the earthquake had not yet swallowed up everything.

Our experience in that little country place was sometimes amusing. I call to mind one occasion when Adelaide gave a party - for although war was at its height Southern people continued to "eat, drink, and be merry", not withstanding tomorrow we may die. Our cottage was small and without considering its limitations - the spirit of hospitality overruling discretion and good judgment - so numerous were the guests that some of them were obliged to sit on the stairs of the porch, and fortunately as the weather was hot, managed to find comfortable seats under the trees in the garden; however, it was war times and all unheard of experiments were excusable. The entertainment went off with great éclat. The corporal man was administered to abundantly and everybody was happy. Fifteen months were passed in that sleepy little place consisting of about six families. Each house was hidden in clumps of trees and literally every man lived under his own vine and fig tree. Never have I seen such grape vines. In our garden was one scupanong vine, covering at least an eighth of an acre. One could sit in its body and feast upon the luscious fruit, picking the grapes one by one for that species never grow in bunches - always a twig holding two or three. Figs were in abundance and in fact no want of excellent fruits and meals was then known. Flour was scarce and high. About the close of the war we paid in Confederate money about fifteen hundred dollars for a barrel of flour. Corn meal was abundant; coffee was very scarce and as substitute sweet potatoes cut into small pieces and burned were considered satisfactory. Some persons preferred peanuts burned, other liked wheat parched. All imported goods were enormously high - of course, very scarce owing to the blockade. Thanks to kind Providence we never suffered for want of food and although our clothing was homely it was like everybody's, so that all being in the same boat no criticism could be made - indeed we were better off than many for our good friend, Mr. Doize - and I must say, like the Irish, Lord have mercy on his soul - sent us from Charleston where he got goods through the blockade a large box of clothing. Poor fellow, he lost all earthly goods, and still worse lost his mind, and afterwards died in a hospital in New York. We sent his remains to

New Orleans and from his wife I received a letter of thanks. His story is a sad one. His father, a French refugee, died in Baltimore; his mother I suppose was dead, and to this boy - then about 18 years old - was left the care of three little sisters. He brought them to the Frederick Convent and it was there that I knew them. Your grandmother whose heart was always touched at misfortune, particularly in a case so appealing to sympathy, was kind to those orphan children whose brother treasured it sacredly. This little episode is grateful to me as a reminder of a noble nature.

I have lost the thread of my story and will now go back to our little hamlet. Excepting the family of the Carters, there were no persons of high social standing there - all respectable and thrifty; a few without slaves, belonging naturally to the plain class. I note an occasion rather amusing. A young girl informed me that she had come from Macon the day before and in the car was seated near her a police office who had in charge two "ladies" and two "gentlemen" whom he was taking to the penitentiary.

The Carters were persons of aristocratic descent and highly cultured. It was a treat to hear Mrs. Carter soft, gentle voice in conversation, so indicative of high breeding. Major Napier, another neighbor, called often to see us. He had seen better days, but through misfortune incident to the times was obliged to sell his little farm. It was a nice place, of about one hundred acres and on it a small house that was in fact only a cabin. I persuaded your father to purchase it. The land was good for cotton and peas. We thought it a good thing to buy and at the same time help the Major out of his temporary embarrassment. We remained at Scottsborough until the alarm of Sheridan's approach hurried us off to Augusta, and there, in a most dilapidated house - but the best that could be found - we passed a winter of unspeakable discomfort. Fortunately we had kind friends there and but for that our sojourn would have been dismal in the extreme. A cord of sympathy bound us all together. We suffered the same terrors of suspense and bodily privations. No clothes, except the homely homespun, as it was called, a kind of striped cloth woven by the country people on looms manufactured years and years before; no bread but that made of cornmeal, no meat but the most indifferent, and of that but very little - in fact brought down to the slimmest necessities of life, and thankful for that. The danger of taking Augusta averted - Savannah being the objective point - we returned to Milledgeville. Your father bought a load of spun cotton which we found convenient as a medium of exchange - the country people being no longer willing to take Confederate money. I can see as now, with our load of children and luggage, crowded into a car kindly placed at our disposal by the President of the Georgia railroad, starting off for Milledgeville. Louis, then about ten years of age, was perched upon the top of the bales of cotton and enjoyed immensely that novel mode of transit. Aunt Ariana hired for us a comfortable house in Milledgeville and contribution of necessary furniture made by friends answered well for our comfort. Times were hard; we managed however through agreeable society and general conviviality to pass quite a bright summer.

Everybody felt that the war was coming to an end and the hope of returning to home and friends was made manifest in word and action everywhere. It was there that my little James. my last child, was born. In November 1865, war over, we left Georgia for Maryland. An old worn out ship we had to take at Savannah. Such a voyage; everybody deadly sick; even you, almost a baby, did not escape. Heaven favored me. I had no time to be sick, for the charge of a baby three months and seven sick children were quite enough to appeal to mercy. To enjoy the sweet one must take the bitter. In four days New York was sighted. What joy to see signs of life. We piled into an omnibus and went to a hotel and - upon a breakfast of buckwheat cakes and sausages - the first seen in four years - we poor pilgrims feasted to repletion, and with renewed strength continued our journey, reaching Baltimore in good time, where our good brother-in-law, Mr. Gorter, met and took us to his house - the home of peace and plenty - where with a smile of welcome my dear sister Mary embraced us.

A short time after my arrival in Maryland, I went to visit my friend, Miss Teresa Jamison. Observing on the mantel in her drawing room, a photograph of your father, I inquired how she happened to have it. She told me that it had a curious history. A lady from Baltimore had attempted to go south and was taking for me a bag several articles - amongst them this picture sent by my Mother. When crossing the Potomac she learned that the Union soldiers were watching upon the Virginia shore for persons running the blockade, and becoming alarmed she threw the bag into the river. The tide washed it ashore on the Maryland side. The photograph was recognized and sent to Frederick to Miss Jamison. This is the same picture from which a full sized portrait of your father was made and now hangs in the State House in Annapolis.

Owing to an enactment of the Republican Legislature of Maryland, requiring every Marylander to take what was called the Iron Clad Oath - to the effect that he had never sympathized with the South, your father was obliged to leave the State and in order to practice his profession came to New York, a city which offered more inducements than any other, being Cosmopolitan in character. New York seemed to be the haven of rest and hope to all victims of the Civil War. The Southerner who claimed the most aristocratic lineage, who had counted his slaves by the hundreds - officers of Navy and Army, in fact men from all ranks in life - were to be found in New York, occupied in menial services trying to make a living. I have been told that not more than five or six professional men held their ground and that your father and Judge Roger A. Pryor were the only two lawyers, of the many, who remained.

In April 1866 we journeyed into New York with our nine children and there your father at the age of 45 years entered again into the battle of life. I have often thought how courageous to go into a strange land, in an unsympathetic community, weighed down, as he was, with a load of nine children, all dependent upon a brain that ought to have been exhausted from care, responsibility, and harrowing suspense during four long years. How kind was Providence to him to sustain nerve and brain under the fearful struggle for existence which followed those dark days after the close of the war. Knowing his high strung, sensitive organism I often wondered from whence came this heroic courage -- this daring effort to stem the tide of unrelenting misfortune and not sink in its steps. Truly it was courage engendered in a transcendent sense of duty to his children. The burden was heavy -- seemed overpowering -- but manfully he shouldered it and marched on though staggering under its weight.

We took a house in Brooklyn and in the course of time made friends. One family in particular, near neighbors, I found congenial and with pleasure recall them. The head of the house, a kind generous friend, always sympathetic and ready to do a good turn -- we were all very fond of. He had his little weaknesses, not unusual to a man of his temperament -- an inordinate admiration for the fair sex. An old Irish woman was asked by his wife to look at his portrait just finished. The old woman's criticism was quite apt. She said: "Ah, indeed, it is just like him; but in truth it is not for the good of his soul that he has them eyes in his head." It is sad indeed that all these dear friends have passed away.

My dear Child, my monitor warns me that length is not strength; hence heeding this admonition, I close these scant memories which drawn from a span of 89 years are but flying fragments caught as they come and go; but one there is immutable, dearest and sweetest, sacredly sealed in this heart -- it is the memory of the constant affection of my daughters and their devoted husbands, to whose solicitude and generosity are due comforts unsparingly given and gratefully enjoyed.

Devotedly,

Mother

90 Greene Avenue
Brooklyn, New York
March 14, 1913

Appendix V

Somerset – from the Court Records

The day-to-day lives of our colonial ancestors can be seen through the colorful prism of the judicial records which they left behind. The Somerset County Court or Council was not merely a judicial forum, it was the governing body of the county, presided over by its Commissioners or Justices of the Peace who were appointed by the Provincial Governor. The judicial (court) records therefore contain the complete history of the county government and all its deliberations, the criminal cases, civil suits, routine business, laws, and proclamations—matters such as how tobacco was to be weighed, who would operate the ferries, collect taxes, build the pillory, which ministers were properly accredited, and determination of the ages of servants and slaves (for tax collection purposes). The Council met four or more times a year (usually January, March, June, August or September, and November) in formal sessions which might last for several days or weeks. In between sessions the individual Commissioners were empowered to take action as needed to settle disputes, maintain order and hear petitions. Some of these actions were entered afterwards into the court records, apparently out of chronological sequence, but important as a matter of formal record.

The records included here are mostly concerned with actions involving the Polk family or others closely associated with them. Other items, particularly the earlier ones, are included to convey insight into the Somerset world in which the family lived. They are a fascinating glimpse back in time to the period from Robert Polke's arrival until the start of the American Revolution. There are no surviving Somerset court records for the period 1683-1687 but it is not likely that they would include any mention of Robert and Magdalen or their family in any case since they probably did not arrive until the end of that period. The earliest record of Robert Polke in Maryland is in the warrants for Polkes Folly and Polkes Lott which were issued on 20 November 1687 by the Provincial Land Office. There is no mention of any Polk in the 1687-89 Somerset Judicials. Robert's first appearance in the Court records is in August 1690 when he is listed as a juror in several trials. He did sign the Address of Loyalty that was sent by the citizens of Somerset to their new Sovereigns, William and Mary, in November 1689. That document is now in the British Public Records Office.

The entries through 1710 are all direct transcripts from the records. This is done so readers can gain some appreciation for the color and character of Somerset and the people who inhabited it at that time. Some of the later entries are just abstracts summarizing the action.

SOMERSET JUDICIAL RECORDS 1687-89
[MSA C 1774-6, Loc. 1/48/2/33]

10 [11 June 1689] Petition of Rev. William Trail for altering of road
*The peticon of Mr William Traill Minister Shewing how that he is Setling of a
New plantation on pocomoke and that the first Clearers of the Main Roads there
have not been well acquainted with the ground for that the roade that now is, is
both bad way, and about, by what it may be made, and runs through the Middle
of what ground your peticoner hath to Cleare for a Corne feild, your peticoner
Craves Leave to alter the said Roade by his plantacon at his owne Charges
Nearer & better way for the Inhabitants thereabouts who are likewise willing
thereto & your peticoner will pray. This Court haveing taken the premisses into
their Consideracon Ordered that if The peticoner performes according to the
Contents of his peticon that he may alter the Roade as prayed provided it be noe
damage to the Neighbours or Others*

SOMERSET JUDICIAL RECORDS 1689-90
[MSA C 1774-7, Loc. 1/48/2/34]

19 [13 November 1689] Address of Loyalty written
*This same day viz the 13th of 9ber There was an address by the Grand Jury to
the Wor'll Court humbly craving there Wor'ps and freemens concurrence
therein and that it may be with all speed sent to their majesty's ~~~-
Immediately after the Justices of the Court signed the Address, and so did many
others that attended the court. Then the Court Ordered that the aforesaid
Address when finished should Be sent over the bay, in order to be presented to
there Ma'ties. It was then likewise Ordered by the Court that when the said
Address was sent over the Bay that it should be certifyed there that the Court
had appointed and made Mr. William Brereton high Sheriffe of this County
instead and (in) place of Capt. William Whittington.*

*The same day the Court Ordered the Grand Jury One gallon of Rum to be had of
mr. Andrew Whittington (innkeeper), payable from the County's Levey.*

Address of Loyalty to William and Mary
The previous entry refers to the Address of Loyalty which was duly sent to the
provincial government in St Marys and afterwards to the British sovereigns,
William and Mary in London. The document may now be found in the British
Public Records Office, in Colonial Office records file CO5/718. It is transcribed
in the Archives of Maryland, Vol. 8, p.138, under the title "An Address of the
Inhabitants of the County of Somersett Nov'er the 28th 1689":

*To the King and Queen most Ex't Maj'ty Wee your Majesty's subjects in the
County of Somersett and Province of Maryland being refreshed and encouraged
by your Majestys great and prosperous undertakings, and by your late gracious
letter to those of this Province, do cast ourselves at your Majesty's feet humbly*

desiring and hopefully expecting the continuance of your Maj'tys care of us, as our Case and Circumstance doe or may require, in the confidence whereof wee resolve to continue (by the Grace of God) in the Profession and defence of the Protestant religion and your Majesty's Title and interest against the French and other Papists that oppose and trouble us in soe just and good a cause not doubting but your Majestys wisdom and clemency will afford unto us all needful suitable Aid and Protection for securing our lives and liberty under Protestant Governors and Government, and for enabling us to defend ourselves against all Invaders. Thus praying for your Majestys long and happy Reigne over us. Wee know ourselves to bee (with due Reverence and sincerity) your Majestys Loyall Obedient and humble Subjects.

The document was signed by 238 citizens of Somerset, including Robert Polk, William Polk, William Trail, David Brown and members of other families closely associated with them—Alexander, Knox, McKnitt, Owens, Gray, Pollett, Porter and Wilson. Unfortunately, it is a contemporary transcript and not the original, so does not contain the actual autographs of the individual signers.

67 [15 March 1689/90] Affadavit of William Pattent, Scotch-Irishman
[Although there is no known direct relationship of the Patton (Pattent) family with the Polks, this passage is notable in revealing a resentful attitude held by earlier settlers towards the newly arrived Scotch-Irish – a reaction seemingly repeated in this country with every wave of new arrivals to the present day. It is also very likely the first recorded use of the term "Scotch-Irish" in American records as a descriptor of the immigrant Ulster-Scots.]

I William Pattent was at worke at James Minders and one night as I was at worke Mr Matt: Scarbrough came into the house of sd Minders and sett down by me as I was at work, the sd Minder askt him if he came afoot, he made answer again and sd he did, saying that man meaning me calling me Rogue makes me goe afoot also makes it his business to goe from house to house to ruinate me, my Wife and Children for ever. I made answer is it I Mr. Scarbrough. and he replyed and said ay you, you Rogue, for which doing ile whip you and make my Wife whipp to whipp you, and I answered if ever I have abused (you) at any time, or to any bodies hearing, I will give you full satisfaction to your own Content. You Scotch Irish dogg it was you, with that he gave me a blow on the face saying it was no more sin to kill me then to kill a dogg, or any Scotch Irish dogg, giving me another blow in the face. now saying goe to yr god that Rogue and have a warrant for me and I will answer it.   Wm. Patent

103 [10 June 1690] Trial of Matthew Scarbrough for contempt
Their Ma'ties   Somersett County
Ag't
Matthew Scarbrough
The Jurors for their Maties being sworne upon the holy Evangelists at a Grand Jury held for the body of this County the second tuesday in March last doe

present and find that Matthew Scarbrough of this County Gent att Snow hill in Bogatoe norton hundred and within the jurisdiction of this Court, most proudly arrogantly and contemptuously and malitiously utter publish, and with a loud voyce did declare his contemptuous malitious and seditious mind agt their Maties authority now in being in these words that Mr. Samuel Hopkins had granted a warrant to the Constable to sumon none to theese Burgesses but Scotch Irish men. which was a great abuse to your Ma'ties Comrs for this County thrfore yr Ma'ties attorney craves judgmt agt the sd Scarbrough according to Law,

James: Sangster. Clk. Indts.

The abovesd Indtmt was produced in Court but not read, a litle while debated between the Court & Scarbrough and the matter Quasht.

Their Ma'ties	*Somersett County*
Ag't	*March Court*
Matt. Scarbrough	

The Jurors for the Maties being sworne upon the holy Evangelists at a Grd Jury held for the body of this County last past doe present and find that Matthew Scarbrough of this County at the house of James Minor in the hundred of Bogetenorton Anno. '89. his Ma'ties peace then and their did not keep, but their M't'ies. Comrs did abuse and contemne, Calling Capt David Browne Rogue & Dogg, and in an oppirous manner stile him the scotch Irish mens God, and upon the matter aforesd did beat and wound William Pattent of this County, taylor, saying affirming and his wicked intent wth a loud voyce declaring that it was no more sin to kill the sd Pattent than it was to kill a dogg not regarding that due respect by the law of God he ought and should give to Magistracy but in despite of their power & authority in it by law invested by perticularizing the sd Capt David Browne in the name of the whole did tacitly imply his contempt to the sd power Their Maties Attorney craves judgmt may be entered agt the sd scarbrough according to Law in that case made and provided.

James Sangster. Clk. Indt

The Indtmt being Read The sd Scarbrough referrs him Selfe to the judgmt of the Court. who having heard the Evidences Sworne and examined doe give their opinion that the sd Scarbrough is guilty of some parts of breach of their Maties. Peace and therefore Orders the and Said Scarbrough to find Security for his good behaviour till next Court And thereupon Came Henry Lynch and John West and did confess them Selves to be indebted unto their Maties in £5 pr man, Scarbrough in £10, sterling money to levied upon their goods and Chattels for their Ma'ties. use ～ The Condicon of which Recognizance is such that if the abovesd Matt Scarbrough be of the good behaviour to all their Ma'ties. leige people of this Province from the day of the date till the second tuesday in August then this Recog. to be voyd and of none effect otherwayes to be and remain in full power force and vertue.

147 [12 August 1690] Case of Walter Taylor vs. Samuel Hopkins; Robert

Polke on Jury

[This entry marks the first appearance of Robert Polke in the Somerset Judicials. It also is the first of several related actions involving Samuel Hopkins and Walter Taylor. Hopkins complained bitterly of the verdict reached in this case and sought to have it reversed. Taylor was eventually convicted of fraud. See below, Somerset Judicials 1690-91, folios 6, 63 and 99.]

Walter. Taylor Plt.   *Somerset County ~~*
agt
Mr. Samuel: Hopkins Dft
Declaration being Read. Issue was joynd. and the whole Cause referred to a Jury of twelve men duely impannelled & Sworne.- Mr. Samuel: Hopkins of this County was Sumoned to answer unto Walter Taylor of the same County in an action of the Case. And whereupon the plt by his Attorney John Taylor comes and sayes about the month of August last past the sd Samuel Hopkins did buy of the plt twelve Cutts of Cypresse Timber for the which the sd deft did promise to pay unto the sd Taylor, twenty two yards of the best sort of the whore kill linnen of lockoram breadth which sd linnen to pay doth utterly deny to pay although often thereunto required by the plt, but part of the Timber hath received and the rest there being theire for him to receive, but could not carry it at that time by which fraudulent means the plt saith he is damnified to the value of fourty four yards of the like linnen and thereupon brings his suit.
                       Taylor pr Quer   *Pledges of prosecuting*
                                           John Doe   Rich Roe.

Jno. Taylor was not admitted to plead at Barr his Bro: Walter for him Selfe did manage the matter} Taylor. Plt.
Plea in Barr of the accon Hopkins Dft
And whereas the deft by James Sangster his Attorney Comes and defend the force and injury &c. and saith that plt his accon ought not to have 1st., because the defend't is ready to hold Covenant and bargain with the plt, upon the delivery of the 12 Cutts of Cypresse Timber; 2ly. The plt by the delivery of part as he alleadges hath not named the quantity being conscious of the fraudulency and deceit of the same, paying the defendt with halfe the quantity of Cutts that he agreed for, thereby cheating the defendt, and spoiling the timber, as may appear upon view; 3ly. whereas the plt confesseth that he hath not carryed all the Cutts tacitly implying that the whole must be delivered, and good sound & Suffitient Cutts before satisfaction, till such delivery and payment denyed, thereupon no cause of accion   *Sangster per defendt.*
Then was these three following papers preferred to Court & Jury. (1st) Wee the persons whose names are here under Subscribed were requested by Samuel: Hopkins Senior to view A percell of Cypresse Timber standing in the sd Hopkins tobacco house, which timber Hopkins aforesd declareth (was) Sent him by Walter Taylor or his Order. Now wee the sd persons subscribors as aforesd to hereby Certifie & make known unto all persons whom these may or doth Concern that wee have deliberately, viewed, scanned and compared the sd timber, both as to quantity and quallity and also the dementions and wee the sd

254

persons having expended Considerable time and some pains aforesd we find as
followeth, to witt the quality of the said Timber to be good and to be the
proceeds of very large and great trees that have made double stuffe
(Long description of cuts of lumber follows)
That is to say two breadths of Stuffe called peices or quarters of each Cutt of the
shortest lengths of timber for wee find the said timber to be of divers lengths, the
Major part of that Sort, the quarters are more properly the peices to be four foot
Six inches long other peices to be four foot eight inches, and other peices to be
in length five foot five Inches and having viewed the heart breadth peices of that
Sort of timber and of the said dementions as to length as aforesd, and
comparing the sd outside breadth of quarters with the inside breadth or heart
quarters or peice hath properly belonging to it, some three quarters and Some
two quarters and wee also find, that each cut of what we have viewed of the sd
timber, or at least what in our best judgmts of the timber makes a Cutt each cut
hath transparently yielded eight heart quarters while sd quarters are peices
plainly appears to be the choice and best of the quarters in Complemt of timber
aforesd, notwithstanding Severall of the sd eights of heart quarters are riven
into two peices and when any timber is so riven out that is to say sixteen peices
of the second or heart breadth from a Cutt there must needs be thirty two
quarters or peices of the firsts or out side breadth belonging to the sd 16 heart
peice, in every such Cutt which two Sums or numbers aforesd being added
together makes 48 peices improperly called quarters in a Cutt, The best of the
timber (not yet mentioned in perticulars though included in the whole Complaint
viewed were find to be in length 6.foot 6 inches and not to aford losse of the
quarters or rather the peices viewed as aforesd then 16 to the Cutt of some Cutts
and 24 peices of or in other Cutts, and wee Certifie and declare the premises
upon the best of our experience and knowlege and will deposed thereupon if
required thereunto and that wee connot find in the whole Complaint;. of timber
of all dementions aforesd one quarter or peice of four foot long or of six foot
long wee the within Subscribers and viewers do further Certifie upon our
deliberate Consultation & calculation of the said timber within mentioned, that
there is nor cannot possibly be contained in 50 peices (of the length 6.foot Six
inches, in number twenty six quarters or peices of timber, wee can neither in
judgmt or reason, or conscience apprehend that there is one Cutt and a halfe of
timber in that this we certifie under our hands the day and year within
mentioned   Edward [E H] Hammon
                            John [I H] Hammon   Wm Richardson

To the Worships
Humbly offered that the Controversie will be the more easily and justly desided
as the following queries are truly or erroniously answered, first whether any
part of a Cutt of timber, or ought else can be the whole, Secondly whether the
dementions of the length or lengths be not a manifest breach of the said bargain,
and visibly and realy damnifying to the buyer, for if too short the buyer is
clearly frustrate if too long then it consequently & necessarily follows that the
buyer must either perform the Major part of the sellers labour, or lett his timber

255

lye useless, for all men knows it must be all Sawn over again which is the great part of the whole work, so in Justice and equity there cannot be halfe due from the buyer, supposing the bargain be complyed with in all other points which is positively disowned by me in the Cause depending. ~~~ Sam: Hopkins

I beseach the Courts and Juryes well weighing and Considering of what is so highly preferred and pleaded for as a Custom this I humbly offer to prove to the satisfaction, that although there may have formerly been some thing of reason for it or equity in it which I know nothing of, yet I now know very Well if ever any such thing were, length of time and Corrupt fraudulent, guilfull used by Cypress timber men hath near worn it out, so that -- become the greatest peice of deceit, and one of the formidablest Cheats in the whole world and to mantaine and keep it up I doe in Submission to the more competent judgments affirm, that is the very next to establishing of iniquity by a law, and to defend it in its reputation & Credits as some would have it. Is every jott as bad as defending the turkist Alchoran sett forth by Mahomett & I most humbly begg of the Worll. Court that they will defend me imolested untill I make it evidently appear which is all I crave

S Hopkins ~~~

The Jury having thus heard the whole matter as also four Evidences Sworn for defendt, goes forth whose names are as followeth viz. John Bossman William Robinson John Bowns Alexander Thomas Moses Fainton Robert Polke Ralph Milbourn Samuel Shewell John Tarr William Bossman Thomas Oxford Matt Scarbrough who being returned do bring in this following verdict viz. The Jurors find for the Plt. given in by John. Bosman forem. Indmt. Ordrd to be entered upon the verdict ~~ The Origll Coppies of the three last papers sent to Mr Hopkins according to his Order.

156 [14 August 1690] Trial of George Seaward for embezzling various items; Robert Polk on Jury

Wm. Woodland being Sworne saith that George Seaward said that he would stand in his owne defence and cutt off the leggs of any Majestrate or other Officer that should come to apprehend him, and said he would so doe although he killd him, and in Order thereto whetted or Sharpned an Adds and Carried the same about him three dayes.

Anne Woodland Swears that G. S. deluded her and her sonn to Run away with him and that there was a hogg and a halfe and four bushells wheat to be provided for the voyadge for biskett, That George Seaward told her he had hired John Ellis to Carry him away, that he was to allow him a Bill about 1800. of either Phill Lynes or Coll Darnalls, which said Bill belongs to the Estate of Jonas Seaward Deced. ~~~

Imbezleing the Papers and Raceing out Severall accots.
   Wm. Woodland Evidence.
Unrigging the Sloop. Abuse of the Widdow Breach of the Sabbath}

Wm Woodland and his wife Evidences.
A Dantzick Case ownd by G:S:(as Imbezld Chargd) but pretended twas his owne
A Bill of Thomas Everdens Owned by G: S: about 1500 lb tobacco.
One Accot. Instanced to be Crost out or Raced, was Rich Whartons.
Evidence Wm. Woodland.
That the sd George hath Ripped up and Sold and Embezled Oke planke from the
Sloop that belongs to the Estate of his decd Brother and sold the same for drink,
on Board Capt. Samuel Paule. &c. That the sd George hath purloined Sold and
made away for drinke as aforesd a Considerable quantity of Tarr formerly by
his decd Brother provided for the triming and repair of the aforesd Sloop
whereby she is all togeather unfurnished and uncapable of any imploy &c.
Memorandum The feather Bed and the Blocks Packed up for the March
Sam. Merchment & his wife and Archibald White Sworne agt the sd Seaward
The aforesd George Seaward being Called to the Barr, where all the foregoing
proceedings were fairly red before the said Seaward, who pleaded not guilty,
and for his tryall, put himselfe upon a Jury, which Jury was duely impannelled
and Sworne whose Names are as followeth. Viz. John Bossman Lawrence
Crawford William Robbinson John Bowns Alexander Thomas Moses Fainton
Robert Polk Ralph Milbourne Sam'll Shewell John Tarr William Bossman
Matthew Scarbrough, who having heard the whole matter as also five
Evidences Sworne agt the Seaward (viz) Samll Merchmt and his Wife, Archibald
White Benjamin Keizer & Wm. Woodland, goes forth to determine the same, the
day following do bring in this following verdict (Viz.) Wee the Jurors finds
George Seaward guilty of fact and also guilty of Contempt of authority, except
the Charge of hogg stealing. Given by me John Bossman. forem. ~~ G.S.
desired Mr Lane might plead for him, which was denyed pr Court.
  Before which Verdict was returned, the sd George Seaward made his
Escape and Run awayand att the request of John Ellis of this County Senior,
Hue & Cryes Issued forth after the sd Seaward.

163 [14 August 1690] Trial of Daniel Selby for refusing assistance to Constable; Robert Polke on Jury

Their Ma'ties   *Somerset County ~~*
  agt
Daniel Selby
The Jurors for their Maties. being Sworne upon ye holy Evangelists at a County
Court held for the body of this County doe present and find that Daniel Selby of
this County Planter, hath most audaciously arrogantly and contemptuously
Refuse and deny to be aiding and assisting to William Wouldhave Constable
after that the said Selby had been twice required in their Majesties Names by the
said Wouldhave Constable, who upon the 19th. of May was in pursuite of James
Minor Cordwinder, which sd Miner was their Maties Prisoner and excaped from
the Constable and by him found at the house of the said Selby. Now their Maties.
Attorney Comes and sayes that whereas the sd Minor by vertue of a Warrant
from Mr. Samuel Hopkins One of their Maties.Comrs for this County was
apprehended (on Examination of Evidence for fellony Comitted by his Nigro and

*him Selfe, by the sd Constable and from him escaped, where the said Selby did
not only entertein, but after the Constable had there retaken the said Minor did
peremterily deny his assistance, but did aid defend and abscond the prisoner
whereby he escaped and frustrated judgment & condigne punishment according
to Law. Wherefore their Maties. Attorney Craves judgmt may be entered agt the
said Selby for his Contempt of their Maties authority and buse of Government
according to Law &c.*

James: Sangster. Clk. Indtmt.

*The Deposition of William Wouldhave their Maties Constable in Bogatenorton
hundred, saith that being imployed and impowered by Samuel:Hopkins one of
their Maties Justices of the Peace to apprehend and Secure the body of James
Minor, and in Order thereunto to Comand aid and assistance from any person
or persons as the Deponent should so cause, the said Deponent making search
for the said Minor, did find him in the house of mr Daniel Selby, and the sd
Minor resisting and laying violent hands on the deponent your Deponent did
Comand the said Daniel Selby, in their Maties names to aid and assist him, the
which he the said Selby peremptorily refused saying it was not his business
neither would he doe it but in stead of assisting as was required he was the only
cause of the said Minors escape. your Deponent telling the sd Selby he could not
answer what he had done, the sd Selby replyed that the Deponent had no
business there, the sd Minor being escaped but not farr from the said house it
being the 19th of this Instant Month at night your Deponent desired the sd Selby
to advize the said Minor not to stand it out against authority for it would be
worse for him, or with him so doe and so departed the sd Selbyes house for that
night, And the next morning repaired thither again to see what might be effected
in the premisses but all to no purpose, The said Minor made his escape towards
Accomack, this your Deponent, saith and further saith not.
Sworne before me this 26th. day of May 1690   William Wouldhave
Wittness my hand   Samuel Hopkins*

*The Indictment and Deposition being Read before the sd Selby at the Barr, to
which sd Selby pleaded not guilty and for tryall put himselfe upon a Jury. which
Jury was legally impannelled and duely sworne upon the holy Evangelists whose
names are as followeth viz: John Bozman William Robbinson Jno. Bowns
Alexander Thomas Moses Fainten Robert Polke Ralph Milbourne Samuel
Shewel Jno. Tarr William Bozman Matthew Scarbrough Thomas Oxford who
having heard the totall proceedings goes forth to determine the same. ~
And being returned do bring in this following verdict viz. Wee the Jurors find
Daniel Selby guilty of the Indtmt given in by John Bozman. Which Verdict was
Ordered to be entered. Order likewise the sd Selby give Security for good
behaviour and there upon Came the sd Selby and Capt Wm. Whittington. and
did acknowledge them Selves pr Recognizance to be indebted to their Maties
Selby in £10, and Whittington in £5 sterling money to be levyed on their goods
and Chattells for their Maties uses &c. The condicon of wch Recog. is such that
if the sd Selby be of the good behaviour to all their Maties liege People of this*

Province dureing Courts pleasure, then paying Court fees the Recognicance voyd otherwayes to be and remain in full power force and vertue.

168 [14 August 1690] Lawrence Crawford vs. Jonathan Towers; Robert Polke on Jury

Lawrence: Crawford. Plt.   *Somerset County*
agt.   *Jonathan Towers of this County Cooper was*
Jonathan: Towers. Defdt   *Sumoned to answer unto Mr. Lawrence*
           Crawford of the same County Gent. in a
           plea of trespass upon the Case ~~~~

And whereupon the plt by James: Sangster his Attorney Comes and sayes that mr John: White late of this County deceased and predecessor to the plt did Lett a Certain Plantation Called Newport pannel, on certain Articles between the sd defendt and the said White deceased, where it was Concluded and agreed that what hoggs was or should be raised upon the said Plantation by the defendt, should run in a joynt stock between them, and at the expiration of four years to be equally shared, Now the said plt by his intermarriage with the Extrx and Admrx of the sd Estate hath parted what hoggs did give him an accompt of but the said plt doth find, and here in Court by Evidence doth make it appear that the sd Jonathan defendt hath Clandestinly and Craftily Sold and disposed of five hoggs, to viz One Sow & four Barrows and for them hath recd satisfaction, without the knowledge or Consent of the plt, with a firme and Setled purpose to defraud the plt of the same. wherefore the plt sayes he is damnified and hath losse to the value of Sixteen hundred pounds of tobacco and hereupon brings his suit

     Sangster pr Quer. pled de pr sois. {Jno. Doe   Rich:Roe.}
     Jones Attorney pr defdt.

Declaration being Read, and Issue joynd, the matter being referred to a Jury. which Jury was legally impannelled and duely Sworne, which names are as followeth. Viz. John: Bozman Wm. Robbinson John. Downs Alexander Thomas Moses Fainton Robert Polke Ralph Milbourn Samuel Shewel John Tarr William Bozman Matthew Scarbrough Thomas Oxford who having the whole matter rightly undrstood as also heard four Evidences Sworne for the plt. having recd their Charge goes forth ~~~ And being returned do bring in this following verdict (viz) We the Jurors do find for the plt, damages four hundred pounds of tobacco with Cost of suit. Given in by John: Bozman foreman. Ordr. to enter the verdict ~

172 [15 August 1690] Jonathan Towers vs. Lawrence Crawford; Robert Polke on Jury

Jonathan Towers Plt.   *Somerset County ~~*
  agt.
Lawrence Crawford. Deft
Lawrence Crawford of this County Gent was Summoned to answer unto Jonathan Towers of the same County, cooper in an action of the Case ~~ And whereupon the plt by Edward Jones his Attorney comes and saith that mr

Edward White late of this County decd and predecessor to the defendt did lett a certain plantation unto the plt and at the expiration of six years the plt did remove from the said plantation and left in A tobacco house upon the said plantation Sixteen hoggsheads of tobacco of the plt, And about the last of June or the beginning of July in the year 1689. then the deft came to the aforesaid tobacco house, and then did take and put out of the said tobacco house the aforesaid Sixteen hoggsheads of tobacco belonging to the plt to the great losse and damage of the said plte wherefore the plt sayes he is damnified and hath losse to the value of tenn thousand pounds of tobacco and thereupon brings his suite.   *pr Quer*   *Edward:Jones*   *Issue joynd. //*

And whereupon the defendt by his Attorney James Sangster Comes and defends the force and injury &c and saith that as the plt doth declare he did lease a Certain plantation of Mr John White late of this County deceased, for the terme of six years, which in the first place is altogether false as the lease will make appeare being but four years 2dly the plt doth declare that he the sd plt did lease a certain plantation, but what plantation or where there is nothing more uncertain, the sd Mr John White decd being seized of severall plantations with the names & where they lye ought carefully to have been inserted Otherwise it appears that this plantation by the plt alleadged was no plantation of Mr. John White deceased & consequently the decl false 3dly the plt sayes, that at the expiration of six years he did remove of the sd plantation which is by the defendt granted and further he sayes that he left 16. hogsheads of tobacco in a tobacco house upon the sd plantation which is also false, being a dwelling house. Now herein the plt is herein also uncertain as to the quantity or quality weight or Condition, Sound or rotten, So that no judgmente can pass, if all that the plt doth alleadge thereupon were really true. 4thly the plt alleadgeth that the defendt did take the said 16.hhds of tobacco which in Law terms doth amount to an appropriation which is likewise false & 5thly that the sd defendt did put out of the sd tobacco house the sd 16.hhds of tob. which is by the dft likewise warranted as thus. The plt anno 1688. was tenant by lease paroll, and being lawfully warnd to remove about the latter end of december that instant year the plt did remove leaving his tobacco part in hhds, which was removeable without damage notwithstanding the sd plt being warned as sd is to transport and remove the sd tob. with all other his utensells, yet the said plt obstinately maliciously and with a premeditate intent to damnifie the defdt, the said tobacco would not remove, having sufficient warning and time betwixt Christmas and the first of July following 1689 at which time the defendt had use of the sd house to secure his wheat and lastly the plt sayes he is damnified the value of 10000 lb. of tobacco which is a certain Sum which cannot hold good in law, the principall being uncertain the damages is nor cannot be certain no judgment can be intered but by the whole, that the plt doth and may alleadge is the turing out of the said tobacco, which the defendt. Justifies & sayes that the plt in the sd house had no property, and ought the same tobacco to have removed after notice given to remove the Same, as also the same he ought to have secured from damage the means being in him Selfe and the defdt no wayes being obliged to Secure or keep it, for all men are bound to prevent their owne hurt and if they neglect, the law

*calls it damnum Sin injuria, and they remediless. The defendt likewise sayes
that he could not expose his own Cropp of wheat to the hazzard of the weather
for the saifty of another mans goods, the law sayes. Nemo teneter Exponere Se
in fortuiniis et pericut Likewise Nulle Commodum Capere potest de injuria sua
pria, being so sure maxims in Law that the plts malicious intent plainly appears
in the said vexatious suit Expecting to take benifit by his own wrong Contrary to
the sd rules and reason &lastly the defendt sayes that there is nothing certain in
the whole declaration whereupn judgmt might pass, and it behaveth that
nothing certain be brought into judgment Secundi axioma oportet ut res Certa
deducatur in Judicium and if nothing certain a Non suit follows in Course. J. S..
The plt Craves that the matter in question may be referred to a Jury which by
the Court was granted. Which Jury was legally impannelled and duely Sworne,
whose names are as followeth. Viz John Bozman William Robbinson
John:Bowns Alexander Thomas Moses Fainten Robert Polke Ralph
Milbourne Samuel Shewell John Tarr William Bozman Matthew Scarbrough
Thomas Oxford who having heard the total proceedings, having recd their
Charge goes forth to determine the Same ~~~ And being returned do
unanimously bring into Court this following verdict. Viz. Wee the Jurors do find
for the plt Damages two thousand five hundred pounds tobaccoe with Cost given
in by Jno. Bozman.   4 Evidences sworne for plt.
Which Verdict the Court Ordered to enter*

174 [15 August 1690] Capt. Henry Smith vs. Michael Holland; Robert Polke on Jury

Capt Henry Smith. Plt.   *Somerset County*

~

     agt.

Michael: Holland. deft

*Issue joynd Declaration Read viz Michael Holland of the County of Somersett,
and Province of Maryland Marryner was Sumoned to answer unto Capt.
Henry Smith of the Same County of Somerset and Province Gentll. of a plea that
he render unto him the full and just Sum of two hundred pounds Sterling money
of England which to him he oweth and unjustly deteineth &c. And whereupon
the said Henry by Peter Dent his Attorney saith that the said Michael.the 13th:
day of March in the year of our Lord 1689/90 at Monocan within the
Jurisdiction of this Court, by his Certain bond Obligatory which the said Henry
with the seal of the sd Michael Signed bringeth here unto Court, the date
whereof is the day and year aforesaid acknowledged himselfe to be bound to the
said Henry in the said full and just Sum of two hundred pounds Sterling money
of England to be paid to the sd Henry upon demand, to the which payment well
and truly to be made the said Michael bound himselfe firmly by the said Bill.
Nevertheless the said Michael the said Sum of two hundred pounds sterling
although often demanded the same, to the said Henry hath not rendered but hath
hitherto denyed and doth still deny to the damage of the sd Henry of two
hundred and fifty pounds Sterling and thereof bringeth his suite &c.*

    Dent pr Quer Pleg &c.   *John:Doe Rich: Roe.*

*The Defendant Comes and defends the force and injury and sayes that there is a
certain Bond for two hundred pounds sterling money with a Condition there
unto annexed, But the plt doth not declare for any Bond with a Condition
thereunto anexed and this he gives in Barr.   J.S.*
*And the said Henry by Peter Dent Saith that he hath declared for a Certain bond
to be here in Court produced, which is here ready, and this he prayes may be
enquired by the Court.   Dent*
*The whole matter being wholy referred to a Jury of twelve good and lawfull
men, who was legally impanneld and duly sworn whose names are as followeth
(Viz) John Bozman William Robbinson   John:Bowns Alexander Thomas.
Moses Fainton. Robert Polke Ralph:Milbourn Samuel:Shewell John Tarr
William Bozman Thomas Oxford. William Planner who having viewed the
Bonds and papers as also the Evidences Sworne, having received their Charge
goes forth to determine the Same ～ And being returned do bring in this
following verdict Viz. Wee the Jurors find no Cause of action. Given in pr John
Bozman*

180 [7 October 1690] Devils Island to be included in Monie Hundred

[The John Laws mentioned in this list later became the third husband of
Margaret Polk/Pollett/Tull. The Laws family followed the Polk migration to the
upper Nanticoke region in the 1720-30s.]

*It was Ordered by the Justices in September Court last past, that the Constable
of Mony hundred, take the taxable Inhabitants of the divels Island into his list of
Tytheables, wch Order was forthwith sent to the aforesd Constable. And after
our Burgesses was gone over the bay with the generall List of Taxable persons
in this County, the aforesd Constable (viz) James:Langrell brought to the Clerks
Office a List of the sd Taxable persons upon the divels Island as followeth
The true list of the divels Island*
Dennis Buskey.- 1
Thomas Roe.--- 1
John Winsor ---- 1
John Laws.--
William Laws} 2

191 [Entered October/November 1690] Rev. William Trail power of attorney

This power of attorney was probably drawn up in anticipation of Rev. Trail's
return to Scotland. One of the witnesses, Samuel Davis was also a Presbyterian
minister.

*Somerset County in Maryland ～ Be it known and manifest unto all persons to
whom these presents shall come, that I William Trail of Somerset County Clerk.
for divers good causes and Considerations me hereunto espetially moveing have
made Constituted and appointed and in my place and stead put and authorized
my trusty and welbeloved wife Elinor Traile of Somerset County foresd my true*

*and lawfull Attorney for me and in my name and to my use to enter into hold &
posess all and singuler the lands & Tenements whatsoever to me belonging
within the County aforesd by whch name or title so everknown or calld with all
and singuler the appurtenances thereunto belonging and the same or any part
thereof for me and in my name to view and Survey and the same land or any
part thereof for me and in my name, to bargain sell lease and grant to any
person or persons whatsoever and for Such estates, for life or lives, Inheritance,
and for Such Sum or Sums of money, as to my said Attorney shall be thought
meet and Convenient to the uttermost & best comodity and profit of me the said
William Traile, and the deed or deeds of the same grant or grants So to be made
for me and in my name, to make Seal and as my deed deliver unto the party or
parties to whome the same shall be made or to any other, to his or their use &
uses and Counter parts of the same for me and in my name to accept & receive
and also all Such fines & other Sums of money as shall grow due for the same
for me & in my name and to my use to gather receive and take, and all such
rents duties and arearages of Rents & profits as are already or hereafter shall
become due or payable for out of or concerning the premises or any of them to
receive and also all other debts or Sums of money, tobacco Indian Corne wheat
porke &c as are shall or may become due or payable to me in any part of this
Province of Maryland or in the Collony of Virginia from any person or persons
whatsoever for me and in my name and to my use, to ask sue for leavy recover
and receive and upon the receit of any of the said Sums of money, tobacco
Indian Corne &c. acquittances or other discharges for me & in my name to
make seal and deliver, and for the recovery of any Such debt or debts one or
more attorneys under her to constitute & appoint, and the same at her will &
pleasure to revoke, and all other act and acts, thing & things, device and devises
in the Law needfull and necessary for the recovery of any debt or debts as to the
sd Attorney shall seem meet & convenient in the premisses to act and do giving
& hereby granting unto my said Attorney my full power and authority touching
& concerning the premises to doe execute and finish in all things in as ample
manner to all intents and purposes as I my Selfe might or could do ratifying
allowing and holding firm & stable whatsoever my said Attorney shall lawfully
do or cause to be done in and about the premises or any of them according to
the true intent and meaning of these presents. In Witnesse whereof I have
hereunto Sett my hand and affixed my seal this twenty first day of february in the
year of our Lord 1689/90*

W Traile   ¤ *Sealed* ～

Sealed signed and delivered in the presence of us ～
*George Layfield
Edmund Howard
Mr. Richard Farewell
Samuel Davis*

SOMERSET JUDICIAL RECORDS 1690-91
[MSA C 1774-8, Loc. 1/48/2/33]

36 [10 Feb 1690/91] Trial of Christopher Little for not working on county road

[Note: An orphan boy named Christopher Little was mentioned in Robert Polke's will – most likely the son of the defendant in this trial.]

Their Majesties   *Somerset County ~~*
  Agt.
The Jurors for their Maties being sworne Christopher Little   upon the holy Evangelist at a   grand Jury held for the body of this County the second tuesday in 9-ber last past doe present and find that Christopher Little of this County Planter being lawfully warned and having Suffitient notice from George Betts, Overseer of thier Maties high wayes. for Mony *(Monie)* hundred to attend and mend the sd high wayes in pursuance of an Act of Assembly in that Case made, did willingly, wittingly and wilfully himself absent and therein prove a delinquent, without any Colour of Lawfull excuse, but in Contempt of the sd Law. Therefore their Maties Attorney Craves judgment may be entered agt the said Christopher: Little for his delinquency according to Law &c.

Ja. Sangster Clk Indts ~~~

The above said Christopher Litle was fined two dayes worke & Ordered to pay Court Charges .
Court charges, then the Recognizance voyd, otherwayes to be and remain, in full power, force and vertue. ~ ~

94 [10 June 1691] Trial of William Mason for hog stealing; Robert Polke (Poke) security for Mason

 Their Maties   *Somerset County ~~*
   Agt
Wm. Mason
The Jurors for their Maties at a Grand Jury held for the body of this County the second tuesday in March last past being sworn upon the holy Evangelists: do present and find William Mason of this County togeather withone James: Inglish upon the fourteenth day of Febry Ano. Dom1690/1 did upon a point known by the name of Samphire point in Manokin River within the Jurisdiction of this Court Steal, kill and felloniously carry away four hoggs belonging and of the propper marke of Elinor Cane Widdow, of the value of nine hundred and ninety nine pounds of tobacco, being not only a great damage, detriment and injury to the sd Elinor but also to the good people of this Province. Notwithstanding of the sacred and divine Law of God expressed in the eight Comandement in these words (thou shalt not steal.) and in Contempt of the good Laws and institutions of this their Maties Province thereby dishonouring God giving scandall and evill example to all the good people of this Province, and against the publick peace. Therefore their Maties Attorney Craves judgment may be entered agt the sd Wm: Mason and that he Suffer the pains and punishments by law in the Case made and provided. agt Such offenders &c.

James: Sangster. Clk. Indts.

The Indictment being Read, to wch. the sd Mason pleaded not guilty, and for tryal put himself upn the Countrywhereupon Command was given to the Sheriffe to Sumon twelve good and lawfull men of his vicenage that the matter might be the better understood, which was imediatly performed a list or pannel returned in Court whose names are as followeth. Viz. John Emmett John Smock Wm. Henderson Wm.Denson Wm. Noble Miles Gray Edward Evins Henry Hudson, Senior Bryan Peart Thomas Tull James Langre Aaron Bishop who being duely summoned and Sworn haveing heard the foresd Indictmt. read, as also these eight Evidences following examined and Sworn in Open Court whose names are. Viz Richard Davis Thomas Royall Jno. Royall James. Terril John Bozman John Renshaw John Johnson Paskew Bartlett who having recd their charge are Sent forth to determine the matter. ~~~ And being now returned in Court. being unanimously agreed the plt & deft being called. do give in this following verdict. (viz) We of the Jury find the defendt guilty of the Indictment. Jno. Emmett foreman which verdict as aforesd was Ordered to be entered.

Ordered by this Court that the sd Wm. Mason pay fourteen hundred thirty five pounds of tobacco to Elinor Cane it being the one halfe of the fourfold. Order likewise the sd Mason find good Security for his good behaviour dureing Courts pleasure ~~~ Whereupon came the sd Wm. Mason with his two Securityes. Viz. Robert Poke and Thomas Ryoll and the sd Poke by Recognizance did become bound to their Maties in the sum of Tenn pounds sterling money of England, the sd Poke, and Ryoll in the sum of five pounds like money, due to be leavyed upon their goods and Chattels, Lands & Tennements for their Maties uses &c. ~~~ The Condition of this Recognizance is Such, that if the above bound Wm. Mason be of the good behaviour & abearance to all their Maties Liege people of this Province dureing the Courts pleasure as also pay Court Charge that then this Recognizance to be void and of none effect otherwayes to be and remain in full power force & virtue

95 [10 June 1691] Case against Mary Mackenny for bastardy

The Grand Jury do present and find that Mary Mackenny of this County spinster and of Money Hundred within the Jurisdiction of this Court hath most wickedly sinfully and shamefully commited fornication and born a child to the great dishonour of Almighty God scandall & evil example to all the good people of this Province and in contempt of the good laws and Institutions of the same. Therefore their Maties Attorney Craves judgment may be entered against the sd Offender according to law in that Case made and provided.

James Sangster Clk. Indts.

The Indictmt being read to which the said Mary confessed, and made Oath that Francis Roberts was the father of her Basterd Child ~~~ The sd Mackenny having fitts of sickness, her punishment was remitted and a fine accepted, which was twenty dayes worke and tools with diet to be paid to George Betts Overseer of Mony hundred, also the sd Mary Ordered to find Security for her good behaviour and to keep the County harmless from sd Child. Whereupon came Henry Haylor, and by Recognizance did confess himself indebted to their Maties in the Sum of five pound, for to be leavied on his goods and Chattels Lands and

99 [10 June 1691] Trial of Walter Taylor for fraud in sale of timber; Robert "Poke" on Jury

Walter Taylor is retried for fraud in sale of timber to Samuel Hopkins who unsuccessfully sued Taylor in a civil case. This time Taylor is found guilty. See Somerset Judicials 1689-90:147]

Their Maties   *Somerset Count ~~.*
 Contra
Walter: Taylor
The Jurors for their Maties being sworn upon the holy Evangelists at a Grand Jury held for the body of this County the second tuesday in March last past do present and find that Walter Taylor of this County sawyer upon a bargain and saile of twelve Cutts of Cypress Timber to mr. Samuel: Hopkins of this County Gent. for and in Consideration of 22 pnds of linnen and in Complyance with the said agreement the said mr Samuel: Hopkins, did send one Adam:Spence, and SamuelHopkins Junior to receive the said Cutts Now the said Walter: Taylor not regarding the agreement nor fearing the punishment by law inflicted upon fraudulent cheaters, did send 76: pieces of Cypress timber, avouching and averring, avouching them to be nine 2 cutts of the twelve agreed for, whereas upon view, and upon Oath, there is not of the alleadged nine 2 passing three Cutts, the said Walter having fraudulently and cunningly cheated the sd mr Samuel: Hopkins, by mauling the sd Cutts some into 16: quarters or pieces others into 32: pieces, and the rest into more, and delivered for nine 2 cutts of the 12: only y 6: pieces instead of 8: quarters to the cutt to the said mr. Samuel: Hopkins. Now their Maties Attorney comes and sayes, that the sd Walter Taylor hath not only cheated and cunningly and cossened the said mr. Samuel: Hopkins of six cutts of the nine 2 by him averred to be dilivered, but in like manner to cheat and cozen of the remainder, that is due of the twelve endeavoured, and that the said Walter hath made his practice to cozen and cheat others in the same manner and kind. To the great injry, damage & losse of their Maties good people, of and agt the Laws and institutions of this Province, and therefore craves judgment may be entered agt the sd Walter for this his great and abominable fact according to law in that Case made and provided.

James: Sangster. Clk. Indts

To which Indictment the sd Walter Taylor pleaded not guilty and for tryall put himself upon y Country. And therefore Command was given to the sheriffe of this County to Summon twelve good and lawfull men of his vicenage   that the matter might be the better understood. a List or pannel whereof are returned as followeth. viz) Jno Emmet Wm Denson Miles Gray Edward Ennis HenryHudson Senr Thomas Tull James Langrell Aaron Bishop Samuel Shewall Robert Poke John Porter Thomas Hobbs who being called over by their names, were duely Sworn upon the holy Evangelists, who attends at the Barr to hear the aforesd Indictmt. the Evidences and Depositions hereafter following.

[Several depositions follow]

Charge are Sent forth to determine of the matter. ~~~ which foresd Jury being now returned are called over being unanimously agreed to bring in this following verdict (viz) we of the Jury findeth the defendant guilty of the Indictment. John Emmett wch. verdict was pr Court Ordered to be entered Likewise the said Walter was by order of Court fined four hundred pounds of tobacco. And Ordered to find good Security for his good behaviour ~~ Whereupon came the aforesaid Walter with his two Securities viz. Lawrence Crawford and Teague Riggen. Junior. And the sd Walter. did pr Recognizance acknowledge And Confess himself to owe and be indebted unto their Maties in the sum of tenn pounds Sterling moneys of a piece England and the sd Lawrence Crawford and Teague Riggon like wise indebted to sd Maties in the sum of five pound of the like money, due to be leaived on their goods and Chattels Land and Tennements for their Maties. uses &c.

112 [11 June 1691] Paternity case against Francis Roberts
Their Ma'ties Attorney came and says that the said Roberts hath most wickedly sinfully and shamefully committed fornication and upon the body on Mary Mackenny hath begot a Bastard Child against the laws of the Province. The said Mary Mackennie yesterday having made Oath in Open Court that Fr. Roberts now at the Barr was the father of her Basterd Child as in folio 95. Therefore the Court Orders the sd Roberts to give good Security for his behaviour, as also to keep the County harmless and indemnified from the sd Basterd Child. And whereupon Came the sd Francis Roberts with his two Securities (viz) James Langrell & Jno. Richins and the sd Roberts in Open Court pr Recognizance, did confess him self to owe and be indebted unto their Ma'ties in the sum of twenty pounds Sterling money of England and the sd Langrel & Richins in the sum of ten pounds a piece like lawfull money, due to be leaived on their goods and Chattels lands and tenements for their Ma'ties uses ~ The Condition of which Recognizance is Such that if the above bound Francis Roberts be of the good behaviour and abeareance to all their Ma'ties Liege people of this Province, and shall keep this County harmless and indemnified from charge or trouble by reason of a Basterd Child borne of the body of Mary Mackennie as also to pay all Court Charges then this Recognizance to be void. Otherwayes to be & remain in full power force and vertue. Memorand ~ The said Fra. Roberts in Open Court agreed with the sd Mackennie to give her twelve hundred Pounds of tobacco to keep the forsd Basterd Child twelve months.

165 [30 September 1691] William Knox given custody of Joseph Ward
Joseph Ward Basterd Sonn of Sarah Ward late Servant to Capt. John King was this day brought into Court and being made appearant to the Court that the sd Sarah in her life time gave the sd Joseph her Sonn, to William Knox and this Court Confirms the sd Joseph to the sd Knox till he be one & twenty years of age. the sd Joseph being two years old tomorrow (viz) the first day of October

Ano.Dom. 1691. And the sd Wm. Knox in Courtassumes to give the sd Joseph a yearling Heifer when he attains to the age of Seaventeen years

167 [30 October 1691] Francis Roberts acts as Attorney

Francis Roberts acts as attorney for Richard Lamb in suit against William Cheeseman to collect alleged debt of 2000 pounds of tobacco, without success. *... And the defendt by Peter Dent his Attorney Comes & defends the force & Injury & Saith that the plt is not qualified in Law to Sue or implead the Deft. Neither did the sd William Cheesman Deft ever Seal Sign or diliver any Obligation to the said Francis Roberts or to the sd Richard. Lamb, as the plt in his Decl. hath averred and this he prayes may be enquired of by the Country. Dent pr Dft. The matter being Debated before the Court by the Attorneys, who at length referred their issue to the judgmt of the Court, who having Considered the matter do Ordr a Non Suit agt the plt.*

SOMERSET JUDICIAL RECORDS 1691-92
[MSA C 1774-9, Loc. 1/48/2/35]

175 [9 March 1691/2] Trial of Margaret Kennedy for hog stealing; Robert Polke on Jury

Their Ma'ties   Somerset
Contra.
Margerett Kenneday
Margerett Kenneday of this County Spinster was attached to answer unto their Maties the Second tuesday in August before the worll. their Maties Justices of the Peace, what should be then & there Objected agt her ~~
And whereupon their Ma'ties Attorney Comes and Sayes that the said Margerett not having the fear of God Before here eyes, but instigated by the Divil, did most wickedly, maliciously, Spitefully & felloniously at the house of Stephen Page of Mattapony hundred within the Jurisdiction of this Court, Sometime in the month of October. 1690: Togeather with the assistance of two of the said Stephen Pages Nigroes— Thomas Parramore, and Susanna Parramore, as also the advice Consent, and approbation of the said Stephen and Bridgett his wife Steal, kill, dresse and Salted upp Six large hoggs belonging to Thomas Oxford of the said County and hundred, of the value of nine hundred ninety and nine pounds of tobacco not withstanding that the Sacred and divine Law of Allmighty God, Expressly forbiddeth the Same in the eight Comandement, Saying thou shall not steal, as also the good and wholesome laws and insititutions of this Province, especially agt Hoggstealers, and other Criminals, which Said hoggs as Said is The Said Margarett hath most felloniously Stolne as Said is. To the great Scandall Evil example of others, and against the publick peace. Their Maties Attorney Craves judgment may be entered agt the said Margeret Kenneday according to Law in that Case made and provided, and that she Suffer the pains and punishments by law thereupon inflicted. ~~ James Sangster Clr. Indtmts

The aforesd Indictment being Read, to which the said Margerett Kenneday pleaded not guilty and for tryall put her Self upon the Country, whereupon Comand was given to the sheriffe to bring here twelve good and lawfull men of his Balywick that the matter in hand might be the better known a List or pannel whereof are thus returned as appear in the Margent, being leagally Sumoned, returnd and Sworn upon the holy Evangelists having heard the forsad Indictment read, as also Six Evidences Sworn and examined, receives their Charge and are Sent forth to determine the Same ~~~

[Entered in the margin] *Jurors viz: Henry Hall Walter Talbott Edward Evins John Colhoone William Porter RogerBurkum James Ingram Joseph Bainton John Browne Thomas Tull Thomas Smith Robert Polke*
Evidences: John Pope Robert Johnson Eliz. Lawrence John Tarr Mr. Sam'll Hopkins Martin Troutam.

This following Deposition was likewise read, as followeth, viz: The Deposition of Sam'll Hopkins Senr. this Deponent Saith that being at dinner alias Supper in the house of Mr. Andrew Whittington, as the Deponent remembers at August Court last past) word was brought the Deponent, that Margeret Kenneday would Speak with him. This Deponent imediately went forth to know the said Kennedays business. she came to the Deponent and gave him the relation following, to witt that she now Saw she was a fool for not telling the truth about the hoggs. This Deponent told her that if she had concealed the truth by lying she was a fool indeed, or to that effect, she replyed, though I denyed the killing of the hoggs at the house, yet I alwayes resolved to declare it when I came to Court. and you may remember I told you I had more to say when I came there, then I would speak at that time, Referring as the Deponent understood, to her examination at my house, she added further, that Seeing the Court was broke up, and there Could be no tryall now she had Sent for me to declare the truth to me, though she knew she must be whipt
~~~ she then uttered these words (viz) the hoggs we killed were of three marks, I asked her what hoggs, those that Betty Lawrence had Sworn too, I asked if she owned that she helped or asisted in killing those hoggs, she answered yes, like a fool as I was, & I have undone my Selfe I asked her if she owned what Elizabeth Lawrence had made Oath of at my house she answered Betty has Sworn nothing but the truth. Betty replyed, you know Margeret I told not a word of a lye neither of you nor my Mistress nor no body else. Margaret answered no more you did Betty. I asked if she know whose hoggs they were that they killed, she answered she did not Certainly know, but Some of them they Said was Thomas Oxfords hoggs, then she nominated & described all three of the markes, which she related as abovesd, and promised to declare them the next Court this & more to the Same purpose she very freely & very fullently declared, to the truth of all above written the deponent Can Saifly be deposed witness my hand.
Courts adjourned for a quarter of an hour. Samuel: Hopkins ~~~
And this day to witt the 9th day of March Anno Domini 1691/2 the aforesd Jury as in the Margent Comes in Court the plt & dft being calld as also the Jurors of that Jury, and being all agreed of their verdict which is read as followeteh. viz.

269

Wee of the Jury do find Margeret Kenneday guilty of the Indictment & do valued the hoggs at 800lb of tobacco. Henry Hall foreman

186 [11 March 1691/2] Case of Francis Gunby vs. Thomas Jones for embezzlement of a horse; Robert Polke on Jury

Francis: Gunby Plt   *Somerset County ~~*
Agt.
Mr Thomas: Jones. Dft
Mr. Thomas Jones of this County Gent, was attached to answer unto Francis Gunby of the Same County Joyner in a plea of trespass upon the Case. And whereupon the plt by James Sangster his Attorney Comes and Sayes that in the year of our Lord 1682 the plt had One black horse well known to be the plts by the name of Gunby on the other side the Bay, which said Horse then and there runing. The said Thomas Jones Dft, did then & there take up Sell and dispose of to Mr Daniel Clocker, at the price of three thousand pounds of tobacco. without the plts Order, knowledge Consent or privity, and the plt likewise declareth that the said Jones at his return to this County, the Same did Craftily and Cuningly Conceal from the plts knowledge about the space of nine years, whereby it is apparent that the sd dft did fraudulently and Craftily intend the plt to deceive, and him defraud of both horse and price by the dft imposed, which in reality was an under rate formerly proffered the plt for the said horse. The plt likewise declareth that the premises Considered (viz) that the dft. never had Order either written or verball to dispose of the said horse. his Concealing the Same So long, and his late denyal Satisfaction to the plt, imparts the great abuse and damage of the plt. to the value of Six thousand pounds of tobacco, and there upon brings this Suit   Ja. Sangster pr Que pled
The Dfendt. Saith he is not guilty as by the Decl is averred and puts himself upon the Country The plt also
Edward Jones James Sangster } Attorneys
Decl. Read   issue joynd &ca
Whereupon Comand was given to the Sheriffe to bring here Twelve good and Lawfull men of his Balywick that the matter in hand might be the better understood, a List or pannel whereof are returned as appears upon the left hand [Jurors listed in the side margin: Henry Hall, Walter Talbott, Edward Evins, Jno. Colhoone, Wm.Porter, Roger Burkum, James Ingram, Jos. Bainton, John Browne, Tho. Tull, Tho. Smith, Robert Polke] *being legally Sumoned returned and Sworn upon the holy Evangelists having heard the foresd Declaration & pleas also those following precepts. or papers read. receives their Charge & are Sent forth in Order to return their verdict ~~~~*
———————— [Several attachments omitted]
And this Same day (viz) 11th. of March Ano. 1691/2 the aforesd Jury as in fo:186. appears in Court, the plt & Deft being Calld, as also the Jurors of sd Jury each man by his name and being demanded are all unanimously agreed of their verdict which being read is as followeth Wee of the Jury find for the plt. also we value the horse a 1200lb: of tobacco Henry: Hall. foreman
Which forsd verdict was Ordered to be entered, but for Some reasons given to

Court Sossit Executio *was Ordered till June Court next.*

188 [11 March 1691/2] Trial of Thomas Porter for stealing three pigs; Robert Polke on Jury

Their Ma'ties   *Somerset County ~*
Contra
Thomas Porter
The Jurors for their Maties being Sworn upon the holy Evangelists at a grand Jury held for the body of this County the Second Tuesday in Novemr last pastdoe present and find that Thomas Porter of this County Planter not having the fear of God before his Eyes nor Regarding the good laws and institutions of this their Maties Province, upon the twenty fifth day of July Ao. Dom 1691 did most wickedly and felloniously at hogg neck, within the Jurisdiction of this Court Steal and Carry away three black Boar piggs off and from the Sows belonging to Mr. Francis Jenckins, of the value of One hundred & fifty pounds of tobacco. To the great Scandall, Evil Example and damage, and detriment, not only of the sd mr Francis Jenckins, but also of the good people and inhabitants of this Province, Contrary to the Laws, and agt the publick peace, Their Maties Attorney Craves judgment may be entered against the said Thomas Porter, according to Law in that Case made and provided &c.

James Sangster Clr Indtmts.

The plts and dft being Calld the foresd Indictmt. was read to which the said dft pleaded not guilty and for tryall was referred pr Court to a Jury ~~~~- Whereupon Comand was given to the Sheriffe to bring here into Court twelve good and lawfull men of his Balywick that the matter in hand might be the better known a list or pannel whereof are returned being legally Sumoned, and Sworn upon the holy Evangelists. whose names are as appears upon the left hand. [Jurors names listed in left margin: Henry Hall, Walter Talbott, Edward Evins, John Colhoone, William Porter, Roger Burkum, James Ingram, Joseph Bainton, John Browne, Thomas Tull, Thomas Smith, Robert Polke] *who having heard the foresd Indictmt as also the Oaths of three Evidences bondes the examination of three more with these Depositions following. viz*

October the 19th. 1691. Then Came before me William Layton & Cornelius Anderson & did depose that William: Burch & Thomas Porter had Some words of difference, which difference Porter desired to agree & End it and did Say that if Burch would Comply he would at his own trouble gett Coll. David Browne and Mr James Dashiels to come to his Brother John Hollands for to end the difference   *John Winder ~~~*

Cornelius Anderson
William Layton.

[In side margin] *Evidences Sworne.viz Wm. Burch Cornelius Anderson Wm. Layton Hen. Freaks Tho. Rolph & Tho. Horseman.*

And this day having asd heard the totall proceedings the sd Jury as in the

Margent or left hand after the Charge given, are Sent forth to determine the matter ~~ Which Said Jury being returned in Court, being each man Calld Over by their names are all unanimously agreed Evidences Examined of their verdict, the plts & deft first calld. the verdict is read as followeth ~ Wee of the Jury do find Tho. Porter not guilty of this Indictmt. Hen.Hall forem.

This Court Orders the verdict to be entered. Ordered likewise sd Porter pay the Jurors fees. Ordered likewise the said Porter give Security for his good behaviour dureing this Courts pleasure and for Cost of Suit. whereupon Came the sd Porter & his 2 Securts. viz Wm. Elgate & Tho. Horsman and the sd Porter did acknowledge himself to be indebted to their Ma'ties in the Sum of 10£ Sterl. & his Securities in the Sum of 5£ Sterl apiece to be levied on their good & chattels lands & tennements for their Maties uses &c

The Condicon &ca is that the sd Porter shall be of good behaviour dureing pleasure &c.

189 [11 March 1691/2] Trial of Daniel Selby for selling remains of a carrion cow; Robert Polke on Jury

Their Maties   Somerset ~~
  Contra
  Daniel Selby

The Jurors for their Maties being Sworn upon the holy Evangelists at a Grand Jury held for the body of this County the Second Tuesday in Novem'r last past doe present and find that Daniel: Selby of Mattapony hundred and within the Jurisdiction of this Court sometime Last Spring, did pack up and picle, a Certain lean Carrion Cow, which of poverty died in his own field at the said plantation in the Said hundred, and the Same did pay away for Mertable beef, and thereby did Cheat and Cozne the Merchant, which said Cheat was not only injurious to the private Interest of the buyer, but also to the publick trade and Comerce of the Country and agt the Laws of the Land Their Maties Attorney Craves judgment agt the said Daniel: Selby according to Law, in that Case made & provide.   James: Sangster.

The Indictment being read, to which the sd Selby pleaded not guilty. and this Court refers the tryall to a Jury: ~~ Whereupon Command was this day given to the Sheriffe to bring here twelve good and Lawfull men of his Balywick that the matter might be the better known. A list or pannel whereof are upon the left hand, [Jurors listed in the side margin: Henry Hall, Walter Read, Edward Evins, John Colhoone, Wm. Porter, Roger Burkum, James Ingram, Joseph:Bainton, John Browne, Thomas Tull, Thomas Smith, Robert Polke] who being legally returned Sumoned & Sworn upon the holy Evangelists having heard the aforesaid Declaration, as also the Oaths of the Evidences fairly examined viz of Walter Talbott Mr John Cornish & Mr. James Sangster & James Maynard was Sumoned & examined but not Sworne. which sd Jury as in the Margent having deliberatly heard the totall proceedings receives their Charge and are Sent forth in Order to determine the same And the Same day as abovesd the aforesaid Jury returns in Court, being each man perticuliarly calld over by his name, being asked, are all unanimously agreed of ther verdict. The plts and deft being

272

*calld. sd verdict is read as followeth: Wee of the Jury doe find find that Daniel
Selby is not guilty of the Indictment. Henry Hall, foreman* ~~~~~
*This Court Orders The verdict to be entered. Ordered likewise the sd Selby pay
the Jurors fees.*

228 [June 1692] Robert Polke case on docket for June Court
*N.E.I.—Caps agt Robert Polke to answere unto Andrew Whittington in an accon
of the Case.*
[This probably refers to a suit for debt collection; Andrew Whittington was the
Innholder at Manokin where Court was held. NEI is an abbreviation for *non est
inventus*, meaning not to be found, which is not further explained. The case was
later settled out of court.]

SOMERSET JUDICIAL RECORDS 1692-93
[MSA C 1774-10, Loc. 1/48/2/36]

P-2[No date] Docket for August Court 1692
*Entries Returnable the Second Tuesday in August anno Domini 1692
Robert Poke, planter, answer to Andrew Whittington* (among other entries)

**8 [8 August 1692] Resolution of dispute between George Parks and James
Inglish**
[The agreement entered here had been reached earlier but was placed in the
Court record at this time. It involves two persons who were associated with the
Polk family: George Parks had instructed John and William Polk in the coopers
trade; both of the latter were witnesses to the will of William Porter in 1695.]
*15 March 1691/2 By vertue of the Order of Court Mr Richard Whitty & Wm
Porter hath heard what the wittnesses could say and according to the best of our
judgement have ended and finally concluded the difference in the two pet'ions
betwixt James Inglish & George Parks to which we have ordered the said
Inglish to pay the said Parks nine hundred pounds of tobacco, each man paying
his own charges in Law for his work as wittness our hands and seals.*
                                          Richard Whitty   William Porter

**76 [September Court 1692] Case of Andrew Whittington vs. Robert Polke
settled**
[Among other entries listed in cases settled out of Court, September session]
Andrew Whittington vs. Robert Poke

**141 [11 November 1692] Case of Francis Roberts vs. William Cheeseman
for recovery of a long boat**
[Francis Roberts was married to Anne Polk at this time; he was seldom
successful in Court.]

*Francis Roberts, Plt   Somerset.
        Contra*

273

Wm Cheesman, Dft
Wm Cheesman of this County Planter was attached to answer unto Francis
Roberts of the same County in a plea on the case etc ~~~
And whereupon the Plt by his Attorney James Sangster comes & says that
whereas the Plt did buy one certaine Long Boat of Mr Richard Lamb mariner
which said long boat with her furniture Cable & Anchor did by stress of weather
break away from the said Richard Lambs shipp and so fell into the hands of the
def in the same condicon she was into when she broke away from her shipp and
the said plt the said Boat having purchaed of the owner did demand of the said
Cheesman dft tending him satisfaction for the taking up of the said boat with her
furniture which said boat was of the value with her furniture of six thousand
pounds of tobacco but the sd Defend't craftily & cunningly intending to deceive
& defraud the Pltf of said boat did pretend he should be fully satisfied if the plt
would lend him the sd def the said boat for a small time then between them
agreed and did upon himself assume & to the plt faithfully promise to bring the
said boat to the plt's landing in the same estate & condition as the deft first had
her. Yett the said deft litle regarding the promise & assumption hath not brought
the said Boat, but hath utterly defrauded & cousin --- the plt thereof. Therefore
the plt sayes he is damnified & hath losse to the value of eight thousand pounds
of tobacco & here upon brings this suite.
                    Sangster Qu   Pled
The Doct being read anon was dismist p/ Curia

175 [14 March 1692/93] Trial of Germane Gillett for aiding two pregnant women

[The Gillett (Gullett/Guillette) family were French Huguenot and had arrived somewhat earlier than the Scotch-Irish from Donegal. Robert Polk Jr. married Grace Gullett, daughter of William Gullett, and probably the niece of Germane.]

Their Ma'ties   Somerset.
contra
Germane Gillett
The jurors for their Ma'ties being sworn upon the Holy Evangelists at a Grand
Jury held for the this County in Jan'y 1692 doe present & find that Germane
Gillett of Pocomoke Hundred and within the Jurisdiction of this Court not
having any regard to the good Laws and Institutions of this Province against the
breakers of the said Laws that they may be brought speedily to tryall &
according to the demerit of their fact punished, hath in contempt of the said
Laws & ag't authority upon himself taken to arbitrate, determine & for the
wor'll Court to agree & compound with criminals for their fines & punishment,
concealing some & protecting others from the Laws. And whereas Susannah
Hazard the stepdaughter of the sd Germane in anno 1690 committed fornication
& last winter twelve month brought forth a bastard child at the house of the said
Germane, and in order that the said Susannah might evade & escape
punishment for the same ofence, did convey her out of the County in an
unseemly manner before she had lyen a fortnight of her month, & to this time

*hath continued in contempt of this Government abovesd The said Germane doth
most contemptuously perservere in these known & manifest abuses in that the
said Germane did at his house receive an Elizabeth Kotle a fugitive from
Accamack County in Virginia being with Child of a bastard & before that the
said Elizabeth was brought to bed, the sd Germane did upon himself presume to
compound & agree with the said Elizabeth for her fine & punishment &
usurping the power, authority & jurisdiction of this Court did cause her
subscribe to an Indenture for three years service assuming upon himself to bear
the sd Elizabeth harmeless from all manner of fine or punishment & in
pursuance of the same assumption to agrivate the matter, did heap abuse upon
abuse on the County & Court & in March Court 1692 did present the said
Elizabeth by Anne his wife to the Grand Jury for Bastardy but before tryal the sd
Germane, cunningly & craftily, did sell & dispose of the sd Elizabeth Kotle &
her likewise did transport from the tryal & punishment of this Court inflicted by
law out of the Jurisdiction of this Court, first into Virginia & supposing her not
safe enough there in person did convey her into the Territitories of
Pennsylvania; all which the said premises, hath been acted & done contrary to
the Laws in despite of Authority & abuse to the Government. Therefore the same
considers that the like accons may not be brought into president & avoiding of
so heinious evil example to the Inhabitants. Their Ma'ties Attorney craves
judgement may be entered ag't the sd Germane according to the Law ~~*
James Sangster, Clerk of Indictments

*The foresd Indictment being read to which the said Germane Gillett pleaded not
guilty and for tryal puts himself upon thhe Court & the Wor'll Court referred the
same to the Jury wherefore command was this day given to the Sheriff of this
County to bring here twelve good & lawfull men of his balywick that the matter
might be the better understood, a list or pannel whereof was forth(with)
returned as followeth (viz.) James Curtis, Alexander Thomas, Lawrence Gary,
James Langreen, George Goddard, Wm. Venables, Rich. Cary, Somerset
Dickinson, John Gray, Thomas Gordon, Roger Odowey, Wm. Bowden (12) who
being legally summoned returned & sworn upon the holy Evangelists, who
having heard the foresd Indictment as also these three Evidences for their
Ma'ties sworn & examined, receives their charge & are sent forth in order to
determine the matter ~~~~~~~~~~~~~~~~*

*And this day, viz. the day aforesd the Jurors of this same cause depending
between their MA'ties & the aforesd Germane Gillett returns in Court with their
verdict. The Plts & Dft being called as also the Jurors of the Jury, who being all
unanimously agreed delivers up this following verdict (viz) Wee of the Jury find
no cause for Indictment; James Curtis foreman. W'ch verdict was ordered to be
entered. Evidences sworn for their Ma'ties were Sam'l Alexander, Walter Reed
& Thomas Gillett.*

Ordered p/ Wor'll Court to impannell another Jury.

*Memorandum this following acc't was p/ Ge. Gillett produced in Court & read
Elizabeth Kotle Debit//*
*To 5 bushels of Indian corne paid to Wm. Lucas   To 300 for her lying in
To one hundred for bringing her to bed   To one hundred for a petticoat
To 2 smocks 150   To one paire of shoes 50   To one paire of stokins 50
To small lining for her & her child & the funeral Charge for her <u>Child 200</u>*
totall 1050

*This Indenture made in the year of our Lord God 1691. Witnesseth that
Elizabeth Kotle of Pocomoke in Somerset County in the Province of Maryland
spinster, hath with her own free & voluntary consent put & bound herself to be
with Germane Gillett of Pocomoke in the County aforesd & Province with the
said Germane to abide & dwell for the terme & space of three years from hence
forth fully to be completed & ended ended in the continuall service of her said
Master in all such lawfull imployment & services as shall be required by her
Master or Mistress, & he the sd Germane as Master to the said Elizabeth is to
find her the said Elizabeth meat drink & such cloathing as is usual for such an
Apprentise in her daily calling & imployment & the said Elizabeth for her good
& valuale consideration, is to fulfill & doe her duty according to the premmises,
to the contrary anything herein mentioned notwithstanding. In witness whereof
both parties hath hereunto sett their hand & affixed their seals interchangeably
this 15th of August 1691.   Elizabeth Kottle   Germane Gillett
Witnesses present ~
Samuel Alexander
John Gillett*

186 [15 March 1692/93] Petition of Mary Huett to be released from indenture to Francis Roberts

[Huett had been sold to Roberts for the remainder of her indenture, the length of
which was now in dispute. Huett was also suffering from *morbis gallicus*
(French pox or syphillis) and required treatment.]
*To the Wor'll the Justices of Somerset County in Court sitting. The humble
petition of Mary Huett showeth that your Petitioner was bound by an indenture
to serve four years to one George Barrett in the Province of Virginia which four
years your Supplyant hath well & truly served as followeth, to say three years to
the said Barret & one to Francis Roberts of this County. These are therefore to
pray your worpp's that your Supplyant may be ordered her freedom & your
petitioner as in duty will ever pray.*

[Indenture agreement] *Whereas Mr. George Berrett bought a servant named
Mary Hewett of Mr. Richard Bray which said servant the said Berrett axed the
said Bray if the said Huett was firme and sound and when the said Barrett
brought the said maid Mary home to his house the said Hewett made a very
great complaint & said she was not well and her Master & Mistress axing what
she ailed to make her goe so lame & stradling and at last found it out that she
was very much sore & in such a condition of the Morbis Gallicus & so farr gone*

that without speedy help the said Mary Hewet might have perished in so much (time) that the sd Barret was faine presently for to look for cure & the sd Barrett sent for one Doctor Thomas Fulkes for to undertake the cure of the said Mary Hewet & the said Doctor hath undertaken the Cure & the said Barrett is for to take the trouble upon him at his own house and for to see the said Mary wants for nothing as is fitting for the said Mary which is a great deal of trouble & charge during the time of her cure.

Know all men by these presents that the said Mary Hewet hath before us voluntairie & freely without any fear or threat from her said Master & mistress or any compulsion but hath willingly engaged herself and for to serve her Master Barret the full terme & time of three years after the time of her said service as she is to serve by her first indenture & to serve my said master truely & faithfully in such service as her master shall imploy me in dureing the time of her said servitude & to serve the said George Barret & his Assigns. The said Barret or his assigns is to find the said Hewet sufficient diet washing cloth and lodging dureing her time & at the expiration of her time for to pay her corne & clothes according to the custome of the country as witness our hand & seal the 21th of March 1688/9 Mary Hewets her part of this engagement is in consideration of her abovesd cure

Signed sealed and delivered	Mary Hewet
In presence of us	
Peter Knight	George Berret
Le'od Howson	

Know all men by these presents that I George Berret of Great Wiccocomocoe in Virginia in the County of Northumberland doe assign one woman Servant for the full & whole terme & time of four years to come unto Francis Roberts her name being Mary Hewet as witness my hand this first of March one thousand six hundred ninety one & two ~~~~ March the 1st 1691/2 by me George Berret William Browne John Roberts

The said Mary Hewet and Francis Roberts both appearing in Court It was the ordered that the said Mary have her freedom from Francis Roberts, and that he the sd Roberts pay her corne & clothes.

SOMERSET JUDICIAL RECORDS 1693-94
[MSA C 1774-11, Loc. 1/48/2/37]

46 [14 November 1693] Grand Jury impanelled; Robert Polke a member
The Sheriff of the County returned this following List or panel of the Grand Jury, viz. Randell Revell John Kirke Edward Stockdell Philip Adams Miles Gray George Lane Benjamin Esham William Robinson Edward Fowler Edward Wheeler Samuel Fluellen Thomas Oxford Alexander White Francis Martin Rob't Polke Robert Caldwell Thomas Larramore (17) who were all duely summoned, returned & sworn upon the holy Evangelists, having rec'd

their charge are sent forth ~~~~

46 [14 Nov 1693] Petition of John McKnitt complaining about neighbor's dog
[John McKnitt later moved to Cecil County Maryland and married into the Alexander family which was closely associated with the Polks of North Carolina for several generations. No subsequent entry has been found in court records to reveal the outcome of this case.]

The humble petition of John Mcknitt humbly sheweth. To the wpr'll the Justices of the Peace of Somerset County in Court sitting. That one Amos Parsons hath a Dogg that is accustomed to seaze and bite cattel whereby several of his neighbours cattel is bitten and laimed and perticliarly yr Petitioner hath three cows much damnified by the biteing of the same Dogg and the Said Amos although often required to take up the Dogg and keep him from doing more damage, obstinately refuseth. May it therefore please yr Worpp's to take some course that y'r Petitioner & others may be no more damnified by the said Dogg and yr Petitioner as in duty duty bound shall ever pray &ra ~~~
The abovesd Pe'tion being read it was by the Wor'll Court ordered that Amos Parsons make his persona;; appearance before the Court tomorrow the 15th of this Instant November anno 1693
Ordered likewise that summons issue for He. Miles & James Wallis that they app'r tomorrow as Evid's for Jno Mcknitt agst sd Amos Parsons ~~~~

49 [15 Nov 1693] Presentments to the Grand Jury; Robert Poke informer on Jane Carr
Wee present Frances Williams for Basterdy, ~~ George Wilson Informer.
  sd Fra. was tried this Court
Wee present Jane Carr for bastardy. Robert Poke informer.
Wee present John Moore for stealing two bottles of Wine the 17th day of 8-ber.
  Thomas Oxford Informer.
Wee present John Pope for the Breach of the Sabbath day.
  Mary Swain Informer.
Wee present Katherine Barrech for Basterdy. Nicholas Cornewell Informer.
Wee Present Thomas Relph for buying of a shoat of an Indian.
  Wm Layton Informer.
Randall Revell Foreman
[Robert Polke may have been acting as Constable for Monie at this time; constables typically acted as informer in charges brought before the Grand Jury. Robert was also required to post bond to ensure Carr's appearance in Court. After her conviction John Winser of Devils island and James Knox posted security for her good behavior.]

55-58 [No date] Cases on Docket for January Court
Writs Returnable the Second Tuesday in January Anno Domini 1693
[Among other entries]

Case ag't Jane Carr to answer to their Maties Per presentment for Basterdy
Subp'a Robert Poke Informer ag't sd Carr

Case ag't Rob't Pollock otherwise called Robert Poke of Somerset county
Planter to answer unto Bryan Snee of the same county of a plea of trespass upon
the case

Case ag't Patrick Quatermus to answer unto Robert Polke acc'on of the case
Case ag't Edward Hagan to answer unto Robert Polke acc'on of the case

61 [10 Jan 1693/4] Robert Polke security for Jane Carr
Robert Polke this day entered into recognizance of ten pounds sterling money
for Jane Carr's appearance at next court to answer such things as be then and
there objected against her on behalf of their Ma'ties.

73 [January Court] List of cases settled out of Court
[Among other entries]
Robert Polke ag't Patrick Quatermus } Agreed saith Pirrie (attorney for Polke)
Robert Polke ag't Edm'd Hugan } Agreed saith Pirrie

75-77 [No date] Docket of cases returnable at March Court
Writs Returnable the Second Tuessday in March Anno Domini 1693/4
[Among other entries]
Subp'a James Rauley @ Jane his Wife & Dorothy Panter for Rob't Polke,
Defend't , Bryan Snee, Plt.
Subp'a Mr. Roger Woolford, Mr. Dominick Coppinger, Jay Hobbs & Geo.
Hutchins for Bry~ Snee plt ag't Rob't
    Polke, def
Mary Jones, Wife of Samuel Jones for Robert Polke Defend't Bryan Snee Plt.

87 [14 March 1693/4] Bryan Snee suit against Robert Polke for slander
Bryan Snee, Plt   *Somerset ~*
    contra
Robert Polke, Dft.
Robert Pollock of this County Planter otherwise called Robert Polke was
attached to answer unto Bryan Snee of the same County, Planter, of a plea of
trespass upon the case. And whereupon the said Bryan by Sam'l Worthington
his attorney complaineth that whereas the said Robert Polke about the 12th day
of October Anno Dom 1693 at Manokin within the Jurisdiction of this Court did
several times and at sundry places falsely and maliciously reproach him the
aforesaid Bryan Snee (who then being in good fame and credit & of good repute
amongst his mat'ies good people of this county and by his labour & industry
hath gott a sufficient competency whereby to live credibly on and to pay
everyone their just dues and demands) in reporting that he had secretly and
feloniously stolen and carried away from him the said Robert four yards of new
white Kersey (Cloth) the sd Bryan saith that he never saw, nor did any wayes

medle or concern himself with, nor that the said Robert hath any evidence, colour or pretense for his unjust scandals & false accusations, but meerly out of envy and malice premeditated to prejudice him the aforesd Bryan—Whereby he the said Bryan is damnified to the value of 1000 pounds of tobacco & thereupon brings this sute. Worthington p/ Pltf.

And the Deft. by Robt. Pirrie (his attorney) saith he is not guilty in manner & forme & of this he puts himself upon the Country. Pirrie p/ Deft.
And the Pltf also. Worthington

Whereupon Command this day was given to the Sheriff of sd County to bring here twelve good and lawfull men of his Balywick that the matter in hand might be the better understood. A list or pannel whereof are returned as followeth (viz.) William Boseman, Thomas Walston, John Jones, James Curtis, Jno. Brown, Sam'l Long, Edward Green, Christopher Snoswell, Jas. Hill, Robert Nearn, George Lane, Archibald Smith (12) Who being duely summoned returned & sworn upon the Holy Evangelists who having heard the foresd Declaration & Evidences sworn & examined received their charge & went forth ~~~ And the same day aforesd the said Jurors aforesd makes their return to the Barr in Court, each man being particularly called being all agreed of their verdict. The Plt & Dft being likewise called the verdict is read as followeth ~ Wee of the Jury do find for the Plt. Which verd't this Court orderto be entered & confirms same. And the Court orders the foresd Jury on sd tryall between the sd Bryan Snee & Rob't Polke to enquire into what damages the sd Snee may have sustained in the sd Accon brought, w'ch sd Jury were then sworn in Court, received their charge & are sent forth ~~~ And being returned doe bring in this following verdict viz. Wee of the Jury doe find that Bryan Snee is damnified to the value of four hundred pounds of tobacco which verd't the Court confirms according to Act of Assembly.

98 [12 June 1694] Trial of Jane Carr for fornication

Their Ma'ties   Somerset County
contra
Jane Carr
The Grand Jury for the body of Somerset County the 14th day of November in the year of the Lord 1693 in Manokin within the jurisdiction of this Court do Jane Carr of the said county spinster for that the said Jane not having the fear of God before her eyes but moved by the instigation of the devil hath committed fornication upon her body born a bastard child to the dishonor of God and contrary to the good laws of this Province in this case made and provided. Dent, Clerk.

The indictment being read the said Jane Carr pleaded guilty denying to tell the father of her late bastard child therefore the court ordered the sd Jane thirty lashes on her bare back well laid on until the blood doth show. The copy of which order was delivered to the Sheriffe who executed the same.

Ordered also by this Court that the said Jane give security for her good behavior and fees where upon came the said Jane and for two securities (viz) James Knox and John Winser and the said Jane did per recognizance acknowledges and consent to be bound unto their Ma'ties King William and Queen Mary the just sum of thirty pounds sterling money of England and the securities (viz) James Knox and John Winser in the sum of thirty pounds of like money aforesaid all do to be levied on their goods and chattels and tenements.

The condition of this recognizance is such that if the above bound Jane be of good behavior to all her Ma'ties good people of this Province during the Courts pleasure as also pay all costs of this suite then this recognizance to be void and of no effect otherwise to remain in full power and force as before.

[John Winser (Winsor) was one of the several inhabitants of Devils Island]

132 [13 Sep 1694] Ephraim Wilson ordered to arrange for repair of Manokin Bridge
Ordered that Mr. Ephraim Wilson employ some person to mend the Bridge at the head of Manokin River. And that the sd Wilson or undertaker to be allowed [expenses] for same. [Ephraim Wilson was the son of Rev. Thomas Wilson and Sheriff of Somerset at this time.]

157 [31 Jan 1694/5] Order to inspect work done on Manokin Bridge
Upon motion made to their Wor'fl court above sd by James Knox concerning work done by said Knox to the Bridge at the head of Manokin it ws by the Justices aforesd considered & ordered that Richard Chambers & John Goldsmith do view the sd work done & bridge & make report thereof to our next court to be held in May.

SOMERSET LAND RECORDS Volume 7 (L), 1691-97
[MSA C1778-12, Loc. 1/45/1/8]

[This entry documents a very unusual, probably unique, transfer of property to a woman in a prenuptial agreement. In the colonial period husbands usual acquired control of any property possessed by their spouses at the time of their marriage.]

265 Prenuptial agreement of Ann Polk and Francis Roberts
Be it known to all men whome this present may concern that I Francis Roberts of Dam Quarter in the County of Somerset and Province of Maryland Planter I the said Francis doe for severall good reasons & valuable considerations doe bind and firmly make over unto Anne Polke of the County and Province afsd. all my goods lands and chattels moveables and innmoveables and to be possest with the same during her natural life, and if the aforesaid Anne Polke doth enjoy any child or children by me the aforesaid Francis for they to enjoy and possess the same estate above mentioned but if the aforesaid Anne Polke should enjoy no

child nor by me the aforesaid Francis then she only to enjoy the said estate during her natural life and I the above said Francis doe give this as my free deed gift and grant and for the true performance hereof I the aforesaid Francis Roberts bind myself my heirs Extors admins firmly in the penalty of two hundred pounds sterling money to be paid to the aforesaid Anne Polke and to be paid upon at demand and in the true performance I sett my hand & seal this twenty fifth day of February Anno Domini 1690.

Tests   John Planter, Robert Polke   Francis < FR> Roberts   sealed
Entered on Record this 30th day of April Anno Domini 1695   P J West Clr Cur

437 Francis Roberts lease of land to son John Roberts, alias Grandee
[Francis Roberts was no doubt frustrated by the foregoing agreement which essentially disinherited his son John Roberts by Rachel Grandee. To circumvent this galling constraint he conceived the idea of a long duration lease of his land, an option still within his legal rights. In this document, written six years after the prenuptial arrangement with Ann Polk, he leased a 100 acre tract to John Roberts for a period of 99 years. Although not specifically mentioned by name, the land in this agreement was situated at least partly within the 200 acre tract Elliott's Choice (see Somerset Judicials 1727-30, f.136). The parcel defined within the lease was configured very differently from the parent tract, contained closer to 250 acres rather than the stated 100, must have overlapped other properties, and is mathematically untenable in any case. This scheme inevitably led to consternation in later years and Elliotts Choice became the subject of multiple land commissions.]

This indenture made the forth day of September in the ninth year of the Reign of our sovereign Lord William the third by the Grace of God of England Scotland France and Ireland King defender of the faith and in the year of our Lord God one thousand six hundred ninety seven between Francis Roberts of Dam Quarter in Somerset County in the Province of Maryland of the one part and John Grundee otherwise called John Roberts of the County and Province aforesaid planter of the other part witnesseth that the said Francis Roberts for the love and affection and also for the sum of three thousand pounds of tobacco in hand payed by the said John Roberts whereof he doth acknowledge the receipt hereof and every part and parcel hereof doth truly exonerate and acquit the said John Roberts his heirs executors and admns hath bargained and sold and doth by these presents bargain and sell unto the said John Roberts his heirs executors admns or assigns one tract or parcel of land scituate lying ad being att the head of Dam Quarter Creek on the west side of the said creek begining at a marked beach standing att the head of a ridge commonly called Dogwood Ridge and from thence running south two hundred and fifty perches to a marked pine and from thence running west one hundred and fifty perches to a white oak and from thence running north west to a marked chestnut two hundred and fifty perches binding upon Sam[ll] Jones land and from thence upon a straight course one hundred and fifty perches to the first bounder containing and laid out one hundred acres of land more or less together with all rights profits previous easements and commodities thereunto appertaining and with all and every the appurtenances thereunto belonging to the only proper use and behoofe of him the said John Roberts his heirs executors admins or assigns from the day of the date of these presents until the full term of ninety nine years be fully completed and ended for the consideration above named and paying unto the Lord or Lords of the fee or fees the rents and services that shall become payable and due for the time aforesaid and the said Francis Roberts for himself his heirs executors admins doth covenant and grant to and with the said John Roberts his heirs executors and assigns by these presents following that is to say that he the said John Roberts his heirs and assigns shall and may from time to time and at all times hereafter for the term of ninety nine years aforesaid peaceably and quietly have hold and enjoy the aforesaid land and premises before mentioned without any trouble molestation interruption of him the said Francis Roberts or of his heirs that by vertue hereof and of the statute for transfering uses unto pocessions the said John Roberts may be in actual procession of the above land and premises. In witness hereof I have hereunto sett my hand and seale the day and year above written.

Signed sealed and delivered in presence   *his*
of us ~ John Panter John Jones   *Francis **F** Roberts*
George Hutchins James Woolford   *mark*
Entered on record the 19ᵗʰ day of October1697

SOMERSET JUDICIAL RECORDS 1695-96
[MSA C1774-12, Loc 1/48/2/38]

4 [No date] Docket for August Court
Writts returnable the second Tuesday in August anno Domini 1695
[Among other entries]
Subp'a Rob't Polke Evid for Jno Polke ag't Ephraim Wilson Dft
Subp'a Jno Macknitt Evid for Wm. Polke ag't Ephraim Wilson Deft

21 [10 October 1695] John McKnitt non-appearance for Grand Jury
John Macknitt & Robert Catlin being called did not appear to show cause why they did not attend as Grand Jurymen in March Court being thereto summoned, it was by the Wor'll Court considered & Ordered that they be acquitted from further trouble paying fees.

54 [13 October 1695] John Polke suit against Ephraim Wilson for debts of his client
[This case is unusual in that it attempts to make a lawyer liable for the debts of his absconded client. Not surprisingly it was thrown out by the Court. John's brother, William Polke, brought a similar case with the same result. A later case to attach the debtor's goods was more successful. See Somerset Judicials 1696-98, f. 28]

Contra
Ephraim Wilson, Defend't
Ephraim Wilson of Somerset County Gent attorney for George Parks, Cooper
was attached to answer unto John Polke of the same County Cooper an anon
on the case. And whereupon John p/ Sam Worthington his attorney comes &
saith that whereas the sd George in the year of the Lord 1692 at Manokin in the
Jurisdiction of this Court became indebted to the sd John in the sum of two
thousand pounds of tob'co as p/ acct here in Court appears, & the sd George
being indebted in manner afsd did upon himself assume & faithfully promise
that the afsd sum of tobacco he would well and truely content & pay as
thereunto required nevertheless the sd George the sd sum of tobacco to the said
John hath not paid but going out of this Province hath made the sd Ephraim his
Attorney & several debts of the sd George the sd Ephraim hath rec'd of whome
the above sd sued for hath been demanded but the said Ephraim to pay the same
hath refused, & doth still refuse to the damage of the sd John of four thousand
pounds of tobacco & therefore he brings this sute.

                    Worthington p/ quor pleg

And the defend't by Peter Dent his Attorney defends the force and saith he is not
indebted to the Plt & this he prays may be enquired of by the Court.   *Dent*

And the Plt says to that as Attorney of the sd George the sd Ephraim is indebted
& putts himself upon the Court   *Worthington*

George Parks, Dr		*Per Contra*	*Cr*
To 8000 lbs of Tobacco for Coopers worke		*By tob rec'd in pl*	*1200*
done for sevr'll pr'sons of wch J		*Ball due*	*0800*
was to have 1/4 pt p/ Agreement	*2000*		*2000*
Errors Excepted p/ me *John Polke*			

The issue being joyned as afsd the Court Orders a non sute agt the Plt with cost
alias Executio

55 [13 October 1695] William Polke, Plt vs Ephraim Wilson, Deft.
Similar suit as above to recover 400 lbs tobacco. Same result.

68 [No date] Docket for November Court
Writts returnable the second Tuesday in 9-ber anno Domini 1695
[Among other entries]
Case ag't Georg Parke Cooper to answer unto Jno. Polke plt of a plea of tresps
of the case
Subp'a Rob't Polk Sen'r & Wm. Polke for Jno. Polk plt ag't Geo Parke dft
[This is first instance of the appendage of "Senior" to the name of Robert Polke,
and indicates that Robert Polk (II) is now a person of legal status, certainly a
taxable of age 16 or older. It is also used in mention of Robert Polke as a
member of the Grand Jury in March; see below.]

68 [12 November 1695] Opening of Court Session, November 1695; John Polke Constable for Manokin

At a Court held for the County of Somerset in the Province of Maryland by his Mat'ies Justices of the Peace the 12th day of November in the 7th year of the reign of Sovereign Lord King William the Third over England this anno Domini 1695

Com'rs Present ~ Mr. Fra Jenkins, Mr. Ja- Dashiels, Mr Tho Dixon, Mr Matthew Scarborough, Mr Tho Newbold, Mr Sam Hopkins, Mr Geo Layfield, Mr Jas Round, Mr Edmd Howard, Capt Jno King

Court Called ~ This day the Sheriff made return of the Grand Jury as followeth (viz) Richard Chambers, Rowland Beavins, Stevin Costin, Jno Franklin, John Panter, Wm Jones, John Jones, Wm Bowen, Nic. Evins, Nic. Conowelly, Alex Thomas, Jno Kellam, Miles Gray, Ja- Rawley, Wm Fausett, Sam Jones, Charles Williams, Tho. Pollett, Thomas Wilson, Charles Hall, Jno Turpin, Charles Fausett, Wm Stevenson & Teague Riggen sumon'd but exempted from serving. The foresd Grand Jury being Called did all appear, was then sworn upon the Holy Evangelists according to the form and then the Charges as usually was to them read and so was sent forth upon his Mat'ies acct.

The Coroners were then Called viz Lt Coll John Winder, Mr Edmund Howard, Capt John King, Mr John Browne

The Constables were then called, viz
Thomas Dashiels Constable for Wiccocomico Hundred
James Givan Constable for Nanticoke Hundred
Wm Waller Constable for Mony Hundred
Edward Wheeler Constable for Manokin Hundred
Wm Wilson Constable for Annimessex Hundred
John Broughton Constable for Pocomoke Hundred
John Purnell Constable for Mattapony Hundred
Thomas Powell Constable for BogateeNorten Hundred
And the Severall Constables above sd put into Court the Severall p'sons for the Court to make Choice of and the Wor'll Court made Choice of these Several p'sons for to be Constables for this present year following (viz)
John Waters Constable for Annimessex Hundred
Francis Thoroughgood Constable for Pocomoke Hundred
John Polke Constable for Manokin Hundred
Thomas Walter Constable for Mony Hundred
William Stacey Constable for Wiccocomico Hundred
Thomas Larramore Constable forNanticoke Hundred
Thomas Purnell Constable for BogateeNorten Hundred
Alexander White Constable for Mattapony Hundred

Then was read the Laws made last Assembly -
Proclamation read prohibiting the Transportation of Corne
Ditto Concerning p'sons leaving the Province & going to Southerd
Ord'n from Assembly read impowering Justices to make rules of Court

Ord'n read to return answers to Governor & how business was dispatched in
obedience to Ord'n formerly directed relating to Loyalls
Order read Concerning any Justices dissent in Court
Order read concerning the Vestrymen to give acct of total proceedings

106 [14 January 1695/6] Opening of Court Session; Rob't Polke on Grand Jury

Ordered by this Court that the Sheriff of this County forthwith summon a Grand
Jury to attend on sd Court on behalf of the King ~
A list or pannel whereof are returned as followeth (viz.) John Lane Alex Kyle
Edward Stockdell Rob't Smith Rob't Catlin Sam'l Handy Jno. Roach Jun'r
John Townsend Sen'r Daniel Dennehoe Rob't Polke Abr'am Knott James
Givan Rob't Givan Edw'd Harper Thomas Quillain & Fra. Martin ~~ who
being impannelled summoned & sworn upon the holy Evangelists & having had
their charge read are semt forth to enquire etc ~~

127 [No date] Cases settled out of Court, January Court

Accons Agreed dismist withdrawn etc [among other entries]
Robert Pirrie Plt Rob't Polk Dft – Agreed saith both parties
Peter Elzey Plt Jno. Polke Dft- Agreed saith Wm. Boseman

129-32 [No date] Docket for January Court 1695/6; subpoena issued to Robert Polke, Sen.

Writts Returnable the 2nd Tuesday in Jan'y 1695/6 [Among other entries]
Case ag't George Parke Cooper to answer unto John Polke of a plea of trespass
of the case
Subp'a Rob't Polke Sen'r & Wm. Polk for the Plt.
Case ag't Rob't Polke to answer to Rob't Pirrie plea of trespass of the case
Case ag't Jno. Polke to answer unto Pr. Elzey of a plea of trespass on the case

134 [18 January 1695] James Knox to repair Manokin Bridge

Ordered by the Court that James Knox forthwith repair & mend Manokin
Bridge to Agreement had & made with Ephraim Wilson

134 [10 March 1695/6] Robert Polke, Senior, on Grand Jury

The Court being called the Sheriff of the County made return of his venire, and a
List or panel of the Grand Jury was returned as follows (viz) Rich'd Chambers,
Wm. Parker, Henry Hudson, Char. Nicholson, Leonard Jones Senior, Donnam
Olandman, Rich'd Carey, Robert Johnson, William Dixon, John Powell, Wm.
Sewell, Walter Evans, Afradozi Johnson, Robert Polke Senior, John Blizard,
Arch Smith, Adam Spence, Tho. Quillain, Leo. Jones Jun'r & Thomas Bromley
& four more were returned summoned but gave reasons by others for their non
appearance which was excused, which said Grand Jury being legally summoned
& returned, was then sworn upon the holy Evangelists, and having had the
whole charge read unto them were by the Court sent forth to consult etc ~

SOMERSET JUDICIAL RECORDS 1696-98
[MSA C1774-13, Loc. 1/48/2/39]

9 [9 June 1696] William Polke petition against estate of William Porter

To the Wpr'll the Com'rs of Somerset County in Court sitting ~~~ William Polke humbly showeth that William Porter late of this County stood indebted at his death unto the Petitioner in the sum of eleven hundred pounds of tobacco, humbly prayes Order for the same ag't Elizabeth Porter Adm'x of the sd dec'd estate & your Petitioner as in duty bound shall ever pray etc.

1693 Wm. Porter Dr.

To tobacco pd Fran. Roberts ~ ~ ~ ~ ~ ~ 300		*The said William Polke*
To tobacco pd for you to Andrew Whittington		*having proved his account*
merchant, 1699 ~ ~ ~ ~ ~ ~ ~ ~ ~ ~ ~ ~ ~ 450		*in open Court the Adm'x did*
To the one half of Cooper work done for Capt.		*confess judgement for the*
King and Mr. Kyle ~ ~ ~ ~ ~ ~ ~ ~ ~ ~ ~ 350		*same (viz.) for eleven*
	1100	*hundred pounds of tobacco,*
Errors Excepted p/ me Wm Polke		*for which this Court grants*
		order for with costs alias
		executio

28 [13 June 1696]   John Polke, Cooper, debt suit against George Parke

John Polke Plt   *Somerset.*

vs

George Parks, Dft

George Parks late of this County Cooper was attached to answer unto John Polke Cooper of --- of the case// And whereupon the sd John per Sam Worthington his attorney Comes and Saith that the sd George in the year of the Lord 1690 at Manokin within the Jurisdiction of this Court became indebted unto the sd John in the just Sum of Eight hundred pounds of tobacco as per here in Court produced and the said George being indebted in manner as afsd did assume upon himself & faithfully --- that the afrsd Sum of tobacco he would well & truely content and pay when thereunto required. Nevertheless the sd George but the Same to doe hath refused to the great disadvantage of the sd John of Sixteen hundred pounds of like tobacco & therefore brings this sute, etc.

Worthington per Pltf

And the Defend. Saith they have never Shewd any acct of the works done in Partnership but hath brought an acct done in guess for work done to Several p'sons, neither did they show what of the said acc't they were to have of the issue & puts himself on the Court. Dent per Defdt

And the Pltf Comes and Saith that it was per one fourth part of 8000 pounds of Tobacco for works done & will make appear by Evidence that George Parks hath no amount of 8000 pounds of Tobacco that was gotten by the works done aforesaid and paid Wm Polke 2000 lb tbco which was the same part that the Plt was to have, of this puts himself upon the Court

> *Worthington fpr Plt*

*And the Deft Saith they ought to have shewed to whome the works was done &
at what time & puts himself on the Court also—— Dent*

*And the Plt Saith that he was but Servant to the sd George and that he kept the
acct of what work was done, and this wee had from him which will prove, and
put himself upon the Court also.   Worthington*

[Invoice]   *1690 George Parks Dft*   *Contra*
 To the 4th part 8000 pounds tbco   *By 600 lb allowed for instructing*
 by the setting up in caske in ano 1690   *me in the Coopers trade— 600*
 by George Parke, Wm Polke & myself   *By the 4th of 1600 lb tbco for*
 of Sundry prod——— 2000 lb tbco   *Staves to make up the Cask 400*
                                          By two bar'll Indian Corn   200
                                                                 1200
                                          Balance due   800

Errors Excepted, Per me
> *John Polke*

*The Declaracon being read and the issue joynd the Wor'll Court having
Considered the premises as also the Oaths of the Witnesses doe give judgmt ags
the Dft for the debt declared for according to Declaracon in Case*

34 [13 June 1696] Robert Polke paid for attendance at Court
*Robert Polke this day in open court made oath that he attended as an evident for
John Polke agt. George Parks fifteen days and humbly craved order for the
same which to him was granted*

34 [13 June 1696] William Polke paid for attendance at Court
*William Polke Robert Polke this day in open court made oath that he attended
as an evident for John Polke Pltf agt. George Parks def't eleven days and
humbly craved order for the same which to him was granted.*

41 [August 1696] Subpoena in list of actions returnable in August Court
*Subp'a: John Mcknitt & John Nox Evid. For Wm. Owens Plt agt. Amos Parsons
Dft*

43 [11 August 1696] William Owens claim against estate of William Porter
[Transcription of promissory note]
Wm Owens, Plt   Maryland
  Contra
 Wm. Porters Adm'nx
*This my note shall oblige me the subscriber to pay to Wm Owens on Order the
sum of one thousand nine hundred & eighty two pounds of tobacco convenient
in Somerset County aforesd. Witness my hand
This 25th day of September 1695.   William Porter*

Witness hereof Peter Dent, Matt Kirwan }
This being read and the Admnx Attorney confest judgement for the same. Order
granted thereon with costs alias executio //

51 [13 August 1696] Trial of James Knox for extortion against Ann Sedbury

[Transcription of bond for appearance]

His Ma'tie	*Somerset County in Maryland*
Contra	
James Knox	*William Polke,*

Know all men by these presents that wee James Nox, John Polke and are firmly
bound & justly indebted unto our Sovereign Lord
$\qquad$ *King William the third or his assigns in the*
penal sum of twenty pounds current money of England upon demand, to the
which payment well & truly made wee bind us either and every of us, our heirs,
ex'tors & Admins joyntly or severally in the whole & for the whole firmly by
these presents. In witness whereof wee fix our hands and seals this seventeenth
day of July in the eigth year of the reign of our sovereign Lord William over
England Scotland France & Ireland King & Defender of the faith – Anno Dom
1696. The Condition of this obligation is such that if the sd James Nox be of
good abearance to all his Ma'ties Liege People especially unto Anne Sedbury,
and doe make his personal appearance before our Justices of our next County
Court to be held on the second Tuesday of August next ensueing the date at the
Dividing Creek and then and there to answer what shall be alleaged or objected
agt him on his Ma'ties behalf and stand & abide the Award thereof that the
obligation to be void & of no effect, or else to stand remain and be in full force
power & vertue ~~

The Deposition of Ann Sedbury aged about 44 years or thereabouts saith that
about the 17th Instant James Nox came to the house of John Goldsmith Jun'r &
told this Deponent that he has a warrant & that she must go before a Justice to
answer his complaint, and the Deponent replyed she was willing to go, Old
Mary Goldsmith asked him to read the Warrant, he answered that he would not
humour them, So he went away & came again in the afternoon, and told this
Deponent that now he had a special warrant, and She must goe before Mr.
Boseman and if she would not he would drag her at his horse tail~ but this
Deponent told him that rather then to be foced out in that deplorable condition
would surrender all her interest in the Plantation, upon which the Said Nox writt
a discharge and this Deponent was forced to sign the same, and further saith
not. //

Mary Goldsmith alias Fillpott aged 28 years or thereabouts saith that which is
above written was realy true and uttered in her hearing further saith not ~~~
$\qquad\qquad$ *Anne Sedbury (her mark)*
Sworn before me the day and year aforesd ~~
$\qquad$ *Tho Jones* $\qquad\qquad$ *Mary Fillpott (her mark)*

The foresd bond & Deposition being read the Evidences Sworn & Examined, It did appear to the Wor'll Court that the sd Knox hand misbehaved himself to the sd Anne, as well as abused his authority, for which the said Court did order, as it is hereby ordered that the said James Knox be fyned five hundred pounds of tobacco and that the sum be paid to the use of the Poore of this county and that the sd James give good security for his behaviour fine & fees ~~
[After which Knox made bond for £20 with John Macknitt and John Knox as his securities.]

107 [11 November 1696] John Macknitt paid for attendance at Court
John Macknitt this day made oath that he attended as Evid't on behalf of Wm Polk plt ag't Ephraim Wilson Defd't three days & this court granted order theron.

113 [11 Nov 1696] John Polke claim against estate of Captain John King
John Polke, Pltf
Contra
Extrs of Capt. King, Dft
The said plt. By his acc't this day proved in Court did make appear that the estate pf Cap't John King dec'd stood justly indebted to him the sum of five hundred and thirty three pounds of tobacco, hereupon John West one of the Ex'tors of the sd King confest judgm't for the same, which the Court granted Order for with costs alias executio. //

194 [10 March 1696/97]   Francis Graden age adjudged
Then Mr. Ephraim Wilson brought his servant Boy Francis Graden to be adjudged, who adjudged to be of the age of Sixteen years. [Francis Graden/Craydon appears several times in the land records of Deal Island and the Tangier section of Dames Quarter. He is cited in the Provincial Rent Rolls as rent payer for the tract Locust Hummock on behalf of the widow and orphans of John Polkey.]

194 [10 March 1696/97] Petiton of Robert Polke, Senior, to alter course of road past his property
To his Ma'ties Justices of the Peace for the County of Somerset now in Court Sitting the Humble Petition of Robert Polke Sen humbly showing whereas your Petitioner has lately purchased a Small Ridge of Land Laying betwixt Damn Quarter & Little Mony on the horse Road Commonly Called Justins Ridge and now your petitioner having Cleared a Corn field on the said Ridge and the Road going thru the said Cleared Ground your Petioner desires that your Worp's may be pleased to grant him an order to turne the said Road and to have it go allong the side of the sd Ridge by the Cornfield fense and in so doing your Petion'r as in duty bound shall ever pray.
March 10 1696/7   Rob't Polke, Sen
Then the above Petition was read and it is referred to George Betts Sen overseere of Mony hundred who is to view the said Road and to make Report

whether it be not Prejudicall to the Publick Road

218 [15 April 1697] Petition of John Polky concerning payment to Sheriff
[This individual is most likely not John Polk, the son of Robert and Magdalen
Polke, but the John Polkey/Pelikey, who patented the tract Locust Hummock at
the SW side of Dames Quarter and died in 1703.]
*The humble petition of John Polky April 13th 1697 to the Worp'll Court of
Somereset County sitting. Right Worsp'll Gentlemen whereas your Petitioner
hath due to him one Thousand pounds of Tobacco in Caske for the maintaining
of William Browne deceased and your Petitioner being Ignorant of giving in
before your Worships my accompt at one time notwithstanding, I am indebted to
the High Sherriff tobacco, and if your Worships will be pleased to grant your
Petioner an Order for the said Sum I hope your Petioner may previle with the
High Sherriff to deduct the same so hoping your Worships it taken in
Consideration and grant this my petition and your Petitioner shall ever in duty
be bound to pay.*
*Upon reading the said Petition the Court doe take in Consideration and grant
the said Pelky the tobacco allowed William Browne in the Last Levy*

263 [9 November 1697] William Polke appointed Constable for Manokin
*The following persons are appointed to serve as Constables for the next ensuing
year ~ Annemessix William Planner, jun'r ~~ Pocomoke Isaac Boston ~~
Mattapony Benj. Idolette, jun ~~ Manokin William Polke ~~ Mony George
Hutchins ~~ Wicocomaco James Hardy ~~ Nanticoke Thomas Lannan ~~
Poogatenorton John Powell ~~*

**264 [9 November 1697] James Knox Petition to be discharged from his
bond**
*To the Worp'll Ma'ties Justices of the Peace for Somersett County, James Knox
most humbly showeth that whereas your Petitioner was bound to his good
behavior in august Court anno 1696 and your Pe'tioner having sevilly and
orderly behaved himself amongst his neighbors and others etc humbly prays
your Worships to discharge him of his said Bonds an as in Duty bound shall
pray ~~*
*Then the abovesaid Pe'tion was read and ordered that the said Knox be
discharged of his said bond ~~~~*

**302 [13 March 1697] Legal action by John Polke to secure goods of George
Parks**
John Poalke, Plt
George Parks, Def.
*Sciere facias being returned made known the Dft was called to show cause why
the former judgement should not be continued and execution thereof awarded to
the said John Poalke for nineteen hundred & eleven pounds of tobco who
appearing and having nothing to say agst the said Judgement therefore the court
Confirmed the former judgement with cost of suit alias executio.*

318 [14 June 1698] Order to Ephraim Polke and Francis Roberts
Ordered that Francis Roberts and Ephraim Polke bring the orphants of Thomas Hilman to next Court.

SOMERSET JUDICIAL RECORDS 1698-1701
[MSA C1774-14, Loc. 1/48/2/40]

1 [9 August 1698]   William Polke Constable for Manokin
The severall Constables hereafter mentioned returne their Lists of Tythables (Vizt) William Planner Jun, Ammemessix Benj. Idolett Jun, Mattapony   William Polke, Manokin George Hutchins, Mony James Hardy, Wiccocomacoe Thomas Sherman, Nantecoke John Powell, Baltemore Isaac Boston, Pocomoke John Fansett Bogatenorten Hundred ~~~

4 [10 August 1698] John Polke on Grand Jury
Maryland ~ By the Grand Jury sworne for the County of Somersett August the 9th 1698 Impr. Wee the Jurors (Vizt) Richard Chambers John Jones John Polke Alexander Maddux John Kirke Martin Trentham William Demem James Beuchannon Jeremiah Townsend William Fansett Christopher Nutter John Porter Thomas Cary Thomas Tull, Sen. Archibald Smith John Henry doe present Sarah Gurnell of Pocomoke Hundred for having a bastard child, William Noble informer; Wee present John Pope for abuseung Mr. Matthew Scarborough in calling him rogue and knave and giving him severall other abuses, Witnesses Porter Selby & Daniell Selby; We present Thomas Mumford for Selling of sand instead of tallow, Capt. Erasmus Harrison informer, Margarett Towers, evidence; Wee present James Odougherty for mismarking of Hugh mcNeales shoats, Barnett Ward and Elizabeth Ward witnesses, Hugh McNeale informer; we present Thomas Barnes of authority Richard Chambers foreman
Ordered process issue upon the abovesd presentments

4 [10 August 1698] Orphans of Thomas Hilman assigned to Ephraim Polke and Francis Roberts
Then John Hilman sone of Thomas Hilman Sen, dec'd ordered unto the custody of Francis Roberts who is to apear here next Court and to bring the said Child with him
Thomas Hillman sone of Thomas Hilman, Sen, dec'd. is ordered into the custody of Ephraim Polk who is to apear here next Court and to bring the Child with him

14 [12 August 1698] Ephraim Polke attendance at Court
Ephraim Polke prays payment for two days attendance at court for Parker Selby.

25 [12 August 1698] Condemnation of goods of George Parke for payment awarded to John Polke

*By virtue of a Precept bearing date the 11th day of July ann' Dom'y 1698
returnable to the second tuesday of January following was executed in the hands
of Peter Elzey seven hundred pounds of Tob'co in the hands of James Obratten
six hundred pounds of Tob'co for the use of John Polke who prayed
Condemnation of the same and in Court was granted being the Estate of George
Parke and in 9'ber Court proceeding in the hands of James Inglish four hundred
and fifty pounds of Tob'co*

38 [14 September 1698] John Hilman made ward of Francis Roberts
*John Hilman sone of Thomas Hilman dec'd. aged eight is bound to Francis
Roberts until he arrive to the age of eighteen years, the said Roberts is to give
him one years schooling and at the expiration of his time to give him one cow
and calfe and to cloath him*

55 [9 November 1698] Thomas Hillman made ward of Ephraim Polke
*Thomas Hilman aged four years sone of Thomas Hilman is bound unto Ephraim
Polke till he is of the age of twenty one years who is to give him at the age of
eighteen years one cow and calfe which is to be marked for the child who is to
have all the increase male & female, and to learne the child the trade of a
carpenter & joyner soe far as he can and to give him one year schooling, to the
performance of which the said Ephraim came with his security John Polke and
the said Ephraim acknowledged himselfe by way of recognizance in the sum of
twenty pounds sterl. and the said John in the sum of tenn pounds sterl., the
premises being performed then this recognizance to be void, or else etca ⁓
Taken and acknowledged in Court*

59 [8 November 1698] Petition of William Polke against estate of Major Robert King
Major Robert King was an important figure in Somerset and had been a member
of the Provincial Council during the time of the Maryland Revolution.

*To the worshipfull Court of Somerset County the humble pet'ion of William
Polke humbly sheweth that the Estate of Maj Robert King late of Manokin dec'd
stands indebted unto your Pet'ioner the full and just sum of six thousand four
hundred and forty two pounds of good tobacco as p/ acct here ready to be
produced in Court it may doth appear Your Pet'ioner therefore humbly Craves
your Worships Ord agst the said Maj Kings Estate for the said sum of Tobacco
and you Pet'ioner as in duty bound shall ever pray.   William Polke*

	The Estate of Maj'r Robert King	
1695	*To the Ball of acct having there Reckoned*	*1474*
March 16	*To your assumpsit for Monteith*	*778*
	To your assumpsett for William Alexander	*400*
	To Triming of Casks	*150*
	To nine tunns of Pork Barrels	*3600*
	To the Pastings of 20 Barrells of Porke	*0040*

The Pet'ion on acct being read in open Court and oath made by the above said
William Polke that the same was justly due it is therefore ordered that the said
Polke recover agt Mrs Mary King Admnx of Maj Robert King deceased six
thousand four hundred and forty two pounds of tobacco which the Court granted
order for with cost alias Exec.

71 [24 November 1698] William Polke, Constable, complaint about Nathaniel Horsey

To the Worshipfull Justices of Somerset County in Court sitting the humble
Pet'ion of William Polke Constable for Manokin hundred humbly showeth that
Nathaniel Horsey was picked upon by your Worships to Serve in my Roome as
Constable of Manokin Hundred but the said Nathaniel Horsey Refuseth to serve
notwithstanding I carried your Worships order from under the Clerks hand to
him. Your Pet'ioner humbly desires that some other may be appointed if
Nathaniel Horsey will not serve, that I may be Clear to go about my Business
which lyes not altogether in the County and your Pet'ioner shall ever pray.
Wm Polke
Then this above Pet'ion was read in Court & granted and John Gray appointed
in his Room (stead).

83 [24 November 1698] Ephraim Polke suit against John Porter for debt from joint business venture

Ephraim Polke, Plt   Somerset County
Contra
John Porter, Deft
John Porter was attached to answer unto Ephraim Polke of a plea of Trespass
upon the case --- and so here upon the said Ephraim, Sam Worthington his
attorney Complaineth that on or about the 26th day of 8'ber anno Dom 1697 a
Certain communication was had and held the afsd John and the Ephraim at
Pocomoke within the Jurisdiction of this Court where it was agreed by and
Between the said John and Ephraim to worke together and what Tobacco or
monies or other Commodities could be got by their Working together as afsd—
that the said John should have two thirds and Ephraim one third part, now the
said Ephraim in fact saith that p/ their working together they gott or earned or
did worke to the value of three thousand four hundred and thirty pounds of
Tobacco as p/ a p'tcular acct of the said worke doth appear here in Court, now
the said Ephraim further saith that of the Tobacco gotten as afsd there is eight
hundred and thirty pounds due to him from the said John of which he has rec'd
but one hundred and thirty pounds of the afsd sum, whereof seven hundred reste
(is) still due to the said Ephraim from the said John who hath refused the same
to pay tho often thereunto requested and still doth refuse to the great damage of
the said Ephraim of 2400 lb of Tobacco and thereupon he brings this suit
*   Worthington qu pled/ deft*
And the Defendant by William Boseman his attorney comes and sayes that their
never was any such Communication or agreement between the Plt and Def and

of this for Tryall he putts himself on the Court
            Boseman p/ Def
*And the Plt for Replication saith that the worke according to the acct was jointly
done by Ephraim Polk and John Porter and that he the said Ephraim was to
have one third part which he is ready to prove by his oath and for Tryall puts
himself on the Court.*
            Worthington p/ Plt
*And the Defendant Comes and rejoynes and says as afsd that there never was
any agreement and prays that the Plt may be putt to prove the same and of this
putts himself on the Court also.*
            Boseman p/Def
*Therefore it is considered in the Court that the Plt have nothing for his writ but
be in mercy for his false clamor.*

239 [16 November 1699] Ephraim Polk debt case against John Porter
A continuation of case brought by Ephraim Polk (Pollock/Pollick) against John
Porter alleging that Porter owes Polk 930 pounds of tobacco. Following
accounts had been presented at Court of Adjournment 8 February 1698/9:

1696 August 1 John Porter Debter		*1696 Ephraim Pollock acct*	
		as to John Porter	
To the making of a flax break	080	*To 2 pairs of sho*	140
To 4 days ceating of Syder	080	*To the use of the shop & tools*	350
To 3 days worke in the shop	060	*To seazoned timber*	300
To 4 days in cutting &			
thakeling corne	080	*To Weepeir(?)*	020
To 3 days work paid Johnson Hill		*To glew*	040
for the acct	060	*To 2 dayes of a horse*	040
To 6 days gathering corne	120	*To teaching you to Ree in*	200
To 1 day going to the weaver for you	020	*To 12 days absent from your*	
To 1 day going to Jo: the Smith	020	*service*	200
Finished this acc't 8'ber 26 1696	580	*To 7 months accomodation,*	
For my grinding for your family from		*teaching and lodging*	1400
26th 8'ber 96 to 15th March following	150		2690
To cutting firewood & carting it home		*Errors Excepted p/ me John Porter*	
from 26th 8'ber to 15th March following	200		
	930		

Errors Excepted p/ me Ephraim Pollick

[These accounts had been referred by the Court to John Boseman and John
Browne for audit with instruction to report back to March Court, but took rather
longer.]

*By virtue of the above written order of Court to us directed to auditt and state
the acct betwixt Ephraim Polke, Plaintiff and Mr. John Porter deft after hearing
both parties and considering of both accts we doe find that there is due unto the*

def't five hundred and fifty five pds of tob'co

John Boseman

John Browne

Therefore it considered by the Court that the Plt recover nothing for his Writt but be in Mercy for his false Clamor.

327 [21 March 1699/1700] *Fieri facias* confiming previous Court award to John Polke

Court formally confirms earlier award of 450 lbs/tbco against James Inglish, allowing John Polke to attach his goods and chattels.

365 [August 1700] William Polk and wife Ann, widow of William Owens, on Court Docket

(In list of cases on docket carried over from June session) *Case against Martha McKay, Adm'x of the goods and chattels & credits of Neale McKay late of ths County dec'd to answer unto William Polke & Ann his wife, Adm'x of the goods chattels & credits of William Owens dec'd of a plea that she in her capacity render unto them 4000 lbs of Tob'co which etc ~~~*

408 [13 November 1700] William Polk petition

To the worshipfull Court of Somerset County the humble pet'ion of Wm Polke humbly sheweth that the estate of Wm Knox late of Manokin dec'd stands indebted unto your Pet'ioner the full amount and just sum of twelve hundred and forty seven pounds of porke as by a bill under the said Knoxes hand doth appear. Your pet'ioner therefore humbly craves your Worships order for the said porke ag't the adm'r of the said William Knox and your pet'ioner as in duty bound shall ever pray. Wm Polke
November the 12ᵗʰ 1700

Maryland, Somersett County ~~ This bill bindeth me Wm Knox of the Province & County afsd my heirs Extrs or Admn'rs to pay or cause to be paid unto Wm Owens of the same Province & County weaver his heirs Exec'rs Admn's or assigns the full and just sum of twelve hundred & forty seven pounds of good sweet drest porke to be paid conven't in the said County upon the tenth day of November next or after upon demand as witness my hand & seale this 23d day of march anno Dom 1700   William Knox
Testes Ephraim Wilson   Thomas Jones

The Pet'ion and Bill being read in Court it is therefore ordered by the Justices that the abovesd Wm Polke Adm'r of Wm Owen do recover judgment ag't Robert Stitt Adm'r of the above William Knox the debt in the bill mentioned Vizt twelve hundred forty seven pounds of good sweet drest porke with costs alias ex'io

434 [22 November 1700] Estate of William Owens suit against estate of Neale McKay

William and Ann Polk, as admin of the estate of William Owens, bring suit

against Martha McKay, Administratrix of the estate of Neale Mckay, for 400 lbs/tbco which McKay had promised to Owens in a note dated 9 October 1696. Court orders that the estate should pay, with costs.
[This case confirms that Ann, the widow of William Owens, married William Polk.]

477 [19 February 1700/1] Condemnation of goods of George Parks for payment awarded to John Polke

John Polke, Plt   *Somerset*
George Parks, Def't
Attachment being returned the 2nd Tuesday of January 1700 in the hand of Beynard Ward four hundred and twenty five pounds of tob'co and summoned the said Baynard Ward as Garnisher p/ me John Wolfe Sheriff and the Plt humbly moved the Court for Condemnation of the above said sum of Tab'co which by the Court is Condemned to and for the use of him the said John Polke.

491 [11 March 1700/01] Suit against Francis Roberts for debt owed to estate of Richard Whitty

John Panter and wife Dorothy and George Jones and wife Sarah, administrators of the estate of Richard Whitty, present bill dated 12 December 1685 with balance of 3262 lbs/tbco due from Francis Roberts. Court orders he pay with costs.

507 [11 June 1701] Fine on John Polk for non-attendance

John Poake fined for not attending the Court as petite Juryman when summoned

513 [13 June 1701] Francis Roberts suit against estate of Henry Layton

Francis Roberts Deft (sic)   *Somerset*
George Hutchens etc, Plts (sic)   *George Hutchens and Margaret his*
Wife adm'x of the goods
                                and chattels and creditts of Henry Layton dec'd was attached to answer unto Francis Roberts of an accon upon the case ~~ And whereupon the Said Francis per Sam Worthington his attorney complaineth that at the special instance & request of him the said Henry Layton the said Francis brought a warrant for the said Henry for four hundred acres of Land and passed his bond for the sd warrant payable to my Lord Baron of Baltemore for nine hundred & sixty pounds of tob'co dated the 20th day of Feb'ry ano Dom' 1694 which said warrant was delivered att Damquarter unto the said Henry for which he promised to repay unto the said Francis the aforesaid sum of 960 pounds of tob'co when he should be thereunto required, nevertheless the said Henry in his lifetime the afsd Sum of t'bco to the said Francis hath not paid nor the George & Mary to whom adm'on of the goods & chattels which were the said Henry at the time of his death was committed the same to the said Francis hath not paid tho' often thereunto requested to the damage of the said Francis of 1920 pds oft'bco and thereupon he brings this suit.
The Defts by Wm Boseman their attorney come and defend the force & injury

*when——-)- that they are not indebted in manner & forme and putts themselves
upon the——(the Court).*

*The allegations on both parties being duly weighed and considered by the Court
it is therefore ordered that the plt recover agt the deft as --- the sum of nine
hundred and sixty pounds of tob'co in the dec'd men--- as also the sum of 391 lb
tob'co for the coste & charges in his behalfe laid out and expended & the deft in
mercy ~~*

SOMERSET JUDICIAL RECORDS 1701-02
[MSA C1774-15, Loc. 1/48/2/41]

115 [1 April 1702] Ephraim Polke suit against estate of William Carlisle
[Ephraim lost this case on a technicality but successfully resubmitted it in
November Court. See below. f.199]

Ephraim Polke, Pltf   *Somerset County*
Agt
Alexander Carlile, Deft
*Alexander Carlile, Admn'r of the goods chattles & credits of Wm. Carlisle,
merchant dec'd of a plea of trespass upon the case. And whereupon the said
Ephraim per Sam Worthington his attorney complaineth that whereas William
Carlile in his lifetime on the 23rd day of June ano Dom'y 1699 became indebted
unto the Ephraim att Mony within the Jurisdiction of this Court in the sum of
seventeen pounds two shillings sterling money, it being the ballance of acc't
hereunto annexed as doth appear and the said William being indebted in
manner as aforesd did upon himselfe assume and promise that the aforesaid sum
of money unto the said Ephraim he would well and truly content and pay when
thereunto required nevertheless the sd William in his Lifetime the aforesd sum
of £17-2-00 to the said Ephraim hath not paid nor the said Alexander to whome
admn'on of the goods & chattles were the sd Williams at the time of his Death
was committed though often thereunto requested to the loss & damage of the sd
Ephraim of £30 like money and thereupon he brings this suit ~~*
     Worthington Per qu- pleg

July the 23rd day 1699
A just acc't agt the estate of Wm Carlile dec'd ~

To money lent	25-00-00
To 278 lb of pork at 20d Ster per hund'wt	02-15-00
Subtot	27-15-00
Then his acc't upon his booke agt me	
Being in goods and money	10-13-00
Errors excepted, per Ephra Polke	17-02-00

*Memorandum Vizt May 24th 1701 came Ephraim Polk before me & under oath
upon the holy Evangelists that the within acc't is just & true and that (he) hath
not sent noe part thereof but what he hat given credit for*
Sworne before me the day & year above Written

And the Deft by William Bozman his attorney comes and saith that the plt's decl(aratio)*n is altogether insufficient to maintain his action he having not sett forth in his decl'n to whome he is to ensuit of which he craved his judgm't of the Court   Bozman for Deft Therefore it is considered by the Court here by Reason of the Insufficiency of the plt's decl'n he recover nothing for this his writt butt be in mercy for his false clamour ~~*

199 [25 September 1702] John Polke attendance at Court
John Polke humbly prays o——- for two days attendance on behalfe of Wm Polke plt agt Capt Henry Smith deft and he shall pray ~~
           9-ber 30ᵗʰ 1702 Sworne before me Arnold Elzey (Sic)

208 [25 September 1702] Elizabeth Polkey attendance at Court
Elizabeth (widow of John) Polkey requests payment for 21 days attendance at court on behalf of George Newman against Thomas Shaw.

236 [25 September 1702] Ephraim Polke and James Polke, sawyer, claim on estate of William Carlile
This is rehearing of suit brought earlier by Ephraim Polke for £17/02/00, but lost on a technicality. See above f. 115. In this case James Polke, sawyer, joins Ephraim as a plaintiff in the suit. The text is very similar to previous and is omitted here except for the conclusion -

And the Deft in his capacity by Wm. Boseman his attorney comes & defends the force & injury etc ~ and saith that there is debts of a greater dignity from England vizt one att the Suit of one Westcomb of London and of one duley and now depending in the Provincial Court of the Province & two others depending in this Court one att the suit of Robt Sparke the other att the suit of John Holland which said debts should they be recovered there will not be --- to satisfy the sd debt the plts have declared for   ~   per Curia Boseman for deft

The Allegations on both parties being fully heard & understood by the Court here therefore it is considered that the plts recover agt the Deft adm'r as aforesaid the sum in the decl'n mentioned vizt Seventeen pounds two shillings strl as also the Sum of -- (not entered)-- pounds of tob'co for his cost & charges in this behalfe laid out and expended & the Deft in mercy ~

238 [25 September 1702] William and Ann Polke suit against Capt. Henry Smith
Ann (Owens) Polk, administrator for the estate of William Owens, and William Polke present a note signed by Henry Smith, and witnessed by John Polke, promising to pay 1600 lbs/tbco to William Owens by 20 November 1697. Smith

did not appear and could not be located by the sheriff, so motion was made and granted for attachment of his goods and chattels.

[Capt. Henry Smith was one of the original settlers in Somerset, having come from Accomac at the formation of the County. He brought a rather unsavory reputation with him, including a divorce settlement in Accomac—a very rare occurence in the early colonial period. Initially influential in Somerset, he was one of the County Commisioners in its early period and heavily involved in land speculation. He sold lands in Manokin to William Owens, John Knox and John Polk in 1692, but his affairs deteriorated and he ended up in frequent litigation before the Somerset Court. Eventually he was compelled to leave the county and move to Whorekill in Sussex County, now Delaware.]

SOMERSET JUDICIAL RECORDS 1702-05
[MSA C 1774-16, Loc. 1/45/1/10]

JANUARY COURT 1702/03

19 [25 November 1702] Ephraim Polke and James Polke, sawyer, suit against estate of William Carlile
This entry repeats the case recorded earlier in 1701-02 Judicials, f.236. In this instance mention is made of the Commissary, the Provincial official responsible for probate actions and records. The declaration and result are the same as in the earlier case; only the following is new:

And the Plt for replication comes and saith that for anything by the Deft in his plea alledged he ought not to be debarred of the debt declared for that the Deft hath charged himselfe for soe much money paid to the plts in the acc't given into the Comissarys office as here in Court may appear
      per Curia   Worthington per Plt

The Alligations on both parties being fully heard & understood therefore it is considered by the Court here that the Pltf recover ag't the Deft the ballance of the above acc't Viz't seventeen pound two shillings Sterl' as also the sum of -- (not entered)-- pounds of tobc for their cost & charges in this behalfe laid out and expended & the Deft in mercy ~

SOMERSET JUDICIAL RECORDS 1705-07
[MSA C 1774-17, Loc. 1/45/1/11]

NOVEMBER COURT 1705

1 [14 November 1705] John Polke on Grand Jury
Then was the following List or panel of the Grand Jury by the Sheriff returned and sworn in, viz. Walter Lane, John Parker, Richard Webb, Mark Gendrion, Griffin Thomas, Thomas Wood, William Plannor, Luke Valentine, Michael

Holland, John Beauchamp, Robert Wilson, Marcy Fountain, William Gyles, Richard Shockley, Charles Williams, Walter Taylor, William Turvile

JANUARY COURT 1705/6

33 [9 January 1705/6] Petition by Presbyterian ministers George McNish and John Hampton
Then did Mr. George McNish and Mr. John Hampton their petition exhibit before the worp'll Justices assembled, as followeth ~~~~
To the worshipfull Court of Somerset County in the Province of Maryland the petition of George McNish and John Hampton most humbly showeth ~ That whereas there is an act of Parliament made the first year of the Reign of King William and Queen Mary (which) instituted an Act of Exempting their Majesties Protestant subjects dissenting from the Church of England from the penalties of sundry laws and whereas by the express wish of the said Law we are required to tender ourselves to the Justices of the Peace at the General or Quarter Sessions of the County, Town, Parts or Divisions where we live to take the Oath of Allegiance, take or subscribe the Declarations, & declare our approbation of, and subscribe the Articles of Religion made the thirtieth year of the reign of Queen Elizabeth, excepting such as are excepted in said act. And whereas we in a ready compliance with said Law have already attended and tendered ourselves to take the said Oath and perform everything required in said Law; we do humbly tender ourselves again to your worships as the proper Court held by the Justices of the Peace for this County empowered and required to administer such Oaths and for receiving such subscriptions as are enjoined by the said Act of Parliament.

We therefore your humble petitioners pray that a further consideration of the sd Law we may be admitted to do our duty in compliance with said Law which we are ready to do seeing how all dissenters in all Majesties Dominions have in this Manner qualified themselves and your Petitioners as in duty bound shall always pray ~~~~

The afsd petition being read & by the wor'll Court considered, that whereas a petition from Coventry Parish and another from sd Macknish was to this Court preferred and the same referred to his Ex'lcy's Hon'ble Counsel for result. It is likewise this day by the wor'll Justices again ordered that the sd Hampton and Macknish petition be continued till the aforesd result be returned.

50 [12 January 1705/6] William Polk to recover £50 from Capt. Nicholas Evans and Jeoffrey Gray
William Polk, Pltf., brings suit against Capt. Nicholas Evans, gentleman, of Somerset County and Jeffrey Gray, merchant of Charlestown in New England for £50 persuant to a bond made with Polk on 8 February 1703, the condition being that they deliver a "sound lusty negro woman fit for service between 15 and 25 years of age by 8 February next" (1704). Plea entered by Teodorey

301

Bonner, attorney for Evans, that he is not aware of any defense or answer by his client concerning the action of the plaintiff. Court awards damages to Polk for £50 with defendant to pay cost of suit.

SEPTEMBER COURT 1706

207 [13 September 1706]
Thos Pollitt, Plt vs Ephraim Polk, defd. Agreed, saith in open court. (Settled out of court)

NOVEMBER COURT 1706

210 [12 Nov 1706] John Polke on Grand Jury
Then the Sheriff for Somerset County returned the Panell of the Grand Jury, viz.

Thomas Dashiell	*Francis Joyce*	*John Smith*	*Alexander Brown*
Peter Fassitt	*Nathaniel Hopkins*	*Hugh Poter*	*John Hilliard*
Daniel Jomes	*Edm Beauchamp*	*Walter Reed*	*John Parkes*
Charles Godfrey	*John Polke*	*Golin Fawset*	*David Haszard*
Edward Harper	*Robert Wilson*		

226 [14 Nov 1706] Warrant for arrest of Capt. Nicholas Evans; owes William Polk £50
William Polk, Pltf.   *Somerset*

vs

Capt. Nicholas Evans, deft
Anne, by Grace of God of England, Scotland and Ireland Queen and Defender of the Faith, to the Sheriff of Somerset County, Greeting. We command you that you take Capt Nicholas Evans of Somerset County if he shall return in your bailiwick and him fast keep so that you hand his body before the Justices of afsd County to be held at Dividing Creek the second Tuesday of November next to satisfy unto William Polk of afsd county as well the sum of fifty pounds sterling a certain debt recovered against the said Capt Nicholas Evans of said county and Jeffrey Gray of Charlestown in New England before the Justices of the said court the fifth day of January 1705 whereof they are convict. Also the sum of two hndr'd and forty pounds of tobacco cost of suite. Hereof fail not at your peril & and you there this writ.
Witness John West gent. Chief Justice of afsd court, the 21st day of October in the 5th year of reign of her majesty, anno dom 1706.   Alexander Hall Clk

The return of sd writt cepi corpis   Per Wm. Worthington Sheriff

230 [15 Nov 1706] John Mulrine placed as ward to John Polke
                    To Mr. Wm Kible, Constable, appointed & sworn
                    & to Mr. Jonathan Raymond to execute & return
Somerset County. John West one of her Ma'ties Justices of the Peace for County

afsd sendeth greeting etc. that whereas John Ryne al's Mulrine has this day to me complained of the bad usuage cruelty & Inhumanity of his father in Law (viz) Connor Obryan with his merciless way of correction as to me was made apparent by the many wounds upon his naked body contrary to the good laws of this Province. These are therefore in her Ma'ties name to will & require as also to charge & command you to bring before the wor'll Justices in Court sitting on Tuesday next the body of him the said Connor Obryan there & then to answer to the complaint afsd & to all such matters & things as shall be then objected ag'st him on behalfe of our Sovereign Lady the Queen & for so doing this shall be yr Warrant dated at Monocan this 8th day of 9-ber in the fifth year of the Reign of our sovereigh Lady Anne by Grace of God of England Scotland France & Ireland Queen, Defender of the Faith, etc Anno Dom 1706.
Executed & returned by me Jonathan Raymond

The afsd Warrant & return being read in Court, Connor Obryan was called who appeared & the sd John Ryne al's Mulrine whose wounds was apparently seen by the Court & sd Connor being demanded the reason for his inhuman cruelty seen by the Court & little to say , his wife appearing with black & blew eyes, the Court here having well considered the premises & being well informed of his cruelty to his now wife, mother of sd John Ryne al's Mulrine do put the sd Lad an apprentice to a certain John Polke to learn the trade of a Cooper & to serve him the sd John Polke till he be 21 years of age & the sd John be oblidged to bestow on the sd John one whole years schooling & at the expiration of his time to give him a set of Coopers tools w'ch he assumes in open Court to perform, considered also by the Court that the sd Connor Obryan be bound to his good behaviour & to give security but for want of security is committed into custody & the Wor'll Court having taken into their serious consideration he not being able to give security took his one bond & Connor Obryan acknowledged himself to be indebted to our sovereign Lady the Queen the full & just amount of seventy pds sterling to be leavied on his goods & chattles for the use of his Ma'ties etc.

The Condition of w'ch recogn is such that if you Connor Obryan do be of good abearance to all her Ma'tys leige people but more especially to your now Wife then this recog: to be null & void otherwise to remain in full power force & vertue in Law to which he says he is content, taken in open Court.

SOMERSET JUDICIAL RECORDS 1707-11
[MSA C 1774-18, Loc. 1/48/2/42]

JUNE COURT 1708

101 William Polk petition for guardianship of William and Anne, orphan children of his brother John
To the worshipfull the Justices of Somerset County now in Court sitting Wm. Polk humbly showeth that when your petitioner's brother John Polk late of this county dec'd left two children behind him, to wit Wm. and Ann Polk who upon

his deathbed he requested that your petitioner and his wife to take care of them to see them educated and brought up Christian like and also to bring up the boy to learn a trade which your petitioner humbly craves that he may have the children ordered unto him per your Worships shall in your prudence and discretion think fit to be done (reasonably) for the orphans and petitioner as in duty bound shall ever pray.

The Court grants the request. James and William Polk post recognizance bond for £10, condition being that William Polk *"do his best endeavor to preserve what parts is delivered to him of their portions left by their deceased father's estate till of age and to return the same with their increase if any and do take care to learn the said William Polk a trade and to read and write and do allow the said William and Anne Polk all necessarys convenient till they shall be of age.*

104 Robert Polk (Jr.) and William Gullett trial for shooting shoats on John Panter's property

Her Majesty vs Robert Polk and William Gullett, laborer, late of Somerset County, Defts. The said Robert and William the fear of God before their eyes not having on or about the 11th day of October in the year of our Lord 1707 at Manny (Monie) in our said county with force of arms that is to say with knives dogs and guns on a certain tract of land and marsh belonging to John Panter of our said county then and there did hunt and three unmarked shoats did feloniously kill and carry away of the value two hundred pounds of tobacco contrary to the peace and against the form of the Act of Assembly in that case made and provided.

  Peter Dent   Clerk.

To which indictment they the said Robert and William pleads not guilty of any breach of her majestys laws and for trial puts themselves on the court. Worthington for Deft. And the Queen also. Dent.

Wherefore command was given to the Sheriff of Somerset County that he cause to come here twelve good and lawful men of his Bailywick to try the issue joined between her Majesty Pltf. and Robert Polk and William Gullett.

At which day came Capt. William Round, Richard Tull, Jr., William Stevenson, Henry Dolman, Robert Wattson, Peter Surman, Afrodocia Johnson, Nathanial Cottman, Edward Martin, Capt. Nicholas Evans, Alexander Carlisle, Henry Bishop, who being duly elected and all sworn and the evidences sworn and deliberately heard and the charges given return with this verdict we the jury do find the deft. guilty of hunting upon Mr. Pannters land after being forewarned. William Round foreman.

The verdict being not full the Clerk of Indictments humbly prayed the court that the said jury may be recommended to their room who after some space return with the same verdict as aforesaid. Where upon they were recommended and return with the same verdict. Recommended the third time and return immediately with the same verdict aforesaid. Recommended the fourth time and after some space return with this verdict we of the jury find the defendant not guilty. Ordered the verdict be entered. Considered by the court here that the said Robert Polk and William Gullet be acquitted of this indictment paying their fees become due according to law and to give bonds for their good behavior.

[Note: on f. 132 Robert Polk and William Smith his security make bond for £10 each on condition that Robert Polk "be of good behavior to all her majesties liege people of this province and especially to John Pannther."]

104 Trial of runaway servant of Samuel Rinshaw (Renshaw)
Samuel Rinshaw brought a woman servant to be adjudged for her runaway time who being interrogated by the worshipfull court and demanded how many days she absented herself from her masters service replied eleven days. Wherefore considered by the court here that the said servant serve her said master ten days for one as also three months for the 200 pounds of tobacco paid by her master for the taking her up after the first time of service expired.

106 Petition for legal recognition of Presbyterian meeting house at Manokin
To the worshipfull the Judge and Justices of the Court of Somerset County humbly showeth that whereas diverse persons in and about Manokin of the Presbyterian interest and persuasion have built a Meeting House for the publick exercise of their religious worship and heard(?) by Manokin Bridge & being willing to satisfie the Law according to Act of Parliament in petitioning the county Court where a Meeting House is or shall be erected that it may be put on record; in complyance therefore with the end and design of the law in such case the petitioner in name of the persons foresaid do request that house foresaid may be legally recorded as law will and your petitioners will pray.

The above written petition being read in Court was by the whole Court allowed & ordered that the Meeting House built by the protestant Desenters by Manokin Bridge in Somerset county in Maryland be and is hereby appointed to be a place of worship of Almighty God in; the minister having qualified himself as law required. Entered by order   Alex. Hall, clerk.

[Note: two judges, Capt. John West and Mr. Joseph Gray, dissented because the same question had been forwarded to the Governor's Council and no final answer had been received. See also f.140 below.]

AUGUST COURT 1708

132 Bond on Robert Polk
Robert Polk and William Smith his security make bond of £10 each on condition

that Polk be on good behavior to all his Majesty's high people of this Provvince and especially to John Pannther.

135 [11 August 1708] Petition for John Mulrine's release from apprenticeship to John Polk

John Mulrine called in court made his appearance on a petition exhibited by his mother he being bound to John Polke to learn the trade of a cooper and the said John Polke being deceased would pray the court he the said Mulrine may be restored to his mother. Wherefore the Court entered into judgement and ordered that the said widow Polk give security to learn him the said Mulrine the trade of a cooper and that the said apprentice should remain with the said widow till free. Alex'r Hall post security for £5 sterling.

[Note: John Mulrine was apprenticed to John Polke in August 1706 until age 21; see above, Somerset Judicials 1705-07 f.230.]

139 Johanna Polk brings servant to court to have age recorded

The widow Polk brought servant Thomas Magguire who is adjudged to be of age 13 last May 1708.
[Note. In the Index to 1707-11 Judicials the entry for f. 139 identifies Johanna Polk, rather than Widow Polk.]

140 Petition for legal recognition of Presbyterian meeting house at Rehobeth

This day (viz.) The 10th day of June Anno Dom. 1708 ordered that the new Meeting House built by the Protestant dissenters [Presbyterians] at Rehobeth Town in Somerset County in the province of Maryland be and is hereby appointed to be a house & place for the public worship os Almighty God, the minister thereunto appointed having qualified himself as law required. Entered per order. Alex. Hall Clerk

SEPTEMBER COURT 1708

147 Legal notice regarding Robert Pooke (recorded among other similar notices)

> *To Sam'll Groome, Merchant in London*
> *Maryland—April the First 1705—Exchange for 9/5/0*

At twenty days of this my third of exchange, my first and second not paid, pay Robert Pooke or order the sum of nine pounds five shillings sterling value received and place the same to account of your humble servant.
William Williams Jr.

148 Provincial writ concerning case of James Polk vs. George Hutchins

Writ of Error from Provicial Court to Somerset dated 19 December 1709, received by Court 15 March 1709/10 concerning case of James Polk vs George Hutchins; directs Somerset Court to withhold judgement and penalty against

Hutchins until Provincial Court can hear case; orders James Polk appear in Annapolis on 2nd Tuesday in April 1710. Note: no subsequent record of this case found in Provicial Court proceedings. (See below f. 214.)

151 William Polk on Grand Jury

NOVEMBER COURT 1708

152 [10 November 1708] Robert Polk chosen as Constable for Money (Monie) Hundred
Then were the Constables called which served in 1707 and new constables chosen for the insueing year vizt.

John Hailes for Monocan	*Thomas Stockwell for Annamsex*
Moses Stenton for Pocomoke	*John Ricketts for Baltemore*
Wm. Harris for Wickoocmocoe	*Benjamin Burton for Bogetenorten*
Robert Givens for Nantickoke	*Robert Polk for Money*
Thomas Robins for Mattapany	

164 [16 November 1708] James Polk recognizance for
James Polk accused "for words spoken of the Burgesses which at that time could not be prove his other living out of the county." James bound for £10 for his good behavior with Ephraim Polk as his security, bond for—condition being that James "be of his good behavior and good abearance to all her Majesty's liege people of this province especially the Burgesses of Somerset."

169 [18 Nov 1708] James Polk, Pltf, vs George Hutchins, deft.
Case continued.

MARCH COURT 1708/9

172 [2 March 1708/9] James Polk released from bond
This day James Polk having produced a certificate under hand of John Keene, one of her Majesty's officers that Matthew Graves made oath before him that Mr. John Brown of Patuxent told him that sum of Somerset County Burgesses informed the Governor what was spoken in house. Ordered that said James Polk be released of his bond.

172 Ephraim Polk on jury of 12

172 William and Ephraim Polk on jury of 12.

186 Ephraim Polk on jury

187 [2 March 1708/9] Ann (Polk) Roberts suit vs. John Mulka (Mulkey)
Ann Roberts, widow, Pltf, vs John Mulka, Deft; suit to recover 400lbs/tbco and other items due from Mulka; Samuel Worthington, attorney for Roberts,

presents Mulka's account from 24 December 1707 at Dam Quarter; includes *50 gallons syder, 50 gallons syder the cask to be returned, 400 lbs tbco, washing tub, pare shoes, lye tub*; Mulka appears and admits debt; Court awards for Roberts. as declared, plus 217 lbs/tbco for cost of suit.

188 Ephraim and William Polk on jury of 12.

197 James Polk on jury.

207 Ephraim Polk on Jury of 12.

214 James Polk vs. George Hutchins agreement
James Polk and George Hutchins agree to have representatives arbitrate their dispute; John Jones for James Polk and James McMorre for George Hutchins; action will come to trial if they do not agree by June Court. [See f.283]

215 Andrew Caldwell, Pltf vs James Polk, Deft
Settled out of court, per Samuel Worthington.

AUGUST COURT 1709

234 [11 August 1709] James Polk negro boys ages recorded
James Polk brought a negro boy named "Roger" to be adjudged of his age who was by the Court here adjudged to be twelve years old the date hereof to know when a tithable.

James Polk brought a negro boy named "Acheir" to be adjudged of his age who was by the Court here adjudged to be ten years old the date hereof to know when a tithable.

235 [11 August 1709] Robert Polk brings in list of tithables for Monie
At which day the Constables being called make their appearance and gave in their list of tithables
>   *Thomas Robins, Constable of Mattapony Hundred—lists 146*
>   *Robert Polk, Constable for Monney Hundred—lists 255*
>   *Robert Guian, Constable for Nanticoke Hundred—lists 255*
>   *John Hales, Constable for Manocan Hundred—lists 287*
>   *Moses Honson, Constable for Pocomoke Hundred—lists 394*
>   *Benj. Burton, Constable for Boguerternorten Hundred—lists 232*
>   *Wm. Harris, Constable for Wiccicomoco Hundred—lists 287*
>   *Jonas Shurges, Constable for Baltimore Hundred—lists 162*
>   *Thos. Stockwell, Constable for Annemessex—lists 214*

249 James Polk vs. George Hutchins
Case continued by court.

265 William Polk claims against Joanna, widow of John Polk

William Polk, Pltf. vs Joanna Polk, Deft. Joanna Polk admnx of all and singular the goods, chattels and creditts of John Polk late of Somerset County dec'd was attached to answer unto William Polk of the same County of a plea of trespass upon the the case and whereupon the said William by Peter Dent his attorney complains that wherea the said John in his lifetime to witt the 10th day of March in the year of our Lord 1707 at Monocan within the jurisdiction of this Court was indebted to the sd. Wm. In the sum of two thousand four hundred pounds of tobco and twenty three shillings in money, the balance of an account here in court doth and may appear and the said John to the sd. Wm. in his lifetime in manner aforesaid being indebted did assume on himself and to the said William then and there faithfully promise that he the said John the said sum 2400 pounds of tobacco and twenty three shillings in money the same to the William hath not (though often requested) nor the said Johanna to whom administration of all and singular the goods chattels and credits which were of the said John at the time of the death of the said John hath been committed the same as to the said Wm. hath not paid nor hath either of them paid the same to the said Wm. although the said Johanna to do the same by the sd. William hath been requested but the same to do hath refused and doth still refuse to the damage of the said William of 2500 pounds of tobacco and there upon he brings his suit ~ ~

Items:	*1698 Tobacco due me upon partnership of coopers work*	*2400 lbs*
	1 3/4 gallon molasses	*00-14-03*
	1707 1 1/4 gallon rum for his body and funeral	*00-08-09*
	1 gallon molasses & ½ bushell salt	*00-06-00*
	300 staves lent	*01-09-00*
	Per contra Credit ~	
	By 2 gal. molasses returned	*00-06-00*
	By 300 pipe staves returnes	
	True account, errors accepted, *Wm. Polke*	

Memorandum – That this day being the 22th day of August came Wm. Polk and made oath on the holy Evangelists the above account of two thousand four hundred pounds of tobacco and twenty three shillings in money is due Wm. Polk and he hath received no part or parcell thereof.   Test.   Thomas Dashiell.

And the deft. comes into Court in her proper person and confesses judgement wherefore considerd by the Court here that the Pltf. Wm. Polke recover of the estae of John Polke dec'd 2400 pounds tbco and twenty three shillings in money as also 243 ponds tbco for his cost and charges laid out and expended by means of retaining sd debt. And the deft in Mercy.

NOVEMBER COURT 1709

283 [24 Nov 1709] James Polk vs. George Hutchins
James Polk, Pltf vs George Hutchins, Deft; for debt of £6/6/6, the balance of an

account from 10 February 1705 at Puttuxon, i.e. at Manokin, originally for £12/13/0; Court rules for Polk as declared plus 1579 lbs/ tbco for court costs.

283 Ephraim Polk and Oliver Wallace paid for attendance at court
Ephraim Polke and Oliver Wallace (Wallice) make oath for their attendance at court for 12 days on behalf of James Polke; sworn before Charles Ballard.

329 Ann Roberts vs. John Mulkal (Mulkey)
Case settled out of court

329 James Polk vs. George Hutchins
Case superceeded per writ of error but by default came too late and not produced until March Court 1709/10.

JUNE COURT 1710

381 [6 June 1710] Writ from Provincial Court to stay judgement of Polk vs. Hutchins
Writ of Error from Provincial Court to Somerset Court dated 13 April 1710 concerning case of James Polk vs. George Hutchins; directs that Somerset Court withhold judgement and forward transcripts for hearing on 2nd Tuesday in July; signed by Robert Hall Regent in Chancellery.

413 Suit against John Renshaw, Jun. to give account of estate of Francis Roberts
Petition by Richard Tull and Thomas Hugg, acting in the place of Thomas Pollett and John Polk, the original bondsmen for the estate of Francis Roberts, both deceased, requesting that John Renshaw and wife Anne give a proper account. Granted.

NOVEMBER COURT 1710

423 [8 November 1710] James Polk appointed Constable for Monie (Monney) Hundred

MARCH COURT 1710/11

446 James Polk fined for non-appearance as Constable for Monie
The constables called by their several names (viz) Wm. Noble Pokomoke Hundred, Joseph Atkin Baltimore Hundred, Peter Johnson Mattaponi Hundred, Thos. Ward Annemessex Hundred,Joseph McChester Nanticoke Hundred,,John Scool Wicomico Hundred, James Polk Money Hundred, William SSeby Bogertornorten Hundred. James Polk did not appear. Order he be fined.

453 James Polk Informer
We the Grand Jury do presemt Joseph Huff and Priscilla Barton for cohabiting

together as Man and Wife contrary to the Act of Assembly. James Polk informer. David Spense Foreman.

SOMERSET JUDICIAL RECORDS 1711-13
[MSA C 1774-19, Loc. 1/48/2/43]

NOVEMBER COURT 1711

104 [17 November 1711]   Case of stolen beef; James Polk Constable
Memorandum – That on the 17th of November 1711 Joseph Austen complained to me George Gale one of her Majestys Justices of the Peace for Somerset County that on the 15th instant there was stolen from him out of a conoe at Dam Quarter Creek a parcel of beef and thereupon I granted him a warrant directed at James Polk Constable of Monny Hundred to search suspected places for the said beef (and) if they had any reason to suspect any person to have stolen the same to bring such person before me or some other Justice to be examined. In obedience to which warrant the said James Polk did on the 19th instant bring before me a piece of beef containing about eight pounds weight and likewise brought the body of John Rensher and John Roberts as persons suspected to have stolen the said beef.

The examination of James Polk taken before me George Gale etc. This examinant being sworn on the Holy Evangelist to declare the truth saith that by virtue of the warrant above mentioned he did search the milk house of John Rensher and then found the piece of beef which is above mentioned which the wife of the above said John Austin did suppose to be the stolen beef was given him by the wife of John Marvell and this examinant further saith that he did then go to the wife of John Marvell and asked her if she had given John Roberts that piece of beef and she answered that she would not satisfy him wheather she had or not.

The examination of John Marvell taken before me George Gale etc. This examinant being sworn on the Holy Evangelist do declare that the piece of beef above mentioned could not be any part his beef he having none in his house but cow beef and the piece that was found and produced by the Constable was part of the Cod piece of a steer.

The examination of Wm. Harris taken before me George Gale etc. This examinant being sworn to say the truth saith that he was with Thomas Rensher and a Mulatto wench belonging to John Austin at Dam Quarter Creek on Wednesday and Thursday last they having a canoe which had on board her a carcass of steer beef belonging to John Austin and that during their stay at the said creek part of the said beef was cut and stolen away which was perceived by Thomas Rensher but who stole it knoweth not.

The examination of John Austin taken before me George Gale etc. The 19th of

November 1711 This examinant being sworn on the Holy Evangelist to say the truth saith that he doth realy believe the beef produced by the Constable to be found at John Renshers milk house to be part of that which was stolen from him, and John Rensher and John Roberts had this day deposed him and puts up this complaint and offered to give him a steer and some other considerations if he would proceed no further against them.

The examination of John Rensher taken before me George Gale etc. This examinant saith that he is not guilty of stealing any beef or other things from John Austin or any other person and that he was not at his house when the beef was found there.

The examination of John Roberts taken before me George Gale etc. This examinant saith that he is not guilty of stealing said beef but that he found the said piece of beef (produced by the Constable) hanging on a cedar after the canoe above mentioned was gone from Dam Quarter and he carrying it into John Renshers Milk House and put it there with intent to send it to John Austin believing it to be some of the beef the said Austin had lost. He ownes that when the Constable found it he did say that he had it of Betty Marvell but that was not true and the reason why he said so was that he was taken at a nonplus and did not know what to say.

Case continued to March Court. Bonds for £20 each placed on John Roberts, John Renscher to appear in March Court to answer charges. Bonds for £10 each placed on James Polk, Joseph Austin and William Harris to appear in March Court and provide testimony.

JUNE COURT 1712

153 [4 June 1712] Bastardy case against Joanna Bryan, servant of James Polk

The Queen vs, Joanna Bryan
Memorandum ~ That on the 22ⁿᵈ day of November 1711 there was brought before me at Monny Thomas Burk servent to Oliver Walles (Wallace) of Dorchester County and Joanna Bryan servent to James Polke and the said Joanna did then own herself with child and after her being sworn on the Holy Evangelist to truly declare who got her with child she declared it was Thomas Burke and that it was got sometime about June last which the said Burke denyed to be true.

Somerset County ~ The Jurors of our Sovereign Lady the Queen that now is etc. On their oaths do present for our said Lady the Queen Joanna Bryan servent to James Polke of Monny Hundred in the Parish of Somerset and county aforesaid for that she the said Joanna the fear of God before her eyes not having but being seduced by the instigation of the devil on or about the fifth day of January(June?) 1711 at Monny Hundred in the county and parish aforesaid

312

hath committed fornication and on her body hath born a bastard child to the great dishonor of Almighty God and the breach of her Majestys good laws of this Province.

On the back of this indictment is endorsed, avera ~~ Walter Lane Foreman

And the said Joannna appears and pleads guilty to her indictment and being demanded who was the father of her late born bastard child stood mute and would not confess. Wherefore considered by the Court here and ordered corporal punishment. (Vizt)

To the Sheriff of Somerset County, Greeting. We command you that you take Joanna Bryan to the whipping post and to give her 30 lashes on the bare back well laid on and to make return with the prisoner this 4th day of June 1712. And that Mr. Hopkins see the same order executed.   Signed per order, Alex'r Hall, Clerk.

The return executed per me ~~ Thomas Dashiel Sheriff

James Polk bound for £5 to ensure Joanna Bryan pays fees due because of her case and she serve 12 months extra beyond her agreed time of service.

159 [5 June 1712] William Polk on Jury
Trial of Connor Obryan for stealing 5 pound iron wedge from Edward Wootton. Obryon found not guilty.

163 [5 June 1712] William Polke suit vs. Stephen Coston for debt of 400 lbs of pork
William Polk presents note for eight 50 Lb casks of porke delivered to Coston September 1711. Coston admits debt and found liable. Made to pay Court costs of 260 lbs/tbco.

NOVEMBER COURT 1712

229 [17 November 1712] William Polke suit against Matthew Goldsmith
Case settled out of Court, per Samuel Worthington.

234 [4 December 1712]   James Polke appearance and continuation
James Polk appeared in Court to answer charges. Witnesses for the Queen failed to appear and case was continued until March Court. Bond placed on James Polk and his security Captain Charles Ballard for £20 each for his appearance at March Court.

275 [6 March 1712] Ann (Polk) and John Rensher vs. John Mulka
Mulka had been issued a writ to appear and satisfy a debt allegedly owed to
Ann, wife of John Rensher, from 1709 when she was known as Ann Roberts.
James Knowles, attorney for Mulka, says client had satisfied the debt by
payments of 670 lbs/tbco, one washing tub, one lye tub and two and a half
bushels of Indian corn, and produces a receipt signed by Ann Roberts in 1709.
Court finds for Mulka and assesses court costs and cost of Mulka's legal fees on
John Rensher and Ann (Roberts) Rensher for their false clamor.

280 [7 March 1712/13]   Case against James Polke dimissed
Dismissed the Grand Jury finding the bill ignoramus

JUNE COURT 1713

283 [2 June 1713] James Polke discharged
*Per recog ~~ and this day the Grand Jury finding the indictment ignoramus
indorsed discharged the said James Polke from any further attendance.*

SOMERSET JUDICIAL RECORDS 1713-1715
[MSA C 1774-20, Loc. 1/45/1/15]

66 [2 June 1714] Ephraim Polke vs. John Mackarty, deft.
Case settled out of court per Sheriff.

NOVEMBER COURT 1714

127 [3 November 1714]   Court Convenes
James Polke on Grand Jury
Constables Chosen for the year ensuing (vizt)
*John Pullett (Pollett) for Monocan Hundred, Joseph Polk for Money Hundred,
David Whelon for Baltemore Hundred, Wm. Cord for Mattapany Hundred, Wm.
Poynter for Boquetenorten Hundred, Jeremiah Nocholson for Nanticoake
Hundred, Wm. Coulbourne for Annamessex Hundred, John Disharoon for
Wiccocomeco Hundred, Somersett Dickeson for Pocomoke Hundred.*

156 [12 November 1714] Various Cases settled out of Court
John Fargisson, Pltf. vs. James Polk, deft
Thomas Hugg , Pltf.vs. Phillip Mulkey, deft.
John Scott, Pltf. vs. Magdalen Polke, deft.
The King vs. Thomas Hugg, deft.

JUNE COURT 1715

221 [22 June 1715] James Polke security for Joanna Bryan renewed

The King vs. Joanah Bryan
Per Recog ~ New security required for her appearance next November Court.
James Polke her security did acknowledge himself to be indebted to the King
and his successors due to be levied on his goods and chattels, lands and
tenements, etc.
The condition of this recognizance is such that if Joaneah Bryan do make her
personal appearance before his Majestys Worshipfull Justices of the Peace the
third Tuesday in November next and do stand and abide the judgement of the
said Court then this recog. to be void and otherwise to stand and be in full force.

SOMERSET JUDICIAL RECORDS 1715-1717
[MSA C 1774-21, Loc. 1/48/2/44]

NOVEMBER COURT 1715

3 [16 November 1715] King vs. Joanna Bryan
Per recog ~ New recog. required for her appearance next March. James Polk
her security is £10 for her appearance to stand and abide judgement by the
Court in common form, to which he says he is content.

MARCH COURT 1715/16

15 [20 March 1715/16] The King vs. Joanna Bryan
Somerset County ~ The jurors of our Sovereign Lord the King that now is set
upon their oaths do present for our said Lord the King, Joan Brian.

Joanna Bryan of Somerset Parish in the County of Somerset, single woman. For
that the said Joan, the fear of God before her eyes not having but being seduced
by the instigation of the devil on or about the 17th day of March A D 1713/14 at
Somerset Parish in the County aforesaid hath committed fornication and on her
body hath born a bastard child contrary to his Majestys good laws of this
province and the evil example thereof.

> *Worthington, Clk. Of Indictement*
Ordered that Joannah Bryan be carried to the wipping post and to give her ten
lashes on the bare back well laid on and make return of the prisoner.
> *Alez. Hall, Clk.*
Ordered also that Joanna Bryan give security for the payment of her fees.
Ordered she be committed till she give security. Pleads guilty and says John
Neale is the father.
[Note – John Neal is later listed as a taxable at the household of Joseph Polk (at
Polks Folly) and was a witness to Joseph's will in Dorchester in 1751.]

15 [21 March 1715/16] James Polk on Grand Jury
Panel of 23 grand jurors appointed.

45 [12 April 1716] Ephraim Polke, Administrator, estate of Thomas Walter, vs. Thomas Stevens

Stevens is held liable to estate of Thomas Walter for 5000 lbs/tbco from debt dated 1 June 1713 in Wiccocomico (Wicomico) Hundred which was to be paid in in two 2500 lbs installments in October 1713 and in 1714. Polke claims payment has not been made. Samuel Worthington, attorney for Stevens, produces note signed acknowledging payment by Stephens on various items including 2700 lbs/tbco to Abraham Covington and discharging by Thomas stevens from his debt to Walters.

Court finds Stevens not liable and assesses court costs and legal fees on Polke. [Note – Estate of Thomas Walters was inventoried in Dorchester County at £20/5/8 on 6 May 1715.]

59 [19 June 1716] Walter Quinton, Pltf. vs. Thomas Hugg, deft.

Thomas Hugg, cooper, of Stepney Parish is sued by Quinton for 923 lbs/tbco for note of debt signed on 7 Sept 1709 and never paid. Court finds for Quinton and assesses court costs on Hugg.

[Note – Thomas Hugg married Johanna, widow of John Polk by 1710. This is first of numerous court appearances by Hugg during this period.]

AUGUST COURT 1716

78 [23 August 1716] Phillip Feddeman, Sheriff of Dorchester suit against Ephraim Polk

Feddeman, Sheriff of Dorchester County, sues Ephraim Polk (Polke), administrator of the estate of Thomas Walters (Waters) of Dorchester, for 433 lbs/tbco due for annual county levies not paid by Walters between 1712 and 1714; also demands Polk to appear in August Court in Cambridge, Dorchester County. Court finds for Feddeman and assesses Polke 200 lbs/tbco additional for court costs.

8 [24 August 1716] Colonel Thomas Ennalls, Pltf. vs. Thomas Hugg and Levin Disharoon, Defts.

Ennals sues Hugg and Disharoon as securities for John McCartee against whom Ennalls had obtained a judgment for 502 lbs/tbco from Somerset court in 1710.

103 [9 October 1716] Benjamin Wailes, Pltf. vs. Thomas Hugg, Deft.

Thomas Hugg, plamter of Stepney Parish, is sued for "levies and Sheriff fees and interest" in the amount of 1759 lbs/tbco itemized as follows:

1713 *Thomas Hugg Debt*	
To one levy	*103*
	30
Case John Mulkey	*35*
Account fees at Queens suit for 10.0.0	*185*

19 days Som. Co.	*380*
Copies and bill, Mulkey	*35*
1714 To one levy	*119*
Same on Jacob Taylor	*60*
For fees to Queens suit	*190*
1715 To two levies	*358*
	1495
Interest	*264*
Benjamin Wailes	*1759*

Hugg admits the debt and Court rules for Wailes with 215 lbs/tbco court costs assessed on Hugg.

125 [10 October 1716] Charles Williams sued by Thomas Dashiell for 808 lbs/tbco.

Dashiell complains that during 1710-1712 Charles Williams of Monie (Mannigh) Hundred amassed debts of 2654 lbs/tbco of which 616 was still outstanding. With four years interest at 8% suit is now made for 808 lbs/tbco. Items in the bill of particulars include payments of the county levy, pair of shoes, 3 ½ gallons of brandy, payment of Margaret Tull's account and administrator fees for estate of Richard Tull. [Note—Charles Williams was the third husband of Margaret Polk who was previously married to Thomas Pollett and Richard Tull.]

128 [10 October 1716] Thomas Hugg, cooper, sued by Arnold Elzey

Elzey claims 4000 lbs/tbco for delivery of a"shallop and appurtenances" to Hugg in 1714 as contracted and for which he states he has not been paid. Hugg admits debt. Court awards 1314 lbs/tbco to Elzey and assesses Hugg 329 lbs/tbco for cost of suit.

136 [11 October 1716] James Adams, merchant, sues Thomas Hugg

Adams claims Hugg owes him for purchase made 27 January 1715/16 itemized as follows:

To 26 yds of brown linen, at 7 per	182 lbs of tobacco
To 8½ yds of fine linen at 13 per yd	111 lbs of tobacco
2 doz big buttons at 4 per doz.	
To 2½ doz small at 2 per	013 lbs of tobacco
To 8¼ yds of bed ticking at 10 per yd	
8 hanks of mohair at 8 per	157 lbs of tobacco
To 3 yds of broad cheque at 13 a bale 2 lbs	037 lbs of tobacco
	500 lbs of tobacco

Hugg admits debt and judgment is found for Adams. Hugg also assessed 232 lbs/tbco cost of suit.

220 [20 March 1716/17]   James Polk sues John Nevarr for payment for pine planks

James Polk (Polok, Polloc) brings suit for 9000 lbs/tobacco claiming that John Nevar/Neaver, Innholder of Annapolis, Ann Arundel County, owes him a balance of 4920 lbs/tbco for 6140 feet of "inch pine planks" delivered as of 3rd June 1715. Nevar admits the debt. Court rules for Polk and assesses Nevar 374 lbs/tbco cost of suit.

[Note – James Polk described himself as a ship carpenter in his will.]

221 [20 March 1716/17] Thomas Hugg sued by William Wheatly

William Wheatly sues Thomas Hugg, cooper, for non- payment of 4000 lbs/tbco due from note signed by Hugg on 2 March 1714/15. Hugg admits the debt. Court finds for Wheatly and assesses Hugg 369 lbs/tbco cost of suit.

226 [March 1716/17] Various suits discontinued

John Henry suit vs. Robert Polk dropped due to death of Henry ("Mort est the pltf.")

Henry Spear suit against William Polk settled out of court

Thomas Hugg suit vs. Edward Richards said to be "in custody"

JUNE COURT 1716

271 [21 June 1716] Court order from Somerset to Ann Arundel County for James Polk vs. John Nevar

Maryland ~~ Charles absolute Lord and proprietary of the Province of Maryland and Avalon Lord Baron of Baltemore, We command you that you attach any goods and chattels rights or credits of John Navarr of the City of Annapolis in Annarundell County if they be found in your Bailywick to the value of four thousand and twenty pounds of tobacco debt and four hundred and forty nine cost and when you have the same so attached or any part thereof the same in your custody safe keep so that you have them before the Justices of the County Court to be held at Dividing Creek the third Tuesday of June next then and there to be condemned according to Act of Assembly and for the use of a certain James Polk of Somersett County, planter, unless he the said John Navarr either by himself or his attorney shall appear and answer unto the said James Polk of a plea of trespass upon the case according to the law and that by good and lawfull men of your Bailywick you make known unto the person or persons in whose hands you make the same attachment that he she or they be and appear before the Justices of our said court to be held as aforesaid to show cause if any he she or they may have why the same goods chattels rights or credits so attached in his her or their hands ought not to be condemned according to the law if to him her or them it shall seem meet and how you shall execute this writ that you make known unto our said Justices at the day and place aforesaid and have you then and there this writ. Witness Charles Ballard, Gent. Chief Justice of our said court this 20th day of March in the second year of our dominion anno 1716/17.

Worthington
Alex'r Hall, Clk.

And the Sherriff now returneth on the back of the said attachment that he hath attached in the hands of Benjamin Wailes three thousand pounds of tobacco.

AUGUST COURT 1717

377 [23 August 1717] Thomas Hugg sued by George Benston
Benston claims Hugg owes him 8000 lbs/tbco per note signed in Stepney Parish 26 March 1716. Hugg does not appear and the Sheriff says that Hugg could not be located and that a notice of attachment had been left at Hugg's last abode. Court finds for Benston, with 216 lbs/tbco added for cost of suit.

398 [24 August 1717] Thomas Hugg sued by Enoch Barinton
Barinton presents note for 1500 lbs/tbco signed by Hugg 27 January 1715/16 at Nanticoke. Sheriff states that Hugg is not to be found in his bailiwick but he had left a notice at Hugg's abode. Court finds for Barinton with 238 lbs/tbco added for cost of suit.

414 [August 1717] Items taken from docket
Henry Spear, Pltf. vs. William Polk, Deft. settled out of court
Thomas Hugg, Pltf. vs. Edward Ricketts, Deft. Discontinued – "Pltf. runaway"

NOVEMBER COURT 1717

469 [22 November 1717] Writ of attachment on goods and chattels of Thomas Hugg for George Dashiell
Writ from Somerset Court to Sheriff Thomas Dashiell signed by Chief Justice Charles Ballard 2 September 1717 instructs Dashiell to attach any goods or belongings of Thomas Hugg up to the value of 1750 lbs/tbco, to satisfy his debts to George Dashiell. Sheriff attaches 1300 lbs per James Ruark and 380 from a Mr. Allen which is in turn assigned to George Dashiell and Francis Allen who are enjoined to return it should Hugg make good on his debt.

SOMERSET JUDICIAL RECORDS 1718
[MSA C 1774-22, Loc. 1/45/1/16]

MARCH COURT 1717/8

69 [March 1717/8]   Ephraim Polk suit against Richard Knight
Ephraim Polk (Polke) complains that Richard Knight of Coventy Parish purchased following items from him for 546 lbs/tbco on 9 Aug 1711 for:

2 lbs ginger   24

½ lb of powder	18
4 ½ lb of shot	27
4 ½ gallons of sider	32
1 bushell wheat	45
1 double wheel	400
	546

and had not made payment. Pok requests a writ of attachment for 546 lbs/tbco
plus 242 lbs, cost of suit. Granted by Court.

NOVEMBER COURT 1718

177 [18 November 1718] Thomas Pollitt presents Michael Christopher
Thomas Pollitt brings Michael Christopher before the Court which adjudges his
age as 10; Pollitt agrees to teach him the trade of a shoemaker.
[Note – Thomas Pollitt (Jun.) was second son of Thomas Pollitt (Sen.) and
Margaret Polk.]

SOMERSET JUDICIAL RECORDS 1719
[MSA C 1774-23, Loc. 1/48/2/45]

MARCH COURT 1718/9

24 [March 1718/9] Ann (Polk) Rensher sued by Benjamin Wailes
Benjamin Wailes complains that John Rensher, dec'd, owed him for various
items totaling 1191 lbs/tbco. Court finds for Wailes against Ann Rensher,
administratrix for Rensher's estate, with 219 lbs/tbco added for cost of suit.

JUNE COURT 1719

83 [June 1719] William Polk obliged to mend his fences
Upon complaint of Margaret Cains(?) Court orders William Polk to rerout the
road around his fence and also to keep his horses according to the law.

SOMERSET JUDICIAL RECORDS 1719-22
[MSA C 1774-24, Loc. 1/45/1/17]

13 [22 August 1719] Thomas Hugg required to pay security
Thomas Hugg, deft. vs. His Lordship ~ Security of £10 required against his
appearance at November Court with John Caldwell, and to be of good behavior,
especially to Rev. Alexander Adams, and not to depart without the license of the
court.

NOVEMBER COURT 1719

15 [17 November 1719] William Polk fined for disrespecting Court
Ordered that summons be issued to William Polke that he appear this Court to

shew cause why he hath contemned the authority of this court. (Polke) made his appearance and could shew no cause wherefore it is considered by the court thereby he be fined 400 pounds of tobco for the use of the scool (school) *and to give security for his fine and fees. At which day came Thiomas Layfield and with the principall Wm. Polke did acknowledge themselves to be indebted to their Lordships the Proprietaries of the Province each in ten pounds due to be levied on their goods & chattels lands & tenements for the use of his Lordships toward the maintenance of a free scool if they fail in the condition.*

The condition is such that if Wm. Polke do pay his fine and all fees that become due by law by means of his contemning authority and be of peace then his recognizance to be null and void, other wise to stand and remain in full force & virtue in the law taken in court, to which they say they are content.

SOMERSET JUDICIAL RECORDS—August 1722
[MSA C 1774-25, Loc. 1/45/1/15]

AUGUST COURT 1722

416 [22 August 1722] William Knox chooses his guardian
William Knox came into Court and prayed Liberty to choose his guardian which is granted and the said Wm. Knox chose Wm. Owens his guardian.

429 [22 August 1722] Thomas Hugg sued by John Caldwell
Note dated 3 July 1720 states that Thomas Hugg is indebted to John Caldwell for 6000 lbs/tbco from 7 November 1720 and he is required to attend August Court if he wishes to object. Hugg does not appear and judgement is awarded to Caldwell with 196 lbs/tbco added for cost of suit.

SOMERSET JUDICIAL RECORDS—November 1722
[MSA C 1774-26, Loc. 1/45/1/18]

NOVEMBER COURT 1722

25 [23 November 1722] James Adams suit against Thomas Hugg
Adams asks Court to confirm the decision of earlier case awarding him 500 lbs/tbco and costs against Thomas Hugg. Sherriff had bee ordered to bring Hugg into ourt but Hugg was not to be found and does not appear. Court confirms former judgment with 422 lbs/tbco costs.

25 [23 November 1722] Lady Baltimore suit against estate of William Trail
Margaret, Lady Baltimore, executrix of the estate of Charles Calvert, Lord Baltimore, brings suit against James Trail, son and heir to (Rev.) William Trail, deceased, for 960 lbs/tbco due from 13 June 1688. Testimony is given that Trail is no longer in the County. Court grants attachments against Trail's estate if any be found.

SOMERSET JUDICIAL RECORDS 1723-25
[MSA C 1774-27, Loc. 1/48/3/1]

JUNE COURT 1723

46 [18 June 1723] Edward Roberts fined for failure to assist with road maintenance

John Miller, current overseer of roads for Damn Quarter, complains that Roberts refuses to assist in road maintenance. Roberts admits guilt and is fined 100 lbs/tbco.

48 [18 June 1723] Mary Roberts prosecuted for negro child

Mary Roberts, servant of John Ricketts of All Hallows Parish, is presented for bearing a negro child. Roberts admits guilt and says the father is a negro slave of Ricketts, named Simon. Court finds her guilty and commands her to serve Rickett until following March I compensation. Ricketts is required to bring her to March Court, under bond of 30 sterling.

NOVEMBER COURT 1723

122 [13 November 1723] Bridge over Manokin

Whereas the bridge over the head of Manocan River is so decayed that it is dangerous to ride or pass over & therefore it is ordered by the Court that Cols Charles Ballard, William Stoughton Esqr & Mr. Levin Gale agree with some person or persons for the repairing of said bridge and the keeping it in good repair, and to make their report at next court etc ~~~~

122 [13 November 1723] No free ferry at Vienna

Upon the motion of Mr. Francis Allen for the licensing a free ferry over Nanticoke River at the Town of Vienna etc ~ It is ordered by the Court that there be no free ferry that is no maintained by the County of Somerset over any part of Nanticoke River for the future etc ~~~~

MARCH COURT 1723/4

145 [17 March 1723/4] Mary Roberts indicted and whipped

Mary Roberts is returned to Court for fornication with "a certain person to this Inquest unknown" and bearing a bastard, born 1 September 1723. Roberts says that *she is guilty thereof and submits to the Mercy of the Court but hath not the wherewithal to pay her fine for the fact afsd. Whereof it is considered by the Justices here that the said Mary Roberts be whipt with ten lashes at the public whipping post on the bear back well laid on until the blood appear.* John Ricketts (Rickords) is bound for 10 pounds sterling for payment of the varies officers fees generated by the action.

256 [18 November 1724] Mary Kavanaugh to be sold at auction to pay £7/4 fine for stealing

Whereas a certain Mary Cavanough a servant being convict for the felonious stealing of certain goods and chattels belonging to a certain Merrick Ellis and John Bannister, and at expiration of the said Mary Cavanoughs service Mr. Jos. Gray her master according to Act of Assembly returned her to the County Court of Somerset to be sold to satisfie unto the said Merrick Ellis and John Bannister the four fould of the value of the goods from them stolen which four fould does amount to seven pounds four shillings; etc ~~ thereupon it is ordered by the Court that according to said Act of Assembly the Sheriff of Somerset County sell the said Mary Cavanough at publick sale to the biggest bidder not exceeding seven years to satisfie unto the said Merrick Ellis and John Bannister the value of the goods afsd stolen.

Whereupon the said Sheriff returns to this Court that he did sell the said Mary Cavanough at publick sale for three thousand thirty one pounds of tobacco to a certain Wercott Gray ~~

MARCH COURT 1723/4

272 [16 March 1724/5] Bond to heirs of Ephraim Polke

Somerset County ~~ Know all men by these presents that we John Laws, John Jones and William Turpin all of Somerset County in the Province of Maryland are beholden and firmly bound unto Magdalene, Charles, Elizabeth, Priscilla, Ann, Mary, Joseph and Ephraim Polke, orphans of Ephraim Polke dec'd in the full and just sum of two hundred and forty four pounds sixteen shillings to be paid unto the said orphans their heirs adm'ns or assigns to which payments well and truly to be made and done we bind ourselves and our heirs executprs and admins jointly and severally in and for the whole family by these presents sealed with our seals and dated the 16th day of March anno dom 1724.

The condition of the above obligation is such that if the above bound John Laws his heirs executors and adm'ns do well and truly pay or cause to be paid unto the above said Magdalene, Charles, Eliz, Priscilla, Ann, Mary, Joseph and Ephraim, Polk's orphans and their heirs executors adm's or assigns the full and just sum of one hundred and twenty two pounds eight shillings being the just balance due to them from their said father's estate when they shall attain full age according to act of Assembly then the above obligation to be void otherwise to remain in full force & virtue.

Sealed and delivered	*Charles Radcliffe*	*John Laws*
In presence of	*Thomas Haywood*	*Jn⁰ Jones*
		Wm Turpin

SOMERSET JUDICIAL RECORDS 1725-27

[MSA C 1774-28, Loc. 1/48/3/2]

JUNE COURT 1725

20 [15 June 1725] James Polk trial for contempt of one of the Justices
Note is made from previous court (16 March) that "William Stoughton *Esqr one of the Justices of the County afsd made Complaint that a certain James Polke of Somerset County Planter had abused him and said he did not do him Justice and thet he owed him a spite oe Ellse he would not have done as he did.*" The Sheriff was ordered to bring Polk to next court, where he now was.
Whereupon the said James Polk in his Own proper person appears and being demanded if he had any thing in his own defence to Offer &^c But the said James Polk had Nothing in his own defence to offer that was Materiall and the Matter of fact afd being proved upon him by the Oath of Severall Witnesses &^cWherefore it is Considered by the Court here thisfifteenth day of June ann Dom One thousand Seven hundred twenty five that the said James Polk be fined to his Lordship for the fact afd five hundred pounds of tobacco thereupon thesaid James Polk paid five pounds Curr.^t money in the Lieu of the said five hundred pounds of tobacco which was accepted of by the Court thereupon the Said James Polk is discharged he paying the Severall Officers their Fees

AUGUST COURT 1725

52 James Polk discharged from bond
Polk appears according to recognizance bond issued at March Court and is discharged.

NOVEMBER COURT 1726

185 David Polk brings negroe boys to have age adjudged
Tom and Attey, negro boys belonging to David Polk, are adjudged to be ages 12 and 10.

198 Thomas Hugg suit against James Smith
Continuation of case from August Court. Smith acknowledges debt and judgment is rendered that Hugg recover one young cow and calfe from Smith, and 285 lbs/tbco for costs and charges.

MARCH COURT 1726/7

251 Pricilla Polke, Executrix of William Polke, brings suit against Thomas Gordon
Claim is made against Gordon for a debt of £12/10 owed to the estate of her late husband William Polke (of Dorchester). The Sheriff, Francis Allen, having brought Gordon to Court asks the Justices to require special bail on Gordon to

assure payment should judgement be rendered agaist him. So ordered. John Caldwell and John Jones post bond and Gordon requests that his case be heard at next court.

252 William Robinson suit vs John and Henry Polk for negligent destruction of his property.
Levin Gale, attorney for Robinson, accuses John and Henry Polk of causing destruction of grasses, trees and five hundred "fence railes" by starting a fire which spread onto Robinson's property on 10 March 1725. (John and Henry were sons of James Polk, aged approximately 16 and 17 at the time.) The case was originally brought in June Court 1726 but had been continued several times. Jury called and finds for Robinson. Damages of £5 and 1356 lbs/tbco awarded.

SOMERSET JUDICIAL RECORDS 1727-30
[MSA C 1774-29, Loc. 1/48/3/3]

AUGUST COURT 1727

18 [15 August 1727] Elizabeth Roberts appears for recognizance entered before William Stoughton for her good behavior toward a certain Darby McDorman. He being present and having nothing to allege Elizabeth Roberts is discharged from her fee. Likewise John Roberts also appears and is discharged.

39 Priscilla Polk, admin. for William Polk vs. Thomas Jordan.
Settled out of court.

NOVEMBER COURT 1727

41 [21 November 1727] George Mills, aged seven months, made servant to James Polke
Isabella Mills, spinster, brings her son George Mills, alias Fitzgerald, into Court and binds him *unto James Polk until he arrives to the age of twenty one years, he being eight months old the fifth day of December next. The said George Mills to serve the said James Polke his heirs and assigns in all Lawfull Service as the said James Polke should imploy him in or about during the term afsd.* Polke to teach Mills to read, provide him food, lodging and clothing, and a two year old mare at the expiration of his service.

AUGUST COURT 1728

92 Commission on Friends Denyall, Kirkminster and Maidenhead
Commission to investigate the boundaries of Kirkminster, Friends Denyall and Maidenhedd requested by John Caldwell. Joseph Venables, Ebenezer Handy, Thomas Humphryes and John Roach appointed by Court on 22 September 1726. Affadavits taken from Thomas Hearn (aged about 40), John Lion (58), Robert Hastins (44), Thomas Hugg (45) and Phenix Hall (80) on 10 Ovtober 1726. All

attest to certain trees/stumps as being the first bounders of the various tracts.

115 [20 August 1728] *James Strawbridge, Negro Dick adjudged 10 years of age.*

118 Commission on tract Purgatory on Devils Island
Commission to investigate the bounds of Purgatory, on Devils Island, requested by Thomas Roe. Commission consisting of Levin Gale, George Dashiell, Robert Jones and John Laws appointed by Court on 23 April, 1726. Depositons taken from John Laws (aged about 50) and George Hutchins (57) at the house of Thomas Roe on Golden Quarter at Devils Island on 14 June 1726. Laws attested

That about twenty five years ago he was with Coll. Whittington atakeing up a piece of land for Thomas Roe at the Devill's Island and he carried the chain and when they had runn a piece of land called Graves End at the upper end of the said land there was a post set up in the marsh which he saw set down to the best of his remembrance and Thomas Roe's land called Purgatory went on the south east side of the land called Graves End and that the first bounder of the land called Purgatory was set at the point called Egles nest point and as Coll Whittington runn the length of the land called Graves End this deponent carried the chain above the land called Purgatory two or three times to try the breadth of it being the land then taken up and further saith not.

Similar statement taken from Hutchins.

131 David Polk, suit vs. William Robinson
Case settled out of Court.

NOVEMBER COUR 1728

135 [19 November 1728] David Polk appointed constable of Monie for ensuing year.

136 Petition by Edward Roberts for a commission to examine boundaries of tract Elletts (Elliots) Choice in Damn Quarter, part of which was leased by his father (Francis Roberts) to John Roberts, alias Grundy, *the bounders of which is much decayed and the evidences very antient and infirm.* Commission ordered: William Stoughton, Thomas Laws and John Laws, gentlemen of Somerset County.

AUGUST COURT 1729

204 [19 August 1729] Ages adjudged.
Dinah, a negro girl of Thomas Pullett, is judged to be age 7.
Tamer, a negro girl of David Polk, is judged to be age 10.

204 Henry Freakes indenture to Johanna Hugg

Henry Freakes son of Henry Freakes is bound by the court to Johanna Hugg until he arrive at the age of 21 years he being seven years of age the 4th day of April last, the said Henry Freaks to serve the said Johanna Hugg in all such lawful service she should employ him in or about the full term of time afsd. In consideration of which said service the said Johanna Hugg promises to learn the said Henry Freaks during his servitude the trade art or mastery of a weaver to read in the bible and find and provide for her said servant meat drink washing lodging and clothing mete for such a servant to have and weare. Whereupon it is ordered by the court that the aforesaid Johanna Hugg give recognisance for complying with the covenants afsd.

Bond of £20 sterling required against goods, chattels, lands and tenements of Johanna Hugg with George Burton her security

MARCH COURT 1729/30

233 [17 March 1729/30] William Polk appointed to Grand Jury

JUNE COURT 1730

259 [16 June 1730] Commission on Elliots Choice
Petition of Edward Roberts for court to appoint persons to examine evidence and take depositions concerning bounders of Elliotts Choice. Petition granted; Thomas Gillis, Henry Ballard, Levin Rigsby, appointed.

SOMERSET JUDICIAL RECORDS 1730-33
[MSA C1774-30, Loc. 1/48/3/4]

AUGUST COURT 1730

2 [18 August 1730]   Petition of Charles Williams to be tax free
Charles Williams (now husband to Margaret Polk) of Damn Quarter states that he is now 80 years old and has lived and paid taxes in Monie Hundred for 60 years. He is "now being past my labour and no longer can work and having no servants to labour for me" requests that he be relieved of paying the county levy. Court rules that he "for the future be tax free."

8 [18 August 1730]   Commission to enquiry on boundaries of Elliotts Choice.
Petition by Edward Roberts to establish a commission granted. Robert King, Thomas Gillis, Henry Ballard and Lewis Rigsby appointed, 6 August 1730.
7 August 1730 depositions taken from Ephrain Wilson, aged 64 years or thereabouts; Capt. John Tunstall, 54; Mr. Thomas Laws, 41 years; William Polk, aged 58 years; Charles Williams, 80 years; Margaret Williams, 60 years; Owen Day, 40 years; Joseph Polk, 41 years; Priscilla Quartermus, 36 years; Henry Ballard, 30 years.

[Note—this deposition is highly informative about first generation offspring of Robert and Magdalen Polk. William and Joseph Polk were their second and seventh sons; Margaret Williams was their first daughter and the widow of Thomas Pollett; Charles Williams was Margaret's third husband and also father-in-law to Ephraim and James Polk; Priscilla Quatermus was daughter of Francis and Ann Polk Roberts and was previously married to her cousin William Polk, son of John Polk, oldest son of Robert and Magdalen.]

Deposition of Ephraim Wilson states that he was on an earlier commission and at that time James Polk declared that he had been employed by Francis Roberts to maul some logs and had felled a pine that Roberts said was the first bounder of Elliotts Choice and the stump of that tree was now located 250 yards south from the dwelling place of Francis Roberts;

Thomas Laws states that he saw Samuel Jones set up a marked post at a pine stump near a marsh side about 250 yards from house of Edward Roberts.

Mr. William Polk aged about fifty eight years or thereabouts being sworn on the Holy Evangelists of Almighty God deposeth and saith that at the time Francis Roberts was married to his sister that the deponent with the said Roberts and severall others was coming from his fathers to a fort house which stood on a tract of land called Elliotts Choice belonging to the said Roberts and this deponent further saith that the afsd Roberts pointing to a large pine which stood by the marsh side about one hundred and fifty yards from the fort house and said that the pine was the first bounder of Elliotts Choice and further saith not.

William [W] Polk

Margaret Williams aged sixty years or thereabouts being sworn on the Holy Evangelists of Almighty God deposeth and saith that about nine years ago the Land Commissioners was about a tract of land called Elliotts Choice and that she the deponent was present and John Roberts said that the pine stump which the deponent now stands by was not the bounder of Elliotts Choice but that it was further down but Richard Wallis, Sen said this (was) the bounder. Likewise said John White and my husband Charles Williams and further saith not.

Margaret [M]Williams.

Joseph Polk aged about forty one years or thereabouts being sworn on the Holy Evangelists of Almighty God deposeth and saith that about twenty five years agoe he was in a peach orchard in company with one John Hillman and that the said Hillman told the deponent he would show him the bounder of Elliotts Choice as Samuel Jones told him and they went to a pine stump standing near a marsh side about two hundred and fifty yards from the dwelling home of Francis Roberts and about South from the said house. The deponent further saith that the said Hillman told him that a cedar post standing by the said stump was put up by Samuel Jones and the said Jones told the said Hillman that it was first bounder of Elliotts Choice and that Samuel Jones took severall young people

328

and told them that the afsd bounder was the first bounder of Elliotts Choice. The deponent saith that John Roberts interrupted James Polk on his oath and then Richard Wallis Sen standing by said that John Roberts was a liar for the afsd pine stump was the first bounder of Elliotts Choice. Likewise John White said John Roberts was a rogue for the pine stump aforesaid was the first bounder of Elliotts Choice and further saith not. Joseph Polk.

Priscilla Quartermus aged thirty six years being sworn on the Holy Evangelists of Almighty God deposeth and saith that Samuel Jones came to her mother Ann Roberts and said I am come to the bounder of Elliotts Choice and that the said Jones went to a pine stump where the deponent now sits near the side of a marsh about two hundred and fifty yards from the dwelling house of Edward Roberts and about South from the said house with the deponent and severall others and there set up a post at the root of the said stump and that Samuel Jones told them that the stump afsd was the first bounder of Elliotts Choice and the deponent further saith that John White Sen had laid his hand on the stump aforesaid and said it was the first bounder of Elliotts Choice and Richard Wallis Sen said father White it is, in the presence of the deponent she being then at the afsd stump and further saith not. Priscilla Quartermus.

Henry Ballard aged thirty years or thereabouts being sworn on the Holy Evangelists of Almighty God saith that he was in Company with the Land Commissioners and was on a tract of land called Elliotts Choice belonging to Edward Roberts which was Maj Charles Ballard, Capt John Tunstall, Mr. Ephraim Wilson and Mr. John Caldwell and that they went to a pine stump standing near a marsh side about two hundred and fifty yards South from the house of Edward Roberts where he then lived and there examined James Poalke on his oath and he said he was employed by Francis Roberts to maule some logs and that he went to to the aforesaid place where the afsd mentioned stump now is and that he went to falling some logg lumber and sometime after Francis Roberts came to the said James Polke and told him he had fell the bounder of Elliotts Choice and that James Polk asked him whether it was the first bounder of Elliotts Choice and that Roberts said it was and there was Patrick Quatermus and some others as declared near the same relating to the same bounder and that the aforesaid Commissioners allowed that to be the bounder of Elliotts Choice and further the said Deponent saith that he new of no other bounder af Elliotts Choice and further saith not.

    Henry Ballard

AUGUST COURT 1731

107 *Bek a negro boy of William Polk is adjudged to be of age 10 years.*

125 James Polke and David Polk appointed to Grand Jury

JUNE COURT 1732

186 *James Polk, Order Orphans Jury*

186 James Polk, appointed on Grand Jury

191 *James Polk (Polike) appears upon his recognisance and was thereupon by the court discharged*

AUGUST COURT 1732

221 [15 August 1732]
Amey, a negro girl of William Polk, is adjudged by the Court to the age of ten years.

233 Janes Polk, juror
Henry Fitzwaters suit against Jos. Caldwell, John Dennis and Isaac Fleming for seizing three mares, his goods and chattels without cause, and mistreating the mares. Fitzwaters claims 10 pounds in damages. Jury denies his claim.

239 David Polk, juror; trial over bet on horse race
Benjamin Holland suit against Joshua Caldwell for failure to pay off a bet on a horse race. Race was between a bay horse belonging to Holland and a gray belonging to James Strawbridge, over a quarter mile track near at race grounds near the Courthouse on 17 November 1731, Holland betting 2000 lbs/tbco agains 2500 by Caldwell. The race was held and Caldwell's horse won but Caldwell was never paid. Jury of twelve, including David Polk (Polek), was called and the case argued. Jury rules that Caldwell had not assumed the liability as claimed. Holland to pay costs for his false clamor.

252 James Polk payment for cost of witnesses at his trial
James Polk ordered to pay cost of attendance for various witnesses in his loosing case against William Gray; Allen Gray, Sen. and George Benston, 90 lbs/tbco each for 3 days attendance each; Patrick Daley and John Denston 60 lbs each for 2 days attendance; James Pope, William Polk (Polek), Allen Gray, Jr. and David Polk (Polek) 120 lbs each for 4 days attendance.

NOVEMBER COURT 1732

256 [21 November 1732] David Polk on Grand Jury

282   Case against Richard Driskill, David Polk, juror
Richard Driskill is accused of assault and battery on James Shirly. Driskill pleads not guilty and jury of 12 is called, including David Polk. When case is heard the prosecutor also accuses Driskill of robbery against one of the jurors. Trial is suspended and jurors dismissed.

DORCHESTER JUDGEMENTS 1733-34
[MSA C704-3, Loc. 1-4-3-44]

321 Award to Robert Polk
Robt. Polk vs. Thomas Williams et al. Dorchester County. You Thomas Williams, Charles Goldsborough and Joseph Allford do confess judgement to Robert Polk for two hundred and four pounds of tobacco and two shillings and six pence current money of your goods and chattles lands and tenements to be made and conveyed in case the said Thomas Wiliams do not pay & satisfy unto the said Robert Polk the said two hundred and four pounds of tobacco and two shillings and six pence current money with the additional cost thereon on or before the tenth day of February next. Taken before me the 11th day of May 1734.

To the clerk of Dorchester County.   *Peter Taylor*

SOMERSET JUDICIAL RECORDS 1733-35
[MSA C 1774-31, Loc. 1/48/3/5]

JUNE COURT 1733

35 [19 June 1733] Suit against James Polk for shooting dog
William Gray, Pltf, seeks 20 shillings damages against Polk shooting his dog; Thomas Bluett is attny for Gray; Polk states that shooting was justified because dog had frequently worried Polk's horse, biting at it in the meadow, and Gray had been frequently warned; Francis Allen attny for Polk; judgement rendered for Polk. Gray assessed 887 lbs tbco for his false clamor.

40 David Polk and Henry Ballard ordered to lay out a road between William Gray's and Thomas Brown's plantation in the pocosons.

AUGUST COURT 1733

54 David Polk's negro boy Peter is judged to be 9 years of age.

56 Trial of Edward Dickerson, David Polk on jury
Edmund Dickerson accused of assault on "a certain Hannah Dickerson" on 1 June 1733. No relationship given. Jury summoned, which includes David Polk. Dickerson founld guilty, fined five pounds of tobacco.

83 David Polk foreman of Grand Jury

MARCH COURT 1733/4

110 [19 March 1733/4] James Polk and Thomas Pollitt on Grand Jury

120 Report by David Polk and Henry Ballard about road installation

Attestation by David Polk and Henry Ballard that they had laid out a road for the inhabitants to the road of Manokin, per direction of Court; beginning at Brereton's Savannah to NW side of Thomas Pollett's plantation, and of Robert Wilson and William Heath's and down the branch side by Abraham Heath's to the fork of river; likewise have opened road between William Gray's and Thomas Brown's plantation. 7 March 1733/4.

138 Court appoints various persons as overseers of different sections of road for the county. Robert Jones is overseer of roads from Joseph Polk's to the head of Little Manny (Monie) and from Capt. Jones to the new Church and from said road of Little Manny to William Jones on Goose Creek and from Little Creek to the head of Phebuses Creek and from William Staughton's to the South end of John Shores' plantation. Thomas Laws is overseer of roads from the thorofare to Joseph Polk's and from Richard Wallace's to the main road. Other appointees as well.

JUNE COURT 1734

150 [18 June 1734] Presentment against Mary Polk

Grand Jury called and present charge against Mary Polk. No specific charge mentioned. Case to be heard at next court.

171 David Polk on Jury, adultery trial

Case was brought against Moses Chaille, Jun., mariner, for adultery, in earlier court, August 1734. Accused and found guilty for begetting a child by Ann More, spinster. Found guilty in a trial with Jury. David Polk one of the Jurors. Final judgement was postponed by Justices several times until present court at which he is fined £3.

AUGUST COURT 1734

186 Report of land commission on Henry Dorman's tract Deep

James Strawbridge and Thomas Brown report on investigation into the bounders of tract Deep at request of Henry Dorman, Jr. Commission issued on 3 May 1734. Depositions taken on 14 May from William Polk, aged 61, Henry Dorman, Sen. aged 61, Peter Fischjarrell, aged 60, Mathew Dorman, aged 56, Abraham Heath, aged 49.

SOMERSET JUDICIAL RECORDS 1735-37
[MSA C 1774-32, Loc. 1/48/3/6]

NOVEMBER COURT 1735

85 [18 November 1735] David and Charles Polk on Grand Jury
Start of November session. Grand Jury impanelled: Samuel Wilson, Walter
Darby, John Trehorne, Robert Givan, Solomon Long, David Polk, John
Schockley, James Strawbridge, Charles Polk, Lewis Disharoon, John Covington,
Philip Selby, William Turpin, Jun., William Cord, Joseph Gray, Isaac Boston,
and John Frich.

**122 [18 November 1735]   John Polk fined for not burning tobacco (among
many others)**
*John Polke being summoned to appear at this Court for not burning of Tobacco
according to the act of assembly in such cases made & provided & foreasmuch
as it doth not appear to the Court here that the said John Polke hath nothing to
object wherefore he hath not burned the tobco afsd Therefore the said John
Polke is fined twenty shillings current money by occasion of the premises afsd*
~~~

NOVEMBER COURT 1736

277 [16 November 1736] David Polk, juror, debt case
Robert McFarling (McFarline) suit against Charles Ramsay; Jury finds for
McFarling

281 David Polk, juror, debt case
Tabitha Parker suit against James McDonald; Jury finds for Parker.

281 David Polk, juror, debt case
Thomas Fletcher suit aginst Abraham Mannering; Jury finds for Fletcher.

300 William Polk, plaintiff, debt case
Suit against William Wye settled out of Court

SOMERSET JUDICIAL RECORDS 1737-38
[MSA C 1774-33, Loc. 1/48/3/7]

JUNE COURT 1737

46 William Polk appointed to Orphans Jury

48 William Polk appointed to Grand Jury

88 Prize for best linen produced in county
Ordered by the Court that James Strawbridge be allowed and have an order on

the Sheriffe of Somerset County for four pounds current money of Maryland he producing here in Court the second best piece of linnen according to act of assembly in such case made and provided (Mary Slingo produced the "first best" piece—£5; Capt Edmund Round took 3rd—£3)
[Note—James Strawbridge was married to Jean Polk, daughter of William Polk, son of Robert and Magdalen Polk]

NOVEMBER COURT 1737

131 Ages of slaves adjudged
Cato, negro boy of David Polk adjudged to be 13
Judy, negro girl of James Polk adjudged to be 15
Phillis, negro girl of James Polk adjudged to be 10
Pleasant, negro girl of William Polk adjudged to be 16

180 James Polk on jury
Trial of James Duffy for stealing.

MARCH COURT 1737/8

191 James Owens chooses guardian
James Owens, son of Samuel Owens, deceased, being above age 14 chooses William Owens as his guardian; court confirms and orders Emmanuel Manlove to deliver said James to William with all his estate, real and personal. William Owens, with James Strawbridge and George Benston, planters of Somerset, pledge bond of £100 to James Strawbridge to deliver all estate both real and personal peaceably and quietly whenever the same should be legally required. [Samuel Owens was a stepson of William Polk.]

261 Joseph Polk, appointed to orphans jury

261 Joseph Polk, appointed to grand jury

262 Nero, a negro boy of Charles Polk, adjudged 12 years of age.

273 James Hugg orphan bond

SOMERSET JUDICIAL RECORDS 1738-1740
[MSA C 1774-34, Loc. 1/48/3/8]

13 James Polk, Juror, criminal case

184 William Polk land deposition

194 James Polk, Juror, criminal case

NOVEMBER COURT 1739

202 Commission on Goldsmiths Delight (100 acres)
Commissioners: John Gray, Henry Ballard and William Jones.

Deposition of William Polk, age about 66. A white oak standing at the south side of a branch called Smith's Branch, about 40 yards from the said branch or thereabouts and about eighty yards from a road leading from William Polk's down Manokin to King's Bridge, was the first beginning of Goldsmiths Delight. Goldsmith had the first land taken out of tract Illchester (Elchester) for which the afsd. tree was the first bounder.

Deposition of John Goldsmith, carpenter, age about 50. Mentions father (unnamed) and William Heath, both agreeing with above account. Mentions himself as a boy in company of his father and Jeremiah Harris seeing a white gum notched with 16 notches. His father said that was the bounder between himself and William Knox, years later affirmed by William Hath [Heath], who specified the tree as standing in a swamp at or about a half mile distance from John Gray's dwelling house.

206 James Polk, Juror, criminal case

218 James Polk, Juror, debt case

220 James Polk, Juror, debt case
Nathaniel Waller, Jr. of Stepney Parish, planter v. John Coulbourne, planter. Waller claimed earlier false arrest and indictment for assault upon Coulbourn. Jury trial, in which Waller was deemed guilty of "false clamour" and obliged to pay Coulbourn 1029 lbs/tbco for costs.

238 David Polk, Juror, criminal case

258 David Polk, Juror, debt case

285 David Polk, Juror, debt case

AUGUST COURT 1740

299 David Polk and James appointed overseers of the roads for Manokin Hundred
David appointed to take place of Thomas Gilliss; to have use of all the male taxable laborers at the plantation of William Alexander, Capt. Thomas Gilliss, James Pope and Thomas Layfield. James Polk appointed in place of George Benston for the ensuing year.

SOMERSET JUDICIAL RECORDS 1740-1742
[MSA C 1774-35, Loc. 1/48/3/9]

AUGUST COURT 1740 (continued)
17 Orphans of William Polk suit against James Quatermus
Jane Polk, John Polk and Ann Polk represented by attorney Robert Jenkins
Henry vs. James Quatermus of Somerset, planter, represented by Francis Allen.
Debt of £15 from 1 May 1738. Dispute was referred to arbitrators Robert King
and Nehemiah King, who found for plaintiffs.
[Note: Plaintiffs are the orphans of William Polk of Dorchester (son of John
Polk), who had died in 1727. William's widow Priscilla (Roberts) had remarried
to Patrick Quatermus.]

99 Ann Venables, an orphan above 14, chooses David Polk, planter, as her
guardian, which is approved by the court. Thomas Gilliss and David Wilson are
sureties for £100.

SOMERSET JUDICIAL RECORDS 1742-44
[MSA C 1774-36, Loc. 1/48/3/10]

NOVEMBER COURT 1742

27 [16 November 1742]
John Woolford and Thomas Brown, petition to modify road from Capt.
Ballard's plantation to the head of St. Peter's Creek and the road to Monie Creek
which runs through both their lands. They have laid a new road which would
have advantages for the public in general. Col. George Dashiell and James Polk
ordered by the Court to view the roads. Following their report, the petitioners
are ordered to turn the road from the head of Westlock's Gutt to the head of
Goose Creek, etc. George Dashiell and George Irving to view the result and
Capt. Henry Ballard named overseer of the new road and to have all the laborers
from Goose Creek upward.

75   Robert Harris and Joseph Riggen petition. They complain that Teague
Riggen and William Fleming have joined their fences and felled trees so as to
close the road to the petitioners' land to the Courthouse Landing, long in use.
The respondents level a similar complaint against the petitioners, etc., for
prejudicial stoppage of useful passage, etc. Ordered that John Gray and James
Polk view the situation and report back, etc. Subsequently an extensive finding
and order was issued on the approved area routes.

83 Commission on Hoggs Down; Thomas Goslee complaint vs. David Polk
Commission hearing and affidavits on Hoggs Down, requested by Thomas
Goslee [Goslin], complaining of encroachment by David Polk, defendant.
Comm.: Henry Ballard, Day Scott, William Jones (Monie) and Purnall Johnson.

336

(Note – this hearing was the basis for David Polk's expansion of his tract Fortune into a much larger tract which was later resurveyed into his son William Polk's tract, White Hall. See Chapter 5.)

Deposition of Edward Sherman [Shirman], age ca 74. Fifty years before he and Richard Kimball were "a horse hunting" at Southern's bridge at the head of Southern's Creek. *On behalf of complainant.*
Commission interpolation: said creek makes out of Wicomico River south of now dwelling plantation of John Palint; the bridge is where the main road goes by where Jonathan Bailey [Baly] formerly lived, called Come by Chance, up to Capt. Handy's ferry.

Deposition of George Bailey [Baly], age ca 80. About 50 yrs before he was told by Richard Stevens, "an old stander or liver" *[resident of long standing]* in the neighborhood, that the bridge was called as said above. *On behalf of complainant.*

Deposition of John Christopher, age ca 72. Affirms above, as told him by his father and Robert Crouch, John Records [Riccords], et al., (many old standers) when he was a boy. Southern's plantation and hands were on south side of mouth of the said creek, now owned by heirs of John Venables. Asked by David Polk, defendant, if there was ever a name for the gut between Bluitt's and Jacob Cordray, he responded in the negative. *On behalf of complainant.*

Deposition of Sarah Honging, age ca 61. When 12, her parents removed from Bennett's Neck to Wicomico river side. Going back and forth during the move, she once rode behind Richard Stevens, who identified the bridge named above, near Jonathan Bailey's plantation. *On behalf of complainant.*
But upon questioning by defendant David Polk *in re* Manlift's [prob. Manlove's] Branch in the area, she recalls 15 or 16 yrs before being with Alexander Carlisle, John McClester and Thomas Bashaw [Beshaw], who named such a branch out of the Wicomico above where Jacob Cordray lives and where said Carlisle did live. *On behalf of defendant.*

Deposition of Sarah Hardy, age ca 56. Affirms depositions supporting complainant above. Mentions her aunt Mary Jarrot, an old woman when the deponent was small. *On behalf of complainant.*

Deposition of George Bailey, *again.* He was told, he thinks, by Richard Jarrot [evidently a cousin], of bounders in neighborhood of Hoggs Down. Details given. *On behalf of complainant and defendant.*

Deposition of Robert Hardy, age ca 46. Sometime after he was married to his last wife, "which is about six years ago", he was hog hunting and came across what he believed was a marked bounder tree, later mentioning it and visiting again with Thomas Goslee and Samuel Bordman (the latter now deceased).

Bordman advised it was a bounder of his uncle Thomas Bashaw. *On behalf of complainant.*

Deposition of Graves Bashaw [Beshaw], age ca 25. Mentions living with his aunt Bordman about 8 yrs before, and discussions with Samuel Bordman (now deceased) *in re* bounders. *On behalf of complainant.*

Deposition of Bridget Davis, age ca 29. About 13 yrs before she lived with her aunt Mary Jarrot. At that time an Ann Davis visited, complaining of sore eyes, for which her aunt recommended "a spring in Southern's Gut as good as the boyling springs at Barron Creek for sore eyes", then visited by Ann Davis and her aunt. Thomas Bashaw's land mentioned near the said gut. *On behalf of defendant.*

Deposition of Col. George Dashiell, age ca 50. About 20 yrs before he was laying out land for Francis Bordman (now deceased), believed by deponent to be part of Hoggs Down. Mentions NW line dividing from William Davis land. *On behalf of complainant.*

Deposition of William Sherman [Shirman], age ca 50. About 29 yrs before he was fishing with Graves Jarrot, who mentioned that someone had encouraged Mr. Truman to run out his land "and take some of my orchard, but I will make them know better [then describing bounders]". Lands of Thomas Winder and Jacob Cordray mentioned. *On behalf of defendant.*

Deposition of James Burn, age ca 60. The second year after he came in the county (which was 23 yrs before next Christmas) he was making tobacco hills near a spring by a place called Inglish Grass. While drinking at the spring, Graves Jarrot came by from fishing with a string of fish, and invited him to talk, saying "Your master will not be angry at your being with me". Jarrot said he "would lay him a bottle of rum or a gallon of sider" if he knew the name of the gut there. Deponent knew it as Old House Gut, but Jarrot called it Southern's Gut. *On behalf of defendant.*
Commission interpolation: The spring is at head of the gut mentioned by William Sherman.

Deposition of William Moor, age ca 53. Thirty-three yrs before he lived with Thomas Bashaw for nine months. He heard Thomas and his brother Andrew Bashaw say their uncle Graves Jarrot's land began at mouth of the gut mentioned by William Sherman and James Burn above. He knew both names, Old House Gut and Southern's Gut, to apply to the same stream. *On behalf of defendant.*

Deposition of Sarah Jackson, age ca 56. For 36 yrs she has known the name Southern's Gutt, from her mother and John Winder and, perhaps Francis Bordman, call it by both names. *On behalf of defendant.*

Deposition of Ann Cordray, age ca 45. Heard her former husband Thomas Bashaw call the gut Southern's Gut, and mentions his uncle Graves Jarrot. *On behalf of defendant.*

Deposition of Katherine Venables, age ca 44. When a small girl her father Robert Truman, old Nicholas Jones and his wife called Southern's Gut Old House Gut, and her father called the creek below that one Cutamatico. *On behalf of defendant.*

Deposition of George Goddard [Gothard], age ca 63. When he was a boy Graves Jarrot told his father that his land began at the mouth of Southern's Gut. This gut was between John Bluitt's and William Venables' land. *On behalf of complainant.*

Deposition of John Goddard, age ca 52. Affirms location of Southern's Bridge. *On behalf of complainant.*

Deposition of Christopher Dowdle, age ca 47. About 20 yrs before he was servant to Graves Jarrot, who showed him a patent and other papers naming Southern's Gut, which the deponent questioned, knowing it as Old House Gut, between his master and Thomas Bashaw. *On behalf of defendant.*

Deposition of William Oshehanah, age ca 63. About 40 yrs before he was servant to Richard Jarrot, at which time George Bailey came and settled on land near Southern's Gut. Describes settling boundary because of an issue involving cutting of trees. Names Thomas Bashaw, John Laten, both since deceased, mentions adjoining tract of Ephraim Wilson. *On behalf of complainant.*

Deposition of Sarah Hardy, *again*. Generally affirms many details, mentions going to church with her husband and her aunt Mary Jarrot. *On behalf of complainant.*

Deposition of Elizabeth Hill, age ca 60. She never knew of any other than Southern's Gut between Graves Jarrot and William Venables, her first knowledge from old John Christopher and old Robert Crouch. *On behalf of complainant.*

94 Thomas Ingram case against Thomas Hacker, planter. On 1 Jan 1742 the parties had agreed to 1000 lbs. of pork to be delivered by defendant. Submitted to arbitration by John Handy and James Polk, who determined that the defendant should make good on commitment and assume costs.

118 Samuel Jones appointed overseer of the roads from Laws Thoroughfare to Joseph Polk's and from thence to the head of Little Creek.

124 *Ordered that a road be cleared from the west side of Dividing Creek from where Denston's Bridges over the creek are, to the main road from Princess Ann Town to Dividing Creek, said road to be cleared on the west side of James Polk's plantation; to be cleared as formerly laid out by Capt. James Martin and Capt. David Wilson. Teague Riggen to be overseer of the same new road from Dividing Creek to the bridges, to James Pope's, and James Polk to be overseer and begin where Riggen leaves off by Pope's, and to clear along the west side of his plantation, with the main road that leads from Princess Ann Town to Dividing Creek.*

SOMERSET LAND RECORDS, LIBER 21 (X), 1744
[MSA C 1778-39, Loc. 1/45-1-24],

161 *Barbados. By this publick act of protest be it made known and manifest unto all men that on the 11th day of the gale(?) hereof before me Richard Husbands, Esq, Deputy Secretary and Notary Publick of this Island personally came and appeared George McChester Master or Commander of the Scow Flying Fish now riding at anchor in Carlisle Bay in the said island William McChester mate and Thomas Lloyd mariner both also belonging to the said vesell who being duly sworn on the Holy Evangelists of Almighty God requested me the said notary to make or draw a protest on their voyage from Virginia bound for this Island on the second day of this instant being in the Latt 35°00' N and Long 69°26' W or thereabouts met with violent hard gales of wind at NW and high seas which obliged them to scud before it under their foresail in which time the sea made severall breeches over the vesell and caused her to leak in her upper works which obliged these appearers to keep both pumps at work for twenty eight hours to free her and these appearers say that by means of the violent hard gales and high seas afs'd they are apprehensive the cargo may be damaged wherefore I, the said notary, at the instance and request afsd did even as I do by these presents publickly and solemnly protest as well against the violent hard hard gales of wind and high seas afsd as against all persons concerned for all costs losses damages hurts detriments prejudices and inconveniencys whatsoever arising to these appearers or any others with them concerned for or by reason or means of the accidents and misfortunes herein before set forth.*

George McChester   *William McChester*

    Thomas Lawyd

In faith and testimony whereof I the said notary have hereunto set my hand and seal of office this twenty fourth day of December 1744

Richard Husbands   *D Sectry*

and Notary Publick

SOMERSETJUDICIAL RECORDS 1745-46
[MSA C 1774-37, Loc. 1/48/3/11]

NOVEMBER COURT 1745

76 [19 November 1745] Nicholas Evans Collier, petition for commission on tract Riceland; David Polk, Robert Givans [Givan], Joseph Cottman, Samuel Fluellin appointed commissioners.

MARCH COURT 1745/6

97 [20 Mar 1745/6] Orphans of John Robinson
Joseph Cottman, James Polk and Patrick Stewart all bound to Mary and John Roberson, orphans of John Robinson (Roberson), decd. for £202/13/01

SOMERSET JUDICIAL RECORDS 1746-47
[MSA C 1774-38, Loc. 1/48/3/12]

AUGUST COURT 1746

163 [19 August 1746] Construction of holding room in brick prison
The Justices agree with Capt. Henry BALLARD to make one Room in the Brick prison at Princess Ann Town, *strong, good and Substantially, by Lineing the Same Room with good white oak Timber, or Scanthing workman Like, Sufficient to keep all Sorts of prisoners that should be Committed to the Custody of the Sheriffe ..., without danger of Escape...*Ballard asked to produce a reasonable estimate for construction thereof at November court; will be authorized to proceed, for allowance in the County Levy.

MARCH COURT 1746/7

224 [17 March 1746/7] Court convenes. John Polk on Grand Jury

229 William Kenigan, orphan, age 10 in May 1746, bound of his own free consent to Joshua Turpin, joiner, as shop joiner. David Polk, planter, surety for £20 bond.

230 James Polk appointed **overseer of the roads** in stead of William Arbuth for the ensuing year.

238 Orphans bond on John Taylor, sureties David Polk and John Huffington [Hoffington]; bound to Betty Taylor, William Taylor, George Taylor, Zettrell Taylor and Levin Taylor, orphans of Abraham Taylor, dec'd., for £270/3/9, until they shall arrive to full age.

253 Lost still; David Polk on Jury

Capell King brings suit against William Dashiell, Jun., for recovery of a still, pewter worm and still tub values at £65, "casually lost," and now in possession of Dashiell who refuses to return. Dashiell contests and Jury is called; David Polk is one of twelve members. They find Dashiell guilty and liable for £20. Justices add 1270 lbs/tbco in damages.

SOMERSET JUDICIAL RECORDS 1747-49
MSA C 1774-39, Loc. 1/48/3/13]

NOVEMBER COURT 1747

22 [18 August 1747] Rev. Charles Tennant, Presbyterian, takes oath as Minister; requests house of James Polk be used for services.
*Whereas the Reverend Mr. Charles Tennant, a **presbiterian Minister**, personally appeared here in his Lordship's, the Right Honourable the Lord Proprietary of Maryland, his County Court of Somerset, and did then and there before his said Lordship's Justices, in court individually sitting, take the Oaths appointed by an Act of parliament made in the first year of King William and Queen Mary, and repeated the declaration, directed by an act of parliament made in the thirtyeth year of Charles the Second, and subscribed the same, and declared his approbation to the Articles of faith in the Church of England, and subscribed to the same (except those articles and part of an article as is disallowed of by such discenting ministers).*
"I desire that you will register the Severall places within mentioned for publick Service and preaching of the Gosple of Jesus Christ, the places are as followeth: at the meeting house at Rockawakin on the head of Wickamoco River, and at the meeting house at Olliphant's, and also at Broad Creek Bridge, and also at the dwelling house of Joshua Caldwell, and also at Wilson Rider's, and also at the house of James Polk's in Princess Ann Town on his Lot No. 2. Sep 23rd 1747."
Charles Tennant
(Note – Rev. Tenant was the son of the Rev. William Tenant, founder of the "log college" in Neshaminy NJ, considered a predecessor of Princeton University.)

29 William Vaughan, orphan
Vaughan, aged 14, of his own free will is bound to Joshua Turpin, joiner, as shop joiner. James Polk is surety, bond of £60.

MARCH COURT 1747/8

46 [15 March 1747] Court convened, David Polk (Polke) on Grand Jury
Note – David Polk appears frequently on grand jury, usually as foreman, in the 1747-49 judicial records. See pp 51, 83, 157, 192, 195, 242, 244. In 1770 he was appointed an Attorney of the Court – see 1769-72 Judicials, p.167.)

78 [20 September 1746] Estate of William Vaughan
Various estates mentioned including that of William Vaughan dated 20 Sep
1746, and evaluated at £83/8/7. John Caldwell and wife Mary, acting executrix.
Estate provides for daughters Sarah Polk, Eliz. Bacon; mentions five others, *all
his children whose names are unknown to this Office.*

79 Payment for court attendance
*Ordered that James Pope recover from Thomas Toadvine for evidence v.
Thomas Pullet.*
*Ordered that David Polk recover from Thomas Pullet for evidence v. Thomas
Toadvine.*

JUNE COURT 1748

102 Suit against William Venables
David Wilson, Samuel Wilson, Thomas Brown, John Gray, George Irving,
James Polk and David Polk bring suit against. William Venables for debt of £28.
Venables does not appear and is defaulted for 336 lbs/tbco plus 22 lbs for costs.

AUGUST COURT 1748

110 [16 August 1748] John Goslee petition for commission on Goslins Lott;
George Dashiell, Day Scott, David Polk and William Dashiell appointed
commissioners

125 David Polk v. John White, merchant. Case discontinued; Polk to pay costs.

NOVEMBER COURT 1748

159 Mary Caldwell, Jethro Vaughan, Ephraim Vaughan bound to Sarah Polk,
Elizabeth Bacon, Levin Vaughan, William Vaughan, Mary Vaughan and
Charles Vaughan, orphans of William Vaughan, decd. Security of £99/15/4.
{Note – Sarah (Vaughan) Polk was wife of John Polk of Little Creek.)

182 David Polk awarded 240 lbs tobacco for attendance at Court and providing
testimony in case of James Weatherly vs. Moses Alexander.

JUNE COURT 1749

269 John White v. Jane (Polk) Strawbridge £4.16.7. Four entire pages devoted
to this, including a reckoning of all the pins and thimbles it took to make
£4.16.7.

276 James Polk, Benjamin Labrius, Jane Waltom recover from Jane
Strawbridge for evidence v. John White.

281 Allen Gray petition for tax-free status for ancient slave Hannah.

283 Jane Strawbridge petition for boundaries of Woolver. Nehemiah King, Thomas Jones, Spencer Hack, Solomon Long named to commission.

DORCHESTER TOBACCO INSPECTION RECORDS 1748-1775
[MSA C707-1, Loc. 1/4/3/39]

Note: The Dorchester Tobacco Inspection Records commenced in 1748 with the passage of "An Act of Assembly for Amending the Staple of Tobacco for Preventing Frauds in his Maiestyes Customs and for the Limitation of Oficers Fees". This required that all tobacco be properly inspected and registered in licensed storage facilities. These records appear in a single volume now kept in the Maryland Archives. The first entries appearing in the records are concerned with the location, construction and cost of the warehouses. There were four of these set up in in Dorchester County, at Ennalls Ferry, Hunting Creek at Nanticoke, Mevell's, and White and Plimouth's. The remainder of the volume consists of the recording of bonds made by the Inspectors and their sureties to properly execute their duties as well as periodic records of inventories at the various storage facilities. Robert Polk of Dorchester (son of John Polk, son of Robert Polk the immigrant) appeared frequently in these records as a witness or surety. Last entry was recorded in 1768. Following is a typical entry in which bond is made on Robert Polk and Thomas Andrew.

24 November 1768. Dorchester County. Know all men by these presents that we Thomas Andrew and Robert Polk of Dorchester County gentlemen are held and firmly bound unto the right honorable the Lord Proprietor of Maryland in the full and just sum of forty eight thousand pounds of tobacco to be paid to the Lord Proprietor his heirs and successors to which payment to be well and truly made and done we bind ourselves our heirs, executors and administrators joyntly and severally in the whole and for the whole by these presents sealed with our seals and dated this twenty fourth day of November Anno Domini 1767—The condition of the above is such that the above named Thomas Andrew shall diligently and carefully view and examine all tobacco brought to the inspection house at N.W. Fork Bridge where he is appointed inspector and all other tobacco which he shall be called upon to inspect and view and shall not receive any tobacco that is not sound well conditioned and merchantable and clear of trash nor receive pass or stamp any tobacco or hogshead cask or case of tobacco prohibited by an Act of Assembly entitled An Act of Assembly for Amending the Staple of Tobacco for Preventing frauds in his Maiesttyes Customs and for Limitation of Oficers fees and shall well and truly and faithfully discharge his Duty in the office of an Inspector according to the Directions of the said Act then the above obligation to be void and of no effect else of force.

> *Sealed and delivered in presence of us*
> *Wm. Ennalls*   *Thomas*
> *Andrew*   *(Seal)*
> *Thomas White*   *Robert*
> *Polk*   *(Seal)*

SOMERSET JUDICIAL RECORDS 1749-51
[MSA C 1774-40, Loc. 1/48/3/14]

MARCH COURT 1749/50

42 Ordered that John Mealy and **John Polk** and their hands be added to James Polk, overseer of the roads.

91 John Polk, Joseph Tillman to be paid 72 lbs of tobacco by Daniel Kelley for attendance to give evidence in case of Kelley v. George Benston.

281 Commission and affidavits on William Heath's properties Wansborough and Hog Ridge. Commissioners Henry Ballard, John Polk, William Smith, Thomas Jones.

284 Case of John White, merchant v. Jane Strawbridge. Bail by James Polk. New trial awarded because jury gave their verdict contrary to evidence and affidavit of witness beyond sea.

SOMERSET JUDICIAL RECORDS 1751-52
[MSA C 1774-41, Loc. 1/48/3/15]

47 David Polk adjudged 96 lbs of tobacco from William Draper.

90 Robert King, William Polk commission.

SOMERSET JUDICIAL RECORDS 1752-54
[MSA C 1774-42, Loc. 1/48/3/16]

MARCH COURT 1753

5 David Polk v. Thomas Gilliss, administrator for estate of Daniel Parr; inventory of Daniel Parr. 250 lbs of tobacco awarded Polk.

74 David Polk, administrator for estate of Daniel Uriah Dulany; William Davis, Joseph Allen, sureties.

124 David Polk, James Polk and Thomas Pollit bound unto Betty Dulany, orphan of David Uriah Dulany, deceased. [David Dulany is mentioned in *Tobacco Coast* as an important shipowner.]

NOVEMBER COURT 1753

144 Joseph Venables judgment v. David Polk. Some argument, but eventually David paid up.

JUNE COURT 1754

195 John Polk v. David Long

AUGUST COURT 1754

226 George Marshall, Adrian Marshall, William and Elijah Boston, Samuel Marshall, James Dikes, Thomas Owen, Richard Boston, William Polk, Elizabeth Marshall, Robert Dukes, Phillip Adams, Thomas Moor and Thomas Marshall recover variously from Samuel Marshall for attendance to give evidence at court.

SOMERSET LAND RECORDS Volume 23 (B), 1753-59
[MSA C1778-41, Loc. 1/45/1/26]

205 [24 March 1758] Evaluation of property inherited by George Dashiell, a minor, by David Polk and Thomas Holbrook.

Maryland Somerset County. We the subscribers being appointed by one of his Lordships Justices of the Peace for the County aforesaid to view the lands and tenements with the appurtenances unto the same belonging that now is in the possession of Major Thomas Marshall guardian to George Dashiell an infant Do certify that we entered the same and inspected as followeth, one brick house fifty feet by twenty & a fifteen foot shed with galass Windows eighty seven lights ten inches by twelve, fourteen ditto cract one hundred and fifty four lights eight inches by ten and eighteen ditto cracked, One brick house ten feet square in good repair one hen house ten feet square one old kitchen fourteen foot square with a outside chimney three corn stacks of round nine logs eighteen feet by five two ditto fifteen feet by five one ditto of sawed logs fifteen by four one old house twelve feet square with a shed one old ditto fifteen foot by ten with a shed both the above much out of repair one old stable twenty one feet by eleven out of repair one old quarter with a outside brick chimney fourty feet by twenty one one barn twenty feet by twenty out of repair wanting sills one old house or office ten feet by five one house of round pine logs twenty feet by fifteen one new fraimed Milk House five feet square and two small Logg Houses one hundred and ninety old apple trees and eighty young ditto and two hundred peach trees and fourty four Cherry Trees and three thousand eighty two panells of fence good, and are of the opinion that the guardian of the aforesaid George Dashiell be permitted to make use of the aforesaid plantation but not to clear any more, there being a considerable quantity cultivated and not timber enough for what is already cultivated, the said guardian paying the quitrents and keeping the plantation with all the appurtenances thereunto belonging in the like repair as when he first received it and paying fifteen pounds current money of Maryland by the year to the orphan which is to the best of our judgements as witness our hands.

      David Polk   Thomas Holbrook

SOMERSET JUDICIAL RECORDS 1754-57
[MSA C 1774-43, Loc. 1/48/3/17]

NOVEMBER COURT 1754

3 James Polk security for Marcey Fountain, innkeeper
Marsey Fountain, innholder, comes here in his proper person and prays that he may be permitted to keep an ordinary or house of entertainment in the County at Princess Anne Town for the use and conveniency of travellers and strangers, as to them respectively shall seem meet, which is by the Court unto him granted. Whereas the said Marsey Foutain together with James Polk and William Pollet of Somerset, planters, his securitys all present here in Court ... if it happens that the said Marsey Foutain do not keep good rules and order and do suffer idle Louts and disorderly Persons to tipple, game and commit disorder or other Irregularities in his Ordinary...

58 Commission on Latons Conveyancy and The Downs
Commission requested by Samuel and Lewis Jones and empowered on 23 March 1754; reports to court on 18 March 1755. Depositions taken on 21 April 1754 from Thomas Laws, aged 65; John Laws, aged 70; William Roberts , aged 26; John Laws, aged 79; Thomas Laws, aged 65; Edward Roberts, aged 62; John White, aged 72; William White, aged 29.

AUGUST COURT 1755

103 [17 August 1755] Rebecca Whittingham sues John Polk for defamation of character.
Whittingham sues Polk for £100 for having called her a "damned whore" in public. Polk disputes the charge and a jury is impanelled: William Turpin, John Piper, Levin Woolford, Teague Riggan, William Brown, William Pollit, Wm. Moore, Michael Dorman, William Warwick, Joseph Scroggin, Ahab Costen and Zorobabl King. Jury finds for Whittingham. Court awards her £4 and 1 pound of tobacco. Polk also charged costs of 776¾ lbs/tbco.

Note: a similar case immediately preceded this one in which Whittingham sued William Owens for defamation because he accused her of stealing a "gamine of bacon." No jury called but Court ruled for Whittingham, awarded damages of £4, and assessed Owens costs of 376¼ lbs/tbco.

MARCH COURT 1756

171 Commission on Davids Destiny
Commission formed 21 August 1755 at petition of William Roberts to investigate bounds of Davids Destiny.

Deposition by Edward Roberts, aged about 63, attests that about 50 years earlier his father Francis Roberts indicated a white oak stake that was the first bounder of Davids Destiny; now replaced by a cedar post; also confirmed by Ephraim Polk Sen, Robert Polk and James Polk. ...and this deponent by setting his foot on the spot where he was showed that the first bounder stood and by digging in the marsh found part of white oak or log, the place grown over by marsh where the afsd stake or log was found. In the ground the afsd stake stood about thirty yards towards the west ward of a small gut called Festelowe Gutt, a small gut issuing out of Williamsons Creek, and further saith not.

Deposition of Matthew Wallace, aged about 59, attests that about 31 or 32 years earlier John Grandee stated the first bounder was about 10 feet from side of Fistolo Gutt, to westward side, and this deponent saith that he heard John Grandee say that Edward Roberts or Poke burnt the bounder down the place described to be about twenty eight yards from the mouth of the aforementioned gutt and about twenty seven yards to the southward of the cedar post described in Edward Roberts deposition and further saith not."

SOMERSET JUDICIAL RECORDS 1757-60
[MSA C 1774-44, Loc. 1/48/3/18]

MARCH COURT 1757.

6 [17 March 1757] Land Commission, Bare Ridge; David Polk deposition
Report on a commission requested by Samuel Handy for his tract Bare Ridge. Depositions by Ephraim Wilson, Thomas Jones, Levin Wilson, William Turpin. 24 Nov 1756. The deposition of David Polk, age 51 or thereabouts: about 10 or 12 years past he was employed by one Abraham Heath to run the lines of a parcel of land [Handy's Ridge]; Hannah Goldsmith, age 55, mentions old John Gray; James Polk, age 55.

8 Various Polk and Tull payments for testimony in Court.

JUNE COURT 1757

39 [16 June 1757] Joshua Polk tried for assault
Joshua Polk indicted and fined for assault on William Benston on 1 February
1757. Polk admits guilt and fined £1 (On f.51, Benston receives 22 lbs in
tobacco for appearance in court.)

40 Bastardy case against Tabitha Shaver, servant of William Pollitt
Tabitha Shavers, a servant of William Pollitt, is tried for fornication and
bastardy. The father is a negro "unknown to the jurors." The child, named
Rachell, is to be a servant until age 31, for which Pollitt paid 50 shillings to the
Sheriff of Somerset. Shavers has seven years added to her term of service to
Pollitt.

AUGUST COURT 1757

52 [17 August 1757] Elizabeth Clark apprenticed to George Pollitt
Elizabeth Clark, an orphan (age not stated), enters an indenture agreement to
serve George Pollitt until age 16, who "shall and will during the term aforesaid
learn his afsd apprentice to read well in the bible, and to knit, sew and spin and
weave and likewise find and provide for his apprentice meat, drink, washing,
lodging and clothing sufficient for such an apprentice to have and hold during
the term afsd." Pollitt is required to post £30 bond with William Pollitt and
Christopher as securities.

64 William Anderson trial for assault on Joshua Polk.
William Anderson is accused of assault on Joshua Polk. William Hayward is
prosector for County. Anderson pleads not guilty and Jury is called which finds
for Anderson who is discharged.

NOVEMBER COURT 1757

83 [15 Nov 1757] James Polk case against Jarvis Ballard for theft of trees
James Polk brings suit against Jarvis Ballard for alleged theft of 50 pine trees,
valued at £10, and 50 oak trees also valued at £10. Claim is made that Ballard
did break and enter on Polk's "close" Smith's Resolves on 1 March 1756 to cut,
split and remove the trees. The case been in court and continued several times
previously. Jury is called and finds for Polk who is awarded 5 shillings, Ballard
to pay court costs.

90 George Mills, David Polk and Joshua Polk to recover 120 lbs of tobacco
each from James Polk for 5days attendance at court in case of Polk vs. Jarvis
Ballard, William Polk 96 lbs for 4d.

126 March Court 1758. Joshua Polk to recover 48 pounds of tobacco from
William Allen for attendance at court in case against. George Farrington.

127 [20 March 1758] David Polk serves as one of the presiding Justices

128   Josiah Polk qualification as a lawyer; examination conducted by William Hayward and Levin Wilson.

JUNE COURT 1758

[21 June 1758] David Polk serves as one of the presiding Justices

139   Whittington King commission named for Kings Choice. Nehemiah King, William Polk, William Gray and James Polk commissioners.

140   Commission on Roberts Lott, belonging to Charles Williams. Depositions of Rencher Roberts alias Grandee of Worcester Co, age 46, mentions John Williams about 25 yrs past whose father bought land from Francis Roberts; Thomas Roberts, alias Grandee of Somerset Co, age 41; Matthew Wallace of Somerset, aged 62; for the defendant Capt. James Polk, Edward Roberts, age about 65; William Roberts, age 29, mentions statement of William Polk, Sen. seven years earlier.

AUGUST COURT 1758

[16 August 1758] David Polk serves as one of the presiding Justices

152   William Polk suit against John Callaway
Suit is brought for per note signed by John Callaway, planter, on 5 February 1763. Josiah Polk represents William Polk. Judgment is made against Calloway for £30 and court costs. Special bail on Isaac Callaway as security.

SOMERSET JUDICIAL RECORDS 1760-63
[MSA C 1774-45, Loc. 1/48/3/19]

Note: Josiah Polk appears numerous times in this volume as a defense attorney for clients in Somerset Court. These appearances are not included here.

AUGUST COURT 1760

47   Thomas Tull estate accounts by Solomon Tull and wife Rachel. Thomas Lindsay, Henry Polk sureties. Representatives: Charles, Handy, Samuel, Levin, Rachel Tull—children.

51 [18 November 1760] Grand Jury named: Abraham Outten, Thomas Ward Jr., William Ballard, Joseph Cottingham, Thomas Dixon, Coulbourn Long, Isaac Costin, Elijah Conway, Jonathan Hickman, William Nutter, Thomas Dashiell, William Waller, William Rencher, John Weatherly, Spencer Harris, William Gray, James Polk, John Tull, George Farrington, William Heath. Presentments and indictments v. Jacob Crouch, John Goddard, Mary Martin, Rachel Martin, John Newman, Aaron Starling, Young McGlachlin, James Polk, Benjamin Higgins, William Caldwell; presentments v. Isabell Stuart, Mary Milbourn, Elizabeth Wilson, Sarah Tully, ____ McGrady; and William Haly and John Jones; ignoramus.

53 Thomas Pollitt Petition for Land Commission
Thomas Pollitt requests a commission to investigate the boundaries of his tracts Trouble and Dentry. Court appoints Levin Gilliss, Thomas Holbrook, Thomas Gilliss and Charles Leatherbury.

57 Grand Jury hears case for indictment against William Hailey of Somerset parish for assault on James Polk on 7 October 1765. Polk testifies. Jury returns no true bill.

MARCH COURT 1761

65 [17 March 1761 James Polk appointed to lay out a road
Thomas Pollit and others petition court to lay out a road connecting from head o Wicomico Creek to a landing on the creek. Court appoints Thomas Gillis and William Polk to lay out a road from George Pollit's to the head of the creek and report back to court.

73 His Lordship vs. James Polk, planter of Somerset Parish. Assault upon William Hailey. Polk does not contest "for the saving costs, labor and expenses." Fined 10 sh. [On f.79, Hailey recovers £8 from Polk for same.]

JUNE COURT 1761

86 [16 June 1761] **William Pollit trial for assault**
William Pollit brought into course to answer a charge of assault on Stephen Redding. Pollit does not contest and is fined sixpence.

90 William Furnace [Furniss] commission and affidavits of tracts Fair Spring and Double Purchase. Depositions of James Furnace, 57, cf. S side Back Creek, Levin Wilson and William Furniss (his brother) division; dep of William Catlin, 78; Aaron Tilman, 64; James Furniss (again, several times)—cf. James Strawbridge, Jr., who informed him about 40 years past that Mr. Ephraim Wilson made a resurvey on his land on the S side of Back Creek at which time

Wilson settled a post between his land and Srawbridge's Fair Spring—now owned by William Furniss. Strawbridge present at the setting of the post. Deposition of William Polk, 30.

AUGUST COURT 1761

99 [18 August 1761] James Polk appointed to lay out a road
William Taylor, Jun. petition court to redirect road from Princess Ann to George Pollit's that currently runs through his property. Court appoints James Polk and Thomas Jones to look at the road and report back to court.

103 William Pollit sues William Hath for assault
Pollitt brings suit against William Hath (Heath) for an assault that occurred in previous year. Pollitt represented by Wm. Hayward and Hath by Littleton Dennis. Agreement is reached in side discussion for Hath to pay 17 shillings in damages and pay court costs.

106 18 August 1761] Commission on tracts Trouble and Dentry
Commission appointed on 22 November 1760 at request of Thomas Pollit to hear testimony on bounders of tracts Trouble and Dantry. Depositions taken 20 January 1761 from Thomas Gilliss aged 65, William Pollet, aged 40, Edmund Smullen, aged 29, and Ambrose Fitzwaters, aged 30.

MARCH COURT 1762

120 [16 March 1762] David Polk appointed to lay out a road
Inhabitants living near Barron Creek petition court for road to be laid out from from head of creek to the Warehouse of the creek. Court appoints David Polk and Ephraim King to lay out a road and report back to court.

130 [16 March 1762] Trial of Abagail Johson for fornication and begetting a bastard with a negro slave
Abigail Johnson brought before court on charge of fornication and bastardy with a negro slave. She says that she cannot deny the charge and that Hector a negro man slave of Thomas Williams is the father of the child.

Whereupon all and Singular the Premisses being Seen and by the Court fully understood it is Considered by the Court here that for as much as there is due to the County of Somerset Seven Years Service from Such persons as are Guilty of Inordinate Copulation and Likewise the Issue begot by Such Copulation to become a Servant untill it arrive at the Age of thirty One Years, Whereupon it is further Considered that the af^d. Abigal Johnson become a Servant for Seven Years for Such Copulation af^d. And that David the Issue of the af^d. Abigal and begot by the Copulation af^d. become a Servant untill it Arrive at the Age of thirty One Years &^{c}. Whereupon it is Ordered by the Court here that the af^d. Abigal Johnson Return to her Master Andrew Francis Chaney Service and that the Said

Chaney Return her to the Justices of Somerset County Court Immediately after her now Servitude Expire in order to be Sold for the Copulation af^d. Thereupon the Court Made Sale of David the Issue of the af^d. Abigal and begot by the Copulation af^d. unto Andrew Francis Cheney for the term of thirty One Years to Commence from the time of his Birth (he being three Months old) for the Sum of fifty Shillings Cur^t Money which he paid to the Sheriff for the use of the County &^{c}

132 Commission on tract Davids Destiny

Commission appointed on 20 August 1761 at request of William Roberts to hear testimony on bounders of Davids Destiny. Depositions taken 29 Nov 1761 from William Pollet, aged 41, William Polk, aged 32, Francis Roberts, aged 30, and Francis White, aged 38. Testimony given concerns location of bounder on resurvey between Matthew Wallace and William Roberts; mentions ditch cut from old cow bridge at head of Balls Creek where brick chimney of old Samuel Jones was located.

JUNE COURT 1763

223 Provincial Court held in Somerset with Frederick Lord Baltimore presiding. David Polk, among others, appointed Justice of the Peace.

Att a court of his Lordship the Right Honourable Frederick Absolute Lord and Proprietary of the Provinces of Maryland and Avalon Lord Baron of Baltemore &^{c}. held at Princes Ann Town the third Tuesday of June being the Twenty first day of the Same Month Anno Dom. one thousand Seven hundred and Sixty three by his Said Lordships Justices the peace in the Same County to keep Assigned of whom were present
The worshipfull Gentlemen Sampson Wheatley Joseph Gillis Thomas Holbrook His Lordships Justices
Ephraim Wilson, Shrf Thomas Haywarf Clk

Whereupon the Court being Called Sat as above Proceeded to Business in Manner following
His Lordship Commission of the peace being produced here in Court was Openly Read as follows Viz^t.

Frederick Absolute Lord and Proprietary of the Provinces of Maryland and Avalon Lord Baron of Baltemore &^{c}. To Benjamin Tasker, Charles Hammond, Samuel Chamberlain Edward Lloyd Richard Lee Benedict Calvert Robert Jenkins Henry Daniel Dulany Stephen Bordley, John Ridout and Charles Goldsborough Esquires William Hayward Sampson Wheatly, Joseph Gillis Samuel Adams William Winder, Ephraim Wilson Ephraim King, Thomas Jones, John Dennis, Thomas Holbrook Planner Williams William Adams, David Polk Thomas Moor and Isaiah Tilman of Somerset County Gentlemen Greeting know ye that we have Assigned you and Every of You Jointly and Severally our

*Justices to keep our peace within our County of Somerset and to do Equal Law
and Right to all the Kings Subjects Rich and Poor According to the Laws
Customs and Directions of the Acts of Assembly of this Province So far forth as
they provide and where they are Silent According to the Laws Statutes and
Reasonable Customs of England as used and Practised within this Province for
the Conservation of the peace and Quiet Rule and Government of the Kings
Subjects within our Said County and to Chastise and Punish all or Any Person
or Persons offending Against the Said Acts Laws Statutes and Customs or Any of
them According to the directions thereof and to Call before you or Any of you
all those who in our County af^d. Shall threaten to do any bodily harm to Any of
the Kings Subjects or to burn their houses or Otherwise break our peace and
Misbehave themselves to find Sufficient Security of the peace and good
behaviour to us and the Said Subjects And if they Shall Refuse to find Such
Security that then you Cause them to be Committed into Safe Custody untill they
Shall be delivered by due Course of Law from thence...*

227 Abraham Dogan, orphan, bound to Josiah Polk, gentleman, for the trade of
cordwainer; David Polk and— Hall, sureties.

256 Matthias Coston, commission and affidavits on tracts Good Luck and
Second Choice. Depositions of Thomas Gilliss, age 66, James Polk, age 60 and
David Polk, age 57.

SOMERSET JUDICIAL RECORDS 1763-65
[MSA C 1774-46, Loc. 1/48/3/20]

JUNE COURT 1763

1 David Polk a Justice of the Peace
Polk is listed as one of the Justices. [He remains in court for all sessions covered
through August Court 1765]

8 Commission on bounds of tracts Rowde, Somethingworth, Sassers Folly at
petition of William Sasser was established on 5 November 1755. Depositions
taken by various persons on 20 February 1756, including Edward Roberts, aged
63(?), who mentions that 40 years past John Hall, James Polk and Joseph Polk
had indicated a marked pine tree at the head of Little Creek was the bounder of
John Panter's land.

NOVEMBER COURT 1763

40 James Polk, Pltf, vs. Jarvis Ballard, Deft. Polk had earlier charged that
Ballard had cut and taken ten trees and also some fence panels from his
property. Case had been remanded to William Staywood and Thomas Jones for
arbitration. They now present finding that Ballard was guilty as charged. Ballard
is fined 35 shillings to be paid to Polk.

50 Report from commission on Father and Sons Desire and Friends Contention
Commission requested by John White was established on 24 June 1763. Levin Dashiell, George Irving, Thomas Sloss and Robert Elzey appointed Commisioners. Deposition of Edward Roberts, 72, states that 27 years past he had seen Colonel Levin Gale and Colonel George Dashiell at a chestnut post now replaced by a cedar post. Dashiell had asked John White, the elder, and Richard Wallace if they were satisfied with that as bounder, White to South and Wallace to North; they had agreed at the time. The post was located on hill to West of former dwelling of Matthew Wallace, and about 290 yards from a notable large poplar standing about 14 yards from the sound side. A thriving red oak stands about 5 steps from the poplar.

MARCH COURT 1764

93 Jane Strawbridge case against Samuel Hanson, administrator of Josias Hanson
Jane Strawbridge brings suit for against Samuel Hanson, administrator for estate of Josias Hanson, for £15.02.6 which she had given Josias, now deceased, for transmittal to William Strawbridge in Philadelphia. Strawbridge is represented by her attorney, Josiah Polk. Hanson says he has no goods or chattels from Josias's estate with which to pay. Court finds that he should pay from any good and chattels that are collected.

JUNE COURT 1764

106 Joseph Venables, blacksmith, suit against James English for £18.04.9. Josiah Polk is attorney for English, who admits guilt.

210 Ephraim King, petition for commission on tracts Weatherlys Purchase, Pasturage, Slipe. Commission appointed, including David Polk, Thomas Irving, Matthew Cannon, Joseph Venables.

232 Grand Jury indictment of James Polk for assault and battery on William Addams. Polk does not dispute charge, is fined 10 shillings and pays.

SOMERSET JUDICIAL RECORDS 1765-66
[MSA C 1774-47, Loc. 1/48/3/21]

JUNE COURT 1766

125 William Polk suit against John Weatherly, planter, for £130 per promissory note dated 12 Apr 1765. Josiah Polk acts as counsel for William. Court finds for Polk but continues case to August court. Matthew Kemp appears as security for Weatherly.

SOMERSET JUDICIAL RECORDS 1767-69
[MSA C 1774-49, Loc. 1/48/3/23]

AUGUST COURT 1767

1 [18 August 1767] Record of boundary commission formed 20 June 1767 to investigate boundaries of Joseph Morris' and Robert Malone's land Goddards Folly. Commissioners include John Caldwell, Thomas Irving, Benjamin Cottman and David Polk as chairman. They report back on 25 July. Deposition made by George Parsons, aged 59.

NOVEMBER COURT 1767

54 17 November1767] Record of payment made to William Polk pursuant to suit against Thomas Phillips and Richard Tully for 13 shillings plus 2shilling & sixpence costs.

JUNE COURT 1768

132 [21 June 1767] James Polk suit against William Heath for slander
By Josiah Polk, his attorney, Polk complains that he is *an honest subject of our Lord the King that now is, and is a good, true and honest and liege subject...and from his nativity...hath behaved and governed from all perjury...unspotted and unsuspected all the time...much good will and friendship of all his neighbours and others.* [The defendant is accused of] plotting and [maliciously intending to deprive] James of his good name [and to] drive him into publick Contempt and ignominy... On [date unsaid] *1767 at the County afd. falsely and maliticously spoake, published and pronounced with [.....] these false, feigned, scanadalous, malitious and approbrious words following, to wit: "You [to him the said James Polk speaking and him meaning] old perjured son of a bitch, old foresworn dog. If you had sworn the truth yesterday I [the said William himself meaning] would have had that red-headed dog [meaning a certain Benjamin Polk]."* By which words much offense taken, etc., etc. Court finds for Polk Heath is fined six shillings.

NOVEMBER COURT 1768

202 [15 November 1768] Case of William Waller v. John Anderson, blacksmith. Josiah Polk represents Anderson but loses case. Polk makes special bail for Anderson.

SOMERSET JUDICIAL RECORDS 1769-72
[MSA C 1774-50, Loc. 1/48/3/24; only available on microfilm: MSA CR 50,301]

MARCH COURT 1769

1 [21 March 1769] James Buchanan, of Somerset, innholder, approved for license to keep tavern. George Hayward and Josiah Polk of Somerset, gentlemen, are sureties for Buchanan.

JUNE COURT 1769

45 [20 June 1789] Mary Pollet charged with bearing a bastard in June 1769. Admits guilt and fined £3. Fine doubled for not identifying the father. Pollet and William White post security of £50 to protect county from any costs in caring for the child.

45 James Polk trial for assault
James Polk of Somerset Parish, tried for assault and battery on Rachell Robertson on 10 Jan 1767. Polk pleads not guilty. Jury called and finds him guilty; fined 12 shillings.

NOVEMBER COURT 1770

157 [20 November 1770] David Polk petitions court to form a commission to investigate the boundaries of his property, Tammaroons Ridge. Court agrees and appoints Thomas Dashiel, Thomas Holbrook, John Toadwell(?) and Henry Laws.

167 David Polk admitted to the bar
Upon the motion of David Polk to be admitted as an attorney of this Court it is ordered that Mssrs Geo. Hayward and Isaac Handy two of the Attorneys at Law in this court examine the said David Polk as to his knowledge and abilities in the law and that they make report to the court, etc. and afterwards in the same courtcame the afsd Geo Hayward and Isaac Handy and made the following report ~ In pursuance to your Majesties Order we have examined David Polk touching his abilities in the law and find him Qualified to Practiceas an atty in your Court, given under our hands this 21 November 1770 to the Justices of Som. County. Geo Hayward Isaac Handy

MARCH COURT 1771

198 [19 March 1771] David Polk, commission and affidavits on Tamaroons Ridge. Commissioners: Thomas Dashiell, John Caldwell, Thomas Holbrook, Henry Lowes. Lowes and Holbrook reported. Depositions of Joseph Standford, Thomas Pollitt and William Pollitt taken 1 Mar 1771. Joseph Standford, age ca

77: *Brian Snee had made a survey & then lived on the land where we now are and went about 50 yrs past the sd Brian since employed M. Whittington the then Surveyor to run out his Land & came with the said surveyor & this deponent & some other people to this White Oak where we now are & the sd Snee sett his back against this tree which was then a thriving oak tree, and said this was the first bounder of his tract of land called Tamaroon Ridge and that the afd surveyor then began to run the sd land from this tree and that in running round the said Land this deponent went with them and that in the home coming or last course they came within a yard of sd first bounder and that the sd Whittington asked them all whether they had ever seen a survey made that answered so exactly and touching the first bounder this deponent saith further not, and this deponent being asked if [he knew] anything of any other [bounds of] the land, and saith that this gum tree where we are now [was] showed to him by sd Brian Snee as the second bounder of his land called Tamaroon Ridge, and this deponent further saith that he always understood that the edge of the South Easternmost side of a branch where we now are next to where Thomas Pollitt Sen. formerly lived was the division of sd tract of [land] called Tameroon Ridge between sd Pollitt and David Polk and that the sd Pollitt to his knowledge never claimed any part or parcell of the branch to the northward and westward of this divisional boundary and this deponent further sayeth not.* Deposition of Thomas Pollitt, aged 52, omitted. Deposition of William Pollitt, age ca 50. [noted that] *about 27 yrs past a white oake blow'd down in the sd branch and that this deponent & others went to ... David Polk to ask if he might have the said oake & that the sd Polk gave it to him and that this deponent and Jonathan Tull worked up the sd oake. ...Memo: the white oake as mentioned in Joseph Stanford's deposition is a large tree now dead with the back fallen off and stands about 25 yards to the NW & Westward of the cleared land on sd tract belonging to sd Polk where he formerly lived, and the gum as also mentioned ... stands by the side of a swamp, is a living tree & is marked on four sides & the pine stump as mentioned in Thomas and William Pollitts's depositions stands near a roadside & near the corner of George Pollitt's cleared land & on the SE-most side of the branch mentioned in Thomas and William Pollitt's depositions.*

SOMERSET JUDICIAL RECORDS 1772-74
[MSA C 1774-51, Loc. 1/48/3/25]

MARCH COURT 1772

1 [17 March 1772] Case against Samuel Wilkins, tavern keeper. Josiah Polk, prosecutor for the Lord Proprietor, does not appear and the case is dismissed. Wilkins is free to go.

NOVEMBER COURT 1772

77 [17 March 1772] Commission and affidavits on tracts End of Strife, Daniels Chance, Daniels Privilege belonging to Daniel McIntrye. Depositions:

Ephraim King 50; William Polk 42; John Shiles 63; John Furbush 30; Ephraim King (again); Thomas Willing 56.

AUGUST COURT 1773

168 [17 August 1773] James Bounds case against Richard Waller, planter, whose attorney is Josiah Polk. Court finds for Bounds. William Polk provides security for £100.

NOVEMBER COURT 1773

193 [16 November 1773] Josiah Polk, petition to relocate the road from Widow Hayman's to Breedy(?) Bridge, 7 miles leading through deep, bad ground, impassable by carriage. Few persons are available to maintain it. Polk request that it be turned so it leads from Widow Hayman's to intersect the road leading to Eden School which will shorten the distance by 3 miles. Court orders John Adams, Andrew Adams, Joseph Gillis and Thomas Holbrook to lay out the road and report back to the court.

MARCH COURT 1774

224 [21 March 1774] Elijah Linch, orphan, bound of his own free consent to Elijah Cooper as blacksmith. Charles Vaughan, William Polk sureties.

225 John Dashiell, petition for commission on boundaries of tracts Horseys Bailywick, Little Bellain, Phillips Addition. John Adams, William Adams, Thomas Holbrook, William Polk appointed.

SOMERSET JUDICIALS 1774-75
[MSA C 1774-52, Loc. 1/48/3/26]

NOVEMBER COURT 1774

98 [15 November 1774] Thomas Stuart suit vs. Patrick Hart, ditcher. Josiah Polk is attorney for Stuart; Esme Bayly for Hart.

100 Suit for £10 by Samuel Wilkins suit against Gilliss Polk, gentleman, for a cow belomging to Wilkins that was lost onto Polk's property and claimed by Polk. Josiah Polk is attorney for Gilliss Polk. Judgment rendered in favor of the defendant who recovers damages from Wilkins.

MARCH COURT 1775

157 Tax free petitions: Peter McGee, ancient and infirm. William Matthews, ancient and infirm. Nathaniel Roach, ancient and infirm. Abner, Negro belonging to David Polk.

MARYLAND PREROGATIVE COURT RECORDS, 1774
[Testamentary Paper, Box 83, folder 22]

Petition by William Polk
Petitions court to require that Daniel Polk of Caroline County, heir-at-law to late
John Polk of Dorchester County be required to turn over a crop of wheat and
two looking glasses for evaluation as part of the estate inventory. 12 October—
Daniel appeared and stated that the said glasses were part of the estate of Robert
Polk, father of John.

SOMERSET JUDICIAL RECORDS 1775-84
 [MSA C 1774-53, Loc. 1/48/3/27, Film M 1301]
(Special Collections: Criminal Judgments, 1775-1788, including
proceedings from the Court of the Eastern Shore in the Revolutionary
period)

NOVEMBER COURT 1777

137 Gilliss Polk Justice of the Peace
Justices for November Court: William Winder, Joseph Venables, Gilliss Polk,
John Williams, Peter Waters. Sheriff: William Gilliss. Clerk: Thomas
Hayward.

References

ARCHIVAL REFERENCES

AOM	Archives of Maryland; volumes published by Maryland State Archives (MSA); online at MSA website
CELR	Cecil County Land Records, MSA C626
DOLR	Dorchester County Land Records, MSA C712
MDA	MD Prerogative Court Accounts, MSA S531
MDI	MD Prerogative Court Inventories, MSA S534
MDIA	MD Prerogative Court Inventories and Accounts, MSA S536
MDLS	MD Land Office Surveys, MSA S25
MDLP	MD Land Office Patents, MSA S11
MDRR	MD Land Office Rent Rolls, MSA S18
MDTP	MD Prerogative Court Testamentary Proceedings, MSA S529
MDW	MD Prerogative Court Wills, MSA S538
SODB	Somerset County Debt Books, MSA S14
SOJR	Somerset County Judicial Records, MSA C1774
SOLC	Somerset Land Commissions, MSA C1776
SOLR	Somerset County Land Records, MSA C1778
SORW	Somerset Court, Register of Wills, MSA C1815
SOTL	Somerset County Tax Lists, MSA C1812
SXLR	Sussex County (DE) Land Records, Delaware State Archives
WOLR	Worcester County Land Records, MSA C2019

PUBLISHED WORKS

Angellotti	Mrs. Frank M. Angellotti, *The Polks of North Carolina and Tennessee*. Easly SC: Southern Historical Press, 1984.
Barnes	Robert W. Barnes, *Maryland Marriages, 1634-1777; Maryland Marriages,1777-1800; Maryland Marriages, 1800-1820.* Baltimore: Genealogical Publishing Company, 1975.
Barnes	Robert W. Barnes, "Somerset Parish Records, from transcription by Benjamin J. Dashiell." *Maryland Historical Magazine*, Vol. 69, No.4, 1974.
Batchelder	Pauline Manning Batchelder, *A Somerset Sampler*. Salisbury MD: Lower Delmarva Genealogical Society, Gateway Press, 1994.
Bendler	Bruce A. Bendler, *The Manlove Family*. Privately published, New Castle DE, 1987.
Bolton	Charles Knowles Bolton, *Scotch-Irish Pioneers in Ulster and America.* Baltimore: Genealogical Publishing Company, 1967.
Branch	Mary Polk Branch, *Memoirs of a Southern Woman "Within the Lines."* Chicago: Joseph G. Branch Publishing Co., 1912.
Burke	Burke's Peerage, *Presidential Families of the United States*,

	First Edition. London: Burke's Peerage, Limited, 1975.
Butler	David J. Butler, "Presbyterianism in Clonmel, 1650-1977." *Tipperary Historical Journal*, p.81-201, 2003.
Carr	Lois Green Carr, David William Jordan, *Maryland's Revolution of Government, 1689-1692.* Ithaca NY: Cornell University Press, 1974.
Cock	Edward A. Langslow Cock, *Pollock Pedigree, 1080-1950; Compiled from the Ancient Authorities and the Work of Alex Pollock of 1939.* London: E.A.L. Cock, privately published, no date.
Comfort	Anna Lee Polk Comfort, *Our Polk Family*. Middletown DE: privately published, 2015.
Crawfurd	George Crawfurd, *A General Description of the Shire of Renfrew, Including An Account of the Noble and Ancient Families,1710; Continued to the Present Period by George Robertson*. Glasgow: John Smith and Son, 1818.
Craytor	Doyle M. Craytor, *Descendants of David Pollock, 1755-1841.* Privately published: genealogy files, Library of Congress, 1941.
Cutler	Wayne Cutler, et al., *Correspondence of James K. Polk*, 12 Volumes. Nashville, Vanderbilt University Press, 1969-2013.
Derry Cathedral	*Register of Derry Cathedral (S. Columb's), Parish of Templemore, Londonderry, 1642-1703.* Exeter and London, William Pollard & Company, Ltd. (Printed for the Parish Register Society of Dublin), 1910.
Dryden, 1985	Ruth T. Dryden, *Land Records of Somerset County, Maryland.* Westminster MD: Family Line Publications, 1985.
Dryden, 1988	Ruth T. Dryden, *Stepney Parish Records of Somerset County, Maryland*, (Transcription). Westminster MD: Family Line Publications, 1988.
EFT	E. F. T., "Pollock Family Notes," estimated date 1880. Found at gardener's cottage of Castle Pollok, Mearns, Renfrewshire, Scotland, by Mrs. MacBeth, a later occupant; provided in 1997 to Richard H. Pollock, President of Clan Pollock International.
Engert	J. F. Engert, *Pollock: Letters, Queries and Notes* (with 6 ancillary volumes). Barmouth, Gwynned: Railway Ancestors Family History Society, 2002.
Fife	Margaret Ewing Fife, *Ewing in Early America*. Bountiful UT: Family History Publishers (for Clan Ewing in America), 2003.
Footner	Hulbert Footner, *Rivers of the Eastern Shore: Seventeen Maryland Rivers*. Centreville MD: Tidewater Publishers, 1964.
Garrett	Mary Winder Garrett, "Pedigree of the Pollok or Polk Family from Fulbert the Saxon (AD 1075) to the Present Time" (eight articles), *American Historical Monthly* (AHM), Vol. I-IV.

	Nashville: The University Press, 1896-99.
Hall	Gertrude Scott Hall, *Some Paternal Lines of Samuel Warren Hall*. Dover DE: Delaware State Archives, 1951.
Handy	Isaac W. K. Handy, *Annals and Memorials of the Handy Family and their Kindred*, edited by Mildred Handy Ritchie and Sarah Rozelle Handy Mellon. Ann Arbor: W.L. Clements Library, 1992
Hunter	Robert J. Hunter, *Strabane Barony during the Ulster Plantation*. Belfast: Ulster Historical Foundation, 2011.
Lee	Grace Lawless Lee, *The Huguenot Settlements in Ireland*. London, New York: Longmans, Green, 1936. (Reprinted by Genealogical Publishing Company, 1999.)
Lowe	Esther Winder Polk Lowe, "Memories," Lowe Family Papers, MS 1949, H. Furlong Baldwin Library, Maryland Historical Society, 1913.
McKenny	Kevin McKenny, *The Laggan Army in Ireland, 1640-85*. Dublin: Four Courts Press, 2005.
McMichael	James R. McMichael, *Alexander Ewing (1676/7-1738) Descendants: Ireland to America in 1727*. Spring TX: J. R. McMichael, 1999.
Meade	Buford K. Meade, *Report on Surveys on Delaware Maryland Boundaries*. Rockville MD: National Geodetic Information Center, 1982.
Miller	Rebecca F. Miller, *Abstracts of Commissions and Affidavits from the Judicial Records 1717-1767*. Salisbury MD: Millers Choice Genealogy, 1994.
Peale	Charles Willson Peale, *The Selected Papers of Charles Willson Peale*, 5 volumes. Lillian B. Miller, Editor. New Haven: Yale University Press, published for the National Portrait Gallery.
Pogue	Lloyd Welch Pogue, *Pollock/Pogue/Polk Genealogy as Mirrored in History, from Scotland to Northern Ireland/ Ulster, Ohio, and Westward*. Baltimore: Gateway Press, 1990.
Polk, J. F.	Josiah F. Polk, "Polk Family History Notes," MS, written in Washington DC, 1848; W. H. Polk Collected Papers. Special Collections, Margaret I. King Library, University of Kentucky, Lexington KY. (Transcribed in Appendix II.)
Polk, W. H.	William Harrison Polk, *Polk Family and Kinsmen*. Louisville: Bradley and Gilbert, 1912.
Polk, W. M.	William Mecklenburg Polk, *Leonidas Polk, Bishop and General*. New York: Longmans, Green, and Co., 1893.
Polk, W. R.	William R. Polk, *Polk's Folly, An American Family History*. New York: Doubleday, 2000.
Reid	James Seaton Reid, *History of the Presbyterian Church in Ireland*, 2 volumes. New York: Robert Carter & Brothers, 1860.

Roberts   Emerson Bryan Roberts, "The Roberts Family of Wales, Middlesex, Virginia and Maryland," unpublished MS. Nabb Center, Salisbury University, Salisbury MD, undated.

Rountree   Helen C. Rountree, Thomas E. Davidson, *Eastern Shore Indians of Maryland and Virginia*. Charlottesville and London: University Press of Virginia, 1997.

Russo   J. Elliott Russo, *Tax Lists of Somerset County 1730-1740*. Westminster MD: Family Line Publications, 1992.

Sams   Parker Chastaine Sams, *Fighting Charles Reese*. Findlay, Ohio: The Courier Commercial Printer, 1996.

Sloane   Eric Sloane, *A Museum of Early American Tools*. Mineola, NY: Dover Publications, 2002.

Torrence   Clayton Torrence, *Old Somerset on the Eastern Shore of Maryland.* Richmond: Whittet & Shepperson, 1935. (Reprinted by Heritage Books, 2006.)

Touart   Paul Baker Touart, *Somerset, An Architectural History.* Annapolis MD: Maryland Historical Trust; Princess Anne, MD: Somerset County Historical Trust, c1990.

Welsh   Thomas C. Welsh, *Eastwood District History and Heritage.* Renfrewshire: Eastwood District Libraries, 1989.

Whitelaw   Ralph T. Whitelaw, *Virginia's Eastern Shore, A History of Northampton and Accomac Counties.* Richmond: Virginia Historical Society, 1951.

Wise   Matthew Wise, *Boston Family of Maryland*, 2nd Edition. Charlotte NC: Delmar Co., 1986.

Wright   F. Edward Wright, *Maryland Eastern Shore Vital Records, 1648-1725* (MESVR), Second Edition. Silver Spring MD: Family Line Publications, 1982. Also MESVR, 1726-1750; MESVR, 1751-1775; MESVR, 1776-1800; MESVR, 1801-1825

ABBREVIATIONS USED IN TEXT

PF&K   *Polk Family and Kinsmen* (W. H. Polk)

AHM   *American Historical Monthly* (articles by M. W. Garrett)

Index

Fluellin: Samuel, 341
Flynt: Richard, 154
Follett: Guillermo, 51
Forlone Hope, 42
Forlorn Hope, 83, 138, 142
Forlorne Hope, 1, 29, 33, 34, 43, 45,
    47, 53, 61, 74, 132, 139, 141
Forlorne Hopes Addition, 61, 141,
    142
Fortune, 2, 166, 169, 337
Fouch: Hugh, 154
Fountain: Marcey, 347; Marsey, 347
Freakes: Henry, 327
Friends Choice, 67
Friends Contentment, 67
Friends Denial, 66, 83
Friends Denyall, 74, 80, 81, 82, 325
Friggs: Robt, 84
Fromentine: Betsy, 201; Elegius,
    201; Elizabeth, 227; Judge, 199;
    Mr., 227
Front of Locust Hummock, 151, 160
Fulkes: Thomas, 277
Furbush: John, 359
Furnace: James, 351; William, 351;
    Wm., 16
Furniss: William, 351
Gale: George, 70, 311; Levin, 133,
    322, 325, 355; Mary, 235
Garner: John, 19, 81
Garrett: Mary Winder, vii, viii, ix,
    33, 35, 82, 86, 93, 98, 102, 110,
    164, 165, 174; Miss, 165, 166
Garter: James P., 230
Gaylard: James, 22, 155
Gessell: Jane, 16
Gibb: Edward, 156
Gillett: Ge., 276; Germane, 275, 276;
    Grace, 131; John, 276
Gillis: Elizabeth, 92, 184; Joseph,
    359; Thomas, 351
Gilliss: Betsy, 201, 203; Betty, 198;
    Levin, 351; Sally, 198; Thomas,
    335, 336, 345, 351, 352, 354
Gillman: Miss, 198
Gittings: Mrs. John S., 244

Givan: James, 285; Robert, 341
Givans: Robert, 341
Glasgow, 27
Goddard: George, 339; John, 339
Goddards Folly, 356
Golden Quarter, 58, 75, 89, 92, 93,
    94, 107, 109, 111, 161, 170, 326
Goldsborough: Charles, 331
Goldsmith: Hannah, 348; John, 281,
    289, 335; Mary, 289; Matthew,
    313; William, 93
Goldsmiths Delight, 335
Good Luck, 354
Good Will, 58
Gordon: Thomas, 324
Gorter: Mary, 203, 248; Mr., 203,
    248
Goshen, 57
Goshens Addition, 58
Goslee: John, 343; Thomas, 169,
    336, 337
Goslin: Thomas, 336
Goslins Lott, 343
Gothard: George, 339
Graden: Francis, 290
Grande: Mary Roberd, 157
Grandee: John, 22, 23, 68, 157, 282,
    348; Rachel, 22, 64, 157, 282;
    Rencher, 157, 350; Thomas, 350
Graves: Matthew, 307
Gray: Alan, 104; Alen, 104; Allan,
    106; Allen, 104, 159, 330, 344;
    Ella, 159; Ellen, 159, 184; Erin,
    159; Jeffery, 93; Jeffrey, 301, 302;
    John, 104, 159, 184, 294, 335,
    336, 343, 348; Jos., 323; Joseph,
    305; Wercott, 323; William, 97,
    330, 331, 350
Graydon: Francis, 109
Green Pasture, 67, 119, 121
Grey: Allen, 104; Miles, 16
Griffith: Jesse, 187; Mary, 187
Grome: Wm., 16
Groome: Sam'll, 306
Grounde: Rachell, 157

Grubb: Isabella, 213; Judge, 213; Thomas, 213
Grundee: John, 68, 282
Grundey: John, 73; Rensher, 73
Grundy: John, 22, 326
Guilette: Miss, 205
Guillett: Grace, 188
Gullett: Elizabeth, 131; Germane, 274; Grace, 130, 131, 137, 274; Mary, 131; Susanna, 131; William, 131, 274, 304
Gulletts Advisement, 131
Gulletts Assurance, 131
Gulletts Hope, 131
Gunby: Francis, 270
Gurnell: Sarah, 292
Hack: Spencer, 344
Hacker: Thomas, 339
Hagan: Edward, 34, 279
Hailey: William, 97, 351
Hall: (N), 354; Alex., 305; Alexander, 302; Alex'r, 306; Alex'r., 313, 319; Henry, 270, 273; John, 116, 354; Margarett, 16; Phenix, 325; Robert, 310
Hamilton: James, 30
Hammon: Edward, 255; John, 255
Hampton: John, 301
Handy: Capt., 337; Col. George, 202; Hetty, 201; Isaac, 357; John, 339; Mary, 183; Miss, 202; Richard, 202; Samuel, 183, 348
Hanson: Colonel, 233; George, 232; Josias, 355; Samuel, 355
Harcum: Lee, 167; Miss, 197
Hardy: Robert, 337; Sarah, 337, 339
Harmanson: Matthew, 89
Harris: Jeremiah, 335; John, 15; Robert, 336; William, 156; Wm., 71, 311
Harrison: Daniel, 138; Doctor, 231; Erasmus, 292; Martha, 231
Hart: Patrick, 359; Wm., 16
Harthberry, 92, 95
Hast: Daniell, 15
Hastins: Robert, 325

Hath: William, 352
Haversham: Jessie, 240
Hawkins: Miss, 196
Hayes: Elizabeth, 186; Manlove, 207; Priscilla, 186; Rich., 207; Richard, 186
Haylor: Henry, 65, 265
Hayman: Widow, 359
Haynie: Betsy, 198; Charlotte, 198, 199; Esme, 198, 199; Ezekiel, 198; Hampden, 198, 199; Henrietta, 198, 199
Hayward: Geo., 357; George, 357; William, 349, 350; Wm., 352
Haywood: Thomas, 323
Hazard, 53, 56, 57, 110, 119, 121, 125, 130, 133, 134, 138; Susannah, 274
Hearn: Thomas, 325
Heath: Abraham, 106, 332, 348; Matthew, 106; William, 98, 332, 335, 345, 352
Henderson: John, 126; Sarah, 119, 126, 187
Henry: John, 318; Nancy, 185, 201; Robert Jenkins, 336
Hewett: Mary, 276
Hill: Elizabeth, 339; John, 16; Johnson, 295
Hillman: John, 144, 328
Hilman: John, 292, 293; Thomas, 292, 293
Hinshaw: William Wade, 38
Hitch: Mike, 113
Hobbs: Jay, 279; Thomas, 16
Hoffington: John, 341
Hog Ridge, 345
Hoggs Down, 166, 169, 336, 337, 338
Holbrook: Thomas, 347, 351, 357, 359
Holland: Benjamin, 330; Daniel, 154; John, 299; Michael, 261
Hollands: John, 271
Honging: Sarah, 337
Hook: Jeremiah, 15; Joseph, 81

Locust Hamock, 153
Locust Hummock, 31, 107, 109, 121, 149, 151, 152, 160, 161, 290, 291
Loflin: (N), 189
London: Ambrose, 15
Lone Ridge, 141
Long: David, 346; Solomon, 344
Long Delay, 79, 107, 109, 111, 152, 161
Long Ridge, 130
Loss and Gain, 79
Lott, 119, 121, 156
Lotts Wife, 156
Low (Long) Ridge, 53
Low Ridge, 45
Lowe: Adelaide, 237, 238; Anna, 238, 244, 245; Bradley, 242; E. Louis Lowe, 203; Enoch, 226; Enoch Lewis, 226; Enoch Louis, 96, 164; Esther, 164, 165, 166, 203, 226, 244; Esther Winder Polk, 164; Governor, 226; James, 248; Louis, 238, 247; Mr., 233, 234; Paul, 238; Stuart, 244; Victoire, 244, 245
Lucas: Wm., 276
Lynch: Henry, 253
Lynes: Phill., 256
Lyon: John, 113; John C., 3, 28, 114
Macdaniel: Owen, 145
Macdannell: Owen, 145
Macdonald: Governor, 246; Maria, 246
Mackarty: John, 314
Mackennie: Mary, 65, 267
Mackenny: Mary, 65, 265, 267
Mackie: Margaret, 38, 39, 50
Macknitt: Jno., 283; John, 283, 290
Maddox: Robert, 28
Magguire: Thomas, 306
Maidenhedd, 325
Maidens Blush, 125
Makdaniel: John, 145
Makemie: Francis, 18, 19, 26, 27, 75, 80; Rev. Francis, 18
Malibran: Mme., 237

Malone: Robert, 356
Manlove: (N), 185; Ann, 185; Betty, 146, 182, 185; Boaz, 185; Elizabeth, 185; Emanuel, 116, 146; Emmanuel, 107, 115, 334; George, 185; Jonathan, 185; Magdalen, 110, 116, 185; Magdalene, 107; Manuel, 58, 85, 110, 115, 116, 182, 185; Mary, 107, 186; Patience, 107, 110, 116, 186; Sally, 185; Sarah, 185
Mannering: Abraham, 333
Marcy: John G., 241; Lt., 241
Margarets Fancy, 58
Marshall: Leah, 183; Thomas, 346
Martin: Edward, 72, 131; Francis, 16; James, 340; Leuther, 198
Marvel: John, 152, 161
Marvell: Betty, 71, 312; John, 70, 109, 152, 311
Marvells Chance, 109, 152
Marvels Choice, 117
Marvil: John, 151
Mason: William, 34; Wm., 264, 265
Massy: William, 16
Masten: Rhoda, 141, 190; William, 141, 190
Matcha, 16
Matthews: Bailey, 158; William, 359
Maury: Penelope, 206
Maxwell: (N), 187; Ezekiel, 214; Nancy, 187, 214; Nanny, 127
May: Henry, 244
Maynard: James, 272
McBlair: Admiral, 244, 245; Mrs., 244
McChester: George, 340; William, 340
McCleary: Debora, 223; Deborah, 220; Samuel, 220, 223
McClester: John, 337
McCree: Margaret, 223; Robert, 223
McDonald: James, 333; Owen, 145
McDorman: Darby, 325
McFarling: Robert, 333
McGee: Peter, 359

McGrain: Ellen, 159; John, 159
McIntrye: Daniel, 358
Mckay: Neale, 297
McKay: Martha, 296, 297
McKey: Margaret, 39
Mcknitt: John, 288
McKnitt: John, 278
McMorre: James, 308
McNeale: Hugh, 292
mcNeales: Hugh, 292
McNish: George, 301
McRee: James, 223
Mealy: John, 345
Mecuom: Florence, 16
Merchment: Sam., 257
Milbourn: Ralph, 256
Miles: He., 278; Sarah, 86
Miller: Andrew, 19, 81; David, 19,
   81; Jno., 153; John, 91, 322
Mills: George, 325, 349; Isabella,
   325; Susanna, 131
Minders: James, 252
Minor: James, 27, 253, 257
Minors: Mary Magdalen, 186;
   Robert, 186
Mitchell: George, 16
Moanen, 56, 57, 96
Moneen, 92, 99, 146
Monroe: Mary, 202; President, 232;
   Victor, 202
Moor: William, 338
Moore: Betty, 183; Col., 224; Eliz.,
   151, 153; John, 15, 278
More: Ann, 332; Seamore, 162
Morgan: William, 154
Morgans Venture, 57
Morris: Ann, 141, 146, 189;
   Brinkley, 189; Curtis, 189; Daniel,
   141, 146, 189; Hannah, 189;
   Jesse, 189; John, 189; Joseph,
   356; Mary, 189; Rebecca, 189;
   Rhoda, 187, 189; Robert, 189;
   Sarah, 189; Thomas, 189;
   William, 189
Morrow: (N), 184; Betty, 184;
   Elizabeth, 184

Morton: Betsy, 199; John, 199
Mulka: John, 307, 314
Mulkal: John, 310
Mulkey: John, 307, 310, 316; Phillip,
   314
Mulky: John, 77
Mulrine: John, 77, 303, 306
Mumford: Thomas, 292
Napier: Major, 247
Navarr: John, 120, 318
Neal: John, 145, 148; Margaret, 186
Neale: Andrew, 224; Jane, 224; John,
   315; Thomas, 224
Neall: John, 145
Neaver: John, 318
Negro: Abner, 104, 105, 359; Acheir,
   308; Amey, 330; Amy, 106; Att,
   124; Atte, 115, 124; Attee, 124;
   Attey, 324; Atto, 124; Atty, 124;
   Bek, 329; Bess, 72; Binah, 73;
   Caesar, 113; Cate, 115; Cato,.
   334; Cattey, 115; Ceasar, 113;
   Ceesar, 113; Cesar, 113; Cuffee,
   73; Cuffie, 73; Dick, 326; Dinah,
   326; Dooniar, 113; Duen, 113;
   Duna, 113; Dunah, 113; Duner,
   113; Duney, 113; Fender, 147;
   Haner, 104; Hannah, 104, 105,
   344; Hannay, 105; Hanne, 104;
   Hector, 352; Jeffrey, 72, 73;
   Jeffry, 73; Judy, 334; Juner, 113;
   Kate, 115; Katt, 115; Lenda, 104;
   Lunea, 113; Minggo, 138;
   Mumodah, 104; Ned, 115; Nell,
   115; Nero, 334; Obur, 104; Ogy,
   105; Olan, 105; Oleon, 105;
   Oteen, 104, 105; Otern, 105;
   Outten, 104; Owen, 104; Peter,
   331; Phillis, 334; Pleasant, 105,
   106, 334; Prince, 113; Princess,
   113; Quaco, 115; Quako, 115;
   Quoco, 115; Rodger, 123; Roger,
   123, 308; Rose, 148; Sam, 147;
   Sambo, 123; Samboe, 123; Sarah,
   72, 73; Secar, 113; Sib, 123, 124;
   Sibb, 123; Simon, 322; Sip, 124;

374

376

Shirly: James, 330

Shirman: Edward, 337; William, 338

Shook: Joseph, 81

Shores: John, 43, 61, 83, 142;
Nehemiah, 41; Severn, 41;
Thomas, 41; William, 20, 41, 43,
61, 83, 142

Sigsbee: Commodore, 239

Sirman: Elizabeth, 183; Lowder, 183

Sittler: Hetty, 200

Slave: Ogg, 105; Tamor, 105;
Thamor, 105

Slingo: Mary, 334

Slipe, 355

Smart: Mrs., 211, 222, 223; Susan,
224

Smith: Henry, 15, 74, 75, 93, 95,
193, 261, 299; James, 324;
Joanna, 182; Johanna, 59, 74, 78;
John, 12; Samuel, 20, 154;
Stephen, 58; Thomas, 57, 58, 78;
William, 92, 132, 305, 345; Wm.,
57

Smiths Hope, 58, 92, 95

Smiths Recovery, 74, 170

Smock: John, 17

Smullen: Edmund, 352

Snee: Brian, 358; Bryan, 34, 279

Somethingworth, 354

Southerland: Thomas, 81

Sparke: Robt., 299

Spear: Henry, 318, 319

Spence: Adam, 266; David, 20

Spense: David, 311

Spratt: Jane, 224; Susan, 224;
Thomas, 224

Stacey: William, 285

Stahl: John, 19

Stall: John, 81

Standford: Joseph, 357

Standforth: Augustin, 45

Stanfield: Esther, 182; Richard, 182

Stanford: Augustin, 138; Augustine,
1

Starr: Charles, 38, 39, 50; Charles H.,
38

Staughton: William, 332

Staywood: William, 354

Steele: John, 19, 81

Sterrett: Miss, 202

Stevens: Col., 17, 18, 21; Colonel,
26, 75; Margaret, 183; Richard,
337; Thomas, 316; William, 17,
20, 27, 157, 170, 183

Stevenson: William, 131

Stewart: Alexander, 202; Anna, 203;
Charlotte, 199; Dorthea, 36; Dr.,
199; Henry, 202; Hetty, 202; John
H., 229; Letitia, 206; Margaret,
197; Patrick, 341

Stitt: Robert, 296

Stockwell: Mary, 99; Thomas, 99

Stoughton: William, 97, 322, 324,
325

Strawbridge: James, 92, 96, 101, 184,
326, 330, 332, 333, 334, 351;
Jane, 92, 96, 100, 101, 106, 184,
204, 343, 344, 345, 355; Mary,
184; Mary Jane, 184; Mr., 204;
Polly, 204; William, 101, 184,
204, 355

Stuart: Alexander, 228, 232; Andrew,
242; Anna Maria, 166; Esther,
228; Thomas, 359

Suethen: Virginia, 200; Worthington
G., 200

Sumner: Benjamin, 11

Surman: Peter, 131

Swain: Mary, 278

Swan Pond, 57

Talbott: Walter, 272

Tamaroons Ridge, 92, 357

Tameroons Ridge, 95, 168

Tarr: John, 256

Tasker: Barbara, 25, 48, 49;
Magdalen, 17, 25, 29, 37, 48, 49,
128, 180, 193, 203; Roger, 25, 29,
35, 48, 49, 50

Taunton Deane, 156, 157

Taylor: Abraham, 341; Betty, 341;
Dr., 199; George, 341; Jacob, 317;
John, 254, 341; Levin, 341;

Mr., 207; Sidney, 199; Thomas,
338; W.H., 216; William, 166,
201, 202, 218; William H., 35,
191, 192, 193, 202, 211, 212, 216,
220, 222, 223, 224, 228; Wm. H.,
218, 219, 223, 224, 225
Winders Choice, 170
Winser: Jno., 155; John, 278, 281
Winslowe: William, 15
Winsor: John, 20, 23, 262, 281
Wirt: William, 238
Wittys Invention, 170
Wolfe: John, 297
Wood: Thomas, 16
Woodgate: Mary, 133; Mary
Vaughan, 182

Woodland: Anne, 256; Wm., 256,
257
Woolford: James, 283; John, 336;
Roger, 23, 279
Woolver, 344
Wootton: Edward, 313
Worthington: Sam, 284, 287, 294;
Sam., 297, 298; Sam'l, 279;
Samuel, 307, 308, 313, 316; Wm.,
302
Wouldhave: William, 257, 258
Wright: (N), 189; Henry, 142; Miss,
207, 218; Thomas, 141, 142, 145,
146; William, 156
Wye: William, 333